The Libert

INTERIM SITE

PHILOSOPHY AND SOCIETY
General Editor: MARSHALL COHEN

Also in this series:

The Libertarian Reader

Edited by

TIBOR R. MACHAN

ROWMAN AND LITTLEFIELD
Totowa, New Jersey

Copyright © 1982 in this collection by Rowman and Littlefield

All rights reserved. No part of this publication may be
reproduced or transmitted, in any form or by any means, without the
permission of the Publishers.

First published in the United States 1982 by Rowman and Littlefield,
81 Adams Drive, Totowa, New Jersey 07512.

Library of Congress Cataloging in Publication Data
Main entry under title:

The Libertarian reader.

  (Philosophy and society)
  Bibliography: p.
  1. Libertarianism—Addresses, essays,
lectures. 2. Liberty—Addresses, essays,
lectures. 3. Laissez-faire—Addresses, essays,
lectures. 4. Sociological jurisprudence—Addresses, essays, lectures. I. Machan, Tibor R.
II. Series.
JC585.L39 1981   320.5'12   81-22677
ISBN 0-8476-7061-9   AACR2
ISBN 0-8476-7062-7 (pbk.)

Distributed in the U.K. and Commonwealth by
George Prior Associated Publishers Limited
High Holborn House
53154 High Holborn
London WC1 V 6 RL
England

Printed in the United States of America

Contents

PART IV. LIBERTY AND MORALITY

Preface

Despite the rapidly increasing influence of libertarian ideas it is difficult to find a representative collection of contemporary libertarian writings. I believe, therefore, that the present collection of essays will be of great interest to the private reader as well as to university students and teachers.

Libertarian ideas have been detected in the works of ancient thinkers such as Alcibiades, Lykophron, Hippodamus, and Democritus and in medieval writers such as Ockham, Aquinas, and Lessius. However, none of these writers is libertarian in the contemporary sense. The major modern sources of libertarian ideas are, undoubtedly, Locke and Adam Smith and some of the utilitarians and Social Darwinists. But even these writers do not insist on the importance of unrestricted personal freedom, and on the absolute character of the individual's right to life, liberty, and property in the emphatic manner that is characteristic of contemporary libertarianism.

The main characteristics of contemporary libertarianism began to emerge in the writings of the novelist-philosopher Ayn Rand and in the writings of distinguished economists such as Hayek, von Mises, and Milton Friedman. Even so, it is only with the publication of Robert Nozick's *Anarchy, State, and Utopia* that libertarian ideas achieved some kind of respectability in academic philosophical circles. It is one of the main purposes of this volume to make available some of the writings that this newly awakened philosophical interest has produced.

Libertarians agree that liberty should be prized above all other political values. However, they have not reached a consensus on what the best philosophical defense of this conviction is. This anthology attempts, therefore, to provide the reader with representative examples of the main philosophical approaches to the defense of a fully free society. In addition to the argument made familiar by many economists that only a free-market society (as opposed to one that engages in coercive planning) can make a rational allocation of goods and resources, the reader will find (mainly in Part I) defenses of libertarianism founded on traditional, though often on sharply contrasting, moral conceptions. These include natural law and natural right (as well as "entitlement") theories; theories based on ethical egoism as well as those whose ultimate standard is aggregate utility; Hobbesian theories and conventionalist theories; and theories that take the value of liberty to be entailed by the very nature of intentional or purposive actions. But libertarianism can also be defended by moral sceptics as the political doctrine that consorts best with the absence of objective moral values.

In addition to displaying the main theoretical defenses of the libertarian philosophy, the anthology attempts (in Part II) to explore the legal and social, and (in Part

III) the economic, implications of adopting the libertarian framework—or of failing to adopt it. Part IV investigates the relationship between living a moral life and living in a free society.

I wish to thank Jim Feather, publisher of this work, for his encouragement. Marshall Cohen, series editor, has given his support from the start, for which I thank him. Several of my friends, especially Jim Chesher, helped with the selections and editing. I am sorry for having had to exclude some very fine pieces. Finally, I want to thank the Reason Foundation and members of the 1980 Summer Seminar program of the Liberty Fund, Inc., for their support. Ed Regis, Jr., especially, deserves thanks for his good advice.

May 1981
Santa Barbara, CA

PART ONE

Foundations of Liberty

ERIC MACK*

Individualism, Rights,
and the Open Society

There are certain important connections worth discussing between what I shall term ethical individualism, natural or human rights, and the need for an open and unregulated society. By *ethical individualism* I mean the view that the proper and appropriate goal of each human being's choices and actions is his own well-being. I shall refer to the claim that each person should adopt his own well-being as the purpose of his actions as the *individualist principle*. By *natural* or *human rights*, I mean rights that each person has by virtue of some characteristic which he possesses as a human being, and not by virtue of considerations of utility or contractual arrangement. When a person has a natural or human right he has a moral claim against interference of a certain type. When such interference occurs, his rights are violated and the person who brings about the interference has acted in an unjustified way. By an *open* and *unregulated society*, I mean a society in which people are at liberty to pursue, in a great variety of ways, their respective happiness and well-being. Such a society will exist if rights are respected. And, I shall argue, the existence of such a society insures that the concept of rights and the correlative concept of obligation are applicable in judging human action. [1]

There are a great number of issues that I shall not attempt to cover in this paper. I will not provide a detailed philosophical argument for the view that each individual human being should seek to secure and maximize his own well-being. I will, however, say something in favor of the plausibility of this ethical doctrine and of its import. I will not take up the serious and difficult question of the nature of well-being, that is, the question of exactly what constitutes a person's achieving his well-being. Nor shall I deal, in a very technical way, with the transition from the ethics of the individualist principles to the politics of individual rights. The last section of this paper is devoted to a brief discussion of various exemplifications of

Reprinted from *The Libertarian Alternative*, Tibor R. Machan, ed. Copyright © 1974 by Tibor R. Machan. Used by permission of Nelson-Hall, Publishers, Chicago.
*Tulane University.

the basic right against coercion and to the justification of defense against rights-violating actions.

The Individualist Principle and the Principle of Noncoercion

The individualist principle simply claims that, for *any* given individual person, his own life, well-being, and happiness are the things of ultimate value. Ultimately, the only good reason for a particular individual to choose a certain course of action is that this course serves to secure and maximize his well-being at least as much as any other course of action.[2] The individualist principle repudiates sacrifice, where *sacrifice* is construed not as the intelligent ordering of priorities, but as a person's surrender of what is of higher value to his life and well-being for something which is of lower value. With regard to any choice that faces a person, if it is true that one alternative really is of greater value to his life and well-being, then the pursuit of that alternative is nonsacrificial. Of course, the individualist principle does not exclude, but rather recommends, all of those interactions between persons which lead to, and to a great extent constitute, the well-being of life.

As classically conceived, the bearer of natural (or human) rights has a moral claim against at least certain types of interference with his person. The obligation to act in accordance with these claims is the only natural (i.e., noncontractual) obligation that men are subject to. Whenever I speak of rights and obligations, unless otherwise specified, I mean natural, noncontractual, rights and obligations. Historically, the advocacy of the individualist principle (or something like it) and natural rights which are, of course, *individual* rights have often been linked together. Consider the two great classical English political philosophers, Hobbes and Locke. In Hobbes we find a law of nature, "by which a man is forbidden to do, that which is destructive of his life or taketh away the means of preserving the same; and to omit, that by which he thinketh it may be best preserved." The law of nature is distinct from but compatible with the right of nature which "is the Liberty each man hath, to use his own power, as he will himself, for the preservation of his own Nature."[3] Locke also links the moral requirement, that each person preserve himself with the idea of human rights although the connection is of a different sort. He states the connection as follows:

> Everyone as he is bound to preserve himself, and not quit his Station willfully; so by the like reason when his own Preservation comes not in competition, ought he, as much as he can, to preserve the rest of Mankind, and may not unless it do Justice on an Offender, take away, or impair the life or what tends to the Preservation of the Life, Liberty, Health, Limb or Goods of another.[4]

There is a great deal of commonsensical plausibility in the association of the individualist principle with the belief in natural rights. The former maintains that each man's own well-being is a special, numerically unique goal toward which that man can and should act while other men can and should move toward the attainment of their own well-being. The concept of individual rights seems to protect the autonomy of individual goal-seeking. It serves to sanction the moral pluralism involved in each man's pursuing his own life values and to condemn the destruction of this pluralism which takes place when one man interferes, at least in certain ways, with the activity of another. However, despite this plausibility and despite the historical precedent of linking ethical individualism and individual rights, we must seriously consider the possibility that these two doctrines are not compatible.

Why might one doubt the compatibility of the individualist principle and individual rights? Rights always have obligations as their correlatives. If Jones has a right against action *s* performed by Smith, then Smith is obligated *to Jones* to abstain from action *s*. Now there is a certain feature about the concepts of rights and obligations which may suggest that the application of the individualist principle to a given person is not consistent with that person's having obligations, even negative obligations to abstain from interfering with others. And this further suggests that such obligations are not consistent with the general advocacy of the individualist principle.

To bring out this feature, imagine a case of Smith proposing to slit Jones' throat. Jones objects. He claims a right against having his throat slit. He claims, indeed, that Smith is obligated not to slit his (Jones') throat. Assuming the individualist principle, one way of showing that Smith should not slit Jones' throat is to show that this action would not contribute to Smith's well-being. Except for very extreme situations, invoking considerations related to an agent's own well-being will provide good reasons for his abstaining from aggressive acts such as slitting people's throats.[5] However, when Jones claims that he has a right against Smith's slitting his throat, Jones certainly does not *mean* that this action is not in Smith's interest and that Smith should abstain for *this* reason. Jones means that there is something condemnable about the action independently of the disutility of the action for Smith. That is, when Jones invokes his *right* not to have his throat slit and/or Smith's obligation not to slit it, he is claiming that, *aside* from considerations of the usefulness of this action to Smith, the action is unjustified. If the only reason for saying that Smith's slitting Jones' throat is unjustified were the fact that such an action is not in Smith's interest, then while it would be correct to claim that Smith *should* not slit Jones' throat, it would be incorrect to claim that Smith is *obligated* not to slit Jones' throat. In short there is a distinction between "Smith should not do *s*" and "Smith is obligated not to do *s*".

It may be true that Smith should not burn his manuscript (it being a brilliant work which will bring him wealth and happiness), yet it is obviously false that he is obligated to the manuscript not to consign it to the flames.[6] The manuscript has no right against being consumed. If one ascribes a right to Jones, or to any other entity, against a certain action performed by Smith, then there must be some consideration that can be invoked against that action aside from the disutility of the action for Smith. But it may well appear that, given the individualist principle, the only consideration that could be presented to Smith against any action that he might perform is the consideration that the action does not serve his well-being. In short, our problem is this: how can a moral theory be both individualist (endorse the view that ultimately the only end of moral value for any particular person is his own well-being) and also allow for the existence of rights and obligations?[7]

Philosophers distinguish between ethical principles that are teleological and those that are deontic. Although there are philosophical problems with this distinction, I will apply it here though merely as a means of presenting an answer to the question of the compatibility of ethical individualism and individual rights. According to teleological principles, the moral value or moral disvalue of an action is a function of the consequences of the action. According to deontic principles the rightness or wrongness of an action is based on some feature of the action other than its consequences. Often it is said that a deontic principle focuses on a feature of the action itself (as opposed to its consequences). For instance, punishing a guilty person is often said to be right just because *such* actions *are* just.

The individualist principle implies that the only *consequences* which count in determining the moral value or disvalue of an action are the consequences of the action for the agent's well-being. And we have just seen that if, in evaluating Smith's action, one considers only the consequences of the action for Smith, then one can never reach any conclusion as to whether Smith is obligated to abstain from the action. One could never reach any conclusion as to whether Jones has a right against it. Hence, if we are to incorporate judgments about rights and obligations into our moral theory, we must identify an additional and, in the current terminology, a nonteleological, or deontic, ground for considering certain actions to be condemnable. If an action is unjustified on deontic grounds, it is an action from which a person is obligated to abstain. There is a reason aside from its degree of utility for abstaining from it. Given the correlation between obligations and rights, if Smith is obligated to Jones to abstain from action *s*, then Jones has a right against Smith's performance of *s*.

But in searching for a deontic principle on the basis of which we could judge actions to be actions that persons are obligated to abstain from, and hence are actions against which persons have rights, we must be careful that the deontic principle does not clash with the individualist principle. We cannot endorse a deontic principle that may require an individual to sacrifice his own well-being. In addition, we cannot simply pull out of the air a deontic principle which defines rights and obligations. We must see if one flows from the individualist principle.

The aim, then, is to sketch the outlines of an individualist moral theory which subsumes a doctrine of obligations and rights based upon the teleological individualist principle. Any principle which is to define obligations and rights within this moral theory must meet three conditions. First, its employment must be justified on the basis of the individualist principle. Second, there must be a significant sense in which the employment of the deontic principle cannot require that a person forego those actions that best serve his well-being. Third, if the deontic principle does not apply in all cases of human action, there must be a clear rule for determining when it is applicable. Smith will be obligated to abstain from a certain action toward Jones and Jones will have a right against that action, if the deontic principle (*a*) is appropriately invoked with respect to this action, and (*b*) the action is unjustified in terms of the deontic principle.

The following pair of arguments outlines how some actions by Smith may lack justification. In the second argument, the lack of justification does not depend upon the action's failure to be in Smith's interest. Indeed, the second argument indicates how the individualist principle can itself be invoked to produce judgments about obligations and rights and can thereby serve, in the current terminology, as a deontic principle.

1. Why does this action by Smith lack justification? Because Smith is acting as if it is not the case that Smith ought to act in his own interest. (He is acting, say, as if Smith ought to act in Jones' interest.)

Why is it wrong for Smith to act as if it is not the case that Smith ought to act in his own interest? Because all persons ought to act in their own interest, that is, because of the truth of the individualist principle.

2. Why does this action by Smith lack justification? Because Smith is acting as if it is not the case that Jones ought to act in his own (Jones') interest. (He is acting, say, as if Jones ought to act in Smith's interest.)

Why is it wrong for Smith to act as if it is not the case that Jones ought to act in his own (Jones') interest?   ‹

Because all persons ought to act in their own interest, that is, because of the truth of the individualist principle.

The crucial point to be gleaned from a comparison of these two arguments is that there are two distinct ways in which a person can act in a manner which is unjustified in terms of the individualist principle. He can fail to treat his own well-being as his ultimate value. This is an error on the basis of the individualist principle. And he can fail to treat other persons as beings who also have their own unique moral goals. This too is an error on the basis of the individualist principle.

But what, specifically, is meant when we speak of Smith acting as if it is not the case that Jones ought to act in his own (Jones') interest? We mean treating Jones as if he were a being who, lacking any moral purpose of his own, is at the disposal of other persons. Let us suppose that Smith is acting, pursuing certain goals. In the course of this pursuit, Jones is used. That is, as a result of the actions performed by Smith some portion of Jones' life is consumed. Smith acts in a way that would be justified only if that portion of Jones' life were at his disposal, in the same sense that an unclaimed natural resource might be at Smith's disposal.[8] It is actions of this sort, wherein persons used are treated as natural resources at the disposal of the agents involved that are done as if it is not the case that the person who suffers the action ought to act in his own interest. Such actions are ruled out by the individualist principle in virtue of the principle's implication that a person's life is not a free-floating resource that can properly be consigned to any (anyone's) purpose, but that for each person the proper purpose of his life and actions is his own well-being.

When one acts as if it is not the case that a person Jones again, ought to act for his own well-being, one directs that person, or a portion of the life of that person, or actions of that person, toward a goal which is not his goal. When one acts in such a manner, one directs a person to a goal that he has not chosen, or toward a goal he has chosen under an influence which was itself not chosen and which involved his being treated as if it were not the case that he ought to act on his own behalf. Such actions are coercive actions. The deontic principle for which we have been searching can be stated, then, as follows: an action is unjustified if it involves coercion of some person. Note that the presence of coercion is not a teleological ground for ruling the action unjustified. Thus, when an action is unjustified on the basis of the presence of coercion, he who would perform that action is *obligated* to abstain from performing it. There is a reason against the action aside from the possible disutility of the action for the agent. And the person who would suffer the action has a right against it. Stated generally, this is the right against coercion or the right not to be coerced. The only obligation correlative to this fundamental right is the negative obligation to abstain from coercive action.

The Applicability of the Principle of Noncoercion

We know what principle it is that can be developed on the basis of the teleological individualist principle, and that defines obligations and rights: the principle of noncoercion. However, it seems that an unlimited application of the rule against coercion would sometimes require an individual to sacrifice his own well-being. For sometimes men find themselves in situations where they have to choose between acting coercively and surrendering their overall self-interest. To apply the rule against coercion in such cases is to maintain that in these cases persons are obligated to sacrifice their well-being. As we previously noted, we cannot endorse any application of any deontic principle if that particular application would require an individual to sacrifice his well-being. The endorsement of such an application would be incompatible with the advocacy of the individualist principle. The advocacy of the individualist principle, therefore, demands a limitation on the application of the derived principle of noncoercion such that the proper application of the principle never requires an individual to surrender his overall self-interest. It is a matter of utmost importance that this limitation be properly identified. For the range of the proper application of the principle of noncoercion determines the scope of human rights. We must investigate, then, the conditions for the proper application of the principle of noncoercion. In the terminology which I will employ in this investigation, we must see what must be true about person A's performance, at time t, of a coercive action c in order for one to be justified in condemning A's performance of c at t by invoking the principle of noncoercion.

My claim is that it *is* appropriate to invoke this deontic rule in condemning A's performance of c at t if and *only if* A's performance of c at t is not necessary to A's overall well-being. If doing c at t is not necessary to A's overall self-interest, then A is obligated to abstain from the coercive action c; and other persons have rights against A's performing c at t. Clearly, an explication of my claim requires a discussion of the concept of an action being necessary to an agent's well-being. In this discussion I will speak of series of actions which are open to a person at a given point in time t. Each series is defined by its constituent actions and is to be thought of as commencing at t. Except under the most unusual circumstances, a person has an almost infinite number of series of actions open to him. The performance of action c is necessary for person A's well-being only if c is the first constituent of *every* series of actions (of those available to A at t) which serves A's interest at least as well as any other series of actions. This is to say that A's performance of c at t is necessary only if (i) c is the first constituent of a series of actions which is *more* in A's interest than any other series open to him or (ii) c is the first constituent of *every* one of a number of series of actions each of which is as much in A's interest as any other series of actions. Only if one or another of these conditions is fulfilled is it a sacrifice for A to abstain from performing c at t. (Notice, then, that only a small percentage of the actions open to a person—indeed, only a small percentage of the actions which are first constituents of series of actions which are in his interest—are necessary to that person's interest.)

A's performance of c at t is *not* necessary to A's self-interest if there is some other action, say q, which is the first constituent of a series of actions open to A at t and which is at least as much in A's interest as the series which commences with c. Action q may be the first constituent of a series of actions that is more in A's interest than any other series. Here it is obvious that A can nonsacrificially abstain from doing c at t. Indeed, the individualist principle requires that A choose q over c at t. Action q may be the first constituent of a series of actions that is (along with a series commencing with c) as much in A's interest as any series of actions open to A at t. In such a case it is still true that A can nonsacrificially abstain from doing c at t. The individualist principle requires only that at t he do c or q (or some other equally beneficial action). It is perfectly consistent with the individualist principle that A abstain from one of these actions. In fact, he must abstain from either c or q for he can only perform one of them. Hence as long as A's performance of coercive action c at t is not necessary to A's self-interest, there is no inconsistency in advocating the individualist principle and claiming that A is obligated to abstain from c at t. In general then, when an action s is not necessary to A's well-being, A can abstain from performing s and still act as he should according to the individualist principle. Hence, if the performance of s is not necessary, it is *possible* for A to be obligated to abstain from s. Fulfilling this obligation would not require that A abstain from acting as he should act on the basis of the individualist principle. If the performance of s is not necessary for A, then B *can* have a right against A's doing s. Of course, A *will* be obligated to abstain from action s only when (a) s is not necessary to his well-being and (b) the performance of s involves the coercion of others. B will have a right against A's performance of s only when this act is not necessary for A *and* it involves the coercion of B. In terms of the applicability of this deontic principle which states that coercive acts are unjustified, we are saying that it is appropriate to invoke this principle whenever the action in question is not necessary to the well-being of the agent. And if the action is coercive, the agent is obligated to abstain from performing it, and he who would suffer its performance has a right against it.

As an illustration of these points, consider the case of two men adrift on the open sea with a plank which can only support one man. Let us assume that in this case it serves the well-being of each man to survive, even if this survival costs the other's life. In this case, there is only one possible series of actions for each man that is sufficient for achieving his well-being. These actions are necessary for each of the men. In such an emergency case, rights are significantly absent. Each man ought, given the individualist principle and the assumptions in the case, to seek his own survival at the expense of the other. But neither can be said to have a right to survival. For to ascribe this right to either party would be to ascribe to the other party the obligation to allow the first party's survival at the expense of his own life. But the second party cannot be obligated to allow this, since we know that, given the individualist principle, he ought not to allow it. Undoubtedly there are actions for each person that are necessary to that person's life and well-being. Each person must, for instance, breathe. What is significant, however, is that those actions that *are* necessary to a person, and which, therefore, he *could not* be obligated to abstain from, are, in any case, actions which he *does not seem* obligated to abstain from (for example, breathing).

As the plank example illustrates, in abnormal, crisis situations, actions that are necessary to the well-being of the persons involved increase. Concerning the possibility of obligations and rights (the applicability of the principle of noncoercion) in such circumstances, persons are less capable of being the subject of obligations and less capable of being the bearers of rights (that is, the principle of noncoercion does not apply). This also accords with reasonable particular judgments about obligations and rights. Persons are absolved form obligations in crisis situations. The reason that rights appear only when reasonably sane societal conditions prevail, and not in emergency and purely chaotic situations, is that one person, say Jones, can only have rights against another, say Smith, to the extent that coercive actions against Jones by Smith (the actions from which Smith *would* be obligated to abstain, if he *could* be obligated to abstain from them) are not necessary to Smith's well-being. The key feature of reasonably sane societal conditions is that they provide each person with multiple and noncondemnable means of seeking his own well-being. The reason that it behooves all persons to encourage an open society in the sense of the existence of freedom of broad alternatives for the pursuit of well-being is that (with an exception soon to be noted) the man who *must* perform a particular act to preserve his well-being cannot be obligated to abstain from this action. And so, although defense against this act may be justified on the basis of the defender's well-being, the intended victim of the act cannot claim that his right against coercion is threatened. The more open society is, the less likely the occurrence of such necessary acts.

I have been claiming that if action *s* is necessary to A's well-being, then the deontic rule that coercive acts are unjustified cannot properly be invoked, that if *s* is necessary, A cannot be obligated to abstain from s and persons cannot have a right against the performance of *s*. There is an exception to this rule which I shall discuss only briefly. The exception is that the rule against coercive action *does* apply to an action *s* which is necessary for A's well-being *if A himself brings it about that s is necessary*. This exception is to be explained on the basis of the principle that, whereas the course of events (other than one's own actions) can result in one's being absolved from obligation, one cannot absolve oneself from obligation.

Consider Jones and Smith in a modified plank case. In this case, Jones is on the oneman plank and Smith is on an oceanliner that is passing by. We can say that Smith could be obligated (and what is more, *is* obligated) to abstain from causing Jones' death since, presumably, causing Jones' death is not necessary to Smith's overall well-being. However, in this case, Smith, who is the only person to hear Jones' pleas for help, throws himself overboard. He swims toward the plank feeling a deep relief. For he reasons that since causing Jones' death is now necessary to his own overall well-being, he is finally free of the obligations to abstain from causing Jones' death, and he has always wanted to justifiably kill Jones. Yet Smith reasons incorrectly. To suppose that a person's performance of any actions which would make a particular coercive action *c* necessary to that person's well-being is sufficient for relieving that person of the obligation not to do c is to suppose that the existence of his obligation not to do *c* is utterly dependent upon whether he exercises his liberty to perform actions which would make action *c* necessary. The supposition vitiates the meaning of the word "obligation." There are no obligations if one can absolve oneself from the alleged obligations.

Indeed, it is clear that the modified plank case that I have just described is radically different from the first case in which two men, each unexpectedly, find themselves on or near the plank after the oceanliner explodes and sinks. If an action s is necessary to a person's self-interest because *he himself created the necessity for s*, and if alternatives to creating the necessity for s were available and these alternatives did not involve surrender of his well-being, then the person is obligated to abstain from s.

Let us consider one additional example. Suppose that an act of theft becomes necessary to Jones' well-being. Either Jones does not bring this necessity upon himself, or he does bring it upon himself. Suppose that he did not, that, for example, he is an innocent victim in a war devastated country. On the surface, there is no problem. Due to the course of events, Jones must "steal" food. He cannot be obligated to abstain from this action. In the war devastated area, persons do not have rights to the food they possess; not against victims such as Jones. However, the following objection can be raised. Undoubtedly some series of actions other than the series that Jones engaged in would have been at least as much in his interest as the series of actions that he has engaged in. [9]

For example, Jones might have fled the country at an earlier stage in the war. We might wonder whether his failure to do so, his mistake, does not imply that Jones *did* bring it upon himself that the acts of theft were necessary. After all, alternatives to bringing the necessity to steal upon himself, which did not involve the surrender of his well-being, were available to him. [10] But, in Jones' defense, we must note that Jones did not bring it upon himself that the path that he chose required this coercive action. Jones may very well have made a mistake in not fleeing the country. The path he embarked upon while staying in the country, the path which turns out to involve coercive actions as Jones' only means of protecting his well-being, may very well serve his interests less than some alternative path would have. But his making this mistake, and his having brought it about that the theft is necessary are two different things. Other persons are responsible for the theft being necessary. This is implied in Jones' innocence. And this is why the course of events absolves Jones of certain of his natural obligations. If Jones himself had brought this necessity about, for instance, by carefully destroying all his own resources, he would be obligated to abstain from the theft. For there would have been, in this case, another course of action, fully available to Jones which did not require an act of theft and which would have been at least as much in his interest as the course of action which brought about the necessity for and included the act of theft. Of course, in actual cases of human action we must worry about to what extent the agent brings about the necessity for him to act in a condemnable way. This is just one of the complications which tends to block precision in ethical judgments.

The Application of the Principle of Noncoercion

The difficulty of explaining the relationship between an ethics of individualism and a doctrine of noncontractual rights and obligations has been resolved. This was accomplished by deriving the principle of noncoercion in conjunction with recognizing when that principle is properly applied to a particular action. The application of the principle of noncoercion defines the (negative) obligations and the rights to which all persons are subject. The proper application of this principle is such that persons can never be brought to the point that their obligations to others, or the correlative rights of these other persons, require that they sacrifice their well-being. In the final section of this paper I want to display how other human rights can be accounted for in terms of the fundamental right against coercion.

To begin with, let us consider such commonly ascribed rights as the right to assembly or the right to free speech. The phrases *the right to assembly* and *the right to free speech* are misleading. For Jones can be prevented from assembling or from speaking without having his rights violated. For instance, the owner of the place of assembly may choose not to rent his hall to Jones and his cohorts. This may well prevent Jones from assembling, but it does not violate Jones' rights. The hall owner is under no obligation, assuming the absence of a contract, to rent to Jones. It is clear that persons are at liberty to assemble, speak, etc., (always construing such actions as noncoercive) in the sense that they are under no obligation to abstain from assembling, speaking, and so on. But one's right to R, where R represents any activity or sequence of activities, consists in something more than not being obligated to abstain from R. What? Simply the right not to be coerced in attempting to do R, or preparing for, or doing R. It is only from coercive intervention that other persons are obligated to abstain. By letting R stand for *life,* we arrive at the phrase *the right to life* which can be clarified as the right against coercion. Possession of the right to life does not mean that one has a right to be provided with the means for living, or that one has a right against being deprived (say, through competition) of the possession of some specific object or opportunity which would be a means to living. For no one is *obligated* (again assuming the absence of prior contracts) to insure that one has the means to live. Certainly, each man is at liberty to live in the sense of not being obligated to abstain from living. The additional element present in the right to live is simply the right against coercion in attempting, preparing for, and performing life sustaining actions. The right to life consists in the fact that under normal societal conditions any coercive action, and, *a fortiori,* any coercive action against one's life sustaining actions, is unjustified.

Persons have rights against being lied to and to the keeping of promises that are made to them. In the case of fraud and a lying promise (that is, a promise that is made with the intention of not keeping it and is not kept), it is clear that he who perpetrates them uses or manipulates the object of the fraud or lying promise in much the same way as trained animals are used in circus acts. The failure to fulfill any promise (under normal conditions, and ignoring any possible "escape clauses" built into the promise) will violate the rights of the person to whom the promise was made if, on the basis of the expectation produced by the promise and its subsequent frustration, the person to whom the promise was made is rendered less capable of attaining his own goals. What I have in mind is this. Promises produce expectations; and, given these expectations induced by the promiser, persons may reorder their plans, goals, and actions. The fact that the expected (promised) event does not occur renders the person who received the promise and reordered his plans less efficacious as a direct result of the promise that was made to him. Thus, his power to act, to achieve his own goals, is reduced without his consent and not merely through the withdrawal of any privilege which he enjoyed. Such a reduction of goalseeking efficacy is another instance of coercion. I shall postpone a discussion of the right against threats of coercion until after my remarks on property rights.

Persons have specific rights to property. I shall be concerned only with discussing the original right to any piece of property, assuming that nonfraudulent contractual transfer of property already rightfully possessed is not problematic. The classical account of the right to property in the tradition in which this essay falls is the doctrine enunciated by John Locke.

> Every man has a property in his own person. . . . The labour of his body and the work of his hands, we may say are properly his. Whatsoever, then, he removes out of the state that nature hath provided and left it in, he hath mixed his labour with it, and joined to it. Something that is his own, and thereby makes it his property.[11]

I think that in basic spirit Locke's position is correct (despite the apparent definition of property in terms of property). But this Lockean doctrine can be better expressed in terms of the investment of (some of) the time of one's life and the right against being deprived of this investment. We have seen previously that all persons have a right against the consumption by other persons of portions of their lives. The creation of a right to property merely provides another instance of this right. For persons invest and thereby save up portions of their lives by intentionally directing their actions toward the production of specific and nonfleeting objects and states of objects. A man has a right to the tool he fashions out of an unclaimed stone by virtue of the fact that he cannot be deprived of the tool without depriving him of the invested time involved in fashioning it. A man has a right to a field by virtue of the fact, and to the extent, that it cannot be used by others without depriving him of the time invested in clearing and otherwise preparing it.

The case of the right against threats of coercion is more difficult.[12] Suppose A threatens B as follows: "Your money or your dissertation manuscript"; and B succumbs to this threat by handing over his money. Now, there is a clear sense in which what B has done, he has done voluntarily. Consider the fact that he clearly *decides* to hand over the money. But since this action is voluntary, must one not conclude that A's acquisition of B's money involves no violation of B's rights? Certainly A is free to accept voluntary contributions from B. So what if A *did* make a certain factual prediction, namely, that if B did not hand over the money, his manuscript would be incinerated. The key to seeing what *is* wrong with successful threats begins with the observation that the threats that appear to be rights violating are those threats wherein the threatened party has a right to the object which is threatened (or a right to perform the action whose prevention is threatened). The phrase "your x, or your y" is revealing here. For it shows that what the threatener offers is an exchange, an exchange that will be found to be advantageous to the threatened party. And the sense in which he who succumbs to the threat acts voluntarily is directly linked to this exchange; he is willing to give up his money in return for not having his manuscript burnt.

But there is a great problem in assimilating this "exchange" to other cases of voluntary exchange. The problem is that what A offers B in exchange for B's money is not something that A has a right to—indeed it is something to which B has a right, namely, B's manuscript. Hence, although B's manuscript is in A's power, it is not A's to exchange in the sense that is required if A's receipt of B's money is to be part of a paradigmatic voluntary exchange between A and B. B does voluntarily offer to A his (B's) money as the price for his (B's) manuscript, but what B receives in exchange from A (the manuscript) is not A's to offer. We have an invalid exchange, just as the exchange would be invalid if A offered C's automobile in exchange for B's money. A cannot *rightfully* deliver the proffered goods. Hence, B's voluntary surrender of the money may be rescinded because of A's default. B, or his appointed agents, may properly take such steps as are necessary to reclaim his money.

The justification for self-defense cannot follow the same pattern as, say, the establishment of the right to property or the right against frauds. For the latter are fundamentally rights against coercion and are correlative to obligations on the part of other persons to abstain from coercive and manipulative actions. In the case of self-defense, we want to justify *actions* directly. The right against certain aggressive actions is *not* identical with the right to perform defensive acts, acts which in the absence of prior aggression would themselves be rights violating. Unfortunately, from the fact that action *s* violates A's rights it does not follow that A has a right to forcibly defend himself against *s*. This point is the central feature of any well-developed pacifistic position. Nor can it be overturned. It can, however, be circumvented by invoking the limitation on the applicability of the noncoercion principle which we have previously noted. That is, A cannot be obligated to abstain from action *d* if the performance of action *d* is necessary to A's life and/or well-being. The performance of defensive acts (including, say, the commissioning of a defensive agent) in the face of rights-violating aggression is necessary to the well-being of the intended victim, A. Thus, A cannot be obligated to abstain from such actions. He is at liberty to perform them, that is, he is not obligated not to perform them and the aggressor has no right against them.

Notes

1. For an excellent historical overview of the parallel growth of ethical individualism, the recognition of individual rights, and the breakdown of feudal social structure see: Michael Oakeshott, "The Masses in Representative Democracy," in *American Conservative Thought in the Twentieth Century*, ed. W. F. Buckley, Jr. (Indianapolis: Bobbs-Merrill, 1970), pp. 103-123.

2. For a detailed argument in favor of the individualist principle see Eric Mack, "How to Derive Ethical Egoism," *The Personalist*, Autumn 1971, pp. 735-743, and the references cited therein. For a detailed discussion of noncoercion and the applicability of the latter principle see: Eric Mack, "Egoism and Rights," *The Personalist*, Winter 1973, pp. 5-33.

3. Thomas Hobbes, *Leviathan*, ed. Michael Oakeshott (Oxford: Basil Blackwell, 1966) p. 84.

4. John Locke, *Two Treatises on Government*, ed. Peter Laslett (Cambridge: Cambridge University Press, 1967) p. 289.

5. See especially Nathaniel Branden, "Rational Egoism Continued," *The Personalist*, Summer 1970, pp. 305-313.

6. Of course, Smith may have a *contractual* obligation to other persons to abstain from burning the manuscript. More on contractual obligations later.

7. Note that one *cannot* argue as follows: since each person's acting for his own well-being has moral value, each person should act in such a way that each other person may act for *his* (the latter's) well-being—as long as such actions themselves do not prevent some third party from acting in his respective self-interest. For this argument assumes that the individualist principle implies that Jones' acting for Jones' well-being is a valuable end for Smith—hence, Smith ought to pursue this end. But the individualist principle involves no such implication.

8. Hence the obscenity of Commissioners of Human Resources.

9. To be strictly correct, "nor a greater number/degree of coercive actions" should be added to the antecedent.

10. To be strictly correct, "nor a greater number/degree of coercive actions" should be added at this point.

11. Locke, *Two Treatises*, p. 306.

12. On this issue I am indebted to Mary Sirridge for her insightful suggestions.

J. CHARLES KING*

Moral Theory and the Foundations of Social Order

It has frequently been suggested that in order for a society to survive, to say nothing of its flourishing, the persons who make up the society must to a large extent share basic moral beliefs and be prepared to act on them for the most part. Philosophers of law have observed that even if one conceives of laws as orders backed by threats, most people must obey the orders willingly if a legal system is to be possible.

Yet, clearly, a society may survive in spite of deep moral division among those who live in it. What follows is an attempt to clarify the relationship between morality and the foundations of social order. [1]

I shall advance an understanding of moral theory that suggests a way in which some shared moral principles are necessary for a society to endure. Further, I shall argue that in learning this lesson we discover a powerful line of argument in support of an individualist moral stance which in turn provides the moral background for justification of the social and political views characteristic of classical liberalism.

In Part I I shall explain my conception of moral theory. In Part II I will use this conception to defend an interpretation of natural rights. Finally, in Part III I will outline a view of natural duty which provides the link between morality and social order. The long preliminary explication of moral theory is a necessary precondition for explaining the conclusions concerning morality and society.

I. Moral Theory

a. Moral Theory in Historical Perspective

The basic problem of moral theory since the 17th century has been how to incorporate morality into the steadily growing scientific view of the world. This problem has grown and been defined as modern science has grown into a more and more complex and successful paradigm of knowledge.

*Liberty Fund, Inc.

In most versions of the pre-scientific, medieval conception of the world, the place of human beings is very clear. As special creatures of God, human beings have a special place in creation and in God's plan for the world. As prince of his creation, God is rightly the moral ruler of humans. His laws are their appropriate moral principles. Further, in the most common version, God has built his laws into humans so that the path to their happiness is through keeping his laws.

As this picture is presented in great writers such as Saint Thomas, it presents an intellectually and emotionally enthralling set of answers to the deepest questions of human life. In regard to moral principles it presents a careful and authoritative grounding.

The modern period has seen, of course, the attempt slowly to replace the world view on which this moral structure is based. As the new sciences gradually undermined the cosmology of the medieval world view, its tenets about moral authority were also undermined. As we have learned to think of humans as products of evolution on a small planet, in a small system in an obscure arm of an obscure galaxy, we have had to try to adjust the foundation of our moral beliefs accordingly.

The task has not proved easy. Most of the great moral philosophers of the modern period have been trying to carry out this transition. Their problem has been to discover a way to replace the clear and straightforward picture of moral authority as flowing from God with some alternative foundation.

Thus Kant looks to the nature of reason, or Hegel to the unfolding of Spirit, or Mill to the happiness of the social group. But each of them must offer a complex and difficult way to replace the simple picture of morality as grounded in God's command.

The measure of their failure is the fact that most of our contemporaries either hold the position that there is no ground for moral principles (some emotive or other non-cognitive view of morals) or else still cling to the old world view in some form or other. For all the greatness of past thinkers, the basic problem of replacing the paradigm of morality as authority has not been met.

To be sure, another possibility has often been explored. Hobbes used it, but gave in to authority after all. Kant, and Mill and many others paid lipservice to it. Nietzsche was its prophet. If God is dead, then men must become Gods. If there is no longer God to impose values then we must make our own. This alternative is to base morality in the individual human being, but to have no morality of authority.

The real alternative to authority is a morality based on the individual interests of individual human beings. This is the kind of alternative which I advocate. My basic claim is that moral principles are sound only if they can be justified from the point of view of actual human beings seeking to obtain their own actual ends in life.

Even those philosophers who have seen themselves as proponents of individualism have usually ended up subjecting actual individuals to the authority of some part of themselves, or of the general welfare, or what would have been decided in a bargaining session they did not attend and find irrelevant. I shall address my arguments to real individuals, who know their desires (however confused these may be) and who can be expected to accept no principles which they cannot see to be in their own interests (remembering always that their interests may be broadly or narrowly focused in regard to others).

b. Why Moral Theory?

I now want to consider the intellectual role of moral theory. General principles of action are an inescapable requirement for human life as we know it. Human beings must constantly choose courses of action, and those courses of action must have at least the minimal results of providing food, water and shelter if humans are to live.

But each moment of human life presents the possibility of an indefinitely large set of alternative choices. We must have various general principles to allow us to organize the many particular choices we must make.

These principles need not be thought out or even explicitly formulated in every case. Many of them we may scarcely even give a thought, although if we were asked about them we could see that we do guide our choices in these ways.

Neither must principles which guide our choices be very grand. They may be so simple as the resolve that one must avoid sweets, brought to bear as one contemplates a richly laden pastry tray. But, however grand or simple, one must use various general principles in facing the almost limitless array of possibilities offered by even the most prosaic human life.

From the viewpoint of an observer only, one could call these supposed "principles" merely observed regularities in the choices of an individual. But the use of principles cannot be understood only from the standpoint of an observer in this way.

We are all, as human beings, actors as well as observers. Principles are more than mere observed regularity of choice, because they *guide* our choices. They play a role in leading us to choose as we do. Thus for an agent to adopt or hold a principle is much more than for him to believe that he will regularly act in a certain way. It is for him to *intend*—or *resolve*, or at least be *inclined* to act in that way. As a guide to his conduct the principle helps to produce the action he chooses.

Of course, principles do not always determine conduct. I may have resolved to follow the principle of foregoing sweets, but may on a particular occasion yield to the blandishments of a particular pastry tray. But this does not change the fact that principles are absolutely necessary for human conduct. If one tried to confront each and every possibility of human life as an individual choice with no reliance on general principles as guides, one would never be able to organize one's life well enough even to obtain water, food, and shelter for survival.

Each human being then, employs a large array of principles in making the choices which his life involves. Obviously, the principles themselves may at times conflict, or indicate mutually exclusive courses of action so that other, more general, principles must be brought to bear in deciding how to act.

The special claim of moral principles is to be the final court of appeal in the process. Moral principles are those principles which purport to show how we should act when all things are considered. When one is told that an action would be morally wrong, this purports to be the final answer to the question whether one should do it. It purports to override other considerations such as that it would be enjoyable, or one's neighbors would approve, or the authorities demand it.

These are very large claims. Is there really any reason to suppose that any group of principles plays such a crucial role? Could any principles really make out a case for being granted such a role? Here one begins to ask difficult theoretical questions, but this highly abstract route is not really the one most of us take in coming to questions of moral theory.

We learn a set of principles (some of which we would later call moral principles) as children. In our early years most of us accept the teachings of our elders (both in their words and their deeds) uncritically—or at least after minimal resistance. As we grow, however, natural occurrences of life tend to lead us to question the moral principles we have learned as children. For example, we may meet people whom we like or respect, but who differ from us on matters of moral principle. Or we may find that principles we learned earlier do not really and honestly seem to us to guide our choices correctly. Or the principles we have learned may be a part of a total cultural or religious outlook which we have come to doubt or disbelieve.

In these and many other ways we may be brought to question the principles we have learned as children. This questioning does not necessarily imply that we hold incorrect principles, or even that we will change them. It does imply, however, that we must think about what reasons we have for accepting the principles we do.

To be sure, many people may never reach this stage. They may live a whole life depending on the emotional reactions which result from their early training and later reinforcement as guides to moral choice. Doubtlessly many people have found happiness in a life of simple acceptance of the tastes and standards of their family, community or culture. Often one may even appear wise by very seriously repeating one's traditional judgments in the face of all life's problems.

But it is pointless to debate whether this is a desirable condition because for most humans it is impossible. Most human beings, including those in no way inclined to the life of intellectuals, are simply too inquisitive or too reflective always to be at ease with the principles they have learned as children.

The process of reflecting on or questioning one's moral principles is the first step toward moral theory. It is, however, only a first step. While most people do put some critical thought on moral principles few pursue the matter very far. Some accept an easy answer of one kind or another, some quickly become bored and drop the matter. Others, finding it more and more difficult, finally give up in despair. Moral theory is the result of pressing on and on in search of answers to one's doubts and questions about moral principles. It raises the questions "Should we follow moral principles?" and "If so, which ones?" and takes them on, no holds barred, and with no time limit.

As with any other intellectual task taken with complete seriousness, moral theory has developed a literature, a set of received positions, a list of great figures, and even a niche among the accepted academic disciplines. Nonetheless, for all the technicalities thereby engendered, moral theory remains the task of following to the bitter-end the question how best to conduct one's life.

c. Two Concepts of Moral Skepticism

In order to explain the kind of intellectual task moral theory involves, it is helpful to consider the challenge of the moral skeptic—the person who believes that moral judgments cannot be justified.

A distinction between two kinds of doubt about moral principles is drawn very early in the philosophical literature, at least as early as Glaucon's challenge to Socrates in Book II of Plato's *Republic*. Glaucon wants to be shown not only the nature of justice but also what reason there is to practice justice. He is bothered by the possibility of two different failings on the part of moral principles. One would be that it is impossible to know the nature of justice, thus impossible to know what things really are just and what things really are not just. The other would be that even if one could tell the just from the unjust, one might not have been provided with sufficient reason to suppose that one should practice justice rather than injustice.

If moral principles are to be final principles of conduct—that is, if they are to be genuine practical principles which guide our actions and do so as a final court of appeal—then surely those principles must make some claim upon our action. But to make some claim upon our action they must make some claim upon our motivation. We must be shown some reason related to our purposes, our motives, in acting which would lead us to acknowledge these principles as guiding our conduct.

Moral principles may, for example, suggest that we should forego acting upon some current desire. But we clearly do have motivation to act on the desire. If moral principles are to suggest that we act against desires, some motivating factor must be contained in them.

Thus, I distinguish two different kinds of moral skepticism. One I call cognitive moral skepticism. The other, motivational moral skepticism.

I take cognitive moral skepticism to be the view that truth conditions for moral judgments are in some way or other defective so that it is impossible to determine their truth or falsity. Such claims may be advanced on varying epistemological grounds. One might claim simply that it is impossible to determine truth conditions for moral judgments. (Of course, one must then find some other reason for their persistent presence in ordinary life and speech.) Or one might claim that the ways in which moral judgments are used in ordinary life and speech are so vague and confused that it is impossible to determine any truth conditions for the way in which the terms are actually used. Or one might claim that moral judgments are of such a character that they simply could not meet some test for truth and falsity which one held to be the only way for arriving at effective truth conditions. Leaving aside philosophers, some claims of these kinds or some combination of these kinds of claims doubtlessly underlie the conviction of most sophisticated intellectuals that moral judgments cannot be justified.

By motivational moral skepticism, I understand the view that even if one can determine the truth conditions for moral judgments in some way or other, one nevertheless can provide no reason why persons should govern their conduct according to principles of right or justice or whatever.

It is surprising that while it has had advocates, this kind of moral skepticism has not been more popular than it has. People have been so often asked to sacrifice themselves, their own inclinations, or their own most deeply felt desires to purported moral principles, that one wonders why so few have actually asked boldly, "But look, what reason have you really given for acting on these principles at all?" I suspect that one reason for this is that the grounding for moral principles has been assumed in so many situations to be found in religious beliefs. The grandeur of God, the possibility of eternal damnation or the ill will of a powerful church may serve to silence questions even though they have little or nothing to do with one's real inclinations in regard to his moral principles. (Of course, if God really will send you to Hell for not obeying certain laws, that is a powerful reason for obeying those laws!)

The more common phenomenon in our time, however, is for people who do not believe for a minute that they are in danger of Hell to accept some moral principle without question because it retains an emotional force originally based on religious beliefs which they do not hold. In this way people are led to follow or at least to feel guilty for not following principles which go completely against their desires without asking, "But why should I acknowledge that as a principle?"

In arguing the reasonableness of the motivational skeptic's question I do not claim that his question is unanswerable. As I mentioned, the answer that you may run afoul of God is a very good answer, if true. The answer that acting in such and such a way will make you happy is a good one, if true. The point is that one has every reason, when confronted with a purported moral principle, to ask if one really has reason to follow it. Such reason may exist, but it may not. For example, the purported principle may be based on seeking ends one simply does not wish to attain, or it may be mistaken how best to attain ends one does desire. Even if one is presented with a conceptually convincing account of how the principle is linked to the way terms like "right" are ordinarily used and how one may judge what things are right, it remains sensible to ask, "But why should I act that way?" Good answers may be forthcoming, but the motivational skeptic is correct in asking for them.

While I argue that in the end there is no reason to accept in general the claims of the moral skeptic, I would also suggest that a fuller appreciation of the strength of the case of the motivational skeptic might have saved much moral philosophy, particularly in the twentieth century, from its air of redundancy and emptiness. Too often moral philosophers have written with the assumption (stated or unstated) that all enlightened people shared their basic moral views, and that what was required was only the discovery of a theory which would yield these views as a consequence. This charade was easier to keep up because we so often chose such trivial examples—the notorious returning a book which one had promised to return to a friend—as subjects for analysis.

The claims of the motivational skeptic should remind us that genuine moral inquiry is not a matter of debate only for carefully refined professors all of whom share each other's outlook, but must also be addressed to persons who genuinely disagree concerning moral questions.

The motivational skeptic will always suspect that we are trying to put something over on him—that a moral philosopher is trying to convince him on some spurious ground to act in a way the moral philosopher himself happens to approve or desires to bring about. Study of moral philosophy has convinced me that the motivational skeptic is often right about this and that far from being paranoid he is often merely being realistic.

Space limitations do not allow me to subject specific theories to the test of the motivational skeptic here, but the reader can easily imagine how such a skeptic would react to various of the usual moral theories. To the universalistic utilitarian, he might say, "But I just do not care about the welfare of everyone. I certainly don't make it equal with my own welfare. I care about myself, my family and my friends, but your universalistic principle just doesn't make a claim on me."

To the Kantian he might say, "I understand why I must avoid contradictions in my scientific beliefs. A theory involving contradiction will lead me to expect

experiences which do not result. I see little reason, however, to avoid your contradictions of the will or pragmatic contradictions. You may say that in acting or
choosing I *imply* something universal which non-universalizable actions contradict. What does that matter to me? I see no difficulty for my plans in that. Of
course, it would be a disaster if everyone always lied, but they don't so I may as well
gain an advantage this time. Your supposed penalty of contradicting my own will
seems no penalty at all to me. I *intend* no universal prescription in acting. What
you claim is implied is your problem."

By extending these rather rough and ready illustrations to the very long task of
examining a specific theory, one can come to grasp the importance of the doubt of
the motivational skeptic.

Another lesson we learn from considering two kinds of skeptical doubt concerning moral principles is that moral theory must attend to both of these problems at
once. Starting as it presumably does from the fact that moral judgments are made
and that moral principles are appealed to in ordinary life and argument, albeit
sometimes obliquely, and attempting to bring some order and understanding to
such claims, moral theory must attempt a two-sided task. It must provide plausible
final principles for conduct which could conceivably offer answers to the kinds of
problem that arise in human relationships and in decisions about human conduct.
But, at the same time, it must offer such principles not only in a way that would be
understandable and usable but also in a way that makes claims on the motivations
of individual human beings. This necessity for being argued in such a way as to
show individual human beings why they have reason to act on moral principles
seems, in fact, to provide a key for the actual content of the principles as well.

Thus, the task of moral theory becomes one in which guidelines may be drawn
from two very different directions which come together in moral theory. It must,
after all, provide a theoretical structure—one in which the desired moral terms
such as "good," or "right," or "justice" can be given a satisfactory intellectual
account. But given the nature of the principles involved—that is, the claim to
provide final guides for conduct—the intellectual account can be provided only if
in doing so one has shown what claim on the conduct of individuals these principles make. Notice that the problem is not merely one of explaining why people
might actually act on a principle, but one of showing what good reason they have to
act on a principle—that is, what reason internal to their own motivation would lead
them to accept a particular principle.

This need not be a motivation they already feel. Part of the task of moral
philosophy may be to show persons that their interests require them to act in ways
in which they would have thought they would prefer not to act. Nonetheless, the
point cannot be avoided that if a principle is to be justified as a moral principle one
must not only present truth conditions for its use, but must also present these in
such a way as to show why that kind of thing makes a claim on motivation to act.

To this point I have slurred over the notion of the motivation of individuals. It
must be addressed more directly. I do not intend to suggest that to acknowledge a
principle as a moral principle is therefore automatically to act on it, or that people
always act on the moral principles they believe they have a good reason to accept.

I intend the notion of motivation employed in the conception of motivational
skepticism as what I might call rational motivation. I assume that a person seeks a
disparate set of ends in life and that in order to show a person a good reason for

acting in some way or other, we must show some connection between that action and the ends the person seeks. Since I apply the notion of moral skepticism to moral principles including principles of good, it is not enough to say that one must simply show the person that the thing is good. Rather, the good itself must be linked to the ends which a person seeks in life. Thus, in suggesting that we might show a person a rational motivation for acting according to a particular principle, I intend to suggest that we must show the person how acting according to that principle will contribute to the ends which he seeks in life.

This is not to place a strictly egoistic requirement upon justification for moral judgments since the question of whether the requirement is egoistic is one of the centeredness of ends.[2] A person may seek ends relating primarily to himself, or he may seek ends relating primarily to other persons or to some combination thereof. This is not really the issue with which I am dealing at this point, although I certainly have no objection to calling my account egoistic. I simply find the term confusing because it has been used in so many different ways in the philosophic literature.

To some the concept of rational motivation seems unduly crass. They apparently think that the business of philosophy should be to show us what we ought to desire rather than to try to draw links to actual desires. But this is to flatter philosophy falsely. Neither philosophy nor any other study can show persons what their most deeply felt desires should be. Philosophy does not (much as some would like it to) make people. It must address actual people rationally. But actual people do have desires and preferences. We may try to show a person points of conflict in those desires. We may try to demonstrate that if one really wants y, then one must seek x, etc. But if we are to address principles to actual people then we must advance principles which make a connection to what actual people desire. We only build air castles if we insist on theorizing in terms of what people should desire. To be sure, other factors influence an argument for a moral principle. For example, what aspect of human experience the principle concerns is also important. But, the link to actual motivations cannot be ignored either. Without it we will not produce *practical* principles.

d. Empiricist Moral Theory

The view of moral theory I am suggesting fits easily into an empiricist epistemol-ogy.[3] In order to do so, I must first emphasize that beliefs are the beliefs of an *acting* being. Epistemologists have often been more interested in understanding scientific knowledge and as a result have paid little attention to the usual range of human actions and experiences.

To be sure, humans seek true belief. They seek to understand, explain, and predict experience. But they also seek goals or ends of other kinds. In so doing they try not merely to predict experiences, but to bring some experiences about and avoid others. In so doing they are led by the fact that they desire some things to occur and desire to avoid others.

When we come to fit moral beliefs, i.e., beliefs which provide principles for guiding conduct, into our overall set of beliefs, it is most natural to speak of "justifying" a belief rather than testing it or proving it. This marks, I think, the fact that moral beliefs contain an irreducible element of reference to desires or prefer-ences. Simply put, desire is what moves us to act.[4] Therefore, practical principles,

principles which guide action, must make an ultimate appeal to our desires or motivations.

This has been taken by many to be enough to show that moral beliefs are completely beyond the epistemological pale. But this need not follow. Rather, we learn what the pattern of fitting moral beliefs into our total set of beliefs must be. It must be such as to allow for the fact that moral beliefs have both a cognitive and a motivational side.

This relationship of two differing factors is crucial to my conception of moral theory. If one is attempting to justify a principle of justice, for example, one must provide a way to distinguish cases of justice from cases of non-justice. This is not itself a merely arbitrary task, for the term "justice" has a history and a role in a public language. The theorist need not agree with previous views about what exactly is just, but the general role or function of justice in those views and in ordinary beliefs does provide a restraint on what is even to count as a theory of justice at all.

But the further check on particular moral theories—emphasized by my approach—is the necessity to show how one's cognitive account of justice makes a claim on the motivation of individuals given their individual conceptions of the good. In this way checking back against the desires or preferences of individuals provides a check on moral theory analogous to that provided by sense experience for scientific theory.

I do not want to push this analogy too far because there are differences, but the necessity to address the desires of individuals does provide the sort of outside check on moral theories which can bring the theorist back to earth. Ignoring this restraint has led many thinkers to argue for moral positions which run directly opposite to the most deeply held human desires.

II. Natural Rights

With the foregoing explanations on hand I now want to employ my conception of moral theory to treat some substantive problems so as to bring us back eventually to the link between moral theory and the foundation of social order.

a. Person Relative Theory of Value

It is fairly easy to see that the account of value or goodness to be offered by the kind of moral theory I propose will be in some way relativistic. Three kinds of considerations lead rather immediately to this conclusion. First, people differ in regard to the kinds of things which, even after much reflection, they most strongly desire.

Second, even when people's strongest desires are for similar kinds of things—such as love, security, or adventure—they tend to rank these in different orders of importance. Two persons may desire love and adventure, but one may desire love more while the other puts a greater weight on adventure.

Third, even if people agree on what kinds of things are most desirable, they may disagree concerning for whom they desire them. Some may focus on themselves while others think of family and friends and still others extend their concerns to everyone.

In light of differences of this kind it is hard to imagine that any non-relative account of value could survive the challenge of the motivational moral skeptic. But the implication of this fact must be carefully restricted. It does not follow that judgments of value are non-cognitive or that they are immune from rational justification. It does follow, however, that value judgments—judgments concerning what is good or valuable—will be person relative. They will be relative to the individual set of desires of each person. For present purposes I need not pursue the long task of further elucidating a theory of value along these lines.[5]

In the material concerning right, which follows, I will be assuming that values are person relative. I will assume that each person pursues a more or less well-thought-out conception of the good even if in some cases that conception is fairly far removed from what he would find good for himself if he thought long and carefully about it.

b. The State of Nature

The great challenge of moral theory for one holding a person relative theory of value is the theory of right. While value may be person relative, it is pointless to advance a person relative theory of right. The chief point of a theory of right is to provide principles to check and coordinate the actions of persons pursuing their own version of the good.

This problem is fairly easily handled on an authoritarian moral theory. On that kind of view some other force can be put over against the desires of each individual. But if one argues to individuals one must find a way to show why persons holding very different conceptions of the good should accept common principles as governing their actions. When one looks at questions of right this way, it is not difficult to see why the traditional device of appealing to a state of nature has had continuing use.

In its contemporary understanding, a state of nature is not to be thought of as speculation about a primitive condition. Rather, it is an intellectual construct designed for posing certain questions in moral theory. We are all accustomed to seek whatever we seek in life (i.e., to pursue our conceptions of the good) within a framework of at least some shared principles of right and some degree of political authority. But in moral theory we are questioning both of these.

In order to do so, then, we may sensibly ask what our circumstances would be like with the constraints of shared principles of right and of political authority removed. But we ask the question about persons like ourselves and our associates. The point is to imagine certain constraints as absent in order to discover what reason we have to wish them present (if we do indeed have such reason) and, thereby, also to cast light on what kind of restraint is really needed from our own point of view.

It should be noted that my use of the state of nature is not merely political. I do not use it only to show why one does or does not need political authority. Rather, I also ask that we imagine the restraints of principles of right removed. Thus, not only is the restraint of enforcement of such principles removed, but also the greater restraint of their acceptance by individuals as binding on their conduct. In this way the state of nature technique can be used in arguing for principles of right.

In the state of nature, then, we imagine ourselves as one of a group of persons, living in proximity to one another, each with his own conception of the good which he is seeking to realize. Our question will be what need such persons might find for principles of right and what principles might meet that need.

It should be noted that at this point I make no special assumptions about the conceptions of good of the persons in the state of nature. They can be taken to be as varied as actual conceptions of good are. In fact, they must be so taken—otherwise I would run afoul of my own complaint about moral philosophers' failing to argue to real people. Thus, I make no special assumption about the conceptions of good involved. Some may be very self-centered; others altruistic. Some are presumably quite materialistic; others may be quite spiritual. These kinds of differences are not only permissible, they are crucial if the theory is to avoid the complaint of the motivational skeptic.

It might be thought, however, that even this use of a construct asking what would happen if, means that I have departed from arguing to actual persons, but this does not follow. The questions raised in the state of nature can be addressed to actual persons. The fact that the questions are about hypothetical conditions does not imply that the answers will not apply to real persons. To be sure, some real persons may decide that actual circumstances are for them preferable to what would be decided in the state of nature. But if the state of nature decisions have made out their case in other ways, that is no problem. Room must be left, even by the motivational skeptic, for people to do what is wrong. In arguing to the actual conceptions of the good of actual people, one need not leave each entire conception unchanged—it may be shown, for example, to be an impossible conception. But this must be shown on its own terms. Even though one argues to actual persons, one need not suppose that what is, is exactly what ought to be. To argue about the ideal one always needs some hypotheticals; but this does not keep one from arguing to actual persons with their own conceptions of the good intact.

Nevertheless, since I will be making considerable use of appeals to what persons would have good reason to want or agree to in a state of nature, it will be advisable further to clarify the relationship between the state of nature and actual situations. Since I want to raise questions about the status of certain moral principles and social or political institutions, the state of nature provides a tool for asking what reason one may have for wanting such things by imagining them absent. By this technique we may hope to show the motivational skeptic not only what need he has for moral principles, but also those for which he has need since the need may more or less determine the content of the principles.

But someone might say that while he could see all of this, he could see no reason to obey the principles which would be chosen in a state of nature, because he has a very good position in an actual set of circumstances which admittedly violates those principles. In saying this he gives up much, for he now makes it clear that others who are disadvantaged in his actual set of circumstances actually do not have reason to acknowledge the principles and claims to authority which make that circumstance possible. Thus he appeals only to his power, *but* most of that power will depend on the fact that many persons acknowledge various principles and claims to authority as valid. Of course, many actual tyrants do succeed, but that is not the crucial issue. If our hypothetical person holds to his position he does so only as long as others do not see their own interests with complete clarity. When they do his power evaporates. Thus, the state of nature shows us how to argue about principles and authority. It cannot guarantee, however, that sound principles and legitimate authority will always prevail.

c. *Natural Rights as Negatives*

With the foregoing stipulations concerning value and the state of nature I am ready to offer an interpretation of natural rights and their place in moral theory. We imagine persons like ourselves with the constraints of government and a shared morality removed, each pursuing his own conception of the good. We ask what principles of right such persons would have reason to acknowledge.

My answer is that in a carefully restricted sense all have reason to acknowledge that each is the bearer of certain natural rights. But such claims have been made in so many ways that I must hasten to add that I distinguish between natural rights and natural duties. I will explain my conception of natural rights first and then turn to natural duties in the next section.

While Locke is the best known proponent of natural rights, his account would seem to be of little use for me since it depends on theological beliefs and a rationalist epistemology. Nevertheless, it is with Locke that I will begin.

In attempting to understand Locke's own position simply for the sake of understanding it, I was finally struck by the fact that I was probably looking for too much in trying to justify natural rights. In considering what Locke says in Section Four of the *Second Treatise* about the natural liberty and equality of human beings, I reflected upon the passage in which he says that nothing is more evident than that creatures having been born of the same species and rank with all the same advantages of nature should be equal one with another.[6] This passage seemed to imply an argument that persons were at liberty in the state of nature, and equally at liberty, because none of them in that state had any legitimate mark of authority over any others. There simply was nothing about them that would allow one of them to be able to claim authority over the others.

Further reflection on this point convinced me that I had been looking for too much in searching for a justification of a theory of natural rights. Natural rights merely require that persons be left as they are, that is to say, only two kinds of claims could possibly vitiate the assertion that we have a natural right to act in a particular way. One of those is the claim that we are duty bound to act in some contrary way. The other is the claim that someone has legitimate authority to prevent us from acting in that way.[7] As long as neither of those claims has been justified then we are naturally at liberty to act in such ways as we choose. Thus, I was led to the insight that the claims of natural rights are in one sense basically negative. Those who would advocate natural rights wish primarily to deny claims of authority or obligation in various respects, claiming simply that persons are in those respects still in the state they would be in in a state of nature. There is no legitimate restriction upon them in those respects.

Any attempt to defend a theory of natural rights is bedeviled by the fact that the term "rights" itself not only is sloppily used, but, at best, is a term of systematic ambiguities. The term "rights" may be used in widely differing contexts, ranging from something so trivial as one's rights as a member of a local social club, to something as grand as one's rights as a human being. Because in these different contexts different issues are raised and different standards of judgment are employed, the question of a general philosophical theory of rights is immensely complicated.

For present purposes, therefore, even though I am convinced that the understanding of rights I offer will cover other contexts, I intend to restrict the context to that of natural rights. The presentation of my theory of natural rights is to take place with the concept of the state of nature as outlined in the previous section already on hand. Thus, natural rights in my conception are those rights one would have in a state of nature.

Presentation of a theory of natural rights is further complicated by the fact that the relationship between natural rights and the law of nature in the traditional writers, such as Locke, is a complex and intimate one. From this fact, we learn important lessons for the theory of natural rights. We also encounter, however, serious problems of exposition.

I shall proceed as follows: Having said already that I assume the context of the state of nature I will introduce a proposed definition of the notion of natural rights. This definition should be thought of as the first step in the development of principles within the context of a state of nature. But according to the definition of natural rights as I have already introduced it intuitively, and as I shall present it more precisely, the extent of natural rights will be limited by such moral justifications for limitations on conduct as are forthcoming. These may be demonstrations of duties on the part of the individual or justifications for others to interfere with the conduct of the individual. Thus, in order to have any understanding of the scope of natural rights, one will have to consider what principles of duty might be justified to persons in the state of nature. This is the second step in the development of moral principles in the state of nature and is the analogue of the law of nature in the traditional writers on natural rights.

I propose to define "x has a natural right to y" as "in a state of nature: (a) there is no moral justification on present evidence for the claim that x is obliged or duty bound to refrain from y-ing or to give up y if he holds it and (b) no one has moral justification for preventing x from y-ing, or for taking y from x, or for refusing to surrender y to x, etc." (The alternative clauses merely try to cover the many things y may be and can easily be augmented if necessary on the same pattern for differing contexts.) I propose this definition as a specification of the conception of natural rights as negative which I have already explained. Like any crucial definition in the development of a philosophical theory it requires considerable explanation.[8]

According to the proposed definition, a person has, for example, a natural right to try to preserve his own life if and only if there is no moral justification for either the claim that he is duty bound to give up his life for some reason or the claim that someone else may legitimately take it from him. From the narrow point of view of philosophical theory one could adopt my understanding of rights here whatever his interpretation of the notion of moral justification. My own claims in regard to rights assume the account of moral justification explained in Part I.

I can probably best explain my theory and its advantages by attacking directly the first and chief objection sure to be raised against it. It will be argued that at best I have captured only a part of the notion of a right because to say that someone has a right implies a corresponding duty on the part of others at least to forbear interfering with the exercise of the right. Thus, my account might be thought deficient because, while capturing the idea that the person with a right is at liberty to act in some way, it does not capture the idea that others have *at least* the duty to forbear interfering with such action.

Indeed this opposing view is often held with great confidence. H. L. A. Hart, for example, asserts that Hobbes is simply mistaken in holding that rights are merely liberties.[9] It strikes me, however, that this confidence is considerably overstated. It is true that claims to rights are often advanced in contexts in which, because of a presupposition that everyone has a duty to refrain from interference with rights, the claim to rights is understood to make a claim of restraint on others as well. But it does not follow from this fact that rights imply duties, nor does it follow that rights are to be *defined* in terms of duties to refrain.

If one looks at Hobbes and Locke carefully one sees that they both use the notion of natural rights in conjunction with what they call a law of nature. Locke, for example, says that the law of nature is the restraint in the state of nature which is otherwise perfect liberty.[10] Both Hobbes and Locke speak of the law of nature and the rights of nature as different things. In Hobbes the natural rights are explicitly liberties and the law of nature is a rule of reason governing the exercise of those liberties (although in the absence of a restraining power it doesn't govern very much).[11]

My theory thus follows in the tradition of the early giants of natural rights theory when it makes natural rights the assertion of an initial equal moral liberty within the context of which principles of duty and obligation must be argued. On this view, then, the assertion of a natural right in a given respect asserts that one has been shown no reason to acknowledge a duty or a legitimate authority over one in that respect. Now one might ask, but does it not follow that in that case others are duty bound not to interfere? But I cannot see that it does.

The claim to a right asserts a moral liberty. If x asserts that he has a right to seek to continue his life, he asserts that he is morally at liberty to do so, that he has no duty to refrain from doing so. If, however, he asserts a right to take the lives of others in so doing, and if we can show that he has a duty to refrain from taking the lives of others, then his claim to this second right is incorrect. But notice that if he claims a right to seek to continue his life, he claims a moral liberty. Nonetheless, even though x has no duty to refrain from seeking to continue his life, it does not follow from that alone, that y, another person, is duty bound to refrain from interference in x's life continuing efforts.

The crucial point to see here is that two different lines of argument must be involved when one considers liberties on the one hand and duties on the other. To show that one is morally at liberty to do a certain thing one need only *defeat* or *refute* arguments designed to show that one has a duty to do that thing, but to show that anyone has a duty to do a thing one must present a positive argument answering both the cognitive and the motivational skeptic. Thus, one would expect to find two different terms employed for the conditions shown by these two different kinds of argument, one positive, the other negative. This is what my theory does. One argues for rights on my view by defeating claims that one is duty bound or subject to authority. The question of demonstration of duties, even duties to refrain from interfering with rights, is taken up as a separate question in the next part. Of course, a complete theory of right requires both of these elements to be used together, as they are in the traditional writers, but it is also important to see the two different kinds of argument involved.

This conflation of two different types of argument is the weakness of that view which includes in its analysis of rights the duty to refrain. This view takes its plausibility from the fact that rights and duties are in almost all accounts closely correlated. It is especially plausible in the legal context in which a legislator would have little reason to specify a right save to introduce a duty to respect it or a judge would have little reason to cite a right save to require its respect. This close correlation in the legal context adds plausibility to the inclusion of duty in the very account one gives of the nature of rights. But, such an account should be rejected just because of the difference of supporting arguments already pointed out. In such cases, what we ordinarily understand by what we say would be a poor guide to philosophic theory. In any ordinary situation we depend on a context of usage to provide a background which allows us to accomplish what we wish with our assertions. If we had to speak a language in which absolutely everything had to be spelled out in detail and nothing went without saying, we would never be able to say much to any purpose. But, of course, in a natural language much goes without saying. Thus, for example, pertinent here, if we speak to an audience all of whom may be expected to share the principle that people are not to be interfered with in doing what they have a right to do, then by asserting that we have a right to do x, we also are understood to assert that others have a duty to refrain from interfering with our xing. But this is because of the *presupposed* principle.

Part of the task of philosophic theory is to sort out such questions—drawing the important lines of distinction, etc. Thus, for purposes of philosophic theory I separate the question of rights from that of duties to refrain because of the different considerations required to argue for these two elements. As the foregoing considerations make clear, however, my position is as much a reflection of the usual use of the concept of rights as is the opposing position. Mine, however, has the added advantage of keeping lines of argument straight while allowing us to say what we wish to say using the ordinary rights terminology.

Before turning to the now crucial question of duty, one other traditional objection to theories concerning rights should be noted. It is notoriously true that even among firm believers in natural rights (or in our times in human rights), there is little agreement as to exactly what rights there are. The lists drawn up by different thinkers always seem to differ. Even rights claimed to be "unalienable" in traditional writers seem suspiciously related to social and political disputes of the author's own time. One thus suspects that philosophers and political thinkers are claiming to find sanction in reason and "unalienable rights" for what is really only their own preferred social or political position. Thus, the expectation has grown up that a really adequate theory of natural rights ought to produce a determinate list of exactly which rights people have. If this demand is taken as a reasonable criterion of adequacy, my theory surely fails it, because from my theory one is not able to deduce a once and for all list of natural rights. I suggest, however, that upon examination this supposed objection actually reveals a strength of my theory and an important truth about the theory of rights.

On my theory, one has reason to assert a right only in response to a claimed duty or claimed legitimate authority. Thus, the rights one might find important to assert would differ according to the duties or authorities one found claimed against oneself. Thus, while in one actual social condition, one set of rights might be claimed, in a differing social condition a differing set (although probably not altogether different) might be claimed. But this shows only a strength not a defect of my theory. For my theory makes clear the underlying philosophical basis of claims to rights and shows why such claims can be adopted to differing social conditions. In this respect we learn thereby one important lesson about theories of right in general. It is all too easy to suppose that in seeking principles for judging social relationships, we must give a prescription for designing a complete society, i.e., that our principles must answer all questions about how institutions and relationships should be structured in a society. In fact, we often seem to be looking for a prescription for constructing a society. But, in fact, what we really need are only principles for judging a society and for guiding us in trying to influence its directions. To find principles for judging and even guiding societies one does not need to go so far as to give exact prescriptions for building a society, although at times—such as times of constitutional foundings—such building may be appropriate.

But on this view it is clear that my theory of rights is stronger for claiming no once-and-for-all list of rights, while it can show non-arbitrary reasons why certain lists of rights might be important in particular social circumstances and historical periods. Those rights will seem important which assert the individual's rejection of such attempts to dominate him as are then most current. Nonetheless, the philosophic foundation of such claims is made clear by my theory.

Further, we should note that some conditions are so regularly repeated in human society as to give rise to rights which are relevant in most social conditions of which we have experience. The Lockeian rights to life, liberty, and property still speak to us now because they deal with ways in which our autonomy is still under attack. Thus, since human society seems always well supplied with thieves, con-men, politicians, tax collectors, gurus, and others of that general ilk, the assertion of a right to property is relevant in all social conditions. This is true even for those social conditions in which people are so lost in some kind of tyranny, or have so identified with some system, that they simply could not conceive of asserting their right to property. If they could, or if they came to make such an assertion, their case could be correct, even if in some circumstances it would be pointless to make because so doing would lead to death, prison, or worse. I make this point to forestall the often-made objection that individual rights and particularly property rights are merely an eccentric Western invention. The fact that domination of individuals in some societies is so efficient that they cannot even conceive of asserting their rights, does not imply that they have no rights, i.e., that the arguments showing they have certain duties or are under particular legitimate authority are sound.

III. Natural Duty and Social Order

It may well seem that in arguing for natural rights, I have gone too far on the side of individual liberty. For, given my conception of natural rights as denying claims of duty and authority, combined with the powerful stance of the motivational skeptic as argued in Part I, it may now seem impossible to justify any limit on the liberty of the individual. But this would be disastrous. For as Hobbes has argued cogently, the situation in which each seeks his own conception of the good, unfettered by any enforceable principle of restraint, is a situation of disaster for all.

The challenge for my theory now is to discover whether any principle of restraint can be justified to persons who know their conceptions of the good and know that they have the liberties of natural rights. The problem is to show that even the motivational skeptic has good reason in the state of nature to accept some principle of respect or restraint in regard to the rights of others. Or put another way, the problem is to show that rights, which I have made so broad, do admit of limits using the same exacting standard of the motivational skeptic I have applied to others.

I shall call a principle which all (or more exactly, almost all) have good reason to accept in the state of nature, a principle of natural duty. I follow Rawls in adopting the convention of using "natural duty" to refer to principles of right which apply to persons even without their actual consent, while using "obligation" to refer to requirements based on voluntary acts of our own. [12] The important point to notice is that I claim only that one would have good reason, given one's own conception of the good, to accept the principle of duty. This is compatible with one's later wishing to avoid it, or even with some persons' never actually consenting to it.

But this is a point of some importance when we ask why what one would have good reason to accept in a state of nature matters in an actual situation. The crucial point is that the state of nature device allows us to show actual persons what their own conception of the good requires. It, therefore, allows us to pick out features of an actual situation which would pass the test of the motivational skeptic. Such features, according to my argument, may be justified morally, while others lack such justification.

Thus, the person who rejects the principles of duty will have no reasonable moral complaint if he is punished for his violation, even if he never consented to the principle. Attempts to state such complaints will lead him back to the principle of duty and, thus, to the justice of his punishment.

Let us now return to the main thread of the argument. Continuing to use the analytic device of the state of nature, i.e., persons like ourselves, but without the restraint of government or shared moral principles, we are to ask what principles, if any, persons so situated would have reason to accept as binding upon their conduct and that of others. We must remember that each of these persons knows his or her own conception of the good (at least to the varying degrees actual people do) and is seeking to realize that conception. Their conceptions of the good may be as broadly or narrowly centered in regard to others as those of actual persons.

In order to answer the questions we now face we should first remember our Hobbes. [13] The ingeniousness of Hobbes' argument seems to me to be this: Hobbes tries to show us that in the situation of a state of nature, in which not only is government lacking but also a shared morality capable of any kind of enforcement, each person is *certain* to face disaster. Success in seeking your own goals will imply, in that condition, the frustration of, or danger to, the goals of others. This is one of the few things that would enable people to cooperate long enough to unite against you. Since, as Hobbes points out vividly, the human frame is relatively weak and even the strongest may be destroyed by the weakest, he tries to show us not merely that the state of nature is a state of war, but also that in this way each of us faces certain disaster.

It is crucial to note that Hobbes' own egoism is really irrelevant to this argument. The argument will work as long as we suppose people pursuing their own conceptions of the good. One's conception of the good may extend to good things for other people. Nonetheless, that conception of the good competes with conceptions of the good held by others and leads to the war of each against each in the state of nature in which none can hope to win for very long.

Hobbes' argument here is powerful. One cannot get around it as many try to do simply by saying that Hobbes is a nasty egoist and people are not really that egotistical or nasty. As long as people do, in fact, seek different goals in life and may, in fact, come in conflict with each other, one has the basic premises about value required to make Hobbes' argument work. A crucial point of Hobbes' argument is that even if you are, for your part, willing to leave others alone and secure in their persons and possessions, as long as some are not so content, you are forced to adopt a war-like stance yourself in order to have any hope of attaining what you seek in life. After all, at this stage in the state of nature one has not yet been shown reason to restrict one's action in any way vis-à-vis others. Thus, it may be perfectly rational for another to kill me or rob me without feeling the least compunction about doing so.[14] But knowing that others may rationally act in this way, I have no rational option, but to be prepared to forestall them. Thus, the war of each against each.

Hobbes' argument serves to show a disastrous consequence for all if each simply seeks his own conception of the good in whatever way seems best for him. Thus, it serves to show why each of us, for the sake of his own conception of the good, has good reason to acknowledge some restraint on actions, both his own and those of others. (Actually, I should say that almost everyone has such reason, since there may be exceptions which I will note later although they are of little importance.)

But even if Hobbes does show us why even the motivational moral skeptic has reason to acknowledge, indeed to insist on, some limitation on action, it is not yet clear that he has reason to accept any particular limitation. After all, Hobbes thought that the only way to avoid the war of each against each was for all to acknowledge the unlimited authority of a force great enough to restrain each by fear. The traditional response to Hobbes has been that his cure was as bad as his disease, for one might just as reasonably decide to take his chances in the state of nature fending off individual enemies, as to decide to subject oneself to one overwhelmingly strong enemy. Indeed, in this case, the traditional objection has merit. What one needs to see is what Locke saw to a degree, namely, that general (not necessarily universal) acceptance of principles of conduct could provide a basis for establishing a relatively peaceful association of persons at a cost far less than that of yielding to an unlimited sovereign. Thus, in order to avoid the war of each against each, every person in the state of nature would have reason to acknowledge certain principles as binding on his conduct and that of others.

But then, of course, we must finally come to ask what principles the persons in the state of nature would have good reason to accept. It does no good to say they need the principles to avoid the war if the only way to arrive at the principles is to have the war anyway. The first point for us to see is that the very reason they need a shared principle has a major influence on what principle they have reason to adopt. They need a principle in order to avoid the war or ceaseless conflict, but they are led into conflict because their interests differ. Thus, what they have reason to accept is the *minimal* principle which would enable them to avoid the war. To accept a more extensive principle would yield greater control over their own actions than they have reason to yield, for such control would favor some conceptions of the good over others. The need for a principle is overriding, so they have reason to restrict their own pursuit of the good far enough to attain that end but no further. Thus, the principle which there is reason to adopt in the state of nature is the *minimal* principle which would allow peace.

Further, it must be noted that whatever exact principle one might argue that the persons in a state of nature have reason to adopt, one would have to add the rider that they will have reason to adopt it only if it also contains provision for a practice of punishment. Since all will know that from the point of view of each the absolutely minimal principle will provide that others restrain their conduct while he does as he pleases, some assurance of short-circuiting their strategy is a necessary precondition for the adoption of any principle to be rational. Punishment is just that practice which artificially raises the price of violating the principles of right. Punishment thus finds its moral basis in the fact that it is a necessary condition for the rationality of the principle of duty. Since I have discussed punishment at length elsewhere I shall pursue this point no further now. [15]

Two philosophers might easily agree on all I have said until now, but still disagree on the *exact* formulation of the minimal principles which the persons in the state of nature would have good reason to accept.

It seems clear to me that the minimal principle is one which requires persons to refrain from initiating the use of force against the persons or property of others. Nonetheless, in order to be thoroughly clear and acceptable this principle would require considerable further polishing. Further, corrolaries concerning obligation, restitution, property, and many other matters have to be drawn. In fact, doing so requires several times the length of this already long paper. Fortunately, for present purposes such completion is not necessary. [16] It should be clear that the minimal principle I have argued to will be such as to produce a society with the maximum emphasis on individual choice, and thus a society of individual liberty with a free market economy. But this is only to point to conclusions I have not fully defended here. I can now turn, however, to the relationship of moral theory and social order which I originally proposed to discuss.

First, I would point out that I have been arguing for a philosophical ideal. That is what moral theory does. But the assessment of a particular society using a philosophical ideal is a complex task. [17]

The ultimate basis of the key principle of natural duty in my moral theory is the fact that it makes a social relationship of persons possible, which relationship is necessary from the point of view of each. But, as I have said, many other principles will serve to avoid the war of all against all. Thus, actual societies—based on much more than minimal principles—survive and even prosper to a degree. In morally assessing an actual society we must measure its practices against our ideal, all societies thus far known would to some degree fail that test, but they fail it to different degrees.

Further, social institutions are hard to change. The effects of changing them intentionally are impossible to foresee in great detail. Thus, one must be cautious in deciding how to act on one's assessment of a particular society. A great departure from the pure observance of individual rights may be the best attainable in some places and times. All the likely alternatives may be worse. Still, a moral theory enables one to assess a society and to see the direction in which change should be sought. Further, if my views are sound, moral theory enables us to understand the rational basis of social order. It allows us to see society as not only compatible with, but necessary for, individual liberty and the pursuit of individual good. It also shows us, moreover, how to evaluate social practices morally and shows how much most societies interfere with individuals beyond what is necessary for a sound social order.

Notes

1. An earlier version of this essay was presented to the Annual Meeting of the American Association for the Philosophic Study of Society held at Marquette University, Milwaukee, Wisconsin, October 7-9, 1977. The title and the basic thesis have survived, but the exposition has been completely redone.

2. I borrow the notion of "centeredness" of ends or goals from Robert Nozick, "The Randian Argument," *The Personalist*, 1971, p. 285.

3. In referring to an empiricist epistemology I have the work of W. V. Quine in mind as that I find most plausible, but nothing in my argument as presented here requires that particular example.

4. I discuss this point in greater detail in an essay entitled "The Randian Argument Reconsidered," which will appear in a volume of essays on the thought of Ayn Rand to be published by the University of Illinois Press.

5. Although I would insist on modifications and different emphasis in regard to right, I believe that the theory of value presented by John Rawls in Chapter VII of *A Theory of Justice* (Cambridge, Mass.: Harvard University Press, 1971) is essentially sound. It is the kind of theory I have in mind here.

6. John Locke, *Second Treatise,* Section 4. Cf., the second paragraph of the section.

7. It may well be that this formulation is redundant, since it may be that legitimate authority could be nothing else than one person's being bound to obey the other. But this analysis is open to dispute, and I find that the fuller formulation reminds us of the issues more clearly. I therefore hold to it save for reasons of stylistic flow.

8. I understand definition as a philosophical tool in more or less the way the subject is treated by Quine in *Word and Object* and the way this understanding of definition is extended to moral theory by Rawls in *A Theory of Justice.* The heart of that conception of definition is summed up by Rawls' notion of replacement. That is to say, I do not claim that the definition I have offered is exactly the same in meaning as "x has a right to y," since I don't know how to identify such complicated cases of sameness of meaning anyway. What I claim is that my definition is for the purposes of philosophical theory a more adequate replacement for the notion that x has a natural right to y. Whether this claim is true can be made out only by judgment of the total developed theory. See W. V. Quine, *Word and Object* (Cambridge, Mass.: MIT Press, 1960), pp. 257-262. Rawls, *Theory of Justice*, p. 111.

9. H. L. A. Hart, "Are There Any Natural Rights?" *Philosophical Review,* 1955. Part I, Section B.

10. Locke, *Second Treatise,* Section 6.

11. Thomas Hobbes, *De Corpore Politico,* Part 1, Chapter 1, Section 6. Hobbes presents roughly the same line of argument in regard to politics in *De Corpore Politico, Philosophical Rudiments Concerning Government and Society* (English translation of *De Cive*), and *Leviathan.* I rely on all these sources for the various interpretations of his argument used below. I assume that the basic outline of Hobbes' position is common knowledge. In any case, my use of Hobbes is for constructive purposes in my own theory and is not intended as interpretation for its own sake.

12. While I take this basic distinction from Rawls I do not follow him exactly since his own way of presenting it is tied up with his own theory. For Rawls' discussion see *A Theory of Justice,* Sections 18 and 19, pp. 108-117. It is also well to note that this way of making the distinction is a constructive suggestion. The terms do not work this way in many ordinary language contexts.

13. Hobbes, *De Corpore Politico,* Part 1, Chapter 1, Section 6.

14. I use "rational" here in the simple, straightforward sense of the most efficient means

for attaining ends taken as given. In the case under discussion, if you place no value on my welfare, then taking my possessions may be (for at least the short range) a perfectly rational thing to do.

15.   In an article entitled "A Rationale for Punishment." This paper was delivered at the Seventh Annual Libertarian Scholars Conference, October 1979, in New York City. It was published in *The Journal of Libertarian Studies*, Vol. IV, No. 2 (Spring 1980), pp. 151-165.

16.   I have attempted this much fuller account in a book length manuscript entitled *Rational Individualism: A Moral Theory* for which publishing negotiations are presently under way.

17.   In this discussion I restrict myself to discussing a "society" and do not separate government or the state from other aspects of society. Thus, I leave aside for the purposes of this paper the question between advocates of anarchy on the one hand and the minimal state on the other. In a full treatment I address this question as well. For a very helpful discussion of the problems involved see Tibor Machan, *Human Rights and Human Liberties* (Chicago: Nelson Hall, 1975), Chapter 5.

DOUGLAS RASMUSSEN*

Essentialism, Values and Rights:
The Objectivist Case for the Free Society

In his critique of Robert Nozick's *Anarchy, State, and Utopia*, Samuel Scheffler notes that

> contemporary philosophers who choose to work within the natural rights tradi-
> tion need to explicate their use of natural rights terminology. Given the meta-
> physical associations of the tradition, such philosophers must explain what they
> *mean* by assigning rights to people. They must, further, say something about
> the source of rights, and they must deal with a variety of epistemic questions.
> How do we know what rights people have? What sorts of evidence justify us in
> believing that people do have certain rights but do not have certain others? [1]

These comments are well-taken. Natural rights theorists should explain their view
of rights and why they believe people have certain rights and not others. Moreover,
the metaphysical and epistemological questions that such rights claims raise must
be handled if a natural rights approach is to be even plausible, much less succeed.
This is especially true for libertarian theorists, since Nozick's argument for Lockean natural rights is more dialectical in character than demonstrative. [2] An argument for the natural right to liberty needs to be provided, but is there more that can
be said in favor of such a right?

Though all the issues raised by Scheffler cannot be dealt with here, [3] a sketch of
an overall argument for the natural right to liberty can be given. This argument
takes its inspiration from the writings of the novelist Ayn Rand and is thus called
"the Randian argument."[4] Yet, its interpretation and development are the result of
many sources. [5] The view of rights that this argument will seek to defend is as
follows:

> 'Rights' are a moral concept—the concept that provides the logical transition
> from the principles guiding an individual's actions to the principles guiding his
> relationship with others—the concept that preserves and protects individual

* St. John's University.

morality in a social context—the link between the moral code of a man and the legal code of a society, between ethics and politics.[6]

And:

> The concept of a 'right' pertains only to action—specifically, to freedom of action. It means freedom from physical compulsion, coercion or interference by other men.[7]

Moreover, this human right to liberty is a natural right.

> Rights are conditions of existence required by man's *nature* for his *proper* survival. If man is to live on earth, it is *right* for him to use his mind, it is *right* to act on his own free judgment; it is *right* to work for his values and to keep the product of his work. If life on earth is his purpose, he has the right to live as a rational being. . . .[8] (some emphasis added)

This conception of rights obviously involves many fundamental philosophical issues. This essay will deal with three of these issues and then provide an outline of "the Randian argument." Only those steps of the argument that involve the three philosophical issues to be discussed will be defended here,[9] but at least we shall be able to see the type of argument that is involved in defending the above conception of rights.

The three issues that need to be considered if a natural rights theory is to have any chance of success are: How can we talk about the nature of anything, let alone a human being? How can we speak of a human being having a proper way to live? and, If there is moral knowledge after all, why should government promote liberty and not virtue? These three questions shall provide the focus for the following remarks.

The Nature of Something

The question of whether one can speak of the nature or essence of something is most certainly the type of metaphysical and epistemological question Scheffler had in mind. To say that human beings have rights in virtue of their nature requires that one can state what the nature of a human being is and defend this statement against other accounts of human nature. Yet, to claim that one account of human nature is superior to others is considered by many philosophers as impossible or at best only an account of what is considered important regarding the entity from a certain point of view and not an account of what it really is.

One of the most effective spokesmen for the belief that we cannot know the nature or essence of an entity has been W. V. O. Quine. Quine has argued that Aristotelian essentialism is a "metaphysical jungle,"[10] and that the distinction between essence and accident is without foundation. For example, say that Jones is both a mathematician and a cyclist,

> insofar as we are talking about the object, with no special bias toward a background grouping of mathematician as against cyclist, there is no semblance of sense in the rating of some of his attributes as necessary and others as contingent.[11]

According to Quine no set of features independent of any linguistic system can be said to constitute the nature or essence of an entity. Quine contends that it is only when a certain way of specifying an object is invoked that an object can be said to have necessary as opposed to contingent features, but this distinction between features becomes incoherent when an object is correctly specified in two conflicting ways, e.g., Jones is both a mathematician and a cyclist. If Jones is described correctly as both a mathematician and a cyclist, then Jones is both essentially and accidentally rational and both essentially and accidentally two-legged, for when Jones is described as a mathematician he is necessarily rational and contingently two-legged, and when he is described as a cyclist he is necessarily two-legged and contingently rational. But this is absurd! Jones cannot of himself be, at the same time, both necessarily rational and contingently two-legged and contingently rational and necessarily two-legged. Thus, Aristotelian essentialism cannot be made into a sensible doctrine.

If it is asked, just how much of our account of what a being is is contributed by our way of specifying that being, viz., by our language, and how much is a genuine reflection of reality, Quine contends that this is "perhaps a spurious question,"[12] for we cannot understand the world without a conceptual system. "To talk about the world we must already impose upon the world some conceptual scheme peculiar to our language."[13] The best we can do, according to Quine, is revise our conceptual system bit by bit, as a mariner would rebuild his ship at sea, plank by plank,

> but we cannot detach ourselves from it and compare it with unconceptualized reality. Hence it is meaningless . . . to inquire into the absolute correctness of a conceptual scheme as a mirror of reality.[14]

Thus, Quine's declarations are of a piece with Wittgenstein of the *Investigations* and constitute a transcendental linguisticism. The attempt to say what X really is is considered an error, and wisdom is regarded as accepting one's confinement to a linguistic system.

Given Quine's view, no natural rights argument could possibly succeed, because no account of the nature of man could be considered superior to another. There would be, for example, very little that could be said on behalf of a Lockean view of man as opposed to a Marxian view or vice-versa. Fundamentally different conceptual schemes are employed in both cases, and there could be no way of saying which theory provided an actual insight into the nature of man. In fact, the question of what a human being really is, independent of some ideology, would be meaningless.

The Wittgensteinian version of transcendental linguisticism has been challenged elsewhere,[15] but the Quinean version must be dealt with here. First, it must be noted that Quine's understanding of Aristotelian essentialism is flawed.[16] He assumes that essential and accidental predicates refer to aspects or parts of beings *in rerum natura*. This is a confused view of Aristotle's doctrine of the predicables, and it comes from accepting Porphyry's version of the doctrine—a version which replaces the definition as a predicable with the species term and makes the individual being the subject of predication rather than the species term. When this is done, the doctrine of predicables is changed from a logical doctrine to a metaphysical one. Instead of being an account of the different ways terms may be predicated of each other, it becomes an account of the different ways terms signify things. By including the species term in the list of predicables and by making an individual being rather than the species term the subject of predication, the situation is created where the species term no longer signifies the whole nature of an individual being but only an essential aspect or part. If Socrates is the subject and 'man' is an essential as opposed to accidental predicate, then a bifurcation of the individual into essential and accidental parts results. 'Man' would refer to the essential part of Socrates, "manness," and, let us say, 'snub-nosed' would refer to the accidental part. But in virtue of what is 'man' said to signify what is essential and 'snub-nosed' what is accidental? Given that Socrates is some X which has a variety of predicates that signify aspects or parts of him, how can one say that some one feature (or set of features) ultimately and independently of some interest or concern is essential as opposed to accidental to Socrates? There is nothing in terms of which to make the distinction, for there is no longer any way to signify what Socrates is. This is why Quine's rejection of this view of the essence/accident distinction is dead right! Apart from some way of referring to Socrates, it makes no sense to say some predicates are essential and some are accidental.

None of this, however, needs to be. What must be recognized is that in shifting the incidence of the predicables from terms (universals) to individuals, Porphyry conflated signification and predication. He made the signification of terms—ultimately the different ways things may be said to be—subject to the ways terms are predicated of each other. Terms like 'man' could no longer signify the whole nature of individual men, viz., what Socrates, Plato, and Quine *are*; rather, such terms had to refer (somehow) to what was essential as opposed to accidental in Socrates, Plato, and Quine qua individuals. The essence of Socrates, Plato, and Quine understood in this way was merely some feature(s) possessed by them. They were all X's which *have* properties, features, characteristics, but in and of themselves they were not anything! From this perspective Quine tries and fails to make sense out of the essence/accident distinction.

> Quine's mistake lies in thinking that essence and accident are both relative to the individual. For Aristotle the essence of an individual is the individual itself with all of its accidents: this means there is no distinction between essence and accident in the individual. What is essential is relative to the species. Rationality is essential to some things but essential to them as being the kind of things they are; it is a differentia and the differentia differentiates species, not individuals. [17]

It is the species term—more contemporarily stated, the natural kind term—that tells us what an individual is, and it is relative to this term that the distinction between essential and accidental predicates is made. Quine's cycling mathematician is only a problem for essentialism on the suppositions that essence and accident are determined by reference to the individual and that there is no way of specifying what the individual reality really is. But neither of these suppositions is obvious. In everyday life, in the *lebenswelt*, we do specify what things are, and though the final answer to many what-is-it questions may only be found in science, there is no reason to assume that we cannot specify what an individual really is and thus on that basis determine what is essential and accidental to it.

Qua individuals there are no essential or accidental traits; it is only qua a certain kind of thing—which the species or natural kind term specifies—that certain traits are essential or accidental. The abilities to cycle and do mathematics are uses we make of our rational animality, but it is only the latter that makes us men. A man may choose to cycle or do mathematics, or do both, or he may choose to give one or the other, or both, activities up; but he cannot choose or cease to be a man. The natural kind or species term 'man' is not on the same level of generality as 'cycling' or 'doing mathematics'; it notes that men are animals with a consciousness characterized by the ability to form abstractions, engage in reflection, create language, and exercise choice. It does not, however, note to what forms this conscious animal life will be put. It notes that it must be exercised in *some* way, but that it can be exercised in *any* way. It is the realization that this rational animality must be manifested in *some* way that causes us to say that, for example, Socrates, Plato, and Quine *must* be men—that they cannot be otherwise—and it is also the realization that the rational animality can be manifested in *any* way that causes us to say that, for example, Socrates, Plato, and Quine may or may not be cyclists or mathematicians or both. An individual is neither essentially nor accidentally a cyclist or mathematician. Such an individual is merely manifesting, in one possible form, that which he must be and is—viz., a human being.

It may be objected that this entire response really proves Quine's point, for did not Quine state that the distinction between essence and accident was senseless without a certain way of specifying an object and is this not just what we have exactly argued? The response to this question is "yes," but only in part, for this brings us to the second problem with Quine's criticism of Aristotelian essentialism. Indeed, the Aristotelian view of the essence/accident distinction does require, presuppose, a way of specifying what an object, an individual, is, but it does not hold that this process is determined by an appeal to analyticity.[18] To say what X *is* and thus what X must be is not a result of any analysis of the meaning of 'X'.

Quine seems to assume that admitting that the essential/accidental distinction makes sense only "under a description" or "way of specifying" an object implies that such descriptions and ways of specifying the object are analytic statements or linguistic conventions, and thus it is only in virtue of these that a trait could be considered essential as opposed to accidental. In reality, we could not say what was essential or accidental to the object. As Robert Hollinger notes,

> How are we to tell which of the properties 'necessarily rational' or 'necessarily two-legged' really expresses Jones' 'real essence'? On the assumption that analyticity is the only criterion, there is no way of telling, and indeed no sense to the claim, that this quest is valid.[19]

Yet, this assumes that necessity must be a trait of linguistic terms.[20] If we cannot explain what necessarily belongs to X by an appeal to 'X' 's meaning, frame of reference, language-game, back-ground grouping, etc., then we cannot say anything is necessary to X. It is only because Quine sees 'necessarily rational' and 'necessarily two-legged' as resulting from certain analytic or linguistic ways of specifying Jones that a contradiction ensues—that is, Jones being both necessarily rational and contingently two-legged and contingently rational and necessarily two-legged. If essential as opposed to accidental features were not determined in such analytic, linguistic ways, no contradiction would necessarily result. This, of course, is the very point Aristotelian essentialism notes!

It might seem paradoxical that the thinker most responsible for the demise of the analytic/synthetic division should see necessity as a function of analyticity. Yet, it must be remembered that Quine took logical truths to be necessary in virtue of their form (one way of viewing analyticity) and only objected to analytic truths when it came to defining them as propositions reducible to logical truths via synonyms. It was primarily the issue of synonymy that caused difficulty for the notion of analytic truth. In fact, Quine contended that the determination of 'X' 's meaning was dependent on the entire conceptual scheme. The reevaluation of one statement requires the reevaluation of others for Quine. He rejected analytic truths only in the sense that he rejected the distinction between truths based on meaning and truths based on fact. He actually expanded the former in such a way so as to blur the distinction and thus make all truths dependent on meaning—dependent on an entire conceptual system. This form of transcendental linguisticism will be examined shortly, but it can now be said not to be so unusual for Quine to consider all modes of specifying or describing an object as analytic statements or linguistic conventions, because truths based on fact are understood as part of an entire conceptual scheme.

What, then, are the criteria for determining what X is? How do we determine the what-it-is-to-be, the nature, of X? The answer to this question is beyond this essay's scope and cannot be answered in any complete way here. Yet, it can be indicated what a proper approach to answering this question seems to be. As already noted, the identity conditions of natural kind or species terms are not determined by conceptual analysis and thus have nothing to do with analyticity. The approach that this essay would, at least tentatively, endorse is a procedure stated by Robert Hollinger in "A Defense of Essentialism:"

> My defense of essentialism is the idea that essential traits are specified in terms of empirical laws and hypotheses and that these can be justified by scientific investigation. A statement expressing the essential traits of a species is confirmed in the way any other high-level theoretical hypothesis is confirmed. One method of confirmation . . . is this: if hypothesis H is supported by inductive evidence, leads to accurate predictions, provides plausible explanations of observed data, and fits with a body of theory, then it is at least reasonable to accept that hypothesis, or even think it is true, particularly if it has no rivals, or none as acceptable. [21]

Determining what X *is* is not an a priori or intuitive procedure; rather, it is empirical, and though difficult, it is not impossible. Of course, any complete account of this process would have to provide a non-constant conjunction view of causality[22] and defend the role natures or essences play in scientific explanations, [23] but these do not seem as insurmountable as they once did. Essentialism is a viable position.

The third problem with Quine's position is his claim that since we must use a conceptual scheme—a language—to understand reality, we are "therefore" imposing our concepts on reality and are unable to say what X really is. Moreover, his claim that understanding things as they really are means or implies doing so non-conceptually is problematic too. There are certain implicit assumptions in this position that need to be brought out.

Gilson has remarked that any attempt on the part of a philosopher to avoid the logical conclusion of his position is destined to failure, because what he himself declines to say will be said by his disciples, if he has any; if he has none, it may remain eternally unsaid, but it is there, and anybody going back to the same principles, be it several centuries later, will have to face the same conclusion.[24]

This insight can and should be applied to all forms of the "Copernican Revolution" when it comes to the issue of understanding things objectively. Henry Mansel, a follower of Kant, declares explicitly what is only implied by the transcendental turn.

> With him (Kant) all is phenomenal (mere appearance) which is relative, and all is relative which is an object to a conscious subject. The conceptions of our understanding as such depend on the constitution of our thinking faculties, as perceptions of the senses do on the constitution of our intuitive faculties. Both might be different, were our mental constitutions changed; both probably are different to beings differently constituted. The *real* thus becomes identical with the absolute, with the object as it is in itself, out of all relation to a subject; and, as all consciousness is a relation between subject and object, it follows that to attain a knowledge of the real we must go out of consciousness.[25]

No more eloquent example of Gilson's insight could be offered, for this argument amounts to the claim that to be perceived, to be understood, etc., is not to be real. Yet, if we will but consider what Quine has stated in the previously quoted passages, does he not say just this? Does he not say that to *understand* something objectively—as it really is—we must do so in an *unconceptualized* manner? Indeed, he does! He uses the very impossibility of the task as the basis for characterizing any inquiry in regard to whether we know the real or not as meaningless. Strange as it may seem to some, Quine is following the Kantian tradition.[26]

The unchallenged premise of Mansel's argument is "that any knowledge acquired by a process of consciousness is necessarily subjective and cannot correspond to the facts of reality, since it is processed knowledge."[27] Indeed, the uncritical move from that which is relational to that which is appearance is evident in Mansel's remarks. Yet, even more importantly, there is the confusion of the mode of cognition with the content of cognition. The supposition that if consciousness or knowing operates in a certain fashion, or in more Quinean terms, that if a conceptual scheme is employed in understanding, *then* such processes cannot be reports of the world as it is is a blatant *non sequitur*. The fact that some conceptual system must be employed to understand X does not by itself imply that such understanding cannot be an account of the real. It is only by conflating the mode of cognition with the content of cognition that such an inference could be made plausible. But the mode of existence of the thing known does not have to be the same as the mode of existence of its cognition. If we have learned anything from Aristotle's criticism of Plato's commitment to a world of Forms, it is this, but it is on this very point that Kant, and his followers such as Quine, stumble.

> Failing to distinguish between the *mode* and the *content* of intellectual knowledge, [Kant] regarded the intellect as itself constitutive of the formal element of the *content* of its thought. Whereas it is entirely true that the object of intellectual knowledge is in the intellect in a manner appropriate to the intellect, and that the form of universality is given the object as it is in knowledge, still it is not

true that subjective forms enter into the content of the object known. In direct knowledge the *content* of thought is received, only the manner of its being in thought has been produced by the thinker.[28]

Quine, of course, does not use such language. Quine does not speak of subjective conditions of the intellect determining the form of the content of consciousness. After all, is not Quine an advocate of a behavioristic theory of meaning? Yet, it does not take too much philosophical acumen to realize that Quine has only replaced "subjective conditions of the intellect" with the particular "linguistic system" we have learned. The content of our knowledge has been structured by our language systems and we cannot hope to get outside of them. From the Quinean perspective, it is indeed spurious, futile, and just plain meaningless to talk of knowledge of reality.

It is, however, not necessary to adopt such a Kantian view of knowledge, and much of the reason for adopting it can be avoided by refusing to take the Cartesian step of making the instruments of knowledge—concepts/language—the objects of knowledge. If the Aristotelian tradition teaches us any wisdom, it is the futility of this step.[29] Yet, there is another reason for the adoption of this Kantian view of cognition—namely, the assumption that attaining knowledge of the real involves claiming to know the world as one imagines God knows it, viz., *sub specie aeterni-tatis*. The recognition that human knowing is accomplished in pieces, step by step, is taken as implying that one is simply operating within one's "form of life" or "conceptual system" and thus incapable of knowing reality. Yet, none of this follows. The whole issue of epistemology would be of no concern for an infallible, omniscient being; epistemology exists precisely because man is a being who learns in pieces, step by step, and who must use proper procedures to avoid error. The discovery that man is limited and fallible is not the end of any attempt to know the real, but its beginning! Epistemology begins with this realization.[30] There is, therefore, no reason to view the contention that conceptual apprehension attains the real as somehow requiring the adoption of "God's vantage point" regarding what is known or the admission that human knowing is accomplished in pieces and subject to error, viz., man is limited and fallible, as requiring the abandonment of any attempt to know reality as such. Human beings know the real, but they do so in a human, not a divine, manner.

Facts and Values

Supposing that we can know the nature of entities and even the nature of man, how does this tell us what way a human being should live? The question of how we find values in a world of facts remains. Traditionally, there was no such difficulty, because nature was viewed teleologically. Everything had an end set by nature or God, and this provided the ontological source of values. This view, however, has by and large lost plausibility. Much of science's progress has been accomplished by rejecting teleological explanations, and the arguments for the existence of God are generally regarded as not succeeding. To modern man the only ends in the universe are those set by himself,[31] and there is no reason why he should set his goals one way or the other.

Though there is little reason to accept a universal teleology, it is not altogether obvious that teleological explanations can be eschewed from the entire non-human world. First, it must be recognized that to maintain a place for end-oriented behavior in nature is *not* to prove the existence of God nor to make any statement about the manner of the origin of the species. It is rather to note certain facts that seem to require teleological explanation. Living things grow and develop, but if we try to understand this growth and development only in terms of itself and preceding conditions with no recourse to the end or goal of this growth and development, then a central feature of this process seems to be missed. It appears that living things require teleological explanations in order to be properly understood, and thus the question of whether teleology exists or not comes down to the question of whether the laws in terms of which organic phenomena are explained can be reduced to laws which make no mention of the end or goal of the living process but only how the material constituents of the process interact. As Allan Gotthelf has put the issue,

> In the case of organic development, can one give an account of the process of development solely in terms of laws of chemical interaction, laws which make no mention of the end to be realized, so that in principle one could give a chronological list of sets of chemical transformations of initial and added material such that the end result is a correct chemical description of a mature living organism, without any laws of transformation making any reference to the end result?[32]

If such a reduction can*not* be made, then there is a case to be made for teleology.

In fact, Gotthelf has argued that for Aristotle the primary use of 'for the sake of' concerns the development of a living organism,

> Aristotelian teleology . . . is neither vitalist and mystical, nor "as if" and mechanical. The notion of an irreducible potential for form supplies the proper content to the awareness that for Aristotle organic development is actually *directive*, without implying (as the "immaterial agency" interpretation does) that it is direct*ed;* and it identifies the ontological basis of the awareness that the existence and stages of development can be understood only in terms of its end—by establishing the *identity* of the development is its being *irreducibly* a development to that end, irreducibly the actualization of a potential for form. [33]

Teleology exists, then, because the very nature of living things involves the development toward the form of the mature organism. This end-oriented behavior—this process of pursuing and maintaining goals—is the result of the very nature of a living thing, and if we understand valuation to be a process of pursuing and maintaining goals, this means that values exist because living things exist. As Rand has stated, "the fact that living entities exist and function necessitates the existence of values. . . ."[34] Teleology has a place in nature not because God exists but because living things do.

Given that there is such end-oriented behavior, the end of this behavior, that-for-the-sake-of-which such activity is done, is the life of a living entity. As Rand states,

> Without an ultimate goal or end, there can be no lesser goals or means: a series of means going off into an infinite progression toward a non-existent end is a metaphysical and epistemological impossibility. It is only an ultimate goal, an

end in itself, that makes the existence of values possible. Metaphysically, *life* is the only phenomenon that is an end in itself: a value gained and kept by a constant process of action. Epistemologically, the concept of "value" is genetically dependent upon and derived form the antecedent concept of "life." To speak of "value" as apart from "life" is worse than a contradiction in terms. It is only the concept of "life" that makes the concept of "value" possible.[35]

Yet, to fully appreciate what is meant here, it must be realized that "life" does not exist in the abstract and thus cannot be attained by action that does not conform to a particular living thing's nature. Living is not the same thing in different beings. Living as an amoeba is not living as a plant; living as a plant is not living as an animal, and living as an animal is not living as a human being. So, the mature state of a living being—the full and complete actualization of a living thing's nature—is how the life of a living thing is achieved. Acting in accordance with one's nature is acting to live.

If the foregoing is true, then the goal of *our* natural development is the actualization of our human potential, viz., living as a human being. The unique thing, however, about human nature is that the process of natural development involves volition. Choosing, deciding, etc. constitute the manner by which the natural development of a human being occurs. Human beings have no choice as to what the ultimate end of their actions is—that is set by their very capacity to pursue ends, for it is through the exercise of such a capacity that human life is to be achieved—but whether the actualization of human potential is so achieved is up to them. Thus, living as a human being is the goal of human action and the moral standard by which such action is evaluated.

Just what living as a human being involves and how it is related to liberty will be considered in the next section, but what should be noted now regarding this meta-ethical theory is: 1) It considers teleology to have a naturalistic basis. Teleology is grounded in the thesis that we cannot understand what living things are and how they function except insofar as we understand such functioning as ordered to the maintenance of the entity's life, which for any particular living thing is understood as the living thing's development to maturation. If this thesis should not prove to be true, this meta-ethical theory would fail. 2) It sees teleology as preventing the establishment of the fact/value dichotomy. There are some facts that are inherently value-laden. These facts pertain to living things and their needs and provide the basis for moral knowledge when human beings are considered. 3) It regards human volition as teleological in character, viz., the goal of volition is the attainment of human fulfillment, but the exercise of volition is dependent on the individual human being. Choice is necessary for morality, but choice itself does not determine the moral standard.

Together, these three points provide an answer to a question that has troubled contemporary ethicists. Contemporary ethicists have had difficulty in answering the question "Why should I be moral?" and some[36] have even contended that the decision to be moral must be an arbitrary one. Yet, if a human being has a natural function—a way he should act if he wants to fully realize his potentialities—then this question can be answered. One should practice morality because it will lead to successful human living, to happiness and fulfillment, and these are goals that not only everyone wants but which make the very discussion of ends, goals, and values possible. To ask the question "Why should I want to live successfully?" makes no sense, for the very meaning of 'should' is dependent on the context of pursuing an ultimate end, and for a human being success at being human is just that end. [37]

Virtue and Liberty

Human beings are rational animals; they have the capacity to form concepts. Yet, the process consists of more than merely grasping a few simple abstractions and using words. Conceptually attending to the world is a *method* of using one's consciousness. Conceptualizing

> is not a passive state of registering random impressions. It is an actively sustained process of identifying one's impressions in conceptual terms, of integrating every event and every observation into a conceptual context, of grasping relationships, differences, similarities in one's perceptual material and of abstracting them into new concepts, of drawing inferences, of making deductions, of reaching conclusions, of asking new questions and discovering new answers and expanding one's knowledge into an ever-growing sum. [38]

This process is thinking, and it is man's unique and only way for dealing with the world, for man has no automatic knowledge or course of action to follow.

> His senses do not tell him automatically what is good for him or evil, what will benefit his life or endanger it, what goals he should pursue and what means will achieve them, what *values* his life depends on, what course of action it requires. His own consciousness has to discover the answers to all these questions—but his consciousness will not function *automatically.* [39]

Thinking, conceptualizing, focussing one's consciousness require effort—effort to initiate the activity and effort to maintain it. Thus, rationality and choice are not two separate faculties but distinct aspects of the same conscious act. The act of focussing one's awareness, conceptualizing, is volitional.

Living as a rational animal means living by use of reason. It involves a total commitment to a state of full and active awareness in every aspect of one's life in all of one's waking hours.

> It means a commitment to the principle that all of one's convictions, values, goals, desires and actions must be based on, derived from, and validated by a process of thought. . . . [40]

It also involves the virtues of independence, integrity, honesty, justice, productive-ness, and pride. Rand has done a masterly job of explaining each of these virtues in her works, [41] and so these will not be fully discussed here. Yet, it should be noted that Rand is trying to provide an eudaimonistic account of ethics and should be seen as an advocate of complete self-realization. Her emphasis on reason as the only tool by which human life is achieved does not mean that contemplation and academic pursuits are the only proper vocations for man.

A special comment is necessary regarding the virtue of productiveness. Produc-tive work constitutes the material expression of rationality. Not only is productive work the means by which man secures his sustenance, it is an exercise of his fullest potential—a potential that can only be realized by the fullest use of his mind.

"Productive work" does not mean the unfocussed performance of the motions of some job. It means the consciously chosen pursuit of a productive career, in any line of rational endeavor, great or modest, on any level of ability. It is not the degree of a man's ability nor the scale of his work that is ethically relevant, but the fullest and most purposeful use of his mind.[42]

Living as a human being, as a rational animal, is not something for an elite few. It is within the grasp of all physically normal human beings, and productive work provides the central way by which this is accomplished.

It should be further noted that Rand's eudaimonistic person is not someone who is always striving for happiness in the future, as something to be gained with the achievement of the next goal but never present now. Rather, a person with a fully integrated sense of values, whose emotions and intellect work in harmony, experiences the joy of life in his living. David Norton has expressed this view quite well.

The eudaimonic individual experiences the whole of his life in every act, and he experiences parts and whole together as necessary, such that he can will nothing changed. But the necessity here introduced is moral necessity, deriving from his choice. Hence we may say of him interchangeably, "He is where he wants to be, doing what he wants to do," or "He is where he must be, doing what he must do."[43]

Such would be the achievement of human excellence.

Given this most brief account of human excellence, how does it relate to liberty? The right to liberty specifies a norm for social behavior that protects a necessary condition for human life. Human beings cannot actualize their potentials without conceptually attending to the world and acting on the judgments they form, and they cannot do this if their liberty is violated. As Tibor R. Machan has argued:

Each man must be free to choose to gain the knowledge and perform the actions required for his life,—i.e. if his life is to have the opportunity to be a good one, if he is to have the option between moral and immoral conduct, an option open to him by nature. The choice to learn, to judge, to evaluate, to appraise, to decide what he ought to do must be each person's own, otherwise he simply has no opportunity to excel or fail at the task. His moral aspirations cannot be fulfilled (or left unfulfilled) if he is not the source of his own actions, if they are imposed or forced upon him by others.[44]

The only way that a society can be moral is if it allows its members to *choose* the good. Coercion cannot make someone think, understand, and it separates a person from his action. A person's actions cannot be his own if he has not chosen them. Coercion separates a person from his judgments and makes him act in a manner inconsistent with his own judgment. Force may be used in self-defense and retaliation to protect liberty. It may not be initiated.

It should be realized that the right to liberty involves the right to act to produce, to use, and to dispose of material things in any manner one judges. Man is a material thing, not just a mind, and his fulfillment cannot be achieved if he has not the right to translate his judgments into material form. Freedom of action with respect to material goods is a basic element of the right to liberty. Consistently practiced, capitalism would be the social and economic embodiment of this principle.

For a full discussion of this doctrine of rights one should consult Machan's *Human Rights and Human Liberties*, but from this most brief presentation the rationale for a Lockean natural rights theory can be seen. It remains, however, to discuss the relation between virtue and liberty.

What must be noted from the foregoing comments is the intimate relation between virtue and liberty. Liberty is inherent to the very character of virtue; human excellence cannot be accomplished if a person's actions are not his own. Rand's view of human goodness establishes this connection by showing that conceptual awareness is the process by which man conforms to his nature (actualizes himself) and that this process must be self-initiated and self-maintained. The dichotomy between virtue and liberty so evident in the conservative intellectual movement[45] is completely avoided. The age-old debate as to whether virtue or liberty should be government's purpose is thus avoided too. On the one hand, government should promote virtue, and in order to do this, it should protect each person's right to liberty. On the other hand, government should promote liberty, and to accomplish this it must recognize the natural right to liberty. The practice of virtue requires liberty, and the protection of liberty requires moral knowledge. In other words, a uniting of both ancient and modern political concerns is possible if the foregoing account of virtue and liberty is true.

The Randian Argument

What follows is a step by step account of the argument[46] with which this essay has concerned itself:

1. Life is an ultimate end, and end in itself, for any living thing.
2. To be a living thing and not be a living thing of a particular kind is impossible.
3. The particular kind of living thing an entity is determines what one must mean when talking of "life" with respect to a given entity.
C1 Thus, life as the kind of thing it is is the ultimate value for each living thing.
4. A human being is that kind of living being which can be designated as a rational animal.
C2 Thus, life as a rational animal is the ultimate value for each person.
5. A rational animal is an animal whose mode of consciousness is characterized by the use of concepts, viz., conceptual awareness is the way man is differentiated from the other animals.
C3 Thus, conceptual awareness must characterize one who lives as a rational animal, and one only lives as a rational animal in so far as one engages in conceptual activity. Conceptual awareness is a peculiarly human form of existence.
6. The conceptual mode of cognitive contact with reality is man's only means of determining how to deal with reality so as to sustain his own existence.
7. Actions taken in accord with judgments of how to deal with reality are man's only means of dealing with reality so as to sustain his own existence.
C4 Thus, living as a rational animal means, minimally, acting in accordance with one's own conceptual judgments.

8. Conceptual awareness is not automatic. It must be initiated and sustained by a constant act of volition on the part of the person. Conceptual awareness cannot *exist* save through the person's choice to engage in such a mode of awareness.

9. C4

C5 Thus, a precondition for living the life of a rational animal is that within any given context one be free from interference upon acting according to one's judgment.

10. Since C2

11. And since C5

C6 Anything which threatens the precondition for living the life of a rational animal is of ultimate disvalue.

12. In a social context, the initiation of physical force (and by extension the threat thereof) by one man against another serves to destroy the precondition of living the life of a rational animal, since acting upon one's judgment becomes impossible.

C7 Thus, the iniation of physical force is an ultimate disvalue.

13. C4 and C7 have moral significance, viz., one ought to act as described in C4 and not act as described in C7.

C8 Thus, one human being ought not to initiate physical force against another man.

14. "Rights" is a moral concept determining the limits or boundaries of human interaction.

C9 Thus, one has no right to initiate the use of physical force against another human being.

16. Because of C7, C9 is the ultimate social principle.

C10 Thus, no other social principle or other rights can include the initiation of physical force as their means of being exercised.

There remains much more to be explained and defended regarding this argument. This essay, however, did not purport to present a complete defense. It has rather tried to outline the general features of a way to defend a Lockean natural rights theory. It has also tried to answer briefly some of the metaphysical and epistemological concerns of natural rights critics. Much, however, still needs to be done.[47]

Notes

1. "Natural Rights, Equality, and the Minimal State," *Canadian Journal of Philosophy* (1976): 62.

2. Much of Nozick's work can be seen as an attempt to show that a different conception of justice was derivable by a method essentially similar to that used by Rawls.

3. See Tibor R. Machan's *Human Rights and Human Liberties* (Chicago: Nelson-Hall, 1975) and Douglas B. Rasmussen, "A Groundwork for Rights: Man's Natural End," *The Journal of Libertarian Studies* (Winter 1980): 65-76 for a more complete discussion of some of these issues.

4. See Douglas Den Uyl and Douglas Rasmussen, "Nozick On The Randian Argument," *The Personalist* (April 1978): 184-205.

5. Henry B. Veatch's *For An Ontology Of Morals* (Evanston, Ill.: Northwestern University Press, 1971) and David Norton's *Personal Destinies* (Princeton, N.J.: Princeton University Press, 1976) have aided the development of this argument.

6. Ayn Rand, "Man's Rights" in *The Virtue of Selfishness* (New York, Signet Books, 1964), p. 92.

7. *Ibid.*, p. 94.

8. Ayn Rand, *Atlas Shrugged* (New York, Random House: 1957), p. 1061.

9. Also, see Tibor R. Machan, "Rationale for Human Rights," *The Personalist* (Spring 1971) and Eric Mack, "How to Derive Ethical Egoism," *The Personalist* (Autumn 1971) for a discussion of these issues.

10. W. V. O. Quine, *The Ways of Paradox and Other Essays* (New York: Random House, 1966), p. 174.

11. W. V. O. Quine, *Word and Object* (Cambridge, M. I. T. Press, 1960), p. 199.

12. W. V. O. Quine, *From A Logical Point Of View* (New York, Harper & Row, 1961), p. 78.

13. *Ibid.*

14. *Ibid.*, p. 79.

15. Douglas B. Rasmussen, "Deely, Wittgenstein, and Mental Events," *The New Scholasticism* (Winter 1980).

16. See Edward Black's "Aristotle's 'Essentialism' and Quine's Cycling Mathematician," *The Monist* (April 1968) and Nicholas P. White's "Origins of Aristotle's Essentialism," *The Review of Metaphysics* (September 1972) for a discussion of this point.

17. Black, pp. 293-294.

18. See Douglas B. Rasmussen, "Logical Possibility and Necessary Truth: The Viewpoint From An Intentional Logic," Ph. D. dissertation, Marquette University, 1980 for a discussion of this issue.

19. "A Defense of Essentialism," *The Personalist* (Autumn 1976): 329.

20. See Panayot Butchvarov, *The Concept of Knowledge* (Evanston, Ill.: Northwestern University Press, 1970), chapter 2 for a devastating critique of the linguistic theory of necessary truth.

21. pp. 335-336.

22. See R. Harré and E. H. Madden, *Causal Powers* (Totowa, N.J.: Rowman and Littlefield, 1975).

23. See Banuch A. Brody, *Identity And Essence* (Princeton, N.J.: Princeton University Press, 1980), chapter 6.

24. Etienne Gilson, *The Unity of Philosophical Experience* (New York: Charles Scribner's Sons, 1937), p. 302.

25. Henry Mansel, "On the Philosophy of Kant," in Henry Mansel, *Letters, Lectures And Reviews,* ed. H. W. Chandler (London: John Murray, 1873), p. 171.

26. See Henry B. Veatch, "Is Quine a Metaphysician," *The Review of Metaphysics* (March 1978) for a discussion of this point.

27. Ayn Rand, *Introduction to Objectivist Epistemology* (New York: New American Library, 1979), p. 108.

28. John Frederik Peifer, *The Concept in Thomism* (New York: Bookman Associates, 1952), p. 21.

29. *Ibid.*

30. See Douglas B. Rasmussen, "Austin and Wittgenstein On 'Doubt' And 'Knowledge'," *Reason Papers* (Fall 1974).

31. Some would say, e.g., B. F. Skinner, that teleological explanations should not even be applied to human behavior.

32. "Aristotle's Conception of Final Causality," *The Review of Metaphysics* (December 1976): 231.

33. *Ibid.*, p. 253.

34. Rand, *The Virtue of Selfishness*, p. 17.

35. *Ibid.*

36. Kai Nielsen, "Why Should I Be Moral?" *Methodos* 15 (1963).

37. See Rasmussen, "A Groundwork for Rights: Man's Natural End" for a thorough discussion of this issue.

38. Rand, *The Virtue of Selfishness*, p. 20.

39. *Ibid.*, p. 19.

40. *Ibid.*, p. 26.

41. See her novels *Atlas Shrugged* and *The Fountainhead* for dramatic presentations of this point.

42. Rand, *The Virtue of Selfishness*, pp. 26-27.

43. *Personal Destinies*, p. 222.

44. Machan, *Human Rights and Human Liberties*, 119.

45. See George H. Nash, *The Conservative Intellectual Movement in America* (New York, Basic Books, 1976) for a discussion of this point.

46. This argument is taken, with certain modifications, from Den Uyl and Rasmussen's "Nozick On The Randian Argument."

47. Summer fellowships from the Liberty Fund of Indianapolis, Indiana made certain portions of this paper possible.

MURRAY N. ROTHBARD*

Society without a State

In attempting to outline how a "society without a State"—that is, an anarchist society—might function successfully, I would first like to defuse two common but mistaken criticisms of this approach. First, is the argument that in providing for such defense or protection services as courts, police, or even law itself, I am simply smuggling the state back into society in another form, and that therefore the system I am both analyzing and advocating is not "really" anarchism. This sort of criticism can only involve us in an endless and arid dispute over semantics. Let me ⚡ say from the beginning that I define the state as that institution which possesses one or both (almost always both) of the following properties: (1) it acquires its income by the physical coercion known as "taxation"; and (2) it asserts and usually obtains a coerced monopoly of the provision of defense service (police and courts) over a given territorial area. Any institution not possessing either of these properties is not and cannot be, in accordance with my definition, a State. On the other hand, I define anarchist society as one where there is no legal possibility for coercive aggression against the person or property of any individual. Anarchists oppose the state because it has its very being in such aggression, namely, the expropriation of private property through taxation, the coercive exclusion of other providers of defense service from its territory, and all of the other depredations and coercions that are built upon these twin foci of invasions of individual rights.

Nor is our definition of the state arbitrary, for these two characteristics have been possessed by what is generally acknowledged to be states throughout recorded history. The state, by its use of physical coercion, has arrogated to itself a compulsory monopoly of defense services over its territorial jurisdiction. But it is certainly conceptually possible for such services to be supplied by private, nonstate institutions, and indeed such services have historically been supplied by other organizations than the state. To be opposed to the state is then not necessarily to be ⚡ opposed to services that have often been linked with it; to be opposed to the state does not necessarily imply that we must be opposed to police protection, courts, arbitration, the minting of money, postal service, or roads and highways. *Some* anarchists have indeed been opposed to police and to all physical coercion *in*

* Brooklyn Polytechnic Institute

defense of person and property, but this is not inherent in and is fundamentally irrelevant to the anarchist position, which is precisely marked by opposition to all physical coercion invasive of, or aggressing against, person and property.

The crucial role of taxation may be seen in the fact that the state is the only institution or organization in society which regularly and systematically acquires its income through the use of physical coercion. All other individuals or organizations acquire their income voluntarily, either (1) through the voluntary sale of goods and services to consumers on the market, or (2) through voluntary gifts or donations by members or other donors. If I cease or refrain from purchasing Wheaties on the market, the Wheaties producers do not come after me with a gun or the threat of imprisonment to force me to purchase; if I fail to join the American Philosophical Association, the association may not force me to join or prevent me from giving up my membership. Only the state can do so; only the state can confiscate my property or put me in jail if I do not pay its tax tribute. Therefore, only the state regularly exists and has its very being by means of coercive depredations on private property.

Neither is it legitimate to challenge this sort of analysis by claiming that in some other sense, the purchase of Wheaties or membership in the APA is in some way "coercive"; there again, we can only be trapped in an endless semantic dispute. Apart from other rebuttals which cannot be considered here, I would simply say that anarchists are interested in the abolition of this type of action: for example, aggressive physical violence against person and property, and that this is how we define "coercion." Anyone who is still unhappy with this use of the term "coercion" can simply eliminate the word from this discussion and substitute for it "physical violence or the threat thereof," with the only loss being in literary style rather than in the substance of the argument. What anarchism proposes to do, then, is to abolish the state, that is, to abolish the regularized institution of aggressive coercion.

It need hardly be added that the state habitually builds upon its coercive source of income by adding a host of other aggressions upon society, ranging from economic controls to the prohibition of pornography to the compelling of religious observance to the mass murder of civilians in organized warfare. In short, the state, in the words of Albert Jay Nock, "claims and exercises a monopoly of crime" over its territorial area.

The second criticism I would like to defuse before beginning the main body of the paper is the common charge that anarchists "assume that all people are good" and that without the state no crime would be committed. In short, that anarchism assumes that with the abolition of the state a New Anarchist Man will emerge, cooperative, humane, and benevolent, so that no problem of crime will then plague the society. I confess that I do not understand the basis for this charge. Whatever other schools of anarchism profess—and I do not believe that they are open to this charge—I certainly do not adopt this view. I assume with most observers that mankind is a mixture of good and evil, of cooperative and criminal tendencies. In my view, the anarchist society is one which maximizes the tendencies for the good and the cooperative, while it minimizes both the opportunity and the moral legitimacy of the evil and the criminal. If the anarchist view is correct and the state is indeed the great legalized and socially legitimated channel for all manner of antisocial crime—theft, oppression, mass murder—on a massive scale, then surely the abolition of such an engine of crime can do nothing but favor the good in man and discourage the bad.

A further point: in a profound sense, *no* social system, whether anarchist or statist, can work at all unless most people are "good" in the sense that they are not all hell-bent upon assaulting and robbing their neighbors. If everyone were so disposed, no amount of protection, whether state or private, could succeed in staving off chaos. Furthermore, the more that people are disposed to be peaceful and not aggress against their neighbors, the more successfully *any* social system will work, and the fewer resources will need to be devoted to police protection. The anarchist view holds that, given the "nature of man," given the degree of goodness or badness at any point of time, anarchism will maximize the opportunities for the good and minimize the channels for the bad. The rest depends on the values held by the individual members of society. The only further point that need be made is that by eliminating the living example and the social legitimacy of the massive legalized crime of the state, anarchism will to a large extent promote peaceful values in the minds of the public.

We cannot of course deal here with the numerous arguments in favor of anarchism or against the state, moral, political, and economic. Nor can we take up the various goods and services now provided by the state and show how private individuals and groups will be able to supply them far more efficiently on the free market. Here we can only deal with perhaps the most difficult area, the area where it is almost universally assumed that the state must exist and act, even if it is only a "necessary evil" instead of a positive good: the vital realm of defense or protection of person and property against aggression. Surely, it is universally asserted, the state is at least vitally necessary to provide police protection, the judicial resolution of disputes and enforcement of contracts, and the creation of the law itself that is to be enforced. My contention is that all of these admittedly necessary services of protection can be satisfactorily and efficiently supplied by private persons and institutions on the free market.

One important caveat before we begin the body of this paper: new proposals such as anarchism are almost always gauged against the implicit assumption that the present, or statist, system works to perfection. Any lacunae or difficulties with the picture of the anarchist society are considered net liabilities, and enough to dismiss anarchism out of hand. It is, in short, implicitly assumed that the state is doing its self-assumed job of protecting person and property to perfection. We cannot here go into the reasons why the state is bound to suffer inherently from grave flaws and inefficiencies in such a task. All we need do now is to point to the black and unprecedented record of the state through history: no combination of private marauders can possibly begin to match the state's unremitting record of theft, confiscation, oppression, and mass murder. No collection of Mafia or private bank robbers can begin to compare with all the Hiroshimas, Dresdens, and Lidices and their analogues through the history of mankind.

This point can be made more philosophically: it is illegitimate to compare the merits of anarchism and statism by starting with the present system as the implicit given and then critically examining only the anarchist alternative. What we must do is to begin at the zero point and then critically examine *both* suggested alternatives. Suppose, for example, that we were all suddenly dropped down on the earth *de novo* and that we were all then confronted with the question of what societal arrangements to adopt. And suppose then that someone suggested: "We are all bound to suffer from those of us who wish to aggress against their fellow men. Let us then solve this problem of crime by handing all of our weapons to the Jones family, over there, by giving all of our ultimate power to settle disputes to that family. In that way, with their monopoly of coercion and of ultimate decision making, the Jones family will be able to protect each of us from each other." I submit that this proposal would get very short shrift, except perhaps from the Jones family themselves. And yet this is precisely the common argument or the existence of the state. When we start from zero point, as in the case of the Jones family, the question of "who will guard the guardians?" becomes not simply an abiding lacuna in the theory of the state but an overwhelming barrier to its existence.

A final caveat: the anarchist is always at a disadvantage in attempting to forecast the shape of the future anarchist society. For it is impossible for observers to predict voluntary social arrangements, including the provision of goods and services, on the free market. Suppose, for example, that this were the year 1874 and that someone predicted that eventually there would be a radio-manufacturing industry. To be able to make such a forecast successfully, does he have to be challenged to state immediately how many radio manufacturers there would be a century hence, how big they would be, where they would be located, what technology and marketing techniques they would use, and so on? Obviously, such a challenge would make no sense, and in a profound sense the same is true of those who demand a precise portrayal of the pattern of protection activities on the market. Anarchism advocates the dissolution of the state into social and market arrangements, and these arrangements are far more flexible and less predictable than political institutions. The most that we can do, then, is to offer broad guidelines and perspectives on the shape of a projected anarchist society.

One important point to make here is that the advance of modern technology makes anarchistic arrangements increasingly feasible. Take, for example, the case of lighthouses, where it is often charged that it is unfeasible for private lighthouse operators to row out to each ship to charge it for use of the light. Apart from the fact that this argument ignores the successful existence of private lighthouses in earlier days, as in England in the eighteenth century, another vital consideration is that modern electronic technology makes charging each ship for the light far more feasible. Thus, the ship would have to have paid for an electronically controlled beam which could then be automatically turned on for those ships which had paid for the service.

II

Let us turn now to the problem of how disputes—in particular disputes over alleged violations of person and property—would be resolved in an anarchist society. First, it should be noted that all disputes involve two parties: the plaintiff, the alleged victim of the crime or tort; and the defendant, the alleged aggressor. In many cases of broken contract, of course, each of the two parties alleging that the other is the culprit is at the same time a plaintiff and a defendant.

An important point to remember is that *any* society, be it statist or anarchist, has to have *some* way of resolving disputes that will gain a majority consensus in society. There would be no need for courts or arbitrators if everyone were omniscient and knew instantaneously *which* persons were guilty of any given crime or violation of contract. Since none of us is omniscient, there has to be some method of deciding who is the criminal or lawbreaker which will gain legitimacy; in short, whose decision will be accepted by the great majority of the public.

In the first place, a dispute may be resolved voluntarily between the two parties themselves, either unaided or with the help of a third mediator. This poses no problem, and will automatically be accepted by society at large. It is so accepted even now, much less in a society imbued with the anarchistic values of peaceful cooperation and agreement. Secondly and similarly, the two parties, unable to reach agreement, may decide to submit voluntarily to the decision of an abritrator. This agreement may arise either after a dispute has arisen, or be provided for in advance in the original contract. Again, there is no problem in such an arrangement gaining legitimacy. Even in the present statist era, the notorious inefficiency and coercive and cumbersome procedures of the politically run government courts has led increasing numbers of citizens to turn to voluntary and expert arbitration for a speedy and harmonious settling of disputes.

Thus, William C. Wooldridge has written that

> arbitration has grown to proportions that make the courts a secondary recourse in many areas and completely superfluous in others. The ancient fear of the courts that arbitration would 'oust' them of their jurisdiction has been fulfilled with a vengeance the common-law judges probably never anticipated. Insurance companies adjust over fifty thousand claims a year among themselves through arbitration, and the American Arbitration Association (AAA), with headquarters in New York and twenty-five regional offices across the country, last year conducted over twenty-two thousand arbitrations. Its twenty-three thousand associates available to serve as arbitrators may outnumber the total number of judicial personnel . . . in the United States. . . . Add to this the unknown number of individuals who arbitrate disputes within particular industries or in particular localities, without formal AAA affiliation, and the quantitatively secondary role of official courts begins to be apparent.[1]

Wooldridge adds the important point that, in addition to the speed of arbitration procedures vis-à-vis the courts, the arbitrators can proceed as experts in disregard of the official government law; in a profound sense, then, they serve to create a voluntary body of private law. "In other words," states Wooldridge, "the system of extralegal, voluntary courts has progressed hand in hand with a body of private law; the rules of the state are circumvented by the same process that circumvents the forums established for the settlement of disputes over those rules. . . . In short, a private agreement between two people, a bilateral 'law,' has supplanted the official law. The writ of the sovereign has ceased to run, and for it is substituted a rule tacitly or explicitly agreed to by the parties." Wooldridge concludes that "if an arbitrator can choose to ignore a penal damage rule or the statute of limitations applicable to the claim before him (and it is generally conceded that he has that power), arbitration can be viewed as a practically revolutionary instrument for self-liberation from the law. . . ."[2]

It may be objected that arbitration only works successfully because the courts enforce the award of the arbitrator. Wooldridge points out, however, that arbitration was unenforceable in the American courts before 1920, but that this did not prevent voluntary arbitration from being successful and expanding in the United States and in England. He points, furthermore, to the successful operations of merchant courts since the Middle Ages, those courts which successfully developed the entire body of the law merchant. None of those courts possessed the power of enforcement. He might have added the private courts of shippers which developed the body of admiralty law in a similar way.

How then did these private, "anarchistic," and voluntary courts ensure the acceptance of their decisions? By the method of social ostracism, and by the refusal to deal any further with the offending merchant. This method of voluntary "enforcement," indeed, proved highly successful. Wooldridge writes that "the merchants' courts were voluntary, and if a man ignored their judgment, he could not be sent to jail. . . . Nevertheless, it is apparent that . . . [their] decisions were generally respected even by the losers; otherwise people would never have used them in the first place. . . . Merchants made their courts work simply by agreeing to abide by the results. The merchant who broke the understanding would not be sent to jail, to be sure, but neither would he long continue to be a merchant, for the compliance exacted by his fellows . . . proved if anything more effective than physical coercion."[3] Nor did this voluntary method fail to work in modern times. Wooldridge writes that it was precisely in the years before 1920, when arbitration awards could not be enforced in the courts,

> that arbitration caught on and developed a following in the American mercantile community. Its popularity, gained at a time when abiding by an agreement to arbitrate had to be as voluntary as the agreement itself, casts doubt on whether legal coercion was an essential adjunct to the settlement of most disputes. Cases of refusal to abide by an arbitrator's award were rare; one founder of the American Arbitration Association could not recall a single example. Like their medieval forerunners, merchants in the Americas did not have to rely on any sanctions other than those they could collectively impose on each other. One who refused to pay up might find access to his association's tribunal cut off in the future, or his name released to the membership of his trade association; these penalties were far more fearsome than the cost of the award with which he disagreed. Voluntary and private adjudications were voluntarily and privately adhered to, if not out of honor, out of the self-interest of businessmen who knew that the arbitral mode of dispute settlement would cease to be available to them very quickly if they ignored an award.[4]

It should also be pointed out that modern technology makes even more feasible the collection and dissemination of information about people's credit ratings and records of keeping or violating their contracts or arbitration agreements. Presumably, an anarchist society would see the expansion of this sort of dissemination of data and thereby facilitate the ostracism or boycotting of contract and arbitration violators.

How would arbitrators be selected in an anarchist society? In the same way as they are chosen now, and as they were chosen in the days of strictly voluntary arbitration: the arbitrators with the best reputation for efficiency and probity would be chosen by the various parties on the market. As in other processes of the market, the arbitrators with the best record in settling disputes will come to gain an increasing amount of business, and those with poor records will no longer enjoy clients and will have to shift to another line of endeavor. Here it must be emphasized that parties in dispute will seek out those arbitrators with the best reputation for both expertise and impartiality and that inefficient or biased arbitrators will rapidly have to find another occupation.

Thus, the Tannehills emphasize:

> the advocates of government see initiated force (the legal force of government) as the only solution to social disputes. According to them, if everyone in society were not forced to use the same court system . . . disputes would be insoluble. Apparently it doesn't occur to them that disputing parties are capable of freely choosing their own arbiters. . . . They have not realized that disputants would, in fact, be far better off if they could choose among competing arbitration agencies so that they could reap the benefits of competition and specialization. It should be obvious that a court system which has a monopoly guaranteed by the force of statutory law will not give as good quality service as will free-market arbitration agencies which must compete for their customers. . . .
>
> Perhaps the least tenable argument for government arbitration of disputes is the one which holds that governmental judges are more impartial because they operate outside the market and so have no vested interests. . . . Owing political allegiance to government is certainly no guarantee of impartiality! A governmental judge is always impelled to be partial—in favor of the government, from whom he gets his pay and his power! On the other hand, an arbiter who sells his services in a free market knows that he must be as scrupulously honest, fair, and impartial as possible or no pair of disputants will buy his services to arbitrate their dispute. A free-market arbiter depends for his livelihood on his skill and fairness at settling disputes. A governmental judge depends on political pull. [5]

If desired, furthermore, the contracting parties could provide in advance for a series of arbitrators:

> It would be more economical and in most cases quite sufficient to have only one arbitration agency to hear the case. But if the parties felt that a further appeal might be necessary and were willing to risk the extra expense, they could provide for a succession of two or even more arbitration agencies. The names of these agencies would be written into the contract in order from the "first court of appeal" to the "last court of appeal." It would be neither necessary nor desirable to have one single, final court of appeal for every person in the society, as we have today in the United States Supreme Court. [6]

Arbitration, then, poses little difficulty for a portrayal of the free society. But what of torts or crimes of aggression where there has been no contract? Or suppose that the breaker of a contract defies the arbitration award? Is ostracism enough? In short, how can courts develop in the free-market, anarchist society which will have the power to enforce judgments against criminals or contract breakers?

In the wide sense, defense service consists of guards or police who use force in defending person and property against attack, and judges or courts whose role is to use socially accepted procedures to determine *who* the criminals or tortfeasors are, as well as to enforce judicial awards, such as damages or the keeping of contracts. On the free market, many scenarios are possible on the relationship between the private courts and the police; they may be "vertically integrated," for example, or their services may be supplied by separate firms. Furthermore, it seems likely that police service will be supplied by insurance companies who will provide crime insurance to their clients. In that case, insurance companies will pay off the victims of crime or the breaking of contracts or arbitration awards and then pursue the aggressors in court to recoup their losses. There is a natural market connection between insurance companies and defense service, since they need pay out less benefits in proportion as they are able to keep down the rate of crime.

Courts might either charge fees for their services, with the losers of cases obliged to pay court costs, or else they may subsist on monthly or yearly premiums by their clients, who may be either individuals or the police or insurance agencies. Suppose, for example, that Smith is an aggrieved party, either because he has been assaulted or robbed, or because an arbitration award in his favor has not been honored. Smith believes that Jones is the party guilty of the crime. Smith then goes to a court, Court A, of which he is a client, and brings charges against Jones as a defendant. In my view, the hallmark of an anarchist society is one where no man may legally compel someone who is not a convicted criminal to do anything, since that would be aggression against an innocent man's person or property. Therefore, Court A can only invite rather than subpoena Jones to attend his trial. Of course, if Jones refused to appear or send a representative, his side of the case will not be heard. The trial of Jones proceeds. Suppose that Court A finds Jones innocent. In my view, part of the generally accepted law code of the anarchist society (on which see further below) is that this must end the matter unless Smith can prove charges of gross incompetence or bias on the part of the court.

Suppose, next, that Court A finds Jones guilty. Jones might accept the verdict, because he too is a client of the same court, because he knows he is guilty, or for some other reason. In that case, Court A proceeds to exercise judgment against Jones. Neither of these instances pose very difficult problems for our picture of the anarchist society. But suppose, instead, that Jones contests the decision; he, then, goes to his court, Court B, and the case is retried there. Suppose that Court B, too, finds Jones guilty. Again, it seems to me that the accepted law code of the anarchist society will assert that this ends the matter; both parties have had their say in courts which each has selected, and the decision for guilt is unanimous.

Suppose, however, the most difficult case: that Court B finds Jones innocent. The two courts, each subscribed to by one of the two parties, have split their verdicts. In that case, the two courts will submit the case to an appeals court, or arbitrator, which the two courts agree upon. There seems to be no real difficulty about the concept of an appeals court. As in the case of arbitration contracts, it seems very likely that the various private courts in the society will have prior agreements to submit their disputes to a particular appeals court. How will the appeals judges be chosen? Again, as in the case of arbitrators or of the first judges on the free market, they will be chosen for their expertise and their reputation for efficiency, honesty, and integrity. Obviously, appeals judges who are inefficient or biased will scarcely be chosen by courts who will have a dispute. The point here is that there is no need for a legally established or institutionalized single, monopoly appeals court system, as states now provide. There is no reason why there cannot arise a multitude of efficient and honest appeals judges who will be selected by the disputant courts, just as there are numerous private arbitrators on the market today. The appeals court renders its decision, and the courts proceed to enforce it if, in our example, Jones is considered guilty—unless, of course, Jones can prove bias in some other court proceedings.

No society can have unlimited judicial appeals, for in that case there would be no point to having judges or courts at all. Therefore, every society, whether statist or anarchist, will have to have some socially accepted cutoff point for trials and appeals. My suggestion is the rule that the agreement *of any two courts* be decisive. "Two" is not an arbitrary figure, for it reflects the fact that there are two parties, the plaintiff and the defendant, to any alleged crime or contract dispute.

If the courts are to be empowered to enforce decisions against guilty parties, does this not bring back the state in another form and thereby negate anarchism? No, for at the beginning of this paper I explicitly defined anarchism in such a way as not to rule out the use of defensive force—force in defense of person and property—by privately supported agencies. In the same way, it is not bringing back the state to allow persons to use force to defend themselves against aggression, or to hire guards or police agencies to defend them.

It should be noted, however, that in the anarchist society there will be no "district attorney" to press charges on behalf of "society." Only the victims will press charges as the plaintiffs. If, then, these victims should happen to be absolute pacifists who are opposed even to defensive force, then they will simply not press charges in the courts or otherwise retaliate against those who have aggressed against them. In a free society that would be their right. If the victim should suffer from murder, then his heir would have the right to press the charges.

What of the Hatfield-and-McCoy problem? Suppose that a Hatfield kills a McCoy, and that McCoy's heir does not belong to a private insurance, police agency, or court, and decides to retaliate himself? Since under anarchism there can be no coercion of the noncriminal, McCoy would have the perfect right to do so. No one may be compelled to bring his case to a court. Indeed, since the right to hire police or courts flows from the right of self-defense against aggression, it would be inconsistent and in contradiction to the very basis of the free society to institute such compulsion. Suppose, then, that the surviving McCoy finds what he believes to be the guilty Hatfield and kills him in turn? What then? This is fine, except that McCoy may have to worry about charges being brought against him by a surviving Hatfield. Here it must be emphasized that in the law of the anarchist society based on defense against aggression, the courts would not be able to proceed against McCoy if in fact he killed the right Hatfield. His problem would arise if the courts should find that he made a grievous mistake and killed the wrong man; in that case, he in turn would be found guilty of murder. Surely, in most instances, individuals will wish to obviate such problems by taking their case to a court and thereby gain social acceptability for their defensive retaliation—not for the *act* of retaliation but for the correctness of deciding who the criminal in any given case might be. The purpose of the judicial process, indeed, is to find a way of general agreement on who might be the criminal or contract breaker in any given case. The judicial process is not a good in itself; thus, in the case of an assassination, such as Jack Ruby's murder of Lee Harvey Oswald, on public television, there is no need for a complex judicial process, since the name of the murderer is evident to all.

Will not the possibility exist of a private court that may turn venal and dishonest, or of a private police force that turns criminal and extorts money by coercion? Of course such an event may occur, given the propensities of human nature. Anarchism is not a moral cure-all. But the important point is that market forces exist to place severe checks on such possibilities, especially in contrast to a society where a state exists. For, in the first place, judges, like arbitrators, will prosper on the market in proportion to their reputation for efficiency and impartiality. Secondly, on the free market important checks and balances exist against venal courts or criminal police forces. Namely, that there are competing courts and police agencies to whom the victims may turn for redress. If the "Prudential Police Agency" should turn outlaw and extract revenue from victims by coercion, the latter would have the option of turning to the "Mutual" or "Equitable" Police Agency for defense and for pressing charges against Prudential. These are the *genuine* "checks and balances" of the free market, genuine in contrast to the phony checks and balances of a state system, where all the alleged "balancing" agencies are in the hands of one monopoly government. Indeed, given the monopoly "protection service" of a state, what is there to prevent a state from using its monopoly channels of coercion to extort money from the public? What are the checks and limits of the state? None, except for the extremely difficult course of revolution against a power with all of the guns in its hands. In fact, the state provides an easy, legitimated channel for crime and aggression, since it has its very being in the crime of tax theft, and the coerced monopoly of "protection." It is the state, indeed, that functions as a mighty "protection racket" on a giant and massive scale. It is the state that says: "Pay us for your 'protection' or else." In the light of the massive and inherent activities of the state, the danger of a "protection racket" emerging from one or more private police agencies is relatively small indeed.

Moreover, it must be emphasized that a crucial element in the power of the state is its legitimacy in the eyes of the majority of the public, the fact that after centuries of propaganda, the depredations of the state are looked upon rather as benevolent services. Taxation is generally not seen as theft, nor war as mass murder, nor conscription as slavery. Should a private police agency turn outlaw, should "Prudential" become a protection racket, it would then lack the social legitimacy which the state has managed to accrue to itself over the centuries. "Prudential" would be seen by all as bandits, rather than as legitimate or divinely appointed "sovereigns" bent on promoting the "common good" or the "general welfare." And lacking such legitimacy, "Prudential" would have to face the wrath of the public and the defense and retaliation of the other private defense agencies, the police and courts, on the free market. Given these inherent checks and limits, a successful transformation from a free society to bandit rule becomes most unlikely. Indeed, historically, it has been very difficult for a state to arise to supplant a stateless society; usually, it has come about through external conquest rather than by evolution from within a society.

Within the anarchist camp, there has been much dispute on whether the private courts would have to be bound by a basic, common law code. Ingenious attempts have been made to work out a system where the laws or standards of decision-making by the courts would differ completely from one to another.[7] But in my view all would have to abide by the basic law code, in particular, prohibition of aggression against person and property, in order to fulfill our definition of anarchism as a system which provides no legal sanction for such aggression. Suppose, for example, that one group of people in society holds that all redheads are demons who deserve to be shot on sight. Suppose that Jones, one of this group, shoots Smith, a redhead. Suppose that Smith or his heir presses charges in a court, but that Jones's court, in philosophic agreement with Jones, finds him innocent therefore. It seems to me that in order to be considered legitimate, any court would have to follow the basic libertarian law code of the inviolate right of person and property. For otherwise, courts might legally subscribe to a code which sanctions such aggression in various cases, and which to that extent would violate the definition of anarchism and introduce, if not the state, then a strong element of statishness or legalized aggression into the society.

But again I see no insuperable difficulties here. For in that case, anarchists, in agitating for their creed, will simply include in their agitation the idea of a general libertarian law code as part and parcel of the anarchist creed of abolition of legalized aggression against person or property in the society.

In contrast to the general law code, other aspects of court decisions could legitimately vary in accordance with the market or the wishes of the clients; for example, the language the cases will be conducted in, the number of judges to be involved, and so on.

There are other problems of the basic law code which there is no time to go into here: for example, the definition of just property titles or the question of legitimate punishment of convicted offenders—though the latter problem of course exists in statist legal systems as well.[8] The basic point, however, is that the state is not needed to arrive at legal principles or their elaboration: indeed, much of the common law, the law merchant, admiralty law, and private law in general, grew up apart form the state, by judges not making the law but finding it on the basis of agreed-upon principles derived either from custom or reason.[9] The idea that the state is needed to *make* law is as much a myth as that the state is needed to supply postal or police services.

Enough has been said here, I believe, to indicate that an anarchist system for settling disputes would be both viable and self-subsistent: that once adopted, it could work and continue indefinitely. *How to arrive* at that system is of course a very different problem, but certainly at the very least it will not likely come about unless people are convinced of its workability, are convinced, in short, that the state is not a *necessary* evil.

Notes

1. William C. Wooldridge, *Uncle Sam, the Monopoly Man* (New Rochelle, New York: Arlington House, 1970), p. 101.

2. Ibid., pp. 103-104.

3. Ibid., pp. 95-96.

4. Ibid., pp. 100-101.

5. Morris and Linda Tannehill, *The Market for Liberty* (Lansing, Michigan: privately printed, 1970), pp. 65-67.

6. Ibid., p. 68.

7. E.g., David Friedman, *The Machinery of Freedom* (New York: Harper and Row, 1973).

8. For an elaboration of these points, see Murray N. Rothbard, *For a New Liberty* (New York: Macmillan, 1973).

9. Thus, see Bruno Leoni, *Freedom and the Law* (Princeton, New Jersey: D. Van Nostrand Co., 1961).

PART TWO

Liberty, Law and Society

F. A. HAYEK*

The Use of Knowledge in Society

Many of the current disputes with regard to both economic theory and economic policy have their common origin, it seems to me, in a misconception about the nature on the economic problem of society. This misconception in turn is due to an erroneous transfer to social phenomena of the habits of thought we have developed in dealing with the phenomena of nature.

What is the problem we wish to solve when we try to construct a rational economic order? On certain familiar assumptions the answer is simple enough. *If* we possess all the relevant information, *if* we can start out from a given system of preferences, and *if* we command complete knowledge of available means, the problem which remains is purely one of logic. That is, the answer to the question of what is the best use of the available means is implicit in our assumptions. Stated briefly in mathematical form, it is that the marginal rates of substitution between any two commodities or factors must be the same in all their different uses.

This, however, is emphatically *not* the economic problem which society faces. And the economic calculus which we have developed to solve it, though an important step toward the solution of the economic problem of society, does not yet provide an answer to it. The reason for this is that the "data" for the whole society, from which the economic calculus starts, are never "given" to a single mind.

The peculiar character of the problem of a rational economic order is determined precisely by the fact that the knowledge of the circumstances which we must use never exists in concentrated or integrated form but solely as the dispersed bits of incomplete and frequently contradictory knowledge which separate individuals possess. The economic problem of society is thus not merely a problem of how to allocate "given" resources—if "given" is taken to mean given to a single mind which deliberately solves the problem set by these "data." It is rather a problem of how to secure the best use of resources known to any of the members of society, for

This essay is a slightly revised and abbreviated version of an article which first appeared in *The American Economic Review* Vol. 35 (September 1945). Used by permission of the American Economic Association and F. A. Hayek.

*University of Freiburg.

ends whose relative importance only these individuals know. Or, to put it briefly, it is a problem of the utilization of knowledge which is not given to anyone in its totality.

This character of the fundamental problem has, I am afraid, been obscured rather than illuminated by many of the recent refinements of economic theory, particularly by many of the uses made of mathematics. Though the problem with which I want primarily to deal in this paper is the problem of a rational economic organization, I shall be led again and again to point to its close connections with certain methodological questions. Many of the points I wish to make are indeed conclusions toward which diverse paths of reasoning have unexpectedly converged. But, as I now see these problems, this is no accident.

In ordinary language, we describe by the word "planning" the complex of interrelated decisions about the allocation of our available resources. All economic activity is in this sense planning; and in any society in which many people collaborate, this planning, whoever does it, will in some measure have to be based on knowledge which, in the first instance, is not given to the planner but to somebody else, yet somehow will have to be conveyed to the planner. The various ways in which this knowledge on which people base their plans is communicated to them is the crucial problem for any theory explaining the economic process, and the problem of what is the best way of utilizing knowledge initially dispersed among all the people is at least one of the main problems of economic policy—or of designing an efficient economic system.

The answer to this question is closely connected with that other question which arises here, that of *who* is to do the planning. It is about this question that all the dispute about "economic planning" centers. This is not a dispute about whether planning is to be done or not. It is a dispute as to whether planning is to be done centrally, by one authority for the whole economic system, or is to be divided among many individuals. Planning in the specific sense in which the term is used in contemporary controversy necessarily means central planning—direction of the whole economic system according to one unified plan. Competition, on the other hand, means decentralized planning by many separate persons. The halfway house between the two, about which many people talk but which few like when they see it, is the delegation of planning to privileged industries, or, in other words, monopolies.

Which of these systems is likely to be more efficient depends mainly on the question under which of them we can expect that fuller use will be made of the existing knowledge. This, in turn, depends on whether we are more likely to succeed in putting at the disposal of a single central authority all the knowledge which ought to be used but which is initially dispersed among many different individuals, or in conveying to the individuals such additional knowledge as they need in order to enable them to dovetail their plans with those of others.

Uncommon Knowledge

It will at once be evident that on this point the position will be different with respect to different kinds of knowledge. The answer to our question will therefore largely turn on the relative importance of the different kinds of knowledge: those more likely to be at the disposal of particular individuals and those which we should with greater confidence expect to find in the possession of an authority made up of suitably chosen experts. If it is today so widely assumed that the latter will be in a better position, this is because one kind of knowledge, namely, scientific knowledge, occupies now so prominent a place in public imagination that we tend to forget that it is not the only kind that is relevant. It may be admitted that, as far as scientific knowledge is concerned, a body of suitably chosen experts may be in the best position to command all the best knowledge available—though this is of course merely shifting the difficulty to the problem of selecting the experts. What I wish to point out is that, even assuming that this problem can be readily solved, it is only a small part of the wider problem.

Today it is almost heresy to suggest that scientific knowledge is not the sum of all knowledge. But a little reflection will show that there is beyond question a body of very important but unorganized knowledge which cannot possibly be called scientific in the sense of knowledge of general rules: the knowledge of the particular circumstances of time and place. It is with respect to this that practically every individual has some advantage over all others because he possesses unique information of which beneficial use might be made only if the decisions depending on it are left to him or are made with his active co-operation.

We need only to remember how much we have to learn in any occupation after we have completed our theoretical training, how big a part of our working life we spend learning particular jobs, and how valuable an asset in all walks of life is knowledge of people, of local conditions, and of special circumstances. To know of and put to use a machine not fully employed, or somebody's skill which could be better utilized, or to be aware of a surplus stock which can be drawn upon during an interruption of supplies, is socially quite as useful as the knowledge of better alternative techniques. The shipper who earns his living from using otherwise empty or half-filled journeys of tramp-steamers, or the estate agent whose whole knowledge is almost exclusively one of temporary opportunities, or the *arbitrageur* who gains from local differences of commodity prices—all are performing eminently useful functions based on special knowledge of circumstances of the fleeting moment not known to others.

It is a curious fact that this sort of knowledge should today be generally regarded with a kind of contempt, that anyone who, by such knowledge, gains an advantage over somebody better equipped with theoretical or technical knowledge is thought to have acted almost disreputably. To gain an advantage from better knowledge of facilities of communication or transport is sometimes regarded as almost dishonest, although it is quite as important that society make use of the best opportunities in this respect as in using the latest scientific discoveries. This prejudice has in a considerable measure affected the attitude toward commerce in general compared with that toward production. Even economists who regard themselves as immune to the crude materialist fallacies of the past constantly commit the same mistake where activities directed toward the acquisition of such practical knowledge are concerned—apparently because in their scheme of things all such knowledge is supposed to be "given." The common idea now seems to be that all such knowledge should as a matter of course be readily at the command of everybody, and the reproach of irrationality leveled against the existing economic order is frequently based on the fact that it is not so available. This view disregards the fact that the method by which such knowledge can be made as widely available as possible is precisely the problem to which we have to find an answer.

The Planner's Dilemma

If it is fashionable today to minimize the importance of the knowledge of the particular circumstances of time and place, this is closely connected with the smaller importance which is now attached to change as such. Indeed, there are few points on which the assumptions made (usually only implicitly) by the "planners" differ from those of their opponents as much as with regard to the significance and frequency of changes which will make substantial alterations of production plans necessary. Of course, if detailed economic plans could be laid down for fairly long periods in advance and then closely adhered to so that no further economic decisions of importance would be required, the task of drawing up a comprehensive plan governing all economic activity would be much less formidable.

It is, perhaps, worth stressing that economic problems arise always and only in consequence of change. As long as things continue as before, or at least as they were expected to, there arise no new problems requiring a decision, no need to form a new plan. The belief that changes, or at least day-to-day adjustments, have become less important in modern times implies the contention that economic problems also have become less important. This belief in the decreasing importance of change is, for that reason, usually held by the same people who argue that the importance of economic considerations has been driven into the background by the growing importance of technological knowledge.

Is it true that, with the elaborate apparatus of modern production, economic decisions are required only at long intervals, as when a new factory is to be erected or a new process to be introduced? Is it true that, once a plant has been built, the rest is all more or less mechanical, determined by the character of the plant, and leaving little to be changed in adapting to the ever changing circumstances of the moment?

The fairly widespread belief in the affirmative is not, as far as I can ascertain, borne out by the practical experience of the businessman. In a competitive industry at any rate—and such an industry alone can serve as a test—the task of keeping costs from rising requires constant struggle, absorbing a great part of the energy of the manager. How easy it is for an inefficient manager to dissipate the differentials on which profitability rests. A great variety in costs of production, even when using the same technical facilities, is commonplace in business experience but does not seem to be equally familiar to many economists. The very strength of the desire, constantly voiced by producers and engineers, to be allowed to proceed untrammeled by considerations of money costs, is eloquent testimony to the extent to which these factors enter into their daily work.

One reason why economists are increasingly apt to forget about the constant small changes which make up the whole economic picture is probably their growing preoccupation with statistical aggregates, which show a very much greater stability than the movements of the detail. The comparative stability of the aggregates cannot, however, be accounted for—as the statisticians occasionally seem to be inclined to do—by the "law of large numbers" or the mutual compensation of random changes. The number of elements with which we have to deal is not large enough for such accidental forces to produce stability. The continuous flow of goods and services is maintained by constant deliberate adjustments, by new dispositions made every day in the light of circumstances not known the day before, by B stepping in at once when A fails to deliver. Even the large and highly mechanized plant keeps going largely because of an environment upon which it can draw for all sorts of unexpected needs: tiles for its roof, stationery for its forms, and all the thousand and one kinds of equipment in which it cannot be self-contained and which the plans for the operation of the plant require to be readily available in the market.

I should also briefly mention the fact that the sort of knowledge with which I have been concerned is knowledge of the kind which by its nature cannot enter into statistics and therefore cannot be conveyed to any central authority in statistical form. The statistics which such a central authority would have to use would have to be arrived at precisely by abstracting and then lumping together items which differ as regards location, quality, and other particulars in ways that may be very significant for the specific decision. It follows from this that central planning which is based on statistical information cannot by its nature take direct account of these circumstances of time and place. The central planner will have to find some way to make decisions by leaving them to be made by the "man on the spot."

If we can agree that the economic problem of society is mainly one of rapid adaptation to changes in the particular circumstances of time and place, it would seem to follow that the ultimate decisions must be left to the people who are familiar with these circumstances, who know directly of the relevant changes and of the resources immediately available to meet them. We cannot expect that this problem will be solved by first communicating all this knowledge to a central board which, after integrating all knowledge, issues its orders. We must solve it by some form of decentralization.

But this answers only part of our problem. We need decentralization because only thus can we insure that the knowledge of the particular circumstances of time and place will be promptly used. The "man on the spot" cannot, however, decide solely on the basis of his limited but intimate knowledge of the facts of his immediate surroundings. There still remains the problem of communicating to him such further information as he needs to fit his decisions into the whole pattern of changes of the larger economic system.

Useful Individual Knowledge

How much knowledge does the individual need in order to make these decisions successfully? Which of the events beyond his own horizon of immediate knowledge are of relevance to his immediate decision, and how much of them need he know?

There is hardly anything that happens anywhere in the world that *might* not have an effect on the decision he ought to make. But he need not know of these events as such, nor of *all* their effects. It does not matter for him *why* more screws of one size than of another are wanted at the particular moment, *why* paper bags are more readily available than canvas bags, or *why* skilled labor, or particular machine tools, have for the moment become more difficult to obtain. All that is significant for him is *how much more or less* difficult to procure they have become compared with other things with which he is also concerend, or how much more or less urgently wanted are the alternative things he produces or uses. It is always a question of the relative importance of the particular things with which he is concerned, and the causes which alter their relative importance are of no interest to him beyond the effect on those concrete things of his own environment.

It is in this connection that what I have called the "economic calculus" (or the Pure Logic of Choice) helps us, at least by analogy, to see how this problem can be solved and is being solved by the price system. Even the single controlling mind, in possession of all the data for some small and self-contained economic system, would not—every time some small adjustment in the allocation of resources had to be made—go explicitly through all the relations between ends and means which might possibly be affected. It is indeed the great contribution of the Pure Logic of Choice to have demonstrated conclusively that even such a single mind could solve this kind of problem only by constructing and constantly using rates of equivalence (or "values," or "marginal rates of substitution"); that is, he would have to attach to each kind of scarce resource a numerical index which cannot be derived from any property possessed by that particular thing, but which reflects, or in which is condensed, its significance in view of the whole means-end structure. In any small change he will have to consider only these quantitative indices (or "values") in which all the relevant information is concentrated; and, by adjusting the quantities one by one, he can appropriately rearrange his dispositions without having to solve the whole puzzle *ab initio* or without needing at any stage to survey it at once in all its ramifications.

Fundamentally, in a system in which the knowledge of the relevant facts is dispersed among many people, prices can act to co-ordinate the separate actions of different people in the same way as subjective values help the individual to co-ordinate the parts of his plan.

"Miracle" of the Price System

It is worth contemplating for a moment a very simple and commonplace instance of the action of the price system to see what precisely it accomplishes. Assume that somewhere in the world a new opportunity for the use of some raw material, say, tin, has arisen, or that one of the sources of supply of tin has been eliminated. It does not matter for our purpose—and it is significant that it does not matter— which of these two causes has made tin more scarce. All that the users of tin need to know is that some of the tin they used to consume is now more profitably employed elsewhere and that, in consequence they must economize tin. There is no need for the great majority of them even to know where the more urgent need has arisen, or in favor of what other needs they ought to husband the supply. If only some of them know directly of the new demand and switch resources over to it, and if the people who are aware of the new gap thus created in turn fill it from still other sources, the effect will rapidly spread throughout the whole economic system. This influences not only all the uses of tin but also those of its substitutes and the substitutes of these substitutes, the supply of all things made of tin, and their substitutes, and so on. All this takes place without the great majority of those instrumental in bringing about these substitutions knowing anything at all about the original cause of these changes. The whole acts as one market, not because any of its members surveys the whole field, but because their limited individual fields of vision sufficiently overlap so that through many intermediaries the relevant information is communicated to all. The mere fact that there is one price for any commodity—or rather that local prices are connected in a manner determined by the cost of transport, etc.—brings about the solution which (if conceptually possible) might have been arrived at by one single mind possessing all the information which is in fact dispersed among all the people involved in the process.

We must look at the price system as such a mechanism for communicating information if we want to understand its real function—a function which it fulfills less perfectly as prices grow more rigid. (Even when quoted prices have become quite rigid, however, the forces which would operate through changes in price still operate to a considerable extent through changes in the other terms of the contract.) The most significant fact about this system is the economy of knowledge with which it operates, or how little the individual participants need to know in order to be able to take the right action. In abbreviated form, by a kind of symbol, only the most essential information is passed on, and this is passed on only to those concerned. It is more than a metaphor to describe the price system as a kind of machinery for registering change, or a system of telecommunications which enables individual producers to watch merely the movement of a few pointers, as an engineer might watch the hands of a few dials, in order to adjust their activities to changes of which they may never know more than their reflection in the price movement.

Of course, these adjustments are probably never "perfect" in the sense in which the economist conceives of them in his equilibrium analysis. But I fear that our theoretical habits of approaching the problem with the assumption of more or less perfect knowledge on the part of almost everyone has made us somewhat blind to the true function of the price mechanism and led us to apply rather misleading standards in judging its efficiency. The marvel is that in a case like that of a scarcity of one raw material, without an order being issued, without more than perhaps a handful of people knowing the cause, tens of thousands of people whose identity could not be ascertained by months of investigation, are made to use the material or its products more sparingly; that is, they move in the right direction. This is enough of a marvel even if, in a constantly changing world, not all will react so perfectly that their profit rates will always be maintained at the same "normal" level.

I have deliberately used the word "marvel" to shock the reader out of the complacency with which we often take the working of the price mechanism for granted. I am convinced that if it were the result of deliberate human design, and if the people guided by the price changes understood that their decisions have significance far beyond their immediate aim, this mechanism would have been acclaimed as one of the greatest triumphs of the human mind. Its misfortune is the double one that it is not the product of human design and that the people guided by it usually do not know why they are made to do what they do. But those who clamor for "conscious direction"—and who cannot believe that anything which has evolved without design (and even without our understanding it) can solve problems which we cannot solve consciously—should remember this: the problem is precisely how to extend our utilization of resources beyond the span of the control of any one mind; and, therefore, how to dispense with the need of conscious control, how to provide inducements which will make the individuals do the desirable things without anyone having to tell them what to do.

The problem which we meet here is by no means peculiar to economics but arises in connection with nearly all truly social phenomena, including language and most of our cultural inheritance, and constitutes really the central theoretical problem of all social science. As Alfred Whitehead has said in another connection, "It is a profoundly erroneous truism, repeated by all copy-books and by eminent people when they are making speeches, that we should cultivate the habit of thinking what we are doing. The precise opposite is the case. Civilization advances by extending the number of important operations which we can perform without thinking about them." This is of profound significance in the social field. We make constant use of formulas, symbols, and rules whose meaning we do not understand and through the use of which we avail ourselves of the assistance of knowledge which individually we do not possess. We have developed these practices by building upon habits and institutions which have proved successful in their own sphere and which have in turn become the foundation of the civilization we have built up.

The price system is just one of those formations which man has learned to use (though he is still very far from having learned to make the best use of it) *after he had stumbled upon it without understanding it.* Through it, not only a division of labor but also a co-ordinated utilization of resources based on a similarly divided knowledge has become possible. The people who like to deride any suggestion that this may be so usually distort the argument by insinuating that it asserts that by some miracle just that sort of system has spontaneously grown up which is best suited to modern civilization. It is the other way round: man has been able to develop that division of labor on which our civilization is based because he happened to stumble upon a method which made it possible. Had he not done so, he might still have developed some other, altogether different type of civilization, something like the "state" of the termite ants, or some other altogether unimaginable type. All that we can say is that nobody has yet succeeded in designing an alternative system in which certain features of the existing one can be preserved which are dear even to those who most violently assail it—such as particularly the extent to which the individual can choose his pursuits and consequently freely use his own knowledge and skill.

It is in many ways fortunate that the dispute about the indispensability of the price system for any rational calculation in a complex society is now no longer conducted entirely between camps holding different political views. The thesis that without the price system we could not preserve a society based on such extensive division of labor as ours was greeted with a howl of derision when it was first advanced by von Mises in the early 1920's. Today the difficulties which some still find in accepting it are no longer mainly political, and this makes for an atmosphere much more conducive to reasonable discussion. When we find Leon Trotsky arguing that "economic accounting is unthinkable without market relations"; when Professor Oscar Lange promises Professor von Mises a statue in the marble halls of the future Central Planning Board; and when Professor Abba P.

Lerner rediscovers Adam Smith and emphasizes that the essential utility of the price system consists in inducing the individual, while seeking his own interest, to do what is in the general interest, the differences can indeed no longer be ascribed to political prejudice. The remaining dissent seems clearly to be due to purely intellectual, and more particularly methodological, differences.

MILTON FRIEDMAN*

Freedom Under Capitalism

It is widely believed that politics and economics are separate and largely uncon-
nected; that individual freedom is a political problem and material welfare an
economic problem; and that any kind of political arrangements can be combined
with any kind of economic arrangements. The chief contemporary manifestation
of this idea is the advocacy of "democratic socialism" by many who condemn out of
hand the restrictions on individual freedom imposed by "totalitarian socialism" in
Russia, and who are persuaded that it is possible for a country to adopt the essential
features of Russian economic arrangements and yet to ensure individual freedom
through political arrangements. The thesis I wish to defend here is that such a
view is a delusion, that there is an intimate connection between economics and
politics, that only certain combinations of political and economic arrangements are
possible, and that in particular, a society which is socialist cannot also be democratic, in the sense of guaranteeing individual freedom.

Economic arrangements play a dual role in the promotion of a free society. On
the one hand, freedom in economic arrangements is itself a component of freedom
broadly understood, so economic freedom is an end in itself. In the second place,
economic freedom is also an indispensable means toward the achievement of
political freedom.

The first of these roles of economic freedom needs special emphasis because
intellectuals in particular have a strong bias against regarding this aspect of
freedom as important. They tend to express contempt for what they regard as
material aspects of life, and to regard their own pursuit of allegedly higher values as
on a different plane of significance and as deserving of special attention. For most
citizens of the country, however, if not for the intellectual, the direct importance of
economic freedom is at least comparable in significance to the indirect importance
of economic freedom as a means to political freedom.

The citizen of Great Britain, who after World War II was not permitted to spend
his vacation in the United States because of exchange control, was being deprived
of an essential freedom no less than the citizen of the United States, who was

Reprinted from *Capitalism and Freedom,* Milton Friedman (Chicago: University of
Chicago Press, 1962). Used by permission.
*University of Chicago and Hoover Institution

denied the opportunity to spend his vacation in Russia because of his political views. The one was ostensibly an economic limitation on freedom and the other a political limitation, yet there is no essential difference between the two.

The citizen of the United States who is compelled by law to devote something like 10 per cent of his income to the purchase of a particular kind of retirement contract, administered by the government, is being deprived of a corresponding part of his personal freedom. How strongly this deprivation may be felt and its closeness to the deprivation of religious freedom, which all would regard as "civil" or "political" rather than "economic", were dramatized by an episode involving a group of farmers of the Amish sect. On grounds of principle, this group regarded compulsory federal old age programs as an infringement of their personal individual freedom and refused to pay taxes or accept benefits. As a result, some of their livestock were sold by auction in order to satisfy claims for social security levies. True, the number of citizens who regard compulsory old age insurance as a deprivation of freedom may be few, but the believer in freedom has never counted noses.

A citizen of the United States who under the laws of various states is not free to follow the occupation of his own choosing unless he can get a license for it, is likewise being deprived of an essential part of his freedom. So is the man who would like to exchange some of his goods with, say, a Swiss for a watch but is prevented from doing so by a quota. So also is the Californian who was thrown into jail for selling Alka Seltzer at a price below that set by the manufacturer under so-called "fair trade" laws. So also is the farmer who cannot grow the amount of wheat he wants. And so on. Clearly, economic freedom, in and of itself, is an extremely important part of total freedom.

Viewed as a means to the end of political freedom, economic arrangements are important because of their effect on the concentration or dispersion of power. The kind of economic organization that provides economic freedom directly, namely, competitive capitalism, also promotes political freedom because it separates economic power from political power and in this way enables the one to offset the other.

Historical evidence speaks with a single voice on the relation between political freedom and a free market. I know of no example in time or place of society that has been marked by a large measure of political freedom, and that has not also used something comparable to a free market to organize the bulk of economic activity.

Because we live in a largely free society, we tend to forget how limited is the span of time and the part of the globe for which there has ever been anything like political freedom: the typical state of mankind is tyranny, servitude, and misery. The nineteenth century and early twentieth century in the Western world stand out as striking exceptions to the general trend of historical development. Political freedom in this instance clearly came along with the free market and the development of capitalist institutions. So also did political freedom in the golden age of Greece and in the early days of the Roman era.

History suggests only that capitalism is a necessary condition for political freedom. Clearly it is not a sufficient condition. Fascist Italy and Fascist Spain, Germany at various times in the last seventy years, Japan before World Wars I and II, tzarist Russia in the decades before World War I—are all societies that cannot conceivably be described as politically free. Yet, in each, private enterprise was the dominant form of economic organization. It is therefore clearly possible to have economic arrangements that are fundamentally capitalist and political arrangements that are not free.

Even in those societies, the citizenry had a good deal more freedom than citizens of a modern totalitarian state like Russia or Nazi Germany, in which economic totalitarianism is combined with political totalitarianism. Even in Russia under the Tzars, it was possible for some citizens, under some circumstances, to change their jobs without getting permission from political authority because capitalism and the existence of private property provided some check to the centralized power of the state.

The relation between political and economic freedom is complex and by no means unilateral. In the early nineteenth century, Bentham and the Philosophical Radicals were inclined to regard political freedom as a means to economic freedom. They believed that the masses were being hampered by the restrictions that were being imposed upon them, and that if political reform gave the bulk of the people the vote, they would do what was good for them, which was to vote for laissez faire. In retrospect, one cannot say that they were wrong. There was a large measure of political reform that was accompanied by economic reform in the direction of a great deal of laissez faire. An enormous increase in the well-being of the masses followed this change in economic arrangements.

The triumph of Benthamite liberalism in nineteenth-century England was followed by a reaction toward increasing intervention by government in economic affairs. This tendency to collectivism was greatly accelerated, both in England and elsewhere, by the two World Wars. Welfare rather than freedom became the dominant note in democratic countries. Recognizing the implicit threat to individualism, the intellectual descendants of the Philosophical Radicals—Dicey, Mises, Hayek, and Simons, to mention only a few—feared that a continued movement toward centralized control of economic activity would prove *The Road to Serfdom*, as Hayek entitled his penetrating analysis of the process. Their emphasis was on economic freedom as a means toward political freedom.

Events since the end of World War II display still a different relation between economic and political freedom. Collectivist economic planning has indeed interfered with individual freedom. At least in some countries, however, the result has not been the suppression of freedom, but the reversal of economic policy. England again provides the most striking example. The turning point was perhaps the "control of engagements" order which, despite great misgivings, the Labour party found it necessary to impose in order to carry out its economic policy. Fully enforced and carried through, the law would have involved centralized allocation of individuals to occupations. This conflicted so sharply with personal liberty that it was enforced in a negligible number of cases, and then repealed after the law had been in effect for only a short period. Its repeal ushered in a decided shift in economic policy, marked by reduced reliance on centralized "plans" and "programs", by the dismantling of many controls, and by increased emphasis on the private market. A similar shift in policy occurred in most other democratic countries.

The proximate explanation of these shifts in policy is the limited success of central planning or its outright failure to achieve stated objectives. However, this

failure is itself to be attributed, at least in some measure, to the political implications of central planning and to an unwillingness to follow out its logic when doing
so requires trampling rough-shod on treasured private rights. It may well be that
the shift is only a temporary interruption in the collectivist trend of this century.
Even so, it illustrates the close relation between political freedom and economic
arrangements.

Historical evidence by itself can never be convincing. Perhaps it was sheer
coincidence that the expansion of freedom occurred at the same time as the
development of capitalist and market institutions. Why should there be a connection? What are the logical links between economic and political freedom? In
discussing these questions we shall consider first the market as a direct component of freedom, and then the indirect relation between market arrangements and
political freedom. A by-product will be an outline of the ideal economic arrangements for a free society.

As liberals, we take freedom of the individual, or perhaps the family, as our
ultimate goal in judging social arrangements. Freedom as a value in this sense has
to do with the interrelations among people; it has no meaning whatsoever to a
Robinson Crusoe on an isolated island (without his Man Friday). Robinson Crusoe
on his island is subject to "constraint," he has limited "power," and he has only a
limited number of alternatives, but there is no problem of freedom in the sense that
is relevant to our discussion. Similarly, in a society freedom has nothing to say
about what an individual does with his freedom; it is not an all-embracing ethic.
Indeed, a major aim of the liberal is to leave the ethical problem for the individual to
wrestle with. The "really" important ethical problems are those that face an
individual in a free society—what he should do with his freedom. There are thus
two sets of values that a liberal will emphasize—the values that are relevant to
relations among people, which is the context in which he assigns first priority to
freedom; and the values that are relevant to the individual in the exercise of his
freedom, which is the realm of individual ethics and philosophy.

The liberal conceives of men as imperfect beings. He regards the problem of
social organization to be as much a negative problem of preventing "bad" people
from doing harm as of enabling "good" people to do good; and, of course, "bad" and
"good" people may be the same people, depending on who is judging them.

The basic problem of social organization is how to co-ordinate the economic
activities of large numbers of people. Even in relatively backward societies, extensive division of labor and specialization of function is required to make effective use
of available resources. In advanced societies, the scale on which co-ordination is
needed, to take full advantage of the opportunities offered by modern science and
technology, is enormously greater. Literally millions of people are involved in
providing one another with their daily bread, let alone with their yearly automobiles. The challenge to the believer in liberty is to reconcile this widespread
interdependence with individual freedom.

Fundamentally, there are only two ways of co-ordinating the economic activities
of millions. One is central direction involving the use of coercion—the technique of
the army and of the modern totalitarian state. The other is voluntary co-operation
of individuals—the technique of the market place.

The possibility of co-ordination through voluntary co-operation rests on the elementary—yet frequently denied—proposition that both parties to an economic transaction benefit from it, *provided the transaction is bi-laterally voluntary and informed.*

Exchange can therefore bring about co-ordination without coercion. A working model of a society organized through voluntary exchange is a *free private enterprise exchange economy*—what we have been calling competitive capitalism.

In its simplest form, such a society consists of a number of independent households—a collection of Robinson Crusoes, as it were. Each household uses the resources it controls to produce goods and services that it exchanges for goods and services produced by other households, on terms mutually acceptable to the two parties to the bargain. It is thereby enabled to satisfy its wants indirectly by producing goods and services for others, rather than directly by producing goods for its own immediate use. The incentive for adopting this indirect route is, of course, the increased product made possible by division of labor and specialization of function. Since the household always has the alternative of producing directly for itself, it need not enter into any exchange unless it benefits from it. Hence, no exchange will take place unless both parties do benefit from it. Co-operation is thereby achieved without coercion.

Specialization of function and division of labor would not go far if the ultimate productive unit were the household. In a modern society, we have gone much farther. We have introduced enterprises which are intermediaries between individuals in their capacities as suppliers of service and as purchasers of goods. And similarly, specialization of function and division of labor could not go very far if we had to continue to rely on the barter of product for product. In consequence, money has been introduced as a means of facilitating exchange, and of enabling the acts of purchase and of sale to be separated into two parts.

Despite the important role of enterprises and of money in our actual economy, and despite the numerous and complex problems they raise, the central characteristic of the market technique of achieving co-ordination is fully displayed in the simple exchange economy that contains neither enterprises nor money. As in that simple model, so in the complex enterprise and money-exchange economy, co-operation is strictly individual and voluntary *provided: (a)* that enterprises are private, so that the ultimate contracting parties are individuals and *(b)* that individuals are effectively free to enter or not to enter into any particular exchange, so that every transaction is strictly voluntary.

It is far easier to state these provisos in general terms than to spell them out in detail, or to specify precisely the institutional arrangements most conducive to their maintenance. Indeed, much of technical economic literature is concerned with precisely these questions. The basic requisite is the maintenance of law and order to prevent physical coercion of one individual by another and to enforce contracts voluntarily entered into, thus giving substance to "private." Aside from this, perhaps the most difficult problems arise from monopoly—which inhibits effective freedom by denying individuals alternatives to the particular exchange— and from "neighborhood effects"—effects on third parties for which it is not feasible to charge or recompense them. These problems will be discussed in more detail in the following chapter.

So long as effective freedom of exchange is maintained, the central feature of the market organization of economic activity is that it prevents one person from interfering with another in respect of most of his activities. The consumer is protected from coercion by the seller because of the presence of other sellers with whom he can deal. The seller is protected from coercion by the consumer because of other consumers to whom he can sell. The employee is protected from coercion by the employer because of other employers for whom he can work, and so on. And the market does this impersonally and without centralized authority.

Indeed, a major source of objection to a free economy is precisely that it does this task so well. It gives people what they want instead of what a particular group thinks they ought to want. Underlying most arguments against the free market is a lack of belief in freedom itself.

The existence of a free market does not of course eliminate the need for government. On the contrary, government is essential both as a forum for determining the "rules of the game" and as an umpire to interpret and enforce the rules decided on. What the market does is to reduce greatly the range of issues that must be decided through political means, and thereby to minimize the extent to which government need participate directly in the game. The characteristic feature of action through political channels is that it tends to require or enforce substantial conformity. The great advantage of the market, on the other hand, is that it permits wide diversity. It is, in political terms, a system of proportional representation. Each man can vote, as it were, for the color of tie he wants and get it; he does not have to see what color the majority wants and then, if he is in the minority, submit.

It is this feature of the market that we refer to when we say that the market provides economic freedom. But this characteristic also has implications that go far beyond the narrowly economic. Political freedom means the absence of coercion of a man by his fellow men. The fundamental threat to freedom is power to coerce, be it in the hands of a monarch, a dictator, an oligarchy, or a momentary majority. The preservation of freedom requires the elimination of such concentration of power to the fullest possible extent and the dispersal and distribution of whatever power cannot be eliminated—a system of checks and balances. By removing the organization of economic activity from the control of political authority, the market eliminates this source of coercive power. It enables economic strength to be a check to political power rather than a reinforcement.

Economic power can be widely dispersed. There is no law of conservation which forces the growth of new centers of economic strength to be at the expense of existing centers. Political power, on the other hand, is more difficult to decentralize. There can be numerous small independent governments. But it is far more difficult to maintain numerous equipotent small centers of political power in a single large government than it is to have numerous centers of economic strength in a single large economy. There can be many millionaires in one large economy. But can there be more than one really outstanding leader, one person on whom the energies and enthusiasms of his countrymen are centered? If the central government gains power, it is likely to be at the expense of local governments. There seems to be something like a fixed total of political power to be distributed. Consequently, if economic power is joined to political power, concentration seems almost inevitable. On the other hand, if economic power is kept in separate hands from political power, it can serve as a check and a counter to political power.

The force of this abstract argument can perhaps best be demonstrated by example. Let us consider first, a hypothetical example that may help to bring out the principles involved, and then some actual examples from recent experience that illustrate the way in which the market works to preserve political freedom.

One feature of a free society is surely the freedom of individuals to advocate and propagandize openly for a radical change in the structure of the society—so long as the advocacy is restricted to persuasion and does not include force or other forms of coercion. It is a mark of the political freedom of a capitalist society that men can openly advocate and work for socialism. Equally, political freedom in a socialist society would require that men be free to advocate the introduction of capitalism. How could the freedom to advocate capitalism be preserved and protected in a socialist society?

In order for men to advocate anything, they must in the first place be able to earn a living. This already raises a problem in a socialist society, since all jobs are under the direct control of political authorities. It would take an act of self-denial whose difficulty is underlined by experience in the United States after World War II with the problem of "security" among Federal employees, for a socialist government to permit its employees to advocate policies directly contrary to official doctrine.

But let us suppose this act of self-denial to be achieved. For advocacy of capitalism to mean anything, the proponents must be able to finance their cause—to hold public meetings, publish pamphlets, buy radio time, issue newspapers and magazines, and so on. How could they raise the funds? There might and probably would be men in the socialist society with large incomes, perhaps even large capital sums in the form of government bonds and the like, but these would of necessity be high public officials. It is possible to conceive of a minor socialist official retaining his job although openly advocating capitalism. It strains credulity to imagine the socialist top brass financing such "subversive" activities.

The only recourse for funds would be to raise small amounts from a large number of minor officials. But this is no real answer. To tap these sources, many people would already have to be persuaded, and our whole problem is how to initiate and finance a campaign to do so. Radical movements in capitalist societies have never been financed this way. They have typically been supported by a few wealthy individuals who have become persuaded—by a Frederick Vanderbilt Field, or an Anita McCormick Blaine, or a Corliss Lamont, to mention a few names recently prominent, or by a Friedrich Engels, to go farther back. This is a role of inequality of wealth in preserving political freedom that is seldom noted—the role of the patron.

In a capitalist society, it is only necessary to convince a few wealthy people to get funds to launch any idea, however strange, and there are many such persons, many independent foci of support. And, indeed, it is not even necessary to persuade people or financial institutions with available funds of the soundness of the ideas to be propagated. It is only necessary to persuade them that the propagation can be financially successful; that the newspaper or magazine or book or other venture will be profitable. The competitive publisher, for example, cannot afford to publish only writing with which he personally agrees; his touchstone must be the likelihood that the market will be large enough to yield a satisfactory return on his investment.

In this way, the market breaks the vicious circle and makes it possible ultimately to finance such ventures by small amounts from many people without first persuading them. There are no such possibilities in the socialist society; there is only the all-powerful state.

Let us stretch our imagination and suppose that a socialist government is aware of this problem and is composed of people anxious to preserve freedom. Could it provide the funds? Perhaps, but it is difficult to see how. It could establish a bureau for subsidizing subversive propaganda. But how could it choose whom to support? If it gave to all who asked, it would shortly find itself out of funds, for socialism cannot repeal the elementary economic law that a sufficiently high price will call forth a large supply. Make the advocacy of radical causes sufficiently remunerative, and the supply of advocates will be unlimited.

Moreover, freedom to advocate unpopular causes does not require that such advocacy be without cost. On the contrary, no society could be stable if advocacy of radical change were costless, much less subsidized. It is entirely appropriate that men make sacrifices to advocate causes in which they deeply believe. Indeed, it is important to preserve freedom only for people who are willing to practice self-denial, for otherwise freedom degenerates into license and irresponsibility. What is essential is that the cost of advocating unpopular causes be tolerable and not prohibitive.

But we are not yet through. In a free market society, it is enough to have the funds. The suppliers of paper are as willing to sell it to the *Daily Worker* as to the *Wall Street Journal*. In a socialist society, it would not be enough to have the funds. The hypothetical supporter of capitalism would have to persuade a government factory making paper to sell to him, the government printing press to print his pamphlets, a government post office to distribute them among the people, a government agency to rent him a hall in which to talk, and so on.

Perhaps there is some way in which one could overcome these difficulties and preserve freedom in a socialist society. One cannot say it is utterly impossible. What is clear, however, is that there are very real difficulties in establishing institutions that will effectively preserve the possibility of dissent. So far as I know, none of the people who have been in favor of socialism and also in favor of freedom have really faced up to this issue, or made even a respectable start at developing the institutional arrangements that would permit freedom under socialism. By contrast, it is clear how a free market capitalist society fosters freedom.

A striking practical example of these abstract principles is the experience of Winston Churchill. From 1933 to the outbreak of World War II, Churchill was not permitted to talk over the British radio, which was, of course, a government monopoly administered by the British Broadcasting Corporation. Here was a leading citizen of his country, a Member of Parliament, a former cabinet minister, a man who was desperately trying by every device possible to persuade his countrymen to take steps to ward off the menace of Hitler's Germany. He was not permitted to talk over the radio to the British people because the BBC was a government monopoly and his position was too "controversial."

Another striking example, reported in the January 26, 1959 issue of *Time*, has to do with the "Blacklist Fadeout." Says the *Time* story,

> The Oscar-awarding ritual is Hollywood's biggest pitch for dignity, but two years ago dignity suffered. When one Robert Rich was announced as top writer

for the *The Brave One,* he never stepped forward. Robert Rich was a pseudo-nym, masking one of about 150 writers . . . blacklisted by the industry since 1947 as suspected Communists or fellow travelers. The case was particularly embarrassing because the Motion Picture Academy had barred any Communist or Fifth Amendment pleader from Oscar competition. Last week both the Communist rule and the mystery of Rich's identity were suddenly rescripted.

Rich turned out to be Dalton (*Johnny Got His Gun*) Trumbo, one of the original "Hollywood Ten" writers who refused to testify at the 1947 hearings on Communism in the movie industry. Said producer Frank King, who had stoutly insisted that Robert Rich was "a young guy in Spain with a beard": "We have an obligation to our stockholders to buy the best script we can. Trumbo brought us *The Brave One* and we bought it". . . .

In effect it was the formal end of the Hollywood black list. For barred writers, the informal end came long ago. At least 15% of current Hollywood films are reportedly written by blacklist members. Said Producer King, "There are more ghosts in Hollywood than in Forest Lawn. Every company in town has used the work of blacklisted people. We're just the first to confirm what everybody knows."

One may believe, as I do, that communism would destroy all of our freedoms, one may be opposed to it as firmly and as strongly as possible, and yet, at the same time, also believe that in a free society it is intolerable for a man to be prevented from making voluntary arrangements with others that are mutually attractive because he believes in or is trying to promote communism. His freedom includes his freedom to promote communism. Freedom also, of course, includes the freedom of others not to deal with him under those circumstances. The Hollywood blacklist was an unfree act that destroys freedom because it was a collusive arrangement that used coercive means to prevent voluntary exchanges. It didn't work precisely because the market made it costly for people to preserve the blacklist. The commercial emphasis, the fact that people who are running enterprises have an incentive to make as much money as they can, protected the freedom of the individuals who were blacklisted by providing them with an alternative form of employment, and by giving people an incentive to employ them.

If Hollywood and the movie industry had been government enterprises or if in England it had been a question of employment by the British Broadcasting Corporation it is difficult to believe that the "Hollywood Ten" or their equivalent would have found employment. Equally, it is difficult to believe that under those circumstances, strong proponents of individualism and private enterprise—or indeed strong proponents of any view other than the status quo—would be able to get employment.

Another example of the role of the market in preserving political freedom, was revealed in our experience with McCarthyism. Entirely aside from the substantive issues involved, and the merits of the charges made, what protection did individuals, and in particular government employees, have against irresponsible accusations and probings into matters that it went against their conscience to reveal? Their appeal to the Fifth Amendment would have been a hollow mockery without an alternative to government employment.

Their fundamental protection was the existence of a private-market economy in which they could earn a living. Here again, the protection was not absolute. Many potential private employers were, rightly or wrongly, averse to hiring those pilloried. It may well be that there was far less justification for the costs imposed on many of the people involved than for the costs generally imposed on people who advocate unpopular causes. But the important point is that the costs were limited and not prohibitive, as they would have been if government employment had been the only possibility.

It is of interest to note that a disproportionately large fraction of the people involved apparently went into the most competitive sectors of the economy—small business, trade, farming—where the market approaches most closely the ideal free market. No one who buys bread knows whether the wheat from which it is made was grown by a Communist or a Republican, by a constitutionalist or a Fascist, or, for that matter, by a Negro or a white. This illustrates how an impersonal market separates economic activities from political views and protects men from being discriminated against in their economic activities for reasons that are irrelevant to their productivity—whether these reasons are associated with their views or their color.

As this example suggests, the groups in our society that have the most at stake in the preservation and strengthening of competitive capitalism are those minority groups which can most easily become the object of the distrust and enmity of the majority—the Negroes, the Jews, the foreign-born, to mention only the most obvious. Yet, paradoxically enough, the enemies of the free market—the Socialists and Communists—have been recruited in disproportionate measure from these groups. Instead of recognizing that the existence of the market has protected them from the attitudes of their fellow countrymen, they mistakenly attribute the residual discrimination to the market.

J. ROGER LEE*

The Arrest and Punishment of Criminals: Justification and Limitations

In an earlier paper[1] I argued from premises of ethical egoism and political libertarianism that it was both permissible and desirable to punish some people for some crimes. The present work is given over to a more detailed account of what it is about the character of some crimes that makes it both permissible and desirable to punish them. Having isolated the relevant factor, that allows punishment to be an appropriate response to some actions, I discuss the limitations that are imposed on permissible punishments by the nature of the justifying factors for the institution of punishment generally. Libertarians are very strongly concerned with limitations on permissible behavior imposed by human rights. These concerns are no less operative in the area of punishing criminals. So a libertarian has to look with horror at the sorry history and present practices of punishment, at people's capacity for inhumanity toward each other. However, punishment of a specified sort, for some actions properly called criminal, is justifiable.

I

From my earlier work I take over the conclusions that a libertarian account of punishment ought neither be simply retributivist nor utilitarian. Not utilitarian because considerations of rights will outweigh considerations of consequences. Not retributivist because the point of punishing is to attain features of the good society as ends, and not some sort of duty to right wrongs. The defense of punishment is *teleological* and thus not retributivist. And it is constrained by rights and thus not utilitarian. Again, I argue for these conclusions elsewhere.

*California State University, Northridge

It is a commonplace of libertarian social theory that it is in the interest of each person to live in a society in which there are unimpeded possibilities for freely chosen cooperative interactions. It is a disadvantage, therefore, to have such social relations undermined either by having force initiated on one, or by fraud. It is desirable, therefore, to structure society in such a way that it is possible for individuals to produce, possible for them to enter into cooperative relations with others, or not, as they choose, possible to enter into open and agreed upon (non-fraudulent) trades or to decline to work out such trades as the individuals choose. So it is in the interest of each person in the society to see to it that people deal with each other in terms of freely chosen patterns of interaction—not in terms of force and fraud. I will not argue for the truth of these claims here. They are well argued in other libertarian writings.

While what can be called the harmony principle (that every wrong act directed at another has bad consequences for the actor) is true, its being true does not suffice to insure that a society will contain only those relations that are worthwhile to the individuals involved. Indeed, while there is probably nothing which would insure that all interactions will be of the desired sort, the presence of some sort of institution of punishment will act to make such interactions more the normal course of events.

While it is true that wrongdoers, for the most part, come off worse than right-doers, the average wrongdoer may not know this. In fact, the bad consequences in question often are fairly *recherché*, and while that in no way diminishes them, it does diminish any prophylactic effect that they might have. Second, while any attempt on the part of a person, A, to exploit or attempt to acquire the unearned from B has bad consequences for A, it is by no means clear that in all cases the bad consequences would outweigh the values dishonestly acquired from B. Last, although in all cases in which A acts wrongly toward B, A suffers bad consequences (or the lack of good consequences), it can be and often is the case that B, through no fault of B's own, also suffers bad consequences of A's act, and in some cases the consequences to B are worse than the consequences to A.

There is a set of wrong actions such that, if people perform any of those actions, as a direct consequence of their so doing, someone else, B, undergoes a loss of values. No person, B, who has a reasonable concern for B's own interest can tolerate A's so acting, and consequently each person has the obligation to *defend* against others who would act in the way specified. In civilized societies these defense activities are made subject to both the division of labor and the rule of objective law via the institution of government and it police.

Defense, however, is anticipatory. After the wrong action has been performed, something other than defense is required—restitution first, and then punishment. That is, one very classical reason why we should harm others through punishment is to try to minimize such goings on in the future. But that can't be all there is as an account of the justification of punishment for two reasons.

The first reason is that what is at hand is not a rationale for *punishing* people, but a rationale for inflicting harms on people as part of our self-defense, *because* it contributes to our self-defense. So, if this were all there was to why we should punish people, then we would not have a rationale for punishment which was not also a rationale for telishment. If self-defense through example setting is the reason why we *punish* anybody, why not let it be the reason why we punish *anybody*? For a large number of wrongdoers, the fact that that person did wrong in the past is a poor indication of that person's propensity to do so in the future. So, if eliminating future wrongdoings is at issue, it makes little difference whether the person is innocent or guilty for special deterence. For general deterence, it matters only whether the person is *thought to be* guilty, not whether the person *is* guilty. So, if self-defense, in the form of lowering the crime rates, were the justification of punishment, it would not provide a rationale for punishing only those who are guilty. So it is not a full account of the *justification* of punishment to say that we punish people to create disincentives to future crime.

It is, however, part of our *motive* in punishing people that an anticipated reduction in the crime rate will eventuate. I have argued that this is a reasonable motive. But what has not been argued is that it is permissible to treat people that way, and that is the second reason why the self-defense justification of punishment is inadequate.

The question of the justification of punishment should be divided. First we should ask why it is morally permissible to punish people. Second, we should ask: given that it is morally permissible to punish people, why *should* we punish people? What good reason do we have to think that punishing people for crimes falls within the range of morally preferable things to do? The self-defense justification of punishment is an incomplete answer to the second question. But it does nothing to answer the question: Why is it permissible to punish people?

The answer, of course, is that generally it isn't. It is not generally morally permissible to punish people. Minimally, we should make sure that people are wrongdoers before we punish them. But as the example of a harmless heroin user shows, it is counter-intuitive to suppose that it is permissible to punish just any wrongdoer. So, why is it permissible to punish some wrongdoers? And which wrongdoers?

It is of interest to people generally to live in a society in which there are unimpeded possibilities for freely chosen cooperative interactions and, it is a corresponding disadvantage to them, therefore, to have such relations compromised by persons who introduce force or fraud into the society. This fact, I maintain, goes to specify the minimal conditions for worthy association in society. The purposes for which something is designed constitute goodness for that thing. We do not ever have the opportunity to choose whether or not we will live in society, but we can, counterfactually, specify what our purposes would be in choosing to live in society as opposed to "lone-wolfing" it. Those purposes define the good society and thus define a common good for each of us for whom society is good. We *should,* each of us, act to promote this common good, for it is a good for each of us. In fact, it is a minimal expectation that each of us will avoid compromising the desired relations in the society, that each of us will avoid initiating force or introducing fraud into human relations.

Situations which recur frequently in human relations come to have what I call rational expectation frameworks associated with them. What it is reasonable to expect the parties to do in those recurring situations comes to be fixed in well-known ways through custom and convention. So, by placing ourselves in such recurring situations we license others to require that predicted constraints on our future actions will, in fact, regulate those actions. Since all parties know these constraints on future actions which are associated with a particular recurring social situation, all parties to the situation agree to conform their actions to the constraints of the rational expectation framework by inserting themselves into the situations with which these rational expectation frameworks are associated. Elsewhere, I discuss the nature of these rational expectation frameworks in more detail and explore the relation of these conventions to human rights.[2] Here, I content myself with the rather minimal and intuitively plausible claim that a minimal construal of the rational expectation framework of everyday comings into contact with others is that we are not to introduce force or fraud into such relations.

We have no trans-contextual claim to being a "member in good standing" of society. We have no trans-contextual claim to the treatment of other people in the society as potential parties to cooperative ventures. We have no such claim unless we act in ways that are not destructive of the good to be realized from a society. If we act in ways that are conducive to the common social good, then the obligation of others not to undermine the common social good is an obligation to treat us as of equal standing in the society as possible parties to cooperative ventures. But this claim is conditional. *Minimally,* we have no *claim* to equal treatment as possible parties to cooperative ventures with other members of the society unless we *refrain from damaging the common social good,* that is, *refrain from introducing force or fraud into social relations.* That is a basic part of the rational expectation framework of everyday gettings on with people. If and when we do act to introduce force or fraud into human relations, we lose our claim against others to be treated as a potential partner in cooperative ventures. We lose our *claim* to equal standing in the community which is assembled as a locus of potential cooperations. We lose our claim to free association in the community *because,* by our actions, we have declared ourselves not willing to meet the necessary conditions for such free association, or, more precisely, we have not met the necessary conditions to have a *claim* to the *civil* liberty of free association with others. We would have acted against the rational expectation framework which is associated with every contact with others. We would lose any claim to be persons who *may* play a role in the framework for initiating contacts toward possible cooperations in the future. So, we would lose our claim to the civil liberty of free association in the community.

It is not a natural right that I have to be able to mingle with others, approach them, use property around them, or propose deals to them. The sort of *prima facie* trusting relation of contiguity and community we have with others in our society is a sort of agreed upon conferral of joint status, based on assumptions that the minimal conditions of joint status as members of the society have been met by each of us, and which is done to make possible that good for each of us which is the purpose of society. Those minimal standards are spelled out above, and they are part of the rational expectation framework associated with placing ourselves contiguous with others. When individuals fail to meet them, those individuals remove any claim on us to confer on them the benefit of the assumptions of civility which we have to make to give them civil standing as freely associating members of the community.

The civil liberty of free association to initiate proposals of cooperation is something that we earn by consistently acting in certain ways, avoiding fraud and the initiation of force, by conforming to the rational expectation frameworks which are associated with the situations into which we put ourselves. It is right that this is so, because our having the civil liberty of free association demands of others that they assume that we will behave like that. When we breach this responsibility to earn this treatment from others, we have no claim on them to allow us to freely associate with them.

Once we have lost this claim, we have no grounds for complaint if others fail to confer this liberty on us. This is the basic fact which makes a certain form of punishment of criminals permissible. As a form of punishment for our having undermined the rational expectation framework of everyday life by the introduction of force or fraud into human affairs, the others in the society may withdraw our parole to freely associate with them. That is, they may withdraw our parole to mingle with them, to propose deals to them, and, generally, to place ourselves among them.

Minimally, to achieve this end, the members of the community might make us exile from the community. This could be done by sending us to foreign countries, but that would be a "bad neighbor" policy. Were we to ship our murderers, thieves, and other criminals to foreign countries, those countries would have a viable complaint against us. So, unless our criminals are wanted by other countries, we have no right to ship them to these countries. And in some cases, even if a foreign country would be prepared to accept some of our criminals, reasons of security might make it undesirable for us to send them there. I am thinking about the possibility of "outlaw states" which would serve as a base for crime against other states. We would have no obligation to send our criminals to such an insecure place. In fact, in self-defense, we should not send our criminals to such a place. Yet we are to keep these criminals that we will not send to other countries from associating with us.

What we may do, to realize our ends, is remove criminals to a supervised place from which they cannot leave (though others could join them there if both parties so chose). This practice, if adopted would have the sole effect of denying criminals the civil liberty to mingle among us and to be in physical proximity to us. Second, we could allow mail, telephone, and media contacts initiated by criminals in the penal place with non-criminals in the outside, everyday world. But, since we can deny criminals the civil liberty to propose cooperative ventures to non-criminals, we may "brand" such criminals by insuring that such telephonic, mail, and other media contacts be clearly identified at the outset as originating from a criminal at the penal place. Then it would be up to the citizen at liberty to either grant or not grant the acceptance of such communications and of the deals proposed in them, having first been duly warned about their source.

I believe that the following proposals, if put into practice in a libertarian society, would allow for the legitimate aims of punishment to be met. Certain geographical areas ought to be set off from the rest of the community by the government, to which those who are to be punished would be removed, in which they would be subject to intense surveillance by police to insure the absence of actions against outsiders, and from which they would be denied exit. While in these areas, they would be free to engage in whatever work they desire and amass whatever wealth they are capable of producing, and acquiring through trade, including trade with communities outside the penal place, should outsiders and inmates wish such trade. They should be free to do this, because we have no right to do anything to these people except withhold the civil liberty of free association. That is the only form of punishment that has been justified by the reasoning above. We may not ignore their natural right to undertake actions to produce and to promote their own well-being. If we acted in ways that prevented their so doing, we would violate their rights. We, in fact, violate the rights of criminals in countless ways today, by placing them in jails and prisons which are inhumane places, where people are kept from exercising their rights to lead characteristically human lives.

Any monies made inside the penal place shall be taxed by the government authorities at a rate such that the cost of the intense police supervision and other administrative costs of the area are borne solely by the inmates (it is the wrong-doers who must bear the costs of their wrongdoing, not the other members of the society), and such that restitution is made in a prompt fashion to the victims of their crimes, to the extent that that can be done. Crimes committed within the penal place would be punished by increasing the time to be spent in the penal place and by increasing the tax burden to meet the increased duties of restitution arising out of the new crimes.[3]

I make no comment here about what sort of punishment would be appropriate in non-libertarian societies. It is a feature of libertarian societies that the law is set up only to insure (so far as possible) that the conditions for possible cooperation among freely choosing individuals are met. It does this, in part,[4] by making the initiation of force or fraud a crime. So, the just punishment for a crime is the removal of that for which a pledge has been broken by the introduction of force or fraud into human affairs. What may be removed is the standard civil liberty of free association. One of the drawbacks of a non-libertarian society is that it contains a lot of law that insures that initiations of force, at least, are standard features of that society. The rational expectation framework of everyday life is seriously under-mined. Given the compromised feature of the law, it is very likely that, although that law is better than none, and so is worth enforcing through punishing, there is no way to enforce it justly, and thus, no way to punish justly.

However, it is possible to enforce the law and to punish justly in a libertarian society. A violation of a law there is a violation of the minimal conditions of social interaction. It is permissible to punish people in the way specified above for a libertarian society, because it is permissible to decline to grant a liberty to those who have not earned it. And that is the extent of the permissibility. Nothing more is sanctioned. It is not, for example permissible to kill criminals, to torture them, to deny them avenues for sex or for other pleasures, to make them contemplate their evil ways, to retrain them, to mold them, etc. No sanction for any such behavior comes out of the fact that the criminal has breached the trust which is ordinarily placed in people. So, the very grounds of the permissibility of punishment which comes out of the purposes of society imposes a strict limit on the kind of punish-ment that can be institutionalized in the society. The society may only remove the individual from the conditions of free association as a person who may propose cooperative ventures with others, make the criminal pay for the cost of that supervised exile, and extract restitution to the victim from the criminal. Nothing else has a sanction. Anything else would be abuse of the criminal, in violation of the criminal's rights. Anything else would be inhumane treatment of another human being.

It is not my purpose, in this essay, to develop a sketch of an ideal penal system, but to present a rationale for very limited forms of punishment and show it to be practicable in a libertarian society. What is broadly sketched here is sufficiently unpleasant to make the obscurity of bad consequences overcome by its mere presence as punishment—as an additional bad consequence. The provisions for restitution insure as far as possible that wrongdoers will bear the costs of their wrongdoing. But neither this informative nor the requirement of restitution is, strictly speaking, punishment.

Restitution is done as a civil remedy for the victim. The publicity attaching to this new bad consequence of wrong action, insofar as it deters others from acting wrongly, is defense. Punishment is an action done to a wrongdoer. It is our refusal to grant the civil liberty of free association with a large segment of society. Such a loss of a normal feature of life is severe punishment indeed. And, in part, because of what goes on inside these penal places, the society outside of them remains a place of voluntary association and trade which quickly removes any deviations from that pattern by removing the cause and undoing the effect of such deviations.

II

Two sorts of fine tuning are appropriate for this theory. The first is an account of the relation between the permissibility of punishing and the permissibility of arrest. The second fine tuning is an account of judicial discretion with respect to sentencing. Sometimes we ought not punish even wrongdoers who have acted in ways that go against the rational expectation frameworks to which we demand others to conform their actions. I start with the power of arrest, through a discussion of the ways in which the reasonings of this paper are related to a core notion of jurisprudence which has gone undiscussed to this point.

There is a sense in which all of this ties into the legal notion of presumption of innocence. It is a doctrine of Anglo-American jurisprudence that a person is presumed to be innocent until he is proven guilty. This presumption is an assumption made about people in standard cases. If a person is brought into court on a charge of armed robbery, for example, then all parties formally assume that person's innocence until the government proves guilt, if it can.

It is a helpful paraphrase of what I have said, in the last section of this paper, to say that there is a sort of less articulated presumption of innocence which operates in society at a deeper level than the one which operates in court. People, as I have worked out above, generally treat each other on the basis of an assumption that, by and large, people are safe. We tolerate anybody to mingle freely with us in public places, to approach us with an aim to proposing deals, and in public accommodations, like restaurants and train stations; we enter into all sorts of transactions and associations without having paranoid fears about what our fellow patrons will do to us. We assume that everyone will act in accord with the rational expectation framework of everyday life. That is, we assume that everyone will observe the minimal conditions for worthwhile association in society.

This is a presumption of innocence of sorts. We assume that people will be innocent of the great crimes involving the initiation of force or fraud. Prior to our obtaining probable cause to believe that someone has committed a crime, one has this, what I call "strong presumption of innocence." Of course, it is misleading to say that one *has* this, as if it were a property. It is misleading, because the only sense in which we can be said to have it is that others *confer* this treatment on us. Things could change at any time. The others could stop. Things do, in fact, change if one is detected committing a crime.

The concept of the strong presumption of innocence is useful in answering an important question which, though fundamental to the issues under discussion here, is a different question than the question: Why is it ever permissible to punish people? The question is: Why is it ever permissible to interfere with someone's civil liberty of free association to the extent involved in arrest and binding over for trial? This is a different question than the question why we may punish people, because the practice of arrest is different from punishing. We seek to punish only the guilty. We arrest people and bind them over for trial in an effort to determine whether or not they are guilty and should then be punished. Yet, the arrest and the require- ment that the person stand trial is a revocation of a person's civil liberty of free association. And what justifies that?

The answer is that, in principle, the same thing justifies that that justifies our denying that civil right in punishing. The justifying fact is that the conferral of the strong presumption of innocence is a benefit that has to be acquired from our fellow humans. They may rescind this benefit.

My position is that once there is probable cause to suppose that I have committed a crime, then I lose my strong presumption of innocence. Of course, I will retain my usual judicial presumption of innocence. It is still up to the government to prove in open court that I did, in fact, commit the crime. And the presumption, until they do, if they do, is that I am innocent.

But even if there is a weak or judicial presumption of innocence, there is still probable cause to suppose that I did commit the crime. And that probable cause undoes the strong presumption of innocence. It is because it undoes that strong presumption of innocence that it is morally permissible for the police to arrest me on probable cause, and for the court to bind me over for trial on probable cause. The probable cause attaching me to a crime constitutes a *prima facie* breach of the responsibility I have to earn the civil liberty of free association. It constitutes a breach of the responsibility that I have to earn the response that people make to me in conferring the strong presumption of innocence. It would be unreasonable to suppose that people would still confer this benefit on me in the face of the evidence that it would be unreasonable to do so. So, although one has not been branded a criminal before conviction, it is still the case that arrest and binding over for trial is appropriate.

Others have an interest in not abusing this power of arrest. That interest is the interest which gives them reason to confer the strong presumption in the first place. It is a good for people to get on in society in which the rational expectation framework (the strong presumption) obtains fully. To promote that good for them- selves, people are obliged not to undermine the rational expectation framework of civilized life. Subjecting the innocent to the power of arrest indiscriminately would undermine it. So too would letting the actual perpetrators of crimes go free. Prior to trial and the attendant judicial proof, we don't know which is which. The strictures of probable cause are designed to operate here. Where there is probable cause, there is a ground for removing the strong presumption of innocence to attain the end of not letting the guilty go free. Where there is no probable cause, there is an obligation not to arrest, which is an instance of the obligation to not undermine the rational expectation framework of civilized association.

Once I am arrested, I can no longer freely associate with people. That is just what arrest amounts to. So, once I am arrested, I lose the strong presumption of innocence. Even if I am given an opportunity to bail myself out, I am being given the opportunity only to give security for the temporary conferral of the presumption that I've lost.

I do, however, retain the usual judicial presumption of innocence until I am convicted, if and when I am. If I am not convicted, I am set free and that amounts to my having got back the strong presumption of innocence that I had lost. Even if I am acquitted on a procedural technicality, I reacquire this presumption. I may not deserve to, but the practice of doing so is adopted because it maximizes the good of justice sought from the criminal justice system.

If, however, I am convicted, then the consequences sketched above come into play. I'm sent to the penal institution and I make restitution to the victims of the crime, so far as is practicable. That is, I will lose my liberty of association for a period of time in which I will also be taxed to pay for the upkeep of the penal institution and to make restitution for my crime, to its victims, returning them so far as is possible to their *status quo ante* the crime. All that has been spelled out above, prior to the distinction between the authority to remove the liberty of free association in arrest and in punishment. Here, however, I want to specify a role for judicial discretion in punishing.

Quite often a judge is faced with sentencing in a case in which the criminal is very likely not to ever repeat the crime which had been a unique, spontaneous event in the person's life. Reading of popular magazines, for example, informs me that a typical murderer will be a woman who, in a fit of passion, but after years of abuse at the hands of her husband, on an occasion, impulsively, killed him. Let us say that the criminology statisticians have some way of telling that it is exceedingly unlikely that this person ever will be in a similar situation and then that she never will kill or even be violent in the resolution of disputes again. In this case, our intuitions go to the conclusion that the woman ought not be punished.

Care needs to be taken here. Intuitively, it would be wrong to punish such a woman. Intuitively, *no point* would be served. But this is at best ambiguous. Is it the case that we have no good reason to punish this person, though such treatment would be permissible? Or is it that it would not be permissible to punish this person?

No one, including this woman, has a claim against us in all contexts to the liberty of free association. There is no direct relation to us of a right that demands that we let this person, under the description 'human being,' go free among us. The 'among us' in the last sentence marks a feature of the situation which calls for our consent before claims can be counted.

We each have an obligation to earn the parole of others if we are to have it at all. This woman has not. She has broken the "compact" which demands our granting of the civil liberty of free association. She has benefited from it in the past and yet has not done what is requisite to have earned those past benefits. We are within our rights to withhold the benefit in the future as we would be in refusing to do business with someone after they had taken delivery on a contract and then refused to pay the agreed upon compensation.

If our purposes would be served (including our purposes to be mentioned below in the next section) then we would be within our rights to punish this person. It matters not if the person will never commit the crime in the future, and we know that. What matters is that this person has not done what is required to demand of us that we treat her as someone who should freely associate—she has not behaved in such a way as to earn it from us by her actions. *If* it is in fact to our purposes to punish this woman, then we may. *If,* and I stress the conditional character of this claim, it is in keeping with the *purposes* which motivate us to punish people to punish this person, then we may punish this person.

In the next paragraph I will urge that it will seldom be in our interest to punish such a person. But here I insist that if it is, then it is morally permissible to do so. Of course there are the standard restrictions on even this moral permissibility. Chief is that our treatment of the woman must be universalizable. That is, we must afford here equal treatment before the law. So, if we had a policy of letting all such people go, then she, being such a person, should be let go.

As in the case of the power to arrest, so too with the power to punish. We have an obligation to promote future associations which are in keeping with the rational expectation framework of civilized life. That is, each of us has an obligation not to undermine such gettings on and to promote a situation in which peaceful gettings on will flourish among cooperative people. It is to promote this good that punishment is justified. Now, it is not conducive to this end to incarcerate people who would be parties to worthwhile cooperative social interactions in keeping with the rational expectation framework of civilized life. So, there is a strong initial presumption that it will not be to our purposes in punishing people to punish this woman. It may be our right to do so. *Prima facie*, at least, we ought not do so as it fails to realize our ends. In fact, as we ought not work against our ends, that is a strong *prima facie* ought against the practice.

However, it will not do to make this an exceptionless practice. At times, for example, it would be clear that continuing a practice of freeing husband murderers who murdered impulsively will have the unwanted effect of giving people reasonable betting incentives to murder their disliked husbands on the assumption that one can probably get away with one such murder. There may well be one such case in which it is clear that sending this person to the penal institution will send out a clear message, and in which it is also clear that it doesn't matter that it is this particular person who is ideally suited to be used as a message bearer   anyone else who was similarly situated as guilty would do as well. In that case, it will be conducive to our purposes to punish the murdered and so it will be both permissible and will be desirable, as the *prima facie* undesirability of punishing this person we may well know will never repeat such a crime will have been overcome. But to repeat, very often it will not be to our purposes to do so and in those cases we ought not punish. And so a place for discretion in punishing is preserved.

III

I have specified a reason why it is permissible to punish criminals and have specified one of the reasons why we should punish them—to create a disincentive to crime.

I want to end this essay by specifying another reason we have for punishing criminals. It is, simply, to preserve the integrity of the law and our integrity as people who are committed to the law.

From at least the 1500s onward and probably from even earlier, the punishment of criminals has been a sort of theatre of the integrity of the law. In the times of European monarchies the excessive savageries that were visited on criminals, in public shows of mutilation or execution, were designed to dramatize the over-whelming power of the sovereign, which power was then thought to be the necessary underpinning of the law. Today, the solemn rituals of the courts (at least in movies) constitute a theatre of the rule of law. Ideally, with decent, consistent laws, the administration of justice should be a solemn theatre wherein the assembled citizens express their commitment to the law and their revulsion against those persons who put themselves outside of it by their actions.

This is a necessary theatre. Were we to know of lawbreaking and condone it, then our moral status would be that of an accessory after the fact to a crime and that would be a psychological burden to our integrity that would have to be dispensed with. The absolute eschewing of the criminal through punative incarceration is, in part at least, a ritual with which we purge ourselves and express our commitment to the law.

Randy Barnett and John Hagel have put forth a theory of punishment as restitution[5] which, unfortunately, has attained some adherence in libertarian circles. Barnett and Hagel hold that restitution is the only legitimate "penalty" for crimes. Part of the reasoning that impresses proponents of this view is the claim that only the victims of crime have a right to redress. Since the populace at large is not victimized by crime, the reasoning goes, the government, acting for all the people, has no right to claim redress from the criminal. So that would leave only the criminal and the criminal's victim to work out what is essentially a civil remedy to the criminal act. I maintain that insuring restitution is part of what we should do in criminal proceedings, but that it neither is all or part of what punishment should amount to. What undercuts the argument for the restitutionary view is the fact that the premise cited in the last paragraph is false. The populace at large *is*, in fact, victimized by crime.

Blackstone, in his *Commentaries on the Laws of England*, claims that a crime is always injurious to the king and thus, the king is prosecutor in every criminal action.[6] Now, libertarians are not monarchists. The doctrine of equal standing before the law contravenes that doctrine of privilege and involves commitment to the legitimacy of popular sovereignty. But there is a way in which Blackstone's comment can be updated to apply to a modern popular sovereignty.

I have argued that a crime undercuts the rational expectation framework which each citizen in the society finds to be of value and which governments are set up to preserve. In fact, each citizen is harmed by the undermining of the rational expectation framework. Citizens are harmed in their roles as citizens. It is a civic-social harm. So the citizens, as citizens commanding agencies or government, are the counterparts of Blackstone's king "in whom centers the majesty of the whole community" and are the proper parties to press and prosecute criminal charges. Criminal cases *are* cases of the people v. the criminal.

This parallel goes further. When it comes time to punish those found guilty, then the proper punishment is the people's withdrawal of the blessings of citizenship in the community. The citizens, as citizens, withdraw the status of a citizen in good standing in the community. So, the people are the parties to criminal remedies to preserve the good of each which reposes in the rational expectation framework of civilized association. Punishment to secure those ends is required in the good society, *pace* Barnett and Hagel.

In general, however, punishment is a practice which is designed to help keep society a place for peaceful exchange among reasonable people by: 1) making the cost of deviating from this pattern of interaction by the introduction of force and fraud so high as to make such deviation perspicuously unattractive, thus reducing persons' motives to so act, and 2) expressing people's repulsion by and implementing their dissociation from someone who, by criminal actions, has shown a lack of agreement with the fundamental principle of proper human interaction—to seek a value exchange with another only through voluntary agreement.

The loss of the capacity to freely associate with one's fellows is a form of punishment. This estrangement from others is painful to the one estranged and insures the tranquility of the society, not so much by removal of one likely to act against it (there are probably better indicators of likelihood of future criminal action than past criminal behavior, which only a utilitarian would use), but by the reaffirmation of the basic principle of proper social interaction and of their abhorrence of those who would act otherwise.

Notes

*I am thankful to the Liberty Fund and to the Reason Foundation for a summer fellowship which supported my work on this paper. I am also appreciative of conversations with or comments by Tibor Machan, Herbert Morris, Stephen Munzer and Lawrence Thomas on an earlier draft of this paper. None of these individuals ought be supposed to agree with what is said here. But their criticisms of my earlier work helped me to make this a better work than it otherwise would have been.

1. "Reflections on Punishment," in *The Libertarian Alternative: Readings in Social and Political Philosophy,* ed. Tibor R. Machan (Chicago: Nelson Hall, 1973).

2. "Choice and Harms," in *Regulation or Deregulation,* ed. M. Bruce Johnson and Tibor R. Machan (Cambridge, Mass.: Ballinger Publishing Co., 1982).

3. I make no claims about pairings of ranks of severity of crimes and measures of times of loss of the liberty of free association, though I do think that such coordinations are desirable.

4. The other part is civil law.

5. Randy Barnett and John Hagel, III, "Assessing the Criminal: Restitution, Retribution and the Legal Process," and Randy Barnett, "Restitution: A New Paradigm of Criminal Justice," in *Assessing the Criminal: Restitution, Retribution and the Legal Process,* ed. Randy Barnett and John Hagel, III (Cambridge, Mass.: Ballinger Publishing Co., 1977), pp. 1-32 and 349-384.

6. William Blackstone, *Commentaries on the Laws of England,* Book the fourth, *Of Public Wrongs,* p. 2.

THOMAS S. SZASZ*

The Insanity Plea and
the Insanity Verdict

In 1843, Daniel M'Naghten shot and killed Edward Drummond, private secretary to Sir Robert Peel, whom M'Naghten had intended to kill. The defense was insanity. Evidence was introduced showing that M'Naghten "was labouring under the insane delusion" of being hounded by enemies, among them Peel. Lord Chief Justice Tindal was so impressed by this evidence that he practically directed a verdict for acquittal. The jury found M'Naghten not guilty, on the ground of insanity.[1] As usually told, this is where the story ends. But what happened to Daniel M'Naghten?

Since M'Naghten was acquitted, the reader might think that he was discharged by the court. Until 1843, this is what the word "acquittal" meant in the English language. But M' Naghten's "acquittal" was a precursor to that debauchment of language which, as Orwell taught us, is characteristic of modern bureaucratic societies. *De jure,* M'Naghten was acquitted; *de facto,* he was sentenced to life imprisonment in an insane asylum. He was confined at the Bethlehem Hospital until 1864, when he was transferred to the newly opened Broadmoor Institution for the Criminally Insane. M'Naghten died in Broadmoor in 1865, having been incarcerated for the last twenty-two years of his life.

According to traditional English and American Law, an illegal act is criminal only if it is committed with criminal intent. The law also holds that certain insane persons who commit forbidden acts are not capable of forming the necessary criminal intent and should therefore be judged "not guilty by reason of insanity." This judicial concept requires that some means be found to distinguish persons who commit forbidden acts with criminal intent from persons who commit them without such intent because of insanity. The purpose of psychiatric "tests" of criminal responsibility—one of the oldest of which is named after Daniel M'Naghten—is to do just this.

Reprinted from *Temple Law Quarterly,* Vol. 40, No. 3: 271–82, Temple University, Philadelphia. Used by permission.
*State University of New York Medical Center, Syracuse.

Actually, what does the M'Naghten rule say? It asserts that to establish a defense on the ground of insanity it must be clearly proved that at the time of committing the act the party accused was laboring under such a defect of reason, from disease of the mind, as not to know the nature and quality of the act he was doing, or, if he did know it, that he did not know he was doing what was wrong.

In 1954, the United States Court of Appeals for the District of Columbia, in an opinion by Judge David Bazelon, handed down a decision that displaced the M'Naghten rule and substituted for it what has become known as the Durham rule.[2] According to this decision, "An accused is not criminally responsible if his unlawful act was the product of mental disease or mental defect."[3]

In 1966, the United States Court of Appeals for the Second Circuit, in an opinion by Judge Irving R. Kaufman, handed down a decision replacing the prior rule for the circuit with a new test of criminal responsibility recommended by the American Law Institute.[4] Objecting especially to the M'Naghten rule's emphasis on "defect of reason," Judge Kaufman's ruling provided that "A person is not responsible for criminal conduct if at the time of such conduct as a result of mental disease or defect he lacks substantial capacity either to appreciate the wrongfulness of his conduct or to conform his conduct to the requirements of law."[5]

These new tests of criminal responsibility reflect a longstanding dissatisfaction, in both the legal and psychiatric community, with the M'Naghten rule, which is deemed unsatisfactory because, in Judge Kaufman's words, it is ". . . not in harmony with modern medical science which . . . is opposed to any concept which divides the mind into separate compartments—the intellect, the emotions, and the will."[6] This has been the gist of the argument against the M'Naghten rule: it is old-fashioned and unscientific.

All tests of criminal responsibility rest on the premise that people "have" conditions called "mental diseases," which "cause" them to commit criminal acts.[7] The value of these tests thus hinges on the soundness of this underlying concept.

II

What kind of illness is "mental illness"? Leaders in medicine, psychiatry, government, education, industry, and labor never tire of proclaiming that "mental illness is like any other illness," frequently adding that "mental illness is the nation's number one health problem." This concern about mental illness does not seem to be shared by those who suffer, or might suffer, from it. A 1966 Gallup poll on the question, "What disease or illness do you fear the most?" yielded the following results: On the top of the list: cancer (62%) and blindness (18%); on the bottom of the list: polio (3%) and deafness (1%); not on the list at all: mental illness.[8]

The explanation of this paradox lies in the nature of modern psychiatry and its concept of mental illness. Harold Visotsky, Director of the Department of Mental Health for Illinois, lists "[j]uvenile delinquency, school problems, problems of urban areas, community conflicts, marriage and family counseling, and well-being programs" as among the major concerns of the contemporary psychiatrist.[9] J. Sanbourne Bockoven, Superintendent of the Cushing Hospital in Framingham, Massachusetts, frankly acknowledges, "The condition designated as 'mental illness' is not primarily, basically, or essentially so much a medical concern or responsiblity as it is a vital concern of the . . . state."[10] These statements by prominent phychiatrists—and many other similar opinions could be cited—illustrate the scope of modern psychiatry and the kind of "illnesses" its practitioners treat.

In what sense, then, is a "mentally ill" person sick? To answer this question we must note the several ways in which social roles may be acquired. Some, like hereditary monarch, are inherited; others, like graduate student, are voluntarily assumed; and still others, like convicted criminal, are ascribed to the person against his will.

Typically, the role of medical patient is assumed voluntarily. In the usual course of events, an individual who suffers from pain, discomfort, or disability seeks out a physician and submits to examination by him; the diagnosis—say, diabetes mellitus—is the name the physician gives to the patient's illness.

My purpose in describing what might seem a rather self-evident chain of events, leading from personal discomfort to medical diagnosis, is to show that when we speak of illness we often mean two quite different things: first, that the person displays a certain ("abnormal") *biological condition*; second, that he occupies a certain ("deviant") *social role*. The hypothetical patient mentioned above displays signs and symptoms of his biological condition (for example, sugar in the urine and loss of weight); he also occupies the sick role (for example, he consults a physician and follows his therapeutic recommendations). It is worth emphasizing that biological conditions exist regardless of whether or not they are observed and recognized by human beings, whereas social roles exist only insofar as they are observed and recognized by human beings.

Whereas the role of the *medical* patient is typically assumed voluntarily (though it may sometimes be ascribed to an unconscious person)—the role of *mental* patient may either be assumed voluntarily or imposed on a person against his will. If an individual assumes the role of mental patient voluntarily—for example, by visiting a psychotherapist in his office—his social role is essentially the same as that of a medical patient, or, for that matter, of any client who purchases the services of an expert. If, however, an individual is pressed into the role of mental patient against his will—for example, by being committed to a mental hospital—then his social role most closely resembles that of the criminal sentenced to imprisonment.

III

Both psychiatry and law are concerned with defining which roles are socially legitimate and which are not, and with enforcing conformity to prescribed roles. Institutional psychiatry enforces role conformity by defining role deviance as mental illness punishable by commitment. When, for example, a poor, uneducated, overburdened housewife escapes from her life of drudgery into the pretense that she is the Virgin Mary, the psychiatrist calls the woman "sick" and thus interferes with her playing the role she has selected for herself. [11] This type of prohibition, buttressed by the sanction of confinement in a mental hospital, is similar to the prohibition of the role of bank robber, buttressed by the sanction of confinement in prison.

Why isn't all socially undesirable conduct proscribed by law and punished by penal sanctions? And why isn't all other conduct allowed? Questions such as these are essential to a deeper inquiry into our subject. It must suffice to remark here that our age seems passionately devoted to *not* confronting problems of good and evil, and prefers, therefore, the rhetoric of medicine to the rhetoric of morals. It is as if modern judges had acquired the disability their predecessors had attributed to M'Naghten. M'Naghten, we are told, could not distinguish between right and wrong. Many judges, we may infer from their words and acts, prefer not to distinguish between right and wrong. They speak of mental health and sickness rather than of good and evil, and mete out the penalty of commitment rather than of imprisonment.

In the above-mentioned case before the United States Court of Appeals for the Second Circuit, the moral problem was more difficult to evade than usual, but evaded it was. The defendant, Charles Freeman, had been convicted of selling heroin. He maintained that he was not guilty, by reason of insanity. In reversing the conviction, the court left open the possibility that under the new standards Freeman might be found insane. Yet, if ever there was a moral problem, this was it. The fundamental questions this case poses are whether it is good or bad to sell heroin, and whether or not such conduct should be prohibited by law. (By substituting cigarettes, alcohol, guns, birth control devices, or worthless drugs for heroin, we gain a broader perspective on the type of problem we must face here.) Judge Kaufman's decision is significant precisely because it shifts the emphasis from the moral to the medical. In doing so, it exemplifies the "hysterical optimism" that, according to Richard Weaver, "will prevail until the world again admits the existence of tragedy, and it cannot admit the existence of tragedy until it again distinguishes between good and evil."[12]

As mental illness is unlike medical illness, so the mental hospital is unlike the medical hospital. In contemporary American society, the situation of the medical patient vis-à-vis the medical hospital is essentially that of a buyer vis-à-vis a vendor. A customer need not buy any merchandise he does not want. In the same way, a sick person need not enter a hospital, or submit to an operation, or undergo X-ray treatment, or take drugs, unless he is willing to do so.[13] The patient must give "informed consent" to his physician for any diagnostic or therapeutic procedure; without such consent, the physician is committing an unauthorized invasion of the patient's body and is subject to both civil and criminal sanctions.

It may be thought that the care of patients with communicable diseases constitutes a significant exception to this rule, but this is not so. For example, the *New York Public Health Law* (Paragraph 2223) provides: "1. Any person having tuberculosis, who shall dispose of his sputum, saliva, or other body secretion or excretion so as to cause offense or danger to any person or persons occupying the same room or apartment, house, or part of a house, shall on complaint of any person or persons subjected to such offense or danger, be deemed guilty of a nuisance, and any persons subjected to such a nuisance may make complaint in person or writing to the health officer of the local health district where the nuisance complained of is committed. 2. It shall be the duty of the local health officer receiving such complaint to investigate and if it appears that the nuisance complained of is such as to cause offense or danger to any person occupying the same room, apartment, house, or part of a house, he shall serve notice upon the person so complained of, reciting the alleged cause of offense or danger and requiring him to dispose of his sputum, saliva, or other bodily secretion or excretion in such a manner as to remove all reasonable cause of offense or danger. 3. Any person failing or refusing to comply with orders or regulations of the local health officer requiring him to cease to commit such nuisance, shall be deemed guilty of misdemeanor and on conviction thereof shall be fined not more than ten dollars." There are no provisions in the law authorizing tuberculosis hospitals to hold and treat patients against their will.

The opposite of this is the situation of the involuntary mental patient. (Approximately ninety per cent of hospitalized mental patients in the United States are confined involuntarily.)[14] The mental patient may be compelled, through the power vested in the physician by the state, to submit to psychiatric incarceration and to interventions defined as therapeutic for him.[15]

There is evidence that, from the subject's point of view, confinement in a mental hospital is more unpleasant than imprisonment in jail. "One of my clients," said Hugh J. McGee, "who has served in the prison systems of Florida, Georgia, Virginia, and Maryland, and on road gangs, too, of those states, told me dead seriously that he would rather serve a year in any of them than 6 months in old Howard Hall [at St. Elizabeths Hospital in Washington, D.C.]."[16] The speaker, Chairman of the Committee on Mental Health of the District of Columbia Bar Association, was testifying, in 1961, before a Senate committee conducting hearings on "The Constitutional Rights of the Mentally Ill."

Testifying before the same committee in 1963, Mr. McGee's views were even stronger: "They [the psychiatrists] are punishing him [the defendant] by keeping him in a maximum security ward . . . , which . . . not only amounts to an unconstitutional deprivation of liberty but also amounts to cruel and inhuman punishment. The Court of Appeals has specifically designated persons pleading 'not guilty by reason of insanity' as second-class citizens. When a person acknowledges . . . that he might have had mental disease which caused his criminal conduct . . . he loses his rights—all rights. He loses more rights than a criminal in the penitentiary."[17]

Under New York State's civil commitment laws, an addict arrested for a misdemeanor and for certain felonies may "volunteer" before his trial for a maximum three-year commitment to a mental hospital for a "cure".[18] In doing so, he can avoid prison and a criminal record, because the charge will be dismissed. In practice, less than one in four arrested addicts have chosen commitment, and a large percentage of these have escaped from the hospital before their time was up.[19]

Hospitals for the criminally insane are especially unpleasant institutions. In March 1966 the New York Court of Claims awarded $115,000 to a fifty-seven-year-old man who had stolen $5 worth of candy when he was sixteen and, as a result, spent the next thirty-four years in mental institutions.[20] In his decision, Judge Richard S. Heller characterized the Dannemora State Hospital, where the claimant, Stephen Dennison, had been held for twenty-four years, as an institution that, "although called a 'hospital,' [is] essentially a prison. . . ."[21] In this hospital, continued Judge Heller, where the "illegality" of Dennison's confinement is unquestionable, " . . . the hospital records repeatedly described claimant's behavior as paranoid, or in lay terms, that he had delusions of persecution. If a person is, in fact, being treated unjustly or unfairly, the fact that he perceives, resents, and reacts to the inequity could hardly be regarded as competent and conclusive evidence of paranoia or paranoid tendencies. . . . In a sense, society labeled him as subhuman, . . . drove him insane, and then used the insanity as an excuse for holding him indefinitely."[22]

Excepting death, involuntary psychiatric hospitalization imposes the most severe penalty that our legal system can inflict on a human being: namely, loss of liberty. The existence of psychiatric institutions that function as prisons, and of judicial sentences that are, in effect, indeterminate sentences to such prisons, is the backdrop against which all discussion of criminal responsibility must take place. This is especially true in jurisdictions where there is no death penalty. For what does it matter whether or not the accused was, at the time of the offense, "sane" and criminally responsible, or "insane" and criminally not responsible?

IV

Most words, and certainly *all* words used during criminal trials in courts of law, have strategic import. Their meaning must be inferred mainly from their consequences. The consequences of pleading "guilty" and "not guilty" are clear and generally well appreciated. The consequences of pleading "not guilty by reason of insanity," however, are neither clear nor generally understood. Briefly, they are as follows: If the defense of insanity is not sustained and the defendant is found guilty, he is sentenced to punishment as prescribed by the law and meted out by the judge, much as if he had entered any other plea. If the defense of insanity is sustained, the defendant's fate varies from jurisdiction to jurisdiction. There are two basic possibilities. One is that acquittal by reason of insanity is regarded as being the same as any other acquittal; the defendant walks out of the courtroom a free man. This is what happened to the fictional hero of Robert Traver's *Anatomy of a Murder*.[23] It is what would have happened to Jack Ruby had Melvin Belli's defense strategy succeeded.[24] This outcome is unusual and is becoming rarer every day.

The other course of action, which has been gaining ground rapidly in recent years, is to treat the individual acquitted by reason of insanity as a dangerously insane person from whom society needs the utmost protection. Instead of walking out of the courtroom a free man, such a defendant is forthwith transported to an insane asylum, where he remains until "cured" or until "no longer dangerous to himself and others."[25] This concept and procedure are exemplified in the District of Columbia, where "If any person tried . . . for an offense is acquitted solely on the ground that he was insane at the time of its commission, the court shall order such person to be confined in a hospital for the mentally ill."[26] The American Law Institute rule embodies the same principle of automatic commitment. "Throughout our opinion," wrote Judge Kaufman, "we have not viewed the choice as one between imprisonment and immediate release. Rather, we believe the true choice to be between different forms of institutionalization—between the prison and the mental hospital. Underlying today's decision is our belief that treatment of the truly incompetent in mental institutions would better serve the interests of society as well as the defendant's."[27]

Consider what this means. The judge recognizes the defendant as mentally competent to stand trial; he allows him to enter a plea and defend himself as best he can, and he considers the defendant sane enough to be sentenced to the penitentiary if found guilty. But should the defendant be found "not guilty by reason of insanity," that verdict immediately transforms him into a "truly incompetent" person, whom the judge feels justified in committing to a mental hospital. "In former days," observed John Stuart Mill in his famous essay *On Liberty*, "when it was proposed to burn atheists, charitable people used to suggest putting them in the madhouse instead; it would be nothing surprising nowadays were we to see this done, and the doers applauding themselves, because, instead of persecuting for religion, they had adopted so humane and Christian a mode of treating these unfortunates, not without a silent satisfaction at their having thereby obtained their deserts."[28] This was written when Freud was only three years old and when there was no "scientific psychiatry" to "illuminate" the problem of criminal responsibility.

In short, tests of criminal responsibility cannot be evaluated without knowing whether "acquittal" means freedom or commitment. More important than the semantic differences between the M'Naghten rule and its rivals are the personal consequences for the defendant of successfully pleading insanity. Indeed, preoccupation with the wording of the various rules, in both popular and professional discussions of the subject, only serves to distract attention from the basic issue of social control through legal psychiatry. Actually, where a successful insanity defense means commitment, the well-informed defendant rarely feels that the insanity plea serves his best interest. He tends to avoid this plea, preferring punishment in jail to "treatment" in the mental hospital.

V

What would happen, in jurisdictions where commitment follows automatically upon acquittal by reason of insanity, if the defendant clearly understood this choice? I venture to predict that such pleas would become very infrequent, and perhaps would disappear altogether. Although this is hardly the intention of the "liberalized" rules of criminal insanity, I would consider it a happy outcome. I do not believe that insanity should be an "excusing condition" for crime. The sooner the insanity plea is abolished, or the sooner it disappears because of its dire consequences for the defendant, the better off we shall all be.

But even if the defendant does not elect to plead insanity, so long as the law empowers physicians to incarcerate people in mental hospitals, the law enforcement agencies of the state will be tempted to make use of them. How this might happen was seen in the District of Columbia following the adoption of the Durham rule. Since the plea of "not guilty by reason of insanity" insured an indefinite stay at St. Elizabeths Hospital, judges chose in some cases not to allow the defendant to plead guilty and receive a minor prison sentence, but insisted instead that he plead not guilty by reason of insanity, and, following "acquittal," be committed to the mental hospital.[29] In a decision that side-stepped the constitutional issues involved, the Supreme Court ruled, in 1962, that this tactic was improper, and that, instead of foisting an involuntary plea of insanity on such a defendant, the court ought to initiate proceedings for his civil commitment.[30] This not only leaves commitment intact as a quasi-penal sanction, but recognizes it as the constitutionally proper alternative to a prison sentence.

Whether or not it is constitutional for the state to use mental hospitals to deprive citizens of their liberty is for the authorized interpreters of the Constitution to judge. Until now, the courts have found such detention constitutional. We might recall that earlier courts had found slavery constitutional.

Whatever the courts decide, responsible citizens must judge the matter for themselves. For, regardless of motives, the act of depriving a person of his liberty is a moral and political act. This is denied by the supporters of commitment, who maintain that the involuntary confinement of a person in a mental hospital is itself therapeutic, or that it is a condition necessary for the proper administration of some type of psychiatric treatment (for example, electroshock). In this view, held by many psychiatrists, commitment may be compared to the restraint of the patient on the operating table necessary for the proper performance of surgical treatment. The obvious difference, of course, is that the surgical patient consents to the restraint, whereas the mental patient does not. How, then, shall we decide? Is personal restraint, through commitment, therapy or punishment?

To ask the medical question "What is the proper drug for treating pneumococcal pneumonia?" presents a *technical problem* that the lay person *cannot* be expected to master. The best he can do is to select a competent expert and accept or reject his advice. In contrast, to ask the moral question "Is it justifiable to deprive a person of his liberty in order to treat him for mental illness?" presents an *ethical* problem that the lay person *can* master. If confronted with a choice between liberty and mental health (however defined), he must decide which one he values more highly.

It is an idle hope that a scientific psychiatry will save us from moral problems and moral decisions. If we only let ourselves see with the eyes God gave us and with the courage that only we can give ourselves, we shall see legal psychiatry and involuntary mental hospitalization for what they are: a pseudo-medical system of social controls. This type of psychiatry (it should be kept in mind that it is not the only kind) is a servant of the bureaucratic state, whether it be a totalitarian or a democratic state. To Russian "scientific psychiatry," Valeriy Tarsis was mentally ill; to American "scientific psychiatry," Ezra Pound was mentally ill. A "scientific psychiatry" worthy of the name must begin by accounting for these facts. In doing so, it would lag by only sixty years behind Jack London, who wrote of a bishop who had "obeyed Christ's injunction and got locked up in a madhouse."[31] Why? Because "his views were perilous to society, and society could not conceive that such perilous views could be the product of a sane mind."[32]

VI

Neither the M'Naghten rule nor the Durham rule nor the American Law Institute rule is "humanitarian," for all diminish personal responsibility and thus impair human dignity; nor is any of them "liberal," for none promotes individual freedom under the rule of law. The centuries-old practice of using mental hospitalization as a means of punishing "offenders" has received fresh impetus in our day through the rhetoric of "scientific psychiatry." Contemporary concepts of "mental illness" obscure the contradictions between our pursuit of conflicting policies and objectives—individualism because it promises liberty, and collectivism because it promises security. Through the mental health ethic, psychiatry thus promotes the smooth functioning of the bureaucratic mass society and provides its characteristic ideology. According to this ideology, loss of liberty may be either punitive or therapeutic: If the individual offends because he is "bad," loss of liberty is punishment; but if he offends because he is "sick," it is therapy. From this point of view, deviance is seen as sickness rather than badness, and the individual appears as a patient rather than as a citizen.

This psychiatric perspective on problems of living conceals the fundamental moral dilemma—the characteristic choice—facing us: Do we want to be free men or slaves? If we choose freedom, we cannot prevent our fellow man from also choosing to be free; whereas, if we choose slavery, we cannot permit him to be anything but a slave.

In the final analysis, the insanity plea and the insanity verdict, together with the prison sentences called "treatments" served in buildings called "hospitals," are all parts of the complex structure of institutional psychiatry, which, as I have tried to show, is slavery disguised as therapy. Those who value and wish to defend individual liberty can be satisfied with nothing less than the abolition of this crime against humanity.[33]

Notes

1. *Daniel M'Naghten's Case*, 10 Cl. & Fin. 200, 8 Eng. Rep. 718, 1843.
2. *Durham v. United States*, 214 F. 2d 862 (D. C. Cir.), 1954.
3. Ibid., pp. 874-75.
4. *United States v. Freeman*, 357 F. 2d 606 (2d Cir.), 1966.
5. Ibid., p. 622; see also *Model Penal Code*, par. 4.01, final draft, 1962.
6. *United States v. Freeman, supra*, p. 622.
7. See also *United States v. Currens*, 290 F. 2d 751 (3rd Cir.), 1961.
8. "Disease fear." *Parade*, Feb. 13, 1966, p. 14.
9. Visotsky, H.: "Community psychiatry: We are willing to learn," *Amer. J. Psychiatry*, 122:692-93 (Dec.), 1965, p. 692.
10. Bockoven, S.: "The moral mandate of community psychiatry in America," *Psychiatric Opinion*, 3:32-39 (Winter), 1966, p. 34.
11. For further discussion and documentation, see Szasz, T. S.: "Psychiatric classification as a strategy of personal constraint," in *Ideology and Insanity* (Garden City, N.Y.: Anchor Books, 1970) pp. 190-217; "Involuntary mental hospitalization: A crime against humanity," *Ideology and Insanity*, pp. 113-139.
12. Weaver, R. M.: *Ideas Have Consequences* [1948] (Chicago: Phoenix Books, 1962), p. 11.
13. See, for example, Shindell, S., *The Law in Medical Practice* (Pittsburgh: The University of Pittsburgh Press, 1966), especially pp. 16-32.
14. See *Hearings on Constitutional Rights of the Mentally Ill*, 87th Cong., 1st Sess., Part 1 (Washington, D.C.: U. S. Government Printing Office, 1961), p. 43.
15. See, for example, *New York Mental Hygiene Law*, par. 72 (I).
16. McGee, H.: Statement in *Hearings on Constitutional Rights of the Mentally Ill*, Part 2, *supra*, p. 659.
17. *Hearings on S. 935 to Protect the Constitutional Rights of the Mentally Ill*, 88th Cong., 1st Sess. (Washington, D.C.: U. S. Government Printing Office, 1963), p. 215.
18. *New York Mental Hygiene Law*, par. 206 (5), pp. 210-11.
19. See "Should addicts be locked up?" *New York Post Magazine*, March 6, 1966, p. 3.
20. *Dennison v. State*, 49 Misc. 2d 533, 267 N.Y.S. 2d 920 (Ct. Cl.), 1966.
21. Ibid., p. 924.
22. Ibid.
23. Traver, R.: *Anatomy of a Murder* (New York: St. Martin's Press, 1958).
24. See Kaplan, J. and Waltz, J. R.: *The Trial of Jack Ruby* (New York: Macmillan, 1965).
25. See, for example, *D. C. Code Ann.,* par. 24-301, 1961; *Ohio Rev. Code Ann.,* par. 2945-39, 1954.
26. *D. C. Code Ann.,* par. 24-301 (d), 1961.
27. *United States v. Freeman*, op. cit., p. 626.
28. Mill, J. S.: *On Liberty* [1859] (Chicago: Regnery, 1955), p. 100.
29. See *Cameron v. Fisher*, 320 F. 2d 731 (D. C. Cir.), 1963; *Overholser v. Lynch*, 288 F. 2d 388 (D. C. Cir.), 1961.
30. *Lynch v. Overholser*, 369 U.S. 705, 1962.
31. London, J., *The Iron Heel* [1907] (New York: Sagamore Press, 1957), p. 174.
32. Ibid., p. 163.
33. See Szasz, "Involuntary mental hospitalization," *supra*.

LOREN LOMASKY*

Medical Progress and National Health Care

An individual's access to medical care should not be determined exclusively by his ability to pay the going price. From this starting point, alternative paths beckon. One is that of traditional health care delivery within which eleemosynary and religious institutions figure prominently in providing medical services to those unable to pay. Before the emergence of modern medicine the poor could not expect treatment equivalent to that received by the rich, but this was a general disability of poverty, not specifically a problem of medical access. Indeed, in an era when health care had little positive correlation with health outcomes and hospitals were chiefly places where one went to die, inequities in the provision of medical services were among the least of the burdens borne by the poor.

Medical Progress and the "Right" to Health Care

The ability of medicine to produce favorable results has increased exponentially in this century. At the same time, for understandable reasons, dissatisfaction with the traditional model has also increased. It is criticized as being too haphazard and arbitrary. More fundamentally, it is argued that medical care is a good to which individuals have a right, and that it ought to be distributed impartially in line with the criterion: to each according to his need.[1] Medical care is not simply one consumer good among others; because it bears so directly on life itself as well as

Reprinted from *Philosophy and Public Affairs*, Vol. 10, No. 1 (Winter 1981). Copyright © 1980 by Princeton University Press. Used by permission.
*University of Minnesota, Duluth.

the ability to lead a good life, medical care cannot be left to the vagaries of the market.

But this argument is met with a counterargument that also emphasizes the role of rights. Medical services are, after all, not endowments provided cost-free by a bountiful nature. Rather, they are made available in finite quantities by individuals who must expend effort to produce them. The state can enforce equity in the delivery of these services only by coercing service providers, taxpayers and would-be recipients. State controlled health care is thus founded on wide-spread rights violations.[2]

When right contends with right, the heroic seek victory, the wary hunt for accommodation. It is wariness that will be pursued here.

A Right to What?

It should be obvious that no claim of the form, "persons have a right to X" can be addressed without determining what kind of entity X is. Unless one is clear about what type of good health care is, resulting appraisals of its value and proper apportionment are hobbled. It will be suggested below that arguments for the provision of national health care pay insufficient attention to the changed and changing nature of health care. The following three considerations are preliminary to that argument.

1. 'Health care' denotes a broad, ill-defined genus. Curative and preventive measures differ widely in their urgency; physicians vaccinate the young but also shore up sagging breasts and buttocks. In addition to activities centered around cure or prevention, health personnel carry out a large number of functions that bear little relation to combatting disease. In their "caring" role they reassure the healthy, lend a sympathetic ear to complaints they cannot alleviate, provide counseling that, in a previous age, would have been sought from the clergy, lead the dying out of this life and comfort the bereaved. Moreover, the range of services continues to expand as the medical profession is called upon to carry out tasks formerly fulfilled by other social institutions. Nursing home expenditures multiply more rapidly than any other area within the system of health care delivery. The essentially custodial services they provide were, in the recent past, largely performed by the extended family. Their medicalization proceeds not from any inner logic but as a consequence of extraneous social pressure.[3]

This diversity among health care goods is one factor suggesting the desirability of shifting from broad-guaged discussions of health care as a right to the examination of *particular services* and their optimal distribution.

2. No matter how healthy a society is, its resources are never equal to the totality of the demands placed upon them. Scarcity of goods relative to the possible ways in which they might usefully be employed is the basic postulate of economic science. The opportunity cost of using a resource in one way is the next best use foregone.[4] Only if a resource has no alternative use is it free of cost.

Health care services compete amongst themselves for resources. They also compete with goods quite unrelated to health care. The very success with which they do so is, ironically, a major component of the "crisis" in health care. In 1955 health care expenditures accounted for 4.5% of U.S. gross national product. By 1976 GNP had increased more than 300% yet health care now took 8.7% of that much larger pie.[5] Every dollar spent represents other human wants that go unfulfilled. Again, reference to general health care rights seems less helpful than a close scrutiny of individual component services.

3. Is it within the power of governments to provide full and equal access to health care? If not, then there exists no right to it. Every right must be a right against some specifiable person or group of persons and is a claim for the performance (or omission) of actions which can be brought about (or avoided) by the party in question. For example, in underdeveloped countries beset by a paucity of physicians and supporting medical facilities, there can be no right against the state for extensive health care services. Wealthy nations are blessed with ample medical resources and possess the authority to marshal them for socially desirable goals. Affluence, however, does not eliminate, but instead transforms, the burden of providing full and equal health services.

The first large-scale campaign for universal health insurance in the United States dates back to World War I.[6] At that time Americans were far less wealthy than they are now. Paradoxically, however, they were better equipped to provide genuinely full and equal access to health services. Medicine's power to intervene effectively in crisis situations was then extremely limited. Patients recovered in short order or died, in either case removing themselves from the need for ongoing attention. Chronic diseases, especially those associated with aging, were predominantly dealt with outside of medical contexts. In consequence, little extra benefit could be accorded the richest patients beyond what was available to those of more modest means.

In the last quarter of the 20th century, however, there exist numerous high technology procedures that can be provided to only a fraction of those who could benefit from them. Computerized axial tomography,[7] organ transplants[8] and coronary arteriograms[9] are but three conspicuous therapeutic measures whose use is limited by financial or biological factors. It is incumbent upon those who demand that medical care of the highest quality be universally provided as a matter of right to explain how this can be done. And if it cannot, which would they dispense with: equity or the lives that could be saved by selective use of expansive technology? (I shall return later to this dilemma.)

What the preceding remarks suggest is that there is a wide gulf between medical care being an important human *interest* or *need* and its being a *right*. Interests admit of a wide range of degree and can be freely traded off, one for another. Needs are interests that possess a high degree of urgency, but carry no explicit entitlement to the goods or services of other people. Rights, though, are demands that others *must* comply with; where compliance is impossible or unwarranted no right exists.

The Welfare Case for a National Health Program

Even if health care in all its dimensions cannot, strictly speaking, be made out to be a human right, proponents of a national health program can argue that it is a good that ought to be provided to all irrespective of the ability to pay. Economic impoverishment would then no longer follow in the wake of major illness. Government would be able to address directly the problem of ever rising costs instead of trying to influence at arm's length the fragmented health care industry. Finally, a more rational allocation of scarce medical resources to those who are most in need of them would be achieved. The *de facto* rationing of services by the market would be replaced by explicit consideration of how most equitably to optimize benefits for a given level of expenditure.

Major medical treatments *are* enormously expensive; for many persons the expense occasioned by an illness is its most persistent burden. We are all roughly equal in our vulnerability to debilitating disease or accident. Therefore, everyone would receive benefit from a national health plan that removed the threat of impoverishment as a consequence of medical disability. But this end can be achieved equally well by less sweeping measures. The risk of large economic loss can easily be guarded against by insurance. Its characteristic function is to protect against infrequent, unpredictable events which, when aggregated over a large population, are statistically regular.

Medical insurance is readily available in a variety of forms from private insurance companies. Like fire, automobile and life insurance, it offers a means for persons to pool economic risks that are too great to hazard on an individual basis. Health maintenance organizations (HMOs) represent another and growing means by which pre-payment allows individuals to spread risks. (In addition, HMOs offer service providers added inducement to economize on hospital stays and questionable surgical intervention, thus moderating overall medical expenditures.[10]) The special problems of the poor can be met by cash grants or by health care vouchers exchangeable for prepaid services. Given the availability of these sharply focused means for dealing with unpredictable expense, the threat of major economic loss cannot provide a sound justification for a national health program.

Ever-rising total health care expenditure creates a different dilemma, one that is also far more unyielding. As long as the demand for medical services (especially those embracing high technology) keeps growing, continuous cost increases largely represent an efficient response to consumers' preferences.[11] Of course these preferences can be called into question. Critics of prevailing practices have frequently argued that a more rational allocation of resources would redirect funds away from costly acute intervention procedures to preventive medicine and health education. However, even if this shift in emphasis could be carried out, benefits might prove to be less than anticipated. Annual physical checkups have long been advocated as worthwhile prophylaxis. Although they clearly impose substantial burdens on health care delivery systems, there is little evidence demonstrating significant health gains.[12] Routine mammography to detect breast cancer is now believed to cause more cancer than it uncovers.[13]

Education to alter unhealthy lifestyles would undoubtedly have a momentous positive impact—if we know how to provide it. Wide dissemination of the relevant information may accomplish little: there is probably not a smoker in the country unaware of cigarettes' deleterious effects or a motorcyclist uninformed about the dangers of riding helmetless. In a free society there are limits to how much good one can do for another who isn't very interested.

Governmental control typically features politically motivated decisions and cozy relationships between an industry and its regulators that work against economic efficiency.[14] In addition, there are good reasons to believe that a national health program would be even *more susceptible* to escalating costs than most federal ventures. First, to be workable it would need the support of health professionals. It is therefore unlikely that they will be squeezed very hard in order to realize monetary savings. Witness the boon to physicians' incomes provided by Medicare. Second, few citizens clamor for the purchase of another battleship, and even highly subsidized train fares move few people out of automobiles and airplanes. But health care is a commodity that most people desire. To lower or eliminate out-of-pocket expenses for it will predictably increase demand and thus further burden the public purse. Costs may be shared more evenly, but they will not be small.

The only way a nationalized program can realistically hope to keep costs in line is to enforce strict schedules of permissible treatments for all illnesses. These would be established on the basis of empirical studies detailing cost-effectiveness—assuming that political pressures to act otherwise are avoided. Therapeutic measures failing to come up to the stipulated benefit-per-dollar level would simply be disallowed. In effect, the goal moderating overall costs would be subsumed under that of equitable rationing. So, if the case for a national health program can be made at all, it is on the grounds of enforcing the equal provision of health services based solely on need.

Equality and Health Care

The case for equality in the delivery of health care services may be presented as simply one specification of the general brief for economic equality. But then it is subject to all the standard criticisms that beset rigid egalitarianism. If equality of condition is to be enforced, the liberty to pursue projects that generate differential rewards must be restricted. Substitutes must be found for the motivating force provided by the desire to better one's estate and the fear of seeing it diminished. The intuition that some merit more than others in return for greater effort or services rendered must be set aside. In short, the single-minded pursuit of equality is exceedingly costly in terms of other values surrendered, other goods foregone.

An alternative defense focuses on the special nature of health. The value of experiencing grand opera, vintage Chablis, a Yankee-Red Sox doubleheader or a trek up a mountain will vary greatly from individual to individual. Differences in talents and preferences will render ludicrous any program intent on providing these goods in equal measure to the entire populace. It is clearly preferable to allow individuals to pursue them as they will. But health is different. Whatever else one wants, good health is not only wanted but needed. Failure in securing it jeopardizes all other attainments. Moreover, its absence is rarely an indication of culpability; it is bad luck. Coordinated activity of men in civil society cannot abolish luck but it can ameliorate the stark randomness of its effects. The case for treating health care as a public good, subsidized by the common treasure, is that to do so is the most effective way we have of counteracting the vagaries of nature and providing each person with the preconditions for living a satisfying life.

Classical liberalism's "night watchman" state is devoted to the maximization of liberty, not equality. Yet it is committed to the equal protection of individuals against aggression. It singles out defense as a special good, one to be provided equally to all irrespective of the ability to pay for it. [15] Both aggression and disease are threats to the security of the individual, and one need not have incurred any prior culpability to be vulnerable. Just as civil society and the goods it affords human beings cannot endure in the face of unchecked aggression, the pursuit of individually meaningful projects presupposes minimal standards of physiological functioning. The institution of civil society neutralizes natural advantages possessed in a state of nature by the strong over the weak; similarly, public provision of medical services would mitigate the advantages possessed by the healthy over the sick. Finally, both security from aggression and health are universally regarded as desirable. In securing them, the state is providing its citizens what they *need* and (except for aberrant cases) what they *want*. Thus, no class within society is being favored over any other. An outcome desired by all, and tending to be of equal benefit to all, is a prime candidate on grounds of justice and welfare for public advancement.

The analogy is not perfect. National defense is a public good in the economists' sense of being difficult or impossible to provide to one segment of the community without being extended willy-nilly to all others. Thus, if it were purchased in market transactions by independently acting persons, the existence of free riders would tend to lead to underconsumption relative to the optimum quantity of protection desired. With the exception of some public health measures such as immunization against contagious diseases and the removal of toxic substances from the environment, health services are generally not marked by externalities generating free riders.[16]

A more serious objection to the analogy is that states, of necessity, possess a monopoly on the exercise of coercive force.[17] Being the sole possessors of a right to exercise coercion, governments are obliged to undertake the protection, apprehension and punishment functions that they prohibit their citizens from carrying out on an individual basis. There exists no similar necessity that states monopolize the provision of health services. Health may indeed be a primary human good, but whether it is distributed centrally or by independent contractors is irrelevant to the continued existence of a political order. That is not to deny that states owe obligations to their citizenry respecting health care delivery. A state acts unjustly if it forbids crucial health services to some or all persons or if it promotes economic inequalities that deprive disadvantaged social classes of adequate medical care. It should be noted though that unjust health policies may appear either in states with comprehensive national health care or those without it. In either, services may be discriminatorily distributed, subverted for political ends, irrationally regulated or irresponsive to consumer demand. The desirability of national health care cannot be deduced from a pure philosophical theory of justice; rather, its desirability hinges on whether, in the actual world, it promises to promote a fair and efficient allocation of resources.

The Changing Nature of Health Care

The enormous successes of medicine in the 20th century have altered its face beyond recognition. Gone is the physician who, in his little black bag, carried almost all the essentials of his craft. Technology has dramatically enhanced medicine's power to extend lives, in some cases lives of a greatly diminished quality from that which we take to be optimally livable. Mortality and morbidity remain the chief antagonists of medical practitioners. Battle lines, however, have become blurred as success in warding off death actually increases the prevalence of certain pathological states. Dr. Ernest M. Gruenberg has noted:

In fact, as the result of advances in medical care we are seeing a rising prevalence of certain chronic conditions which previously led to early terminal infections, but whose victims now suffer from them for a longer period. The goal of medical research is to diminish disease and enrich life, but it produces tools which prolong diseased, diminished lives and so increase the proportion of people who have a disabling or chronic disease . . . These increasingly common chronic conditions represent the failures of success. Their growing prevalence and longer duration are a product of progress in health technology. [18]

Among the conditions cited by Dr. Gruenberg are mongolism, senile brain damage and spina bifida. Survival rates for those afflicted have increased dramatically, but little or no progress has been made in either preventing their occurrence or in restoring a semblance of normal functioning. The well-publicized (and anticlimactic) case of Karen Ann Quinlan brought home to many for the first time the fact that medicine's ability to prolong life indefinitely may be not only costly but embarrassing. In restrospect, the 1930s and 40s take on the aspect of a golden age of curative medicine. Victories over disease made possible by "miracle drugs" went hand in hand with victories over death, and the benefits of medical intervention appeared incontestable and unalloyed. Since then not only have major advances been harder to come by, but they are also marked by greater moral ambiguity. That the application of lifesaving technology is always and everywhere an indication of progress can no longer be safely assumed.

When is a therapeutic procedure proven to be a useful member of the medical repertorie? Randomized controlled trials can demonstrate statistically whether a procedure has some effect. They cannot, however, establish that results achieved are indeed benefits or that they justify the costs incurred. These latter questions will be confronted in practice, even if by attempted abdications of responsibility. What remains to be determined is who will pronounce on them: a centralized governmental agency promulgating a unified national health policy or millions of health service providers and consumers acting independently?

Collective vs. Private Choice: Some Examples

A foretaste of the difficulties that would regularly confront a nationalized health program is provided by the debate over Medicaid funded abortion. [19] Each year the nation is treated to a ritualized congressional confrontation that changes no minds, produces no consensus, yet paralyzes essential legislative operations throughout its duration. Few can believe that this public fanning of already polarized attitudes is worthwhile; yet there seems to be no way to avoid it so long as the provision of specific medical services to the poor remains an item for legislative decision. The right of women to procure abortions may have been conclusively established by judicial action, but a democracy must also recognize the right of individual citizens to participate in processes determining how their tax monies will be spent. Either the public treasure will release funds to pay for abortion or it will not; room for compromise is narrowly constricted.

Entirely removing abortion related issues from the public agenda may be neither feasible nor desirable. But this especially futile contest is the direct product of choosing to meet the health needs of the poor through a centrally funded and regulated program. If Medicaid and related welfare measures were replaced by a negative income tax or some other device guaranteeing all persons a minimally adequate income, recipients would be free to purchase those goods and services of greatest personal urgency. Poor persons, if they so chose, could avail themselves of abortions on the same basis as other members of the population. A less sweeping alteration of current welfare programs would be to provide health care vouchers. [20] In either case, we would be spared a situation in which others decide for the poor what specific services they can or cannot have. Perhaps these proposed alternatives are defective on other grounds, but they do point up the advantages of leaving medical questions that touch on basic values up to individual discretion.

By means of amniocentesis dozens of hereditary fetal traits can presently be detected. They range from its sex to the presence of debilitating diseases such as Tay-Sachs or mongolism. Occasionally the procedure is useful for diagnosing a condition that can be treated in utero, but it is also employed to procure information on which the decision whether or not to abort will be based. Will a national health program routinely provide amniocentesis when abortion is intended if results are negative? Or will it attempt somehow to keep to a middle course, allowing procedures leading to the abortion of severely incapacitated fetuses but not, say, those of the parentally disfavored sex? Alternatively, a cost conscious program would require as a condition of coverage that women at risk undergo amniocentesis and abortion when a live birth will entail huge medical costs. These hypothetical policies are not of equal likelihood, but any one of them would engender pitched battles whose outcome would certainly leave large sections of the population dissatisfied. Polyannas may expect the passage of time to ease these problems. Just the reverse will be the case; as techniques of genetic screening and engineering become more sophisticated, moral quandries will ineluctably multiply. Somtimes polarization is the inescapable consequence of forging a national policy, but in this case divisiveness can be minimized by leaving decisions in the hands of private citizens.

The other end of human existence has also been profoundly affected by advances in medical capabilities. The hospital has replaced the home as the usual place to die, and it is increasingly the case that the exact time of death is a matter for choice. Biological function can be preserved in so attenuated a state that physicians have been forced to move toward redefinition of 'death' in order to avoid the ghoulish indefinite preservation of living corpses. [21] But most ethical dilemmas surrounding death and dying are untouched by semantic legerdemain. Unless one supposes that each advance in the power to sustain life creates a corresponding imperative for its universal employment—and also creates the funds to pay for them—there is no simple answer to the question of when to extend life and when to bring about its termination. Here I shall sidestep substantive matters to raise instead a procedural issue: to what extent is it desirable that government intrude upon deliberations at the edge of life?

It is unrealistic to deny that the state does have some legitimate interests. Inevitably it must confront practices that raise the specter of homicide. The law must also establish standards concerning informed consent and the contractual obligations obtaining between patient and physician. But beyond staking out legal terrain within which concerned parties can take their bearings, government may move in either of two opposed directions: it can issue detailed regulations pertaining to the application of lifesaving technology or, within broad guidelines, it can return decision-making prerogatives to individual patients, their families, and physicians. For two major reasons, the latter course is to be preferred whenever possible.

First, individual discretion promotes autonomy. Persons differ in their judgments concerning the conditions under which life is no longer worth living. They will also vary in their willingness to forego other possible satisfactions for the sake of securing incremental health gains. A liberal society is one that values the ability of individuals to direct their own lives. One significant way in which this value can be pursued is to allow people to determine for themselves what course their medical treatments will take. A recent expression of this policy is the granting of legal status to "living wills," documents that spell out conditions under which the signator desires that heroic medical procedures be terminated. The gradual development of hospice programs also provides enhanced opportunities for terminally ill patients to take charge of their own destinies. Instead of being shunted aside as medicine's embarrassing failure, the hospice patient is encouraged to accept the fact of his upcoming death and to influence the conditions under which he will depart from life. As technology continually enlarges the scope for intervention into the process of dying, further methods will be required to ensure that the party most directly affected is able to play a significant role.

Second, an active governmental role in mandating standards for care poses the same danger of political disruption that has already been experienced in the case of publicly funded abortion. All citizens have a fundamental stake in how they and their loved ones will die. Decisions in this sphere do not come easily under the best of circumstances. But burdens will be exacerbated if matters of personal decisions are transformed into public policy questions. Regulation is, in essence, inflexible. If national standards are to be formulated that adjudicate among basic and deeply felt values, diverse groups will want to see their own attitudes enshrined in law. A zero-sum game will develop in which one side's gain is another's loss, and so each will attempt to utilize the political machinery for its own ends.

If the state assumes full responsibility for the provision of health services, it will be unable to avoid dictating standards for the utilization of life sustaining services. Extraordinary means for staving off death are inordinately costly both in monetary terms and in demands placed upon highly trained personnel. If the ability of patients to pay is entirely removed as a factor influencing their use, there will be an increased call for their employment. A national health program that wishes to remain solvent will have to devise some formula for determining when the costs of procuring and employing expensive technology are justified by realizable benefits. If such a formula is not to be subverted from within, little room for exceptions can be permitted. Whatever structure emerges is sure to leave many health professionals and consumers dissatisfied. They will be informed that their own personal discretion must give way before considerations of the public good— as defined by a distant bureaucracy.

It can be objected that constraints upon resources are inevitable regardless of the system by which health care is financed. Nationalization merely shifts the appraisal of costs and benefits from innumerable private hands to one central apparatus. Efficiency is thereby enhanced because policy will be consistently formulated by authorities possessing all the information needed to make rational decisions. Medical services will not be wastefully showered on patients simply because they are prepared to pay for them, nor will they be denied to persons of modest means. As a welcome fringe benefit, patients, their families, and physicians will be spared the necessity of making wrenching choices in cases where objectivity often gives way to emotional pressure.

This response begs several crucial questions. Do health bureaucrats really possess more relevant information than individual practitioners and patients? Surely familiarity with the particular case must count for something. Health services are not provided to faceless pathological syndromes but to persons whose preferences and circumstances are endlessly varied and complexly interrelated. If responsiveness to individual differences is something worth prizing, it is morally obtuse to restrict attention only to data that can be quantified and processed by technocrats. A corollary surmise is that consistency in the dispensation of health resources may not be an unquestioned virtue; perhaps it is the compassionate willingness to accede to individual needs that instead ought to be consistently pursued. And is it a genuine welfare gain if individuals are denied the responsibility of making difficult choices in extremis? An answer in the affirmative reveals an implicit valuing of impotent contentment over psychically demanding self-direction. It is by no means clear that this represents an acceptable ranking.

Deciding when treatment shall cease involves ethical questions of considerable magnitude. A yet more vexing range of dilemmas surround triage: the selection of some for treatment when not all can be saved. If resources are indispensable to a group of persons at peril but too limited to accommodate all, to save one life is to sacrifice another. Our moral principles are severely strained by circumstances that require the balancing of one innocent life against another. Such choices, however, promise to intrude upon us increasingly.

Two classic triage examples are the dangerously overloaded lifeboat and the harried medic patching up carnage from the battlefield. Whatever is done, some salvageable lives will be forfeited. The dreadfulness of these choices though is somewhat softened by the urgency of a crisis situation: action must be immediate and there is little luxury for reflective deliberation. If called upon to justify his actions, an agent could plead that he was reacting instinctively to the needs of the moment.

Contemporary medical technology is responsible for triage situations of a rather different character. A mechanism is devised that is effective against some previously untreatable condition. Unfortunately, only a small percentage of those afflicted can receive treatment. Who shall be allowed to live? Here decision makers are dealing with a series of events predictable well in advance. Since not enmeshed in a precipitously developing crisis, they are privileged to assume the role of detached administrator. There is, however, a price to be paid for this relative ease: whatever standards are developed and employed are subject to close scrutiny. Those disfavored in the selection process are perfectly entitled to ask why. Persuasive answers will not be easily forthcoming.

It is useful to glance at the history of hemodialysis. By provisions of the Social Security Amendments of 1972 (Pl 92-603) the U.S. Federal Government undertook to cover the costs of either dialysis or renal transplant for nearly all those who suffer from chronic kidney failure. Costs are extremely high—in the range of $2 billion annually—but this massive infusion of funds has greatly increased the availability of dialysis machines and, even more importantly, the highly trained staffs needed to run kidney units.[22] Prior to 1972, however, dialysis treatment was available to only a minority of those persons who qualified for it on purely medical grounds. Centers that offered dialysis adopted diverse means for selecting among applicants who passed an initial screening. Some employed committees composed entirely of physicians while others used lay committees. Among the criteria utilized at various hospitals were first-come first-served, drawing lots, and evaluations of expected social worth.[23] The well publicized[24] chronic dialysis selection committee at the Seattle Artificial Kidney Center is reported to have considered whether applicants had been a scout leader, church member or Red Cross volunteer.[25] Two investigators of their procedures have aptly concluded that they rule out "creative nonconformists who rub the bourgeoisie the wrong way but who historically have contributed so much to the making of America. The Pacific Northwest is no place for a Henry David Thoreau with bad kidneys."[26]

I have not referred to this episode in order to pluck from it handy lessons concerning how triage decisions are best arrived at. I believe that there are none. If the dialysis experience is instructive, it is in showing that we possess neither reliable intuitive nor theoretical grounds for making a choice of life against life. Because each human life is owed maximum respect, differential treatment based on precarious judgments of social worth is odious. But to consign individuals to life or death because of the results of a lottery allows impersonal forces to adjudicate in the most deeply personal of crises. Both procedures are more stopgaps than solutions—assuming that it is even possible to speak of a "solution" in such cases.[27] However, I want to address a further question: should triage decisions be left to numerous private groups acting independently, or should responsibility be assumed by a national health care delivery board?

The latter would, I believe, be a profoundly unsatisfactory state of affairs. The least of its drawbacks is that treatment decisions would be thrust into the arena of public choice where diverse groups would lobby intensively for special consideration. It requires little imagination to foresee the young, those with dependents, military veterans, persons holding responsible positions and others all claiming to merit a preferred status. A policy of random selection might appease these contending forces, but it also might appear to each of them as unjustly slighting legitimate merit. The trouble arises precisely because no process of choice presents itself as clearly superior; whichever method is imposed will be open to objections rendering it unstable.

Consider a further complication: wealthy individuals may not be content to leave their survival to the vagaries of a national health care system. Suppose they choose to go outside of the system to procure lifesaving technology; how will authorities respond? If the rich are allowed carte blanche, the egalitarianism of national health care is compromised in a context where the stakes are no less than life and death. If outside access is forbidden by law, the situation is even more anomalous. Persons who are entitled to spend their money for utterly frivolous purposes will be precluded from using it to remain alive.[28] No compensating gain for the poor would be realized—unless a surrender to envy is counted as a gain.

When triage decisions are made by dozens of independent private organizations, rejection is a bitter blow. But it is neither as final nor so laden with ominous overtones as rejection by a governmental board. If a candidate for treatment regards one hospital's selection criteria as unfair he can apply elsewhere. Or, if turned down at one, he may be able to succeed at another.

Rulings promulgated in the name of a national health monopoly are doubly definitive. They carry not only *finality* but also *authority*. Decisions exercised by a handful of administrators at a private hospital may reflect nothing beyond their own idiosyncratic values; national health care, however, serves the entire citizenry and is responsible to it. Triage is never unproblematic, but on what basis could a creature of the state adopt *any* principle of selection? Whoever is excluded can justifiably complain that he is thereby being disadvantaged by the very institution whose special duty is to extend equal protection to all persons. The essential point is not that government will do a poorer job of allocating lifesaving technology than would non-governmental units—although, given the nature of the political pressures to which it is subject, it very well might—but that *this is a singularly inappropriate area for any governmental choice*, no matter how conscientiously it is made. Neutrality among all citizens is a political ideal that is easily subverted and, once breached, difficult to restore. I suggest that this ideal is well worth preserving, and that to establish a precedent of forcing the state to determine that some named individuals shall live and others die is to do that ideal possibly irreparable damage. When such decisions have to be made, it is far better that they be carried out by non-public boards not constrained by obligations of equal protection to an entire citizenry. Flexibility is enhanced, and the implications of unsavory choices are localized.

One objection to this argument is that government can and should avoid the necessity of triage by providing resources sufficient to accommodate all patients. Indeed, precisely this intent motivated the passage of the 1972 legislation providing dialysis treatment to all end-stage renal disease sufferers in need of it. Could not a well-funded national health care program act similarly in all other cases?

The answer is no. There are some shortages that not even unlimited finances can eliminate. The number of persons who can be benefited by organ transplants already exceeds the available supply. As further advances in immunosuppression and surgical technique are realized, the disparity will grow. Transplantable hearts cannot be produced by governmental edict. Further, there is always a gap between the time a procedure is experimentally introduced and its widespread implementation.

In the real world, finances are not unlimited. Money used to counter one life threatening syndrome is unavailable for others. For example, the huge infusion of Medicare funds for kidney disease sufferers could have been devoted to the comparably expensive treatment of hemophiliacs. That it was not may be due only to the greater muscle of the kidney disease lobby. Even if sufficient funds to eliminate all triage situations could be raised, it does not follow that to do so is advisable. A commitment to treat every salvageable patient will shortchange other legitimate health goals as well as competing goods in other spheres. An ironic result of nationalized health care might be that to avoid the undoubted evil of governmental triage, grotesque misallocations of resources will ensue. Is it really desirable that education, housing and general economic advancement be penalized so that a 110 year old patient can receive his third kidney transplant and second artificial heart?

National Health Care and Non-Standard Options

The terms with which a debate is pursued can become frozen while the underlying real dimensions continue to change. This has been the fate of the case for national health care. Its desirability cannot be assessed in a vacuum; as the nature of the commodity health care evolves so too do reasons for and against its provision by the state. The most revolutionary development in medical practice since national health care was initially broached is the increasing prominence of *non-standard options*. By 'non-standard option' I mean a medical service possessing the following three features: (i) Each occasion on which it is delivered entails great expense; (ii) It has little effect on mortality or morbidity configurations for the population as a whole; (iii) Individuals who receive the service are substantially benefited or perceive themselves to be substantially benefited.

Proliferation of non-standard options bedevils egalitarianism in health care delivery. A system that undertook to fulfill all requests on the basis of demonstrated need at no charge to recipients would soon be bankrupt. If non-standard options were excluded from the system but could be secured privately, major inequalities in health care delivery would thereby be reintroduced. Finally, if non-standard options that cannot be offered to all are forbidden to all, government is placed in the uncomfortable position of abridging the liberty of citizens to preserve health and life.

Health care delivery has often been cited as an area in which the case for equality is especially convincing, even self evident. In an important paper, Bernard Williams has maintained, "Leaving aside preventive medicine, the proper ground of distribution of medical care is ill health: this is a necessary truth."[29] I have argued that it is not a necessary truth but rather a seductive falsehood based on an obsolete model of medical care. It does indeed seem intolerable that anyone should die or continue to suffer from disease when, for a relatively small expenditure, his plight can be alleviated. Even on coldly economic grounds, it is irrational not to invest a sum that will be returned many times over in a life of increased productivity. But non-standard options do not fit this model. Their opportunity costs are extremely high, they rarely provide restoration to full health, and the need for them continually outstrips the available supply.[30]

Concluding Suggestions for a Medical Marketplace

I have been arguing that national health care is an idea whose time has come—and gone. That should not be interpreted as a brief for the status quo. Ongoing expansion of the medical role argues against imposing uniformity in the delivery of health services. It is not enough, however, to reject national health care; positive steps should be taken to enable consumers to choose for themselves the goods and services they most want. This requires a genuine marketplace: a sector in which alternative products are offered and where those who receive a good are the ones who pay for it. I conclude with five brief suggestions concerning how diversity and consumer sovereignty can be enhanced:

1. There are better and worse means by which society can respond to the health needs of the poor. Routing all medical care through a monolithic national health service has already been amply criticized. Somewhat preferable would be the provision of a suitably defined "minimum decent standard" of health care. One drawback of this proposal is that not all will agree on what counts as minimally decent. The acrimonious debate over Medicaid funded abortion is a case in point. Also, the poor will still be precluded from acting on their own preferences. Therefore, I suggest instead a cash grant or voucher program enabling the poor to

purchase their own medical services on a prepaid basis. How generous this program should be is a crucial question that cannot be explored in this paper.

2. Influential health care spokespersons should avoid making extravagant claims heralding the accomplishments of highpowered medicine. Such statements lead to unrealistic expectations on the part of consumers and consequent pressure upon the health care system to deliver more than it is capable of providing. Newly developed technology provides genuine health gains, but its effect on mortality and morbidity are inconsequential compared to the dramatic gains realized between the 1930s and 1950s. Predictions are hazardous, but we very probably have reached a point of drastically diminishing returns on the health care dollar. Pessimism concerning future health gains need not follow: health care is not the same as health. There are a great number of steps individuals can take to live longer and healthier lives: avoid smoking, eat breakfasts, get and stay married (especially significant for males), sleep at least seven hours each night, consume alcohol in moderation. These "life-style" patterns are free of cost, undeliverable by professionals but wonderfully responsive to individual choice. Because what individuals can do for themselves far exceeds what can be done for them, we ought to begin to emphasize the former.[31]

3. There is need to expand the variety of health insurance policies and other prepaid packages. Not everyone needs or desires the same level of coverage. I see no reason to suppose that consumers are generally unable to choose rationally how much of their resources to devote to health goods. Nor is there any evidence that welfare gains are realized if central planning boards are vested with the responsibility for such choices. Some persons are very sensitive to increased probabilities of an extended lifespan; they ought to have the opportunity to purchase expensive policies that include coverage for a wide range of non-standard options. Those who place a premium on present consumption should be free to devote only a minimal amount of income to health care coverage. Both will thus be able to maximize expected utility while assuming responsibility for their own choices. A not incidental benefit is that triage dilemmas will be minimized; or rather, *individuals will be making such decisions for themselves* through genuine market arrangements. The prospective demand for some item of expensive lifesaving technology will tend to create its own supply.

4. Consumers of medical services will never reclaim control of their health care programs until what Charles Fried characterizes as "a guild system as tight and self-protective as any we know"[32] is broken. Physicians make virtually all medical decisions and are loath to relinquish any of this power either to public agencies or to consumers. Even the choice of a primary care physician is usually made blind because organized medicine has traditionally anathematized advertising or any other means which would afford consumers the basis for making a cost-conscious selection. Physicians' domination of health care delivery is made possible by a legal structure that grants them unparalleled powers to control entry into the profession, set fees and regulate their own practice. The results are remarkably high incomes and an almost total immunity from normal market forces. Numerous steps could be undertaken to transform this cartel into competitive purveyors of service to an informed clientele: eliminating all bans on advertising, easing the formation of HMOs and other alternatives to fee-for-service medicine, eliminating or drastically abridging entry restricting requirements, allowing patients and pharmacists more say in the selection of prescription drugs and enabling other

health professionals to provide services that do not require a physician's expertise.

5. What ought to be done to hold down the nation's spiraling medical bill? Nothing. To be more precise, external bureaucratic regulation is the wrong prescription for the ills of our health care delivery system. If, as I have suggested above, consumers are afforded the opportunity to make informed purchases in a genuine medical marketplace, they will be able to determine what percentage of their income is devoted to health care. Is 5% of GNP too little, 15% too much? I suggest that there is no a priori answer to these questions. Health care is one among many services persons can choose for themselves in whatever quantity they desire—if they are given the chance to do so.

Notes

1. Variations on this theme abound. See Gene Outka, "Social Justice and Equal Access to Health Care," *Journal of Religious Ethics* 2 (1974) pp. 11-32; Anne R. Somers and Herman M. Somers, "The Organization and Financing of Health Care: Issues and Directions for the Future," *American Journal of Orthopsychiatry* 42 (1972) pp. 119-36; David Whipple, "Health Care as a Right: Its Economic Implications," *Inquiry* 11 (1974) pp. 65-8; Bernard Williams, "The Idea of Equality," in *Problems of the Self* (London: Cambridge University Press, 1973) pp. 230-249.

2. For example, see Robert Nozick, *Anarchy, State and Utopia* (New York: Basic Books, 1974) pp. 232-5; Robert M. Sade, "Medical Care as a Right: A Refutation," *New England Journal of Medicine* 285 (Dec. 2, 1971) pp. 1288-92; Thomas Szasz "The Right to Health," *Georgetown Law Journal* 57 (1969) pp. 734-51.

3. Victor Fuchs, "Economics, Health and Post Industrial Society," *Milbank Memorial Fund Quarterly* 57 (1979) pp. 165-7.

4. See James M. Buchanan, *Cost and Choice* (Chicago: Markham Publishing Company, 1969).

5. U.S. Department of Health Education and Welfare, *Health, United States, 1978*, (Washington, D.C.: Government Printing Office) p. 380.

6. Daniel S. Hirschfield, *The Lost Reform* (Cambridge: Harvard University Press, 1970).

7. Stuart Shapiro and Stanley Wyman, "CAT Fever," *New England Journal of Medicine* 294 (April 22, 1976) pp. 954-6.

8. Nicholas Rescher, "The Allocation of Exotic Medical Lifesaving Therapy," *Ethics* 79 (1969) pp. 173-4.

9. Howard H. Hiatt, "Protecting the Medical Commons: Who is Responsible?" *New England Journal of Medicine* 293 (July 31, 1975) p. 237.

10. An important recent study is Jon B. Christianson and Walter McClure, "Competition in the Delivery of Health Care," *New England Journal of Medicine* 301 (Oct. 11, 1979) pp. 812-8.

11. See Edmond D. Pellegrino, "Medical Economics and Morality: The Conflict of Canons," *Hospital Progress* 59 (August, 1978) pp. 50-55.

12. Richard Spark, "The Case Against Regular Physicals," *New York Times Magazine* (July 25, 1976) p. 10 ff.

13. John Bailar, "Mammography—A Time for Caution," *Journal of the American Medical Association* 237 (March 7, 1977) pp. 997-8; Samuel Thier, "Breast Cancer Screening: A View from Outside the Controversy," *New England Journal of Medicine* 297 (Nov. 10, 1977) pp. 1063-5.

14. Richard Posner, "Regulatory Aspects of National Health Insurance Plans," *University of Chicago Law Review* 39 (Fall, 1971) pp. 1-29.

15. See the discussion in Robert Nozick, *Anarchy, State and Utopia* pp. 26-28.

16. James F. Blumstein and Michael Zubkoff, "Perspectives on Government Policy in the Health Sector," *Milbank Memorial Fund Quarterly* 51 (1973) pp. 395-431.

17. For this characterization of the state see Max Weber, *Theory of Social and Economic Organization* (New York: Free Press, 1947) p. 156.

18. "The Failures of Success," *Milbank Memorial Fund Quarterly*, 55 (1977) p. 5.

19. See Thomas Schelling, "Standards for Adequate Minimum Personal Health Services," *Milbank Memorial Fund Quarterly* 57 (1979) pp. 212-33.

20. Vouchers are an intriguing device for coupling the attainment of social purposes with protection of personal autonomy. In addition, they are flexible: a restrictive voucher plan will resemble a centralized program while less restrictive ones are more like cash grant schemes. In which direction should a health care voucher plan lean? The question is thorny, but, on balance, a minimum of restrictions seems desirable. Four reasons support this assessment: (i) respect for personal autonomy; (ii) the (admittedly defeasible) conviction that individuals are better judges of their health care preferences and needs than are boards of central planners; (iii) the health industry needs a dose of competition more than it does enforced uniformity; (iv) political wrangling over the inclusion of particular services such as abortion are minimized by adherence to a policy of minimal restrictions.

Against these must be weighed the paternalistic concern that individuals will misallocate their vouchers. Much work remains to be done in the foundations of voucher theory. Moral philosophers ought to be involved in this inquiry; the issues are too involved to be left exclusively to the economists.

21. Ad Hoc Committee of the Harvard Medical School to Examine the Definition of Brain Death, "A Definition of Irreversible Coma," *Journal of the American Medical Association* 205 (Aug. 5, 1968) pp. 337-40.

22. See Richard Rettig, "Lessons Learned from the End-State Renal Disease Experience" in Richard Egdahl and Paul Gertman, eds. *Technology and the Quality of Health Care* (Germantown, Maryland: Aspen Systems Corporation, 1978) pp. 153-173; Eliot Marshal, "Rendezvous with a Machine," *New Republic* 176 (March 19, 1977) pp. 16-19.

23. Paul Ramsey, "Scarce Medical Resources," *Columbia Law Review* 69 (1969) pp. 620-92; Jay Katz and Alexander Morgan Capron, *Catastrophic Diseases: Who Decides What?* (New York: Russell Sage Foundation, 1975) pp. 178-96.

24. Especially by Shana Alexander, "They Decide Who Lives Who Dies: Medical Miracle Puts a Moral Burden on a Small Committee," *Life* 53 (Nov. 9, 1962) p. 102ff.

25. Paul Ramsey, "Scarce Medical Resources," p. 659; Renee Rox and Judith Swazey, *The Courage to Fail* (Chicago: University of Chicago Press, 1974) pp. 240-279.

26. David Sanders and Jessee Dukeminier, Jr., "Medical Advance and Legal Lag: Hemodialysis and Kidney Transplantation," *UCLA Law Review* 15 (1968) p. 378.

27. References previously cited concerning the history of dialysis in the United States all deal at greater or lesser length with the ethical bases of triage. For theoretical discussions of this issue displaying significantly varied approaches see: James F. Childress, "Who Shall Live When Not All Can Live?" *Soundings* 53 (1970) pp. 339-55; Nicholas Rescher, "The Allocation of Exotic Medical Lifesaving Therapy;" Robert Young, "Some Criteria for Making Decisions Concerning the Distribution of Scarce Medical Resources," *Theory and Decision* 6 (1975) pp. 439-55.

28. This problem is raised by Charles Fried, "Equality and Rights in Medical Care," *Hastings Center Report* 6 (1976) p. 31.

29. "The Idea of Equality," p. 240.

30. Governmentally provided Catastrophic Health Insurance (coverage for medical expenses above a stipulated minimum) has often been urged as a compromise between a comprehensive national health program and the status quo. Several objections to this policy have been frequently rehearsed: incentives are increased for the use of costly hospital service in place of less costly alternatives; once the floor expenditure has been reached, patients and physicians will have little incentive to minimize further therapy; major medical health insurance is readily available from the private sector. But the foregoing discussion suggests an even more far-reaching objection: non-standard options would, of course, all qualify financially as catastrophic expenses. It would be ironic indeed if universal catastrophic coverage were enacted just as the progress of medical technology renders its provision unattainable.

31. See the discussion in Chapter 2 of Victor Fuchs *Who Shall Live?* pp. 30-55.

32. "Equality and Rights in Medical Care," p. 33.

I would like to thank Paul Menzel, John Troyer and the editors of *Philosophy & Public Affairs* for numerous helpful suggestions.

LESTER H. HUNT*

Some Advantages of
Social Control:
An Individualist Defense

> But a creeping intellectual vice that has never been wholly cured impedes
> seeing social phenomena clearly. It consists in not being able to perceive a
> social function if there is not a specialized social organ to serve it.
> —José Ortega y Gasset

1. Alternative Ways to Regulate Behavior

We sometimes must ask ourselves whether some form of behavior which is
presently legal should be made illegal. Such questions are sometimes discussed as
though the alternatives were either to regulate behavior by means of formal law or
to leave it unregulated. Yet we all are to some extent aware that these are not the
only options. We know that among the many influences on our behavior are social
conventions which proscribe and discourage us from doing things which someone
does not want us to do. If the number of people who want something to be illegal is
large enough to force a public discussion of the issue, then there undoubtedly
already exists—across some section of the population—a convention proscribing
the thing in question. We always have an alternative form of control, however

From *Public Choice*, Vol. 36, no. 1 (1981)
*Johns Hopkins University.

unsatisfactory it may be. In this paper I will discuss some characteristics of the social form of control which tend to make it more efficient than the legal alternative. Of course, this does not mean that we should always choose social control, or even that efficiency considerations on the whole will be in its favor. [1] In some cases, the efficiency advantages will be overwhelmed by costs which will be unacceptable on balance to at least some utility-maximizing legislators. Still, the advantages will always be there and will sometimes be relevant. It should help the rational legislator to know what they are. I will conclude by making a few sketchy remarks about the possible contrasting costs.

The issue I am facing here becomes deeper and more complicated when we notice the obvious fact that the social and legal forms of control are not the only ones. There is also what might be called "individual" control, the influence on a person's conduct of principles he has developed on the basis of his own insight. The thesis of this paper sounds like a watered-down version of James Buchanan's claim, in *The Limits of Liberty,* that the condition of society he calls "orderly anarchy," in which conduct is regulated from sources outside the formal legal structure, is the ideal one and ought to be pursued as far as is practicable. However, he makes a remark which at least appears to directly contradict what I have said:

> Both (orderly) anarchy and formalized constitutional structure must be distinguished from a setting in which individuals behave strictly in accordance with customary or traditional modes of conduct, with little or no connection with rationally selected norms. This alternative is likely to be grossly inefficient, and it must be placed beyond the extreme limits of formalized legal structure in its coerciveness. (1975, pp. 117-118).

Interpreted strictly and literally, [2] this remark suggests a dilemma for anyone who wishes to limit legal control. What Buchanan means by orderly anarchy is a collection of individuals who, more or less independently of one another, formulate their own principles of conduct by means of "something like a Kantian generalization principle" (ibid). In other words, it is what Kant called the Kingdom of Ends, or alternatively, it is Plato's republic—not the lower strata in which the soldiers and artisans live, but the tiny community of the Philosopher Kings. This is undoubtedly a great social ideal but the problem with it as far as legislative decisions are concerned is that there seems to be so little of it in this world. Most people do think about what to do in particular circumstances, but we are relatively thoughtless about the rules according to which these special policy decisions are made—the social analogue of the constitution and the law. If one asks the average decent person why he does not indulge in some seemingly rewarding activity which he regards as immoral—such as theft—one will get no intelligible answer, or something which is too weak to account for the consistency of his behavior. Much of the remainder of his motivation probably comes from a blind obedience to social convention. This brings us to the other horn of the dilemma. If one compares social control on the one hand with individual and legal control on the other, the latter seem to be rational in a way in which the former is not. At least in a democracy, legal enactments are preceded—and, we hope, at least partly based on—some kind of discussion of the issues involved, and it is sometimes followed by more discussion as the effects of the law become visible and remedies for the undesirable ones are proposed. Legal control originates in something like the conscious ratiocination which the philosophers have identified with individual control. In contrast, social control seems to have, as Buchanan says, little or nothing to do with it. The alternatives to legal control so far seem to be, on the one hand, something that is not in plentiful enough supply to be relied upon and, on the other, something which appears to be irrational. So far, legal control seems to be preferable to either of them. A brief consideration of what conventions are like will make the dilemma more vivid and also provide the materials for finding a way out of it.

Consider a rather pure example of convention-regulated behavior: the handshake.[3] For what reason does one shake someone's hand? If "reason" here means "purpose," in some cases there seems to be no reason at all. I have many reasons for going to Professor Schmidt's house, but grasping and pumping his right hand does not seem to serve any of them. Yet, curiously, that is the first thing I do when I get there. The reason one indulges in such behavior is not necessarily some individual purpose of one's own.[4] The most general explanation of our doing such things is simply: that is what people do. This fact, however, does not clearly distinguish conventional behavior from other things people do. A member of a mass movement does what he does because that is what at least some people do, but his behavior is not conventional. However, only some people have this sort of influence over him, and his charismatic leader has more than anyone. In a way, he is subject to individual control, except that he is not the individual who does the controlling. This is not true in the case of convention-following behavior: the "people" who do what we do *also* do it because "that's what people do." That is how conventions are transmitted from one generation to the next: through layer upon layer of more or less thoughtless imitation. Of course, it is plausible to think that every convention originated in the rational insight of some individual, but this does not mean that any convention is still rational when it has been followed imitatively for a long time, as most of them probably have. Consider the obvious irrelevance to one's own behavior of the theory that the handshake originated as a way of showing that one is unarmed. It does me no good to demonstrate to Professor Schmidt that I am not holding a pistol.

A convention, as the Latin root suggests, is a kind of agreement. A convention is a kind of opinion, a certain sort of shared opinion about what is to be done. The fact that it is an opinion is one of many things which distinguishes it from law. A law is not an opinion but, as Plato said, "a speech." Nothing is a law unless it is promulgated by some authoritative person or group, and nothing can be promulgated unless it is formulated in words. Conventions, on the other hand, need not be formulated in words, even in the privacy of anyone's mind. As a matter of fact, one cannot be aware of all the conventions which govern one's conduct—there are simply too many of them. Although it is impossible to count them, we can confidently say that the conventions which govern the conduct of most individuals is greater than the number of laws that govern the subjects of at least some governments. "There are rules for taking and terminating a turn at talking; there are norms synchronizing the process of eyeing the speaker and being eyed by him; there is an etiquette for initiating an encounter and bringing it to an end" (Goffman, 1971, pp. 3-4). I take it for granted that others will tend to respect my claims to certain "territories," but the law protects very few of these: my claims over my house, my yard and the inside of my car. Most of my territories are protected only by conventions: these include most examples of "personal space" (the oval-shaped space of varying size which surrounds me as I walk down the street), "stalls" (such as "my" place, marked with a towel, at the beach), and "use space" (such as the space between me and the picture I am looking at in a gallery).[5] We observe the rules protecting the territories of others and think that behavior which violates them is unseemly, importunate, unfair, rude, and so forth—but we are typically not conscious of the fact that we are indeed observing and applying rules. If we were, we wouldn't be able to do so much of it.

For my purposes, these simple considerations will suffice as an account of what social conventions are. Suppose, now, that there is a community in which some of the inhabitants are considering moving some activity which is widely disapproved of—such as cigarette smoking or homosexuality—out of the domain of social control and into that of legal control. The question is: What advantages are there to leaving it where it is? To eliminate issues which are irrelevant to decisions which are likely to be made in the English-speaking world, I will assume that there are laws which prevent people from enforcing conventions by such means as violence, the threat of violence, and harassment. Virtually all of the penalties imposed for violating the conventions against the activity in question are unpleasant only because they are signs of disapproval. I will also assume that the question of how the activity is to be controlled will be answered democratically.[6]

A Catalog of Advantages

To have a norm which effectively controls behavior, one must have penalties for violation of the norm, and to impose penalties, one must have surveillance of some sort. A striking fact about conventions is that they are part of a system in which the cost of surveillance is close to zero. This is an almost direct consequence of the fact that a convention is a shared normative belief.

Those who share this belief form what might be called a "norm-generating coalition."[7] They alone will conduct surveillance. However, they can be depended on to do it because it is only by noticing violations of one's normative beliefs that we can apply them to the world. To hold a normative belief *is*, in large part, to notice where and how the world falls short of it. People therefore "naturally" tend to notice such things. Since they go through life gathering enormous amounts of information about their surroundings anyway, a small diversion of resources yields a large amount of information relevant to violations of the convention. The town gossips do make special investments in surveillance but, unlike the police, they do it for its entertainment value and from a sense of duty (probably mainly the former) and do not impose a cost on the rest of the community by requiring compensation. They regard themselves as adequately compensated already. It is the nature of social surveillance to raise no free rider problems. If it were conducted entirely by means of onerous specialized activities, everyone would be strongly inclined to let everyone else do it, which would mean that it would never get done. But such is often not the case. Unless there is some special factor present which makes social surveillance physically impossible, the amount which will be conducted without any taxing special effort is apt to be very large. Beyond that, the town gossips and the gossip network they form spontaneously—largely for the sake of a purely private good it produces—will increase that amount beyond what it would be without them. These facts are especially impressive because, where surveillance is concerned, quantity is tantamount to a kind of quality, and anyone who has lived in a small town or taught in a small college knows how great this quantity sometimes is and how effective it can be.

The police, on the other hand, would not be able to collect that much information without imposing enormous pecuniary costs on the community—and doing serious violence to the Bill of Rights. This last is relevant here because it represents a kind of subjective cost. People may find the town gossip irritating, but they tend to find it more obnoxious to be observed by an armed man with the deadly force of the state behind him.[8]

However, the effectiveness of surveillance will be of little interest if the penalties are ineffective. In this respect, social control seems hopelessly weaker than legal control. It is natural to speak of social penalties as differing from legal penalties simply by imposing a lower cost (Johnson, 1970, p. 127) on the violator, as being the more "lax" (Ortega, 1957, pp. 214-15) of the two. It was because of this, and apparently on humanitarian grounds, that Ortega y Gasset thought that social control is preferable to legal control. He suggested that we should rely on social control unless the ancillary social machinery breaks down to the extent that the effectiveness of enforcement is unacceptably small, at which point the law must be called in.[9] However, if we accept this picture—if we think of social penalties as simply being weaker and think of effectiveness of enforcement as the only relevant factor—it is difficult to see any but a trivial role for social enforcement. It would only seem to be fit to enforce what Hobbes appropriately called "small morals," the rules which protect our sensibilities from the little shocks given us by minor acts of rudeness and carelessness in others. It can enforce these norms because the benefits of violating them are so small that they are outweighed even by the paltry penalty of "loss of reputation." If the rewards of breaking a rule are at all substantial, weak penalties will not deter violations. From here it is a short step to the conclusion that every rule which is really important must be part of the law.

However, the idea that social penalties are weaker than legal ones is oversimple and in some cases false.[10] What is peculiar about such penalties is not so much their intensity as the way in which they are distributed; the working of social control tends to be Pareto-optimal, in the sense that it tends to make some people better off and no one worse off. While there are certain tendencies in social control which lead away from this result, there are similar tendencies at work in the law which are much stronger. In some circumstances it can be rational to take this factor as outweighing the weakness of social enforcement when it exists.

Imagine that a respectable husband, after a few drinks at an office party, is kissing his secretary in what he thinks is a secluded place. He looks up and is astonished to find his wife looking at him. Imagine for a moment his scalding misery. If he is at all normal, he would rather lose a large sum of money than encounter that look. It is obvious that, although the only penalty he is suffering is disapproval, there is nothing weak about it. It is also obvious that it is misleading to think of it as "loss of reputation." What he feels is shame. That is, he disapproves of himself, because to some extent he shares the norm which was so far out of his mind a moment ago and is now looking out at him through those eyes. This seems to be the main reason why we tend to treat disapproval, without considering any of its consequences, as a cost: to the extent that we share the principle which is the basis of disapproval, it tends to compel us to apply the principle against ourselves (something we might easily escape doing otherwise). Let us assume for a while—I will tell you when to stop—that it is the only reason we are averse to disapproval.

Consider what happens as a norm-generating coalition forms and grows. To join the coalition is simply to come to have a certain opinion. Each new member is no worse off in his estimation than he was before: if he were, he would return to his old set of opinions (relying, perhaps, on man's impressive talent for self-deception and forgetfulness). It is possible for someone to believe something which he finds depressing, but in that case he apparently prefers believing the truth to believing a delusion (even a comfortable one). ("Better Socrates dissatisfied than a pig satisfied.") It is consistent to prefer to believe the truth and yet wish that the truth were different.

The beliefs here are normative ones: each member of the coalition believes that people—including himself—should act in a certain way. This means that he prefers that *he* act in this way. But this preference is threatened by the fact that violating a rule—any rule—is profitable at some time and in some respect, and now that he is a member he sees these profits as "temptations" to be resisted. One might think that he was better off before he was a member, when he could simply indulge in such things, without acting contrary to his own preferences. However, as the case of the misbehaving husband suggests, the norm-generating coalition has an automatic enforcement mechanism. The member knows that all the other members are constantly engaged in surveillance to some extent, and he knows that if he violated the norm and they found out, they would disapprove and their disapproval affects him as a penalty. Thus, he knows that he is under perpetual threat of enforcement. If the threat—and the enforcement itself when it materializes—helps him to act in accordance with the norm, it increases his utility, helping him to get more of what he prefers (compliance with the norm) and less of what he prefers not having (his own non-compliance).[11] This is so in spite of the unpleasantness of enforcement. If the benefits of leaving the coalition were preferable to the consequences of belonging to it (the results of believing the norm plus the results of enforcement) then he would, according to what I have said above, leave the coalition.

This means that the role of enforcement in the coalition is similar to the role of enforcement in a contract. As Buchanan has pointed out, the enforcing agency in a contract is there to protect something the parties to the contract prefer to have rather than not have—the situation which, in the contract, they have agreed to bring about; that is why they agree to accept enforcement even though its constraining effects constitute a cost (Buchanan, 1974, p. 94). There is also a differ-ence, however. Every contract, including the social and constitutional contracts of Hobbes and Buchanan, creates a prisoner's dilemma situation: for every contract there is a possible situation in which each party would be "better off" if he violated the contract and the other did not. Thus all contracts are unstable and there will no doubt be some cases in which at least one party would really prefer to violate the agreement if he could. He will in a way be frustrated by the enforcement he has agreed to. In the case of the norm-generating coalition, however, there is no prisoner's dilemma situation. If a member breaks the rule, he is worse off in his estimation. This helps to explain why the agent who enforces a contract is an independent third party, while the enforcer of the coalition is, in a way, the member against whom the enforcement is used: it derives its forcefulness from the fact that he agrees with the norm. This means that social control does not pose a problem analogous to one of the most familiar problems of legal control: what has been called "the threat of Leviathan" (Buchanan, 1974, Ch. 9). In contractualist political theory this is sometimes represented by the fact that once we have armed and appointed an enforcement agent—in this case, the state—there is a serious problem about how to confine the agent's coercive actions to those necessary to enforcing the compact. This problem can probably never be solved perfectly because the enforcer is and must be independent of the parties to the agreement. In the case of social control this problem does not appear to arise, because enforcement, as I have described it so far, is not independent in this way.

Though it may be obvious by now, I should perhaps point out that, for approximately the same reason, the enforcement of a norm within its coalition does not present a free rider problem. Within the coalition, enforcement and surveillance are not separate activities: because they agree with the norm, members are penalized by the very fact that others find out. As Goffman remarks: "The scene of the crime, the halls of judgment, and the place of detention are all housed in the same cubicle; furthermore, the complete cycle of crime, apprehension, trial, punishment, and return to society can run its course in two gestures and a glance" (Goffman, 1971, p. 107). Enforcement requires no more onerous specialized activity than surveillance does.

This may be worth mentioning if only because theories of social norms sometimes ignore it. P. M. Blau, a sociologist who uses the methods of economics, has claimed that enforcement must be performed by a "moral entrepreneur" who donates his time to this socially valuable task. (See Heath, 1976, pp. 67-71.) Since penalties are painful, and most of us do not like to hurt people we have no personal cause to be angry with, an especially intense free rider problem develops here. As Anthony Heath, who sympathizes with Blau, has pointed out, "moral entrepreneurship, if it occurs, must be altruistic or moralistic, not self-interested" (p. 157). Heath adds that we may be able to understand why someone would do this if we examine the way in which "the cost of imposing sanctions" varies from one group of persons to another, and speculates that "we may find that the leisured upper classes who have few other things with which to fill their time will be the ones to devote the largest proportion of their leisure to moral entrepreneurship" (p. 158). Given the wide extent of social control in human life, it seems wildly unlikely that the job of enforcement could be performed to any very significant extent by a collection of wealthy hobbyists. The problem to which Heath's rather desperate proposal is addressed is created by the assumption that enforcement *is* a job, essentially similar to what police do in legal control; I hope I have shown that this assumption is not true. [12]

Unfortunately, though, the assumption I introduced earlier on is also untrue in some cases. As Hobbes (1651; I, 13) remarked with some bitterness, human beings tend to become upset about such "trifles" as "a word, a smile, a different opinion, and any other sign of undervalue, either direct in their persons or by reflection in their kindred, their friends, their nation, their profession, or their name." Aside from our aversion to the kind of disapproval which is based on our own principles, we also tend to have a distinct and weaker aversion to disapproval *as such*. By and large, even homosexuals who are "out of the closet" and see nothing wrong with what they do find the widespread disapproval directed against it unpleasant. This tendency makes possible a cost which the coalition imposes on non-members. How strong this tendency is, and how great the cost, is an issue for psychologists to decide. What is more relevant here is the fact that legal control imposes costs which are similar but worse. Punishment by the state is also a sign of disapproval, a much more forcefully expressive one. Further, if the coalition's norm becomes law, the penalties imposed will be ones—like fines, imprisonment, and death—which members and non-members will have equal reason to find unpleasant. They will be distributed equally, and they will simply be added to the ones already imposed on non-members under social control, making them markedly worse off. A move to legal control will be dramatically Pareto-undesirable. [13]

For some norms social control has certain characteristics which make it easier to select norms rationally, characteristics which are absent in the case of legal control. If compliance with a norm does not create a free rider problem, the behavioral effects which would follow if it became an effectively enforced law are roughly the same as what would follow if the coalition were to expand until it included virtually everyone in the community—that is, few people would violate it. If the coalition barely constitutes a majority, the effects will be quite different.

Since the norm can become law when the coalition is barely a majority of the voters, the passage of the law can easily mean an enormous overnight change in behavior. People who supported or sympathized with the norm might then be unpleasantly surprised to find that their interests depended on the norm-violating behavior. This could happen, for instance, to people living in Virginia and North Carolina after cigarette smoking is made illegal. The same sort of information would be acquired if the norm-generating coalition were to spread until it does include virtually everyone, but it would be much less likely to come as a rude shock. People in this situation would have an opportunity to see where their interests lie before serious damage is done and, if the costs thus imposed were not worth the benefits to them, they would defend their interests *before* they suffered the losses they would suffer if the norm were made law. If there were enough people in this situation, we could expect that, as the coalition spreads, opposition to the norm would become more vigorous, and more and better antinorm arguments would be used. This would tend to slow down or even reverse the erosion of the interests of those who are harmed by the norm. It seems very likely that this would stop before they suffered the losses they would suffer under legal control. In the state of equilibrium thus reached, the coalition may still be a large majority of the community; but, depending on circumstances, the position of the people who benefit from the norm-violating activity is still likely to be much better than the one they would have under legal control if the supporters of the law had only 51%. This means that in social control, unlike legal control, those who are in the minority are not necessarily simply losers [14]: laws apply to everyone or no one; the application of existing social conventions is a matter of degree.

As individuals defect from the coalition and new opposition to it appears, what results is the social control analogue of the repeal of a law—except, of course, that it admits of degree. Each unit of this result is vastly easier to obtain than the repeal of a law. The reason for this lies, again, in the fact that a convention is a belief: a belief is a thing which is at least capable of being destroyed by evidence alone. It does not by any means always happen, but it is certainly possible for a person to drop a belief simply because he discovers strong arguments against it. This is important because, in arguing against a norm, those who are harmed by it can make significant gains if they only reduce support of the norm, say, from 70% to 60%. The effectiveness of a convention is a positive function of the number of people in the coalition. [15] This is not true of the relationship between the effectiveness of law and the number of people who support *it*. (Imagine for instance that you and I are the victims of a law supported by 51% of our community and that the staff of the enforcement bureau is drawn almost entirely from that 51%.) Further, even if the victims of a law manage to reduce support of it to below 50%, that is only part of the work of getting rid of the law. Laws are not beliefs and do not immediately disappear when people—any number of people—no longer hold to them.

I said above that if we look only at how conventions and laws originate—through more or less thoughtless imitation on the one hand and through discussion on the other—conventions appear to be less rational than laws. Now that we have looked at reasons why conventions fail to *continue* to exist, we see a dependence on reason which is absent in law. A convention is a belief, and although it is not as such a *reasoned* belief—that is, acquired by thinking—like other beliefs it is amenable to reason in a way in which political institutions are not. A "filter device" tends to reduce or eliminate the effectivenes of conventions which appear to injure the interests of people affected by them, and it does so directly by way of the ability people have to recognize such effects. Since what matters is which rules exist and not where they come from, this is an important fact. [16]

Possible Costs

There is nothing in the nature of social control as such which guarantees that there will be few violations of its norms. In certain circumstances—for instance, when the norm-generating coalition is small or when compliance with the norm presents a free rider problem—there are apt to be many violations. In such cases, the question of whether to bring the matter under legal control will become a public issue if violation imposes costs on people other than the violator and his voluntary partners in the proscribed activity. If this happens, it can be rational for the others—and perhaps for everyone in the community—to prefer legal to social control. In that event, the fact that a law can produce an overnight change in behavior might make law more attractive than convention, and not less, depending on where one stands. I will make a few brief and somewhat obvious remarks about the external costs generated by violators.

One such cost should be separated from the others. Most of us find that our utility is adversely affected simply by being aware that others have certain preferences, regardless of whether these preferences have any other effect on us. We prefer that others not prefer as they do. The capacity to incur this sort of cost varies widely according to the kind of awareness needed to bring it about. At the extreme is the "Puritan": this is the person who is adversely affected by merely having reason to *suspect* that others have certain preferences. [17] Others must actually *see* them acting on their detested preferences in order to be adversely affected. Some heterosexuals don't mind knowing that homosexuals exist but would rather not see two men holding hands. I will call all such costs "intolerance costs."

If the only external costs generated by violating a convention are intolerance costs, then one familiar argument for legal control does not apply. If theft were regulated only by social control, it might be so common that everyone would be better off if it were made illegal—everyone, including those who would continue to steal under the new law (there would be more loot available, *their* property would be protected, etc.). Legal control in that case can be instituted Pareto-optimally. [18] This will be true, though, only if each violator suffers costs as a result of the other violators. Assuming that violators prefer to act as they do, this condition will not be met if they only impose intolerance costs on others. No one is displeased by the mere awareness that others have the *same* preferences he has. There may be a sense in which the intolerance costs generated by the violator's behavior are a "public bad," but in that case whether something is a public bad depends on which public one has in mind. A violator who only imposes intolerance costs on others is not a free rider collecting benefits from their abstinence and will gain nothing if abstinence is made compulsory and universal—he will only lose.

This would seem to mean that with regard to such costs as these the interests of the violator and the coalition conflict to such an extent that it will be rational for the coalition's members to try to move to legal control, thus imposing a pure cost on the violators. This is not necessarily true: it depends on, among other things, what kinds of intolerance costs are going around. Suppose that there are no Puritans in the community and that, in fact, no one suffers intolerance costs unless he actually sees the proscribed preferences being acted upon—people suffer only *mild* intolerance costs. Social control is actually quite effective for eliminating this sort of cost. As I said earlier on, human beings tend to be averse to disapproval aimed at them, even when it is based on principles they do not share. If what the violator does imposes mild intolerance costs on others, it also exposes him to their active disapproval. If that is so, however, it is a rather simple matter for him to eliminate this active disapproval by acting on his preferences in places where the others cannot see him (e.g., at home and, if he is a homosexual, in bars where heterosexuals do not normally go). This seems to be what violators usually do. Most of the people we see near Castro Street in San Francisco are homosexuals, yet we almost never see signs of physical affection there between men. In spite of the fact that the homosexuals in that city have considerable social and political power, aversion to active disapproval drives such behavior indoors (though not into the closet). If only mild intolerance costs are imposed by violation, the disapproval it imposes on the violator actually benefits him in one respect: it gives him a motive to remove the only reason the coalition has for wanting to move to legal control, where he would be worse off.

*   *   *   *   *

I hope nothing I have said will be taken to suggest that the choice between social control and legal control is never a difficult one. Sometimes there is a genuine collision of interests. But my remarks here suggest a consideration which will sometimes make the difficult choice less difficult. In the contexts in which the choice usually occurs, social control appears to be more congenial than legal control to a certain social ideal which might be called "individualism": the notion that, as far as possible, no one should gain at anyone else's expense, and that everyone should have a chance to seek and defend his own interests. For someone who believes in individualism, it can be quite rational to prefer social control even when he suffers some inconveniences under it—even if he is a Puritan, in fact.

The affinity between individualism and social control will probably remind some readers of the closeness of fit which has been said to hold between that ideal and the workings of the market. A closer look will probably reveal a complex system of relationships which both connect and distinguish social control, legal control, and the market. There is an obvious similarity between social and legal control: both are ways of making and executing decisions about how everyone in the community should act; in the market, on the other hand, one decides how one will act oneself. But we have also seen that social control's resemblance to the market is no less important: both take place in the private sector; they are relationships between individuals who stand in a situation which Locke maintained is the "natural" one—no one has a greater right than anyone else to tell others what to do. This is not true of legal control which, however democratic it might be, always includes a central authority with unique rights to issue commands and back them with physical force.

Notes

1. Also, and just as obviously, this does not mean that it will be more just than the alternative. In this paper I will be concerned with utility only, and not with justice: my approach will be economic and not philosophical.

2. I will ungallantly ignore the question of whether this interpretation is the closest of all approximations to what the author means. My concern here is with the troublesomely plausible view it seems to set forth.

3. Except for some refinements, the account in this paragraph is the one given by José Ortega y Gasset: 1957, Chs. 9 and 10.

4. While it is true that I might insult Professor Schmidt if I did *not* shake his hand, I do not necessarily shake his hand in order to avoid insulting him.

5. For a discussion of these and other territories which are protected by convention alone, with comments on the conventions involved, see Goffman, 1971, Ch. 2 and 1967, Ch. 2.

6. In what follows I will frequently use the term "social norm" ("norm" for short) instead of the narrower term "convention" (conventions are social norms which are followed because they are followed). This is not merely to avoid monotony: at such times, what I say is intended to apply to all social norms and, with the same force, to conventions in particular.

7. The phrase is borrowed from Goffman, 1971, p. xii. It is a useful one because in a pluralistic society the coalition will very often be smaller than the community as a whole, in which case we will need to discuss the relations between those within the "coalition" and those on the outside.

8. This is undoubtedly why the police in democratic countries tend to invest their efforts in after-the-fact detection more than before-the-fact surveillance. Many voters would continue to support this system even if something that is already plausible were shown to be true: that a certain amount of increased surveillance would have a much better result in preventing the occurrence of crime than would the same investment if it were turned to increasing detection efforts.

9. For Ortega's account of law as a convention of last resort, see Ortega, 1957, Ch. 12.

10. In some contexts it is a reasonable assumption. This is true of the issue with which Johnson is concerned in the work cited above.

11. This fact disposes of the extreme anti-Puritan notion that there is no social benefit in badgering others about their private pleasures. There is, if the others agree with principles proscribing the pleasures involved.

12. Ultimately, Heath's problem arises from a habit of thought which seems universal among economists: this is the tendency to ask why something is treated as a cost only when it is treated that way on account of its causal consequences. If it is treated as what might be called a "final bad," one simply takes its costliness as a given and inquires no further into the

matter. If we *do* ask why people give disapproval to this status, we see that social penalties need not be imposed by a public-spirited moral entrepreneur.

13. To use a term introduced by Buchanan (1974, pp. 110-115), this means that under legal control the lion's share of the "liberty tax" (the unpleasantness of the fact that one's behavior is restricted by someone else) falls on the ones to whom the tax is not worth paying in the first place. Under social control, it falls on those for whom even the lion's share is worth paying.

14. It is interesting that this characteristic of social control is possessed, although to a greater extent and for different reasons, by the market. For a discussion of the difference, in this respect, between the market and political control in a democracy, see "Individual Choice in Voting and the Market," in Buchanan, 1960.

15. . . . at least if compliance with it presents no free rider problems.

16. For a discussion of "filter devices", see Nozick, 1974, pp. 21-22. See also the "Epilogue" to Hayek, 1979. Lamarck assumed that the organs of animals could only be efficiently organized if their structure originated in a purpose somehow. Darwin's theory illustrates the fact that it is sufficient if structures originate randomly and some mechanism eliminates inefficient ones.

17. So named in honor of H. L. Mencken's definition of Puritanism as "the haunting fear that someone, somewhere, may be happy."

18. In a civilized society, there will be a large number of rules for which this argument is plausible. Apparently, in primitive societies the work of the law—as we think of it—is done entirely by social convention, but that is probably the only sort of society in which such a situation is possible or desirable.

19. This paper was written during a period of residence at the Center for Study of Public Choice at Blacksburg, Virginia. I have benefitted from comments made on an earlier draft by James M. Buchanan, Robert J. Mackay, Gordon Tullock, and Geoffrey Brennan, for which thanks are due.

References

Buchanan, James M., *Fiscal Theory and Political Economy: Selected Essays*. Chapel Hill, University of North Carolina Press, 1960.

———, *The Limits of Liberty*. Chicago, University of Chicago Press, 1974.

Goffman, Erving, *Interaction Ritual: Essays on Face-to-Face Behavior*. Garden City, Anchor, 1967.

———, *Relations in Public*. New York, Harper and Row, 1971.

Hayek, Friedrich A., *Law, Legislation and Liberty*, vol. III. Chicago, University of Chicago Press, 1979.

Heath, Anthony, *Rational Choice and Social Exchange: A Critique of Exchange Theory*. London, Cambridge University Press, 1976.

Hobbes, Thomas, *Leviathan*. 1651 (many editions).

Johnson, David B., "Some Fundamental Economics of the Charity Market." In Thomas R. Ireland and David B. Johnson, *The Economics of Charity*. Blacksburg, Center for Study of Public Choice, 1970.

Nozick, Robert. *Anarchy, State, and Utopia*. New York, Basic Books, 1974.

Ortega y Gasset, José, *Man and People*. New York, Norton, 1957.

JOHN HOSPERS*

Libertarianism and
Legal Paternalism

In his book *Principles of Morals and Legislation* the eighteenth-century philosopher and legislator Jeremy Bentham divided all laws into three kinds: (1) laws designed to protect you from harm caused by other people; (2) laws designed to protect you from harm caused by yourself; and (3) laws requiring you to help and assist others. Bentham held that only the first kind of laws were legitimate; and in general libertarians would agree with him. The third class of laws, sometimes called "good Samaritan" laws, are greatly on the increase today, and their principal examples are not laws requiring you to assist persons in trouble (such as accident victims) although these are on the increase,[1] but rather the laws—both Congressional and bureaucratic law—having to do with income redistribution, such as welfare and food stamps and programs for the disadvantaged. Bentham argued persuasively against these laws as well; but he also condemned laws of the second kind, and it is these I propose to discuss in this paper. Legislation designed to protect people from themselves is called "paternal legislation," and the view that such laws are legitimate and ought to be passed is called "legal paternalism."

I

Legal moralism is the view that the entire nation should be governed by one morality and/or religion, with dissent from the official view being punishable as a crime. Examples of legal moralism are the Catholic Church prior to the Reformation and Iran under the Ayatollah Khomeini.

Legal paternalism is the view that the law should, at least sometimes, require people to act (a) against their will (b) for their own good, in that way protecting them from the undesirable consequences of their own actions. The term derives from the Latin "pater" (father): just as a kind father protects his children against harm and danger, pulling the child away from the speeding car or from the

Reprinted from *Journal of Libertarian Studies*, Vol. 4, No. 3 (Summer 1980).
*University of Southern California.

precipice down which he is about to fall, so the State should protect its citizens, not only against harm inflicted on them by other citizens, but also against harm which they might inflict on themselves. Thus, according to legal paternalists, the State should prohibit drugs because otherwise people might take them, and even if the danger is only to their own health or life the State should protect such values for them if they are too foolish or incompetent to do so for themselves. Or again, the State should protect people from their own profligacy by forced savings, such as social security.

Libertarians, of course, are vigorously anti-paternalistic, believing as they do that people should absorb the consequences of their own actions, and that in any case the State has no right to legislate what people should do as long as their actions harm no one else. The concept of "harm" is admittedly vague:[2] some people would say, for example, that a teacher is harming their children more by teaching them anti-Christian doctrines than by injuring their physical bodies, and if they had their way they would impose not only legal paternalism but a whole system of legal moralism. Most Christians today, however, aware of what would happen if each moral or religious sect tried to impose its views on everyone in this way, would resort to persuasion rather than to force, and however evil they might find certain teachings to be they would stop short of wanting them declared illegal. But disagreement about what constitutes harm continues: some consider X-rated movies harmful, others say the same about nude beaches, and still others would make the same assertion about certain theories of education. Yet most of those who say this (in the case of education at least, often with good reason) would stop short of saying that those who inflict this alleged harm should be subject to civil or criminal prosecution. "Harm" is usually construed by libertarians in accordance with their own political philosophy, to include at least (a) bodily injury, such as assault and battery, (b) damage to or theft of property, and (c) violation of contract, and accordingly it is these that libertarians usually seek to prohibit by law.

II

Even libertarians are not, however, opposed as a rule to *all* paternalism. There are several groups of people in behalf of whom some degree of paternalistic action would be considered proper.

1. *Infants and children.* Infants can not take care of themselves at all, and children cannot in many ways. Children do make decisions, but lacking experience they often fail to comprehend the consequences of their own proposed actions. Views on children's rights are a hotbed of current controversy; but there is probably no parent who has not at some time used coercion in order to prevent some harm to the child or bring about some good. A degree of paternalism concerning children is also embodied in the legal system: for example, if parents demonstrably abuse their children, the State takes the children out of the parents' custody for the children's own good, even if such action may not be in accord with the children's own wishes at the time. The rationale of this is that the parents have proved themselves to be unfit custodians of the children's rights.

2. *The senile.* When an elderly couple can no longer take care of themselves but refuse to leave their home, and when they consistently refuse to pay the utility bills and the heat and light are cut off, it is customary for a near relative to obtain power

of attorney from the court in order to pay the bills and perhaps conduct other business transactions on behalf of the parents even if the parents are unwilling, in order to protect the parents from the consequences of their own actions. Though there has been little discussion of this, it is probable that most libertarians would go along with a degree of paternalism in such cases; at least it would bespeak a certain crassness to say, "If they're so stupid or forgetful as not to pay their utility bills, let them freeze!" Our ordinary assumption is that people are able to estimate to some extent the probable consequences of their own actions, and this assumption is unjustified in the case of senility, just as it sometimes is in the case of children.

3. *The mentally incompetent* (a wider class than "the insane"). This is hardly a clear-cut group. But there are many people who are quite unable to function in the world and quite as unable to fend for themselves as young children. In most states people are at least temporarily institutionalized when they are "in imminent danger of harming themselves or others." Libertarians in general are opposed to the compulsory institutionalization of persons who have committed no legal crimes; but it is not clear that all libertarians would be committed to opposing the non-voluntary incarceration of a knife-wielding psychotic in an aggressive phase when he was bent on killing the children in the neighborhood. Others might approve a person's compulsory incarceration if he was a danger to himself, or even if he was simply unable to function, e.g. to know how to find food or shelter even if he had the money in his pocket.

III

But let us leave these groups aside for the moment. What about "ordinary normal adults"? At least, one would think, we should be totally opposed to any paternalism with respect to them. "Neither one person, nor any number of persons," wrote John Stuart Mill in *On Liberty,* "is warranted in saying to another human creature of ripe years, that he shall not do with his life for his own benefit what he chooses to do with it. . . . The only purpose for which power can be rightfully exercised over any member of a civilized community, against his will, is to prevent harm to others. He cannot rightfully be compelled to do or forbear because it will be better for him to do so, because it will make him happier, because, in the opinion of others, to do so would be wise, or even right."

Mill, a disciple of Bentham, was a utilitarian, and based his ethical conclusions on whatever was for "the greatest good of society." But it is doubtful whether he could justify his strong anti-paternalism on utilitarian grounds. It may be that forcing motorcyclists to wear helmets for their own protection produces in its total consequences more good, e.g. more total happiness and less unhappiness, than the policy of not forcing them—particularly if there are lots of careless riders. It may even be that the policy of having parents arrange marriages produces less unhappiness than having young people (especially when they are emotionally immature) decide these matters for themselves; yet Mill would have them decide for themselves, even make their own mistakes and hopefully profit from them. In fact Mill, not in his *Utilitarianism* but in *On Liberty,* bases his anti-paternalistic stand on quite different considerations. "There is a part of the life of every person who has come to years of discretion, within which the individuality of that person ought to reign uncontrolled either by any other person or by the public collectively." And again, from *On Liberty,* "A man's mode of laying out his existence is the best, not because it is best in itself, but because it is his own mode . . . It is the privilege and proper condition of a human being, arrived at the maturity of his faculties, to use and interpret experience in his own way." Mill here is "saying something about what it means to be a person, an autonomous agent. It is because coercing a person for his own good denies this status as an independent entity that Mill objects to it so strongly and in such absolute terms. To be able to choose is a good that is independent of the wisdom of what is chosen."[3]

The question I now want to ask is, Are libertarians committed to being 100% anti-paternalistic, leaving aside the groups described in the previous section?

We are sometimes paternalistic with non-deranged adults, and believe ourselves to be quite justified in being so. A friend or spouse says to you, "Be sure to get me up at 7 o'clock; my job depends on it. Force me if you have to. No matter what I say at the time, get me up." If you do so, contrary to the person's wishes at the time, do you as a libertarian feel guilt and remorse? No, because even though forcing him to get up at that time is contrary to his wishes as of that moment, it is *in accord with his long-term goals for himself.* We are in a position in which we have to sacrifice either his short-term goal (staying asleep) or his long-term goal (keeping his job), and we consider it preferable to honor his long-term goal.

The attendant at a hospital force-feeds a patient who needs nourishment in order to live but refuses to take it. Should the libertarian say, "If he doesn't want food, it's wrong to force him to take it"—thus letting him die? Surely not. What we will do (or at the very least, may permissibly do) is to go counter to his *present* desires, which may last a day or a week, in order to fulfill his long-term desire (which was constant prior to his present illness), which was to remain alive. When the patient has recovered he may thank us for force-feeding him: "It saved my life." If this happened, would the libertarian still say that the force-feeding was wrong? Even if we have no independent evidence at the time that the patient's attitude was pro-life, we may tentatively infer this from the fact that he has already lived this long, and are justified in having a *presumption* that he wishes to live. If he is grateful to us for saving his life, this alone justifies our previous action; and if he still wants to die after his recovery, he is still alive to make that choice, and there remain many ways in which he can undertake to bring about his own death if he so chooses. Some decisions, once made, are extremely far-reaching, or dangerous, or irreversible—sometimes all three at once, as in the present case. When this is so, we act paternalistically on the person's behalf, so that he can live to freely choose another day.

IV

It is one thing to be justified in doing X; it is another thing to require everyone to do X by law. Is there any justification at all for *legal* paternalism?

Mill himself thought there were occasions when legal paternalism was justified. He held, for example, that a contract by which a person agrees to sell himself into perpetual slavery should be null and void—as indeed it would be declared by virtually any court in the Western world. But why, if a person signs such a contract, should anyone interfere with it? "The reason for not interfering, unless for the sake of others, with a person's voluntary acts," wrote Mill in *On Liberty,* "is consideration for his liberty. . . . By selling himself for a slave, he abdicates his liberty; he foregoes any future use of it beyond that single act. He therefore defeats, in his own case, the very purpose which is the justification of allowing him to dispose of himself. . . . The principle of freedom cannot require that he should be free not to be free. It is not freedom to be allowed to alienate his freedom." The reason for not honoring such a contract is the need to preserve the liberty of the person to make future choices. Paternalism is justified at time t-1 in order to preserve a wider range of freedom for that individual at times t-2, t-3, t-4, etc.

Perhaps this example is extreme, or at any rate unique. Let us return then to our more mundane example, the law (which exists in all the states of the United States except four) requiring cyclists to wear helmets for their own protection. But "for their own protection" is not the only reason why such laws have been passed. It is also for the protection of others—thus falling under the heading of impure paternalism rather than pure paternalism. (A law is purely paternalistic if it is *solely* for the individual's protection; it is impurely paternalistic when it is partly for that reason and partly for other reasons.) Without a helmet, a cyclist involved in an accident is liable to get a permanent head injury, and under present welfare and disability laws he would be a permanent ward of the state, perhaps living on for decades at taxpayer expense. The Supreme Court of Rhode Island a few years ago upheld the helmet requirement on the ground that it was "not persuaded that the legislature is powerless to prohibit individuals from pursuing a course of conduct which could conceivably result in their becoming public charges."

Committing suicide is commonly a criminal offense. (You can be killed for doing it.) Even unsuccessful attempts are punishable. Yet if your life is your own, haven't you the right to take it whenever you wish? What right has the State to command you not to take it? None, we say. Yet the State orders its policemen, when a person tries to kill himself by jumping in the river, to do his best to rescue the would-be suicide provided he can do so "without substantial risk" to his own life. Is there any justification at all for this rule? I believe that such a rule could be defended, for the kind of reason already given: by forcibly preventing a person from taking his life at time t-1, he thereby enables the person to make his own choice later, whereas the person's death would put an end to all future choices. Perhaps the person was in a depressed state of mind which would pass, if he lived; perhaps he was confused, or drugged, or deranged—the policeman is in no position to know when he sees the man jump. It is better to assume that in the long run the man wants to live, than to assume that his continuing and steady disposition (time t-2, t-3. . . . t-n) would be to die. If one assumes that his attempt is only a temporary aberration, and acts accordingly, the rewards may be great; whereas if it is not merely a temporary aberration, but an abiding disposition, then the man will still be alive to make a choice for death at a later time.

Paternalism in such a case represents a kind of *wager* that the person acting paternalistically on his behalf makes: "I'll wager that the long-run trend of your desires is contrary to your apparent wish at the present moment, so I will act to preserve your long-term wish even if it means denying your present, and hopefully temporary, one." In some cases it may even be justifiable, as in the case of teen-age marriages, to have an *enforced waiting period:* when the consequences of the act would be far-reaching and possibly catastrophic, it may be better to make the person wait or hesitate even if he doesn't wish to at the time, just as one makes the person get up even if he doesn't want to at the time. An impulsive suicide leap would have far-reaching and irreversible consequences, so isn't one justified in erring, if at all, on the side of caution? If the weeks go by and the person is still deeply depressed and refuses advice or therapy, then he can, with Marcus Aurelius, weigh the pros and cons carefully and still decide, "The room is smoky, so I leave it."

V

Rather than adopt the simplistic conclusion that all paternalistic action is wrong, I shall adopt a more moderate conclusion: I want to say that the greater the degree to which an act (or a proposed act, or a thought-of act) is *voluntary,* the less justified other persons (or institutions, especially the law) are in behaving paternalistically toward that person. But the key word here is "voluntary." The popular conception of voluntariness, which is shared by most libertarians, seems to me only to skim the surface of the concept. The popular conception, embedded also in most libertarian literature, is that voluntariness means *non-coercion.* As long as you've not been coerced, they believe, your decision is voluntary. But in my view much more than this is required.

1. It is true, of course, that when coercion occurs the decision is not voluntary. But even here there are degrees. The limiting case of coercion is one in which, for example, someone stronger than you are forces your fingers around the trigger of the gun; you resist but without success. In that case it isn't your act at all, but the act of the person who forced you. Still, you were coerced. More typically, coercion consists not of overt physical action but of the *threat* of it: "If you don't hand over your wallet, I'll shoot." Unlike the first case, in threat cases there *is* a choice: you can surrender your life instead of (or probably in addition to) your wallet. But it isn't much of a choice, and it isn't the choice we would have made (handing over the wallet) except for the coercion—we were made to do something we would not voluntarily have done.

Threats too are a matter of degree. Threat of loss of life is more serious than threat of injury; threat of injury is (usually) more serious than threat of loss of employment; and a threat by your mother-in-law to move if you don't do what she asks is still less of a threat—indeed it may be not a threat at all, but its opposite, an inducement.[4] Many libertarians are willing to call it coercion only if there is physical harm or threat of physical harm, but in my opinion this is much too narrow. A threat of loss of a job may not be much of a threat if you can easily obtain another; but if no others are obtainable within a hundred miles, or if your special skill is not one for which there is any longer much demand, or if you would have to move your whole family to another state, the threat of loss of a job could be very serious. In any case it's not a job you would voluntarily have left—you would not have quit it but for the coercion (and it is coercion, threatening the means by which you live, differing only in degree from threat to life or limb).

Indeed, any kind of *pressure* put on you interferes with the voluntariness of your decision. The warden says, "If you don't cooperate with us by joining the group therapy sessions, we'll put you in the hole for two weeks." Surely this compromises the voluntariness of the prisoner's decision. Someone puts pressure on you to make a decision hastily when you wouldn't have made it without the pressure; while this may not be comparable to loss of life or limb, it may seriously compromise the voluntariness of your decision. It may be that laws against duelling are justified because if duelling were legally permitted many people would feel great pressure to preserve their "macho" image by never turning down a challenge, and thus they are (not exactly forced, but) pressured (the sociological pressure here may be enormous) into entering a duel time after time even though they would prefer not to, and would refrain but for the pressure. It's not an outright case of coercion, but there is a continuum between coercion and pressure and when the pressure is of the kind I have described, an individual will be relieved and gratified, and in the long run fulfill his life-plan much more in accordance with his own wishes, if the practice is prohibited by law. (In the film *The Duellists,* this kind of pressure ruins the protagonist's whole life, and how different is that from killing him outright?) There is a certain paternalistic wisdom in the remark of that eminent philosopher Groucho Marx in one of his films, when he wakes from a faint and says, "Force some brandy down my throat!"

Any influence, whether pressure or outright coercion, which keeps it from "filtering through your mind," triggering the decision with partial or no coopera- tion from your untrammeled decision-making faculties, tends to inhibit the full voluntariness of the decision. But freedom from coercion and pressure is only one of the conditions requisite for voluntary action.

2. The decision must be *informed,* based on the facts relevant to the case, and purged of false information. If the merchant tells you it's a real diamond when it's glass, and you pay the price of a diamond, your decision to pay is not voluntary: "You wouldn't have paid that much voluntarily," we say, at least not for a piece of glass. It's not that you were coerced, or even pressured; you were defrauded, that is, you were fed false information in making your decision.

Fraud is only one special case. You think you are drinking water, it was water you asked for and your host at the party brought a clear liquid that looked like water, only it contained poison. Even though no pressure was placed upon you, it is not reasonable to hold that you are voluntarily drinking poison. Drinking the poison is not in these circumstances a voluntary act; drinking water would have been, but that is not what you are doing. Or: you start to walk across a bridge, not knowing that further down the bridge has collapsed (you can't see it through the fog). You know that if it has collapsed you will likely fall to your death, but you don't know that it has collapsed. Since your aim is to cross the bridge and not to commit suicide, your action, based on misinformation, is not voluntary. If a man really thought that when he jumped out of the 20th floor window he would float through the air, would his jumping to his death still be voluntary?

When a patient consents to participate in a medical experiment—he's not threatened, not pressured—but some of the possible serious consequences or unpleasant side-effects of the experimental drug have been concealed from him, one would not say that he consented voluntarily to take the drug. There must not only be uncoerced consent, there must be *informed* consent. Because his consent is not informed, it is not fully voluntary. How informed must it be to be "really informed"? The general formula is: he must be told all the relevant facts prior to making his decision. But this too turns out to be a matter of degree: one could go on forever citing medical facts which *might* turn out to be relevant; can one ever be quite sure one has reached an end of citing such facts? Even if the physician or researcher has cited all the facts he knows, there may still be others he doesn't know which are highly relevant to the patient's decision, even to his life or death. It would seem, then, that a patient can have "informed consent" but not "*fully* informed consent." If full (complete) information is required, the patient's consent must always be something less than fully voluntary. But once again, it is a matter of degree.

When prisoners, or patients in mental hospitals, are encouraged to offer themselves as experimental guinea pigs, it is highly probable that there is always, lurking in the background if not in the foreground, some external pressure (punishment if you don't, reward if you do). But in addition to this, it is seldom indeed that the patient is told even all the relevant information that the physician knows; what happens is more like "How would you guys like to join us in an interesting experiment, which won't take much of your time" and so on. Thus the consent fails of voluntariness in both counts.

It would hardly be an overstatement to say that the consent of children to participate in such an experiment can never be wholly voluntary, and that if "voluntary consent" is required in such a case, it can never be given. Even if the child could reel off all the information an unusually loquacious physician has presented regarding the new medication, the child is not in a position to *appreciate* the force of that information. How many children can really understand the full force of a simple statement like "There's a 50-50 chance that you'll die"? Children can make all kinds of confident assertions, wagers, and challenges, not knowing fully what they really mean. When the twelve-year-old is offered some L.S.D., with the invitation "It'll give you a wonderful high," he may accept it eagerly, as a baby might play with a stick of dynamite or a loaded gun. For this reason, contrary to what some libertarians apparently believe, all such invitations by others should be prohibited by law, for the child's protection. The child cannot give informed consent, much less "educated consent"—and those who would take advantage of the child's incapacity should be met with the full force of the criminal law. To say of the child that "after all he gave his consent" would be ludicrous if its consequences were not so tragic.

3. I believe that there is a third condition that must be fulfilled as well. A person may not be under coercion or outside pressure, and he may be fully informed of the relevant facts of the case, and yet he may make his decision in what I can only describe as an unsatisfactory—or irrational, depending on what that term is taken to mean—*psychological state*. A person may be mentally deranged; but lacking this extreme, he may be in a daze, or drugged, or in an acute state of grief or depression, or just simply confused. Ordinarily when a person is in such a state he could hardly be described as "fully informed," and so his action would fail of voluntariness by the second criterion. But there may well be occasions when he is not pressured and all of the facts are clearly before him, and yet he is in no position to make a decision such as he would make if he were not in such a psychological state. A person in a state of depression might be quite lucid as to the facts, but a recital of ordinarily horrifying facts, such as his own imminent death or the extinction of the entire world, would not move him to any kind of action or response.

I do not wish to say that *any* decision we might label as unwise shows that the person is in such an "abnormal" psychological state; people can certainly act voluntarily and yet foolishly. I only wish to suggest that when a person is in such a mental state as I have indicated, his decisions should not be described as fully voluntary. A psychotic in a highly manic phase may jump out of a second-story window, quite without coercion and in full possession of information as to the probable effects of his action. It is primarily because of the mental state of these persons, not pressure or lack of information, that we hesitate to describe them as fully voluntary.

In discussing human action, libertarians place very great emphasis upon voluntariness. But in my opinion most libertarians conceive it too thinly. "If he was forced, he hasn't acted voluntarily"—this much libertarians all assent to. But too often they fail to see that voluntariness is not as simple as that—that once it is clear that no coercion or pressure has been applied, the action may yet fail of being voluntary. I have argued that the simplistic conception of voluntariness not only fails to do justice to the concept, but is often highly unfortunate in its effects. And I have argued that voluntariness, like so many other concepts, is not a yes-or-no concept but a matter of degree: not only does coercion-pressure itself encompass a broad spectrum of influences, from the application of force at one end to the exertion of subtle psychological pressure on the other, but that even when no external pressure has been applied, an act may be only incompletely voluntary because of its failure to meet the other two conditions.

VI

Whenever I have offered remarks in defense of paternalism in the previous pages, paternalistic action was taken in order to help the person achieve *his own goals*. The man wants to get up at 7 a.m. to keep his job, and by going against his 6 a.m. command we are helping him achieve what he himself (though not at that moment) wants. If a person's suicidal impulse is transitory, we help him achieve his long-term goals—which all, of course, presuppose life—by not letting him kill himself now. Even when laws prohibiting duelling were defended, it was on the assumption that a life freed of this curse is what the person who is constantly being challenged to other duels really wants for himself.

But there is also paternalism which *thwarts* the person's long-term goals. Laws limiting the number of hours per week a person may work are often defended as protecting that person; but what if the person doesn't want any such thing? What if the person wants to work extra long hours this year in order to have money to start a possibly lucrative business next year?

"But," one may say, "surely laws or actions that thwart the person's own goals can't be paternalistic at all, because part of the definition of paternalistic action is that it's for the person's *own good*." Yes, but there's the rub—what is *for the person's good* may not be the same as *what he wants* (even in the long run). Suppose that what would be for his good is to develop his talents so as to have a fulfilling life, but that all he *wants* is to be a bum. Or suppose he is a drug addict, and all he wants for himself even over a life-span is a state of drug-soaked euphoria (he doesn't mind if his life is short as long as it is, by his own standards, sweet). Even if *we* believe, and even if we believe truly, that such a life does not serve *his* good—we think of the wasted talents, what he might have achieved and enjoyed if he had not (on our view) thrown away his life—we are nevertheless faced with the fact that *what we want for him* is not the same as *what he wants for himself.*

Any kind of paternalism which consists of our acting against his will to achieve *our* goals for him, rather than our acting against his (present) will to achieve *his own goals* (assuming, of course, that he is sufficiently mature to have them), is the kind of paternalism which I believe libertarians should condemn. Libertarians have condemned all paternalism without realizing that paternalism may assume both of these distinct forms, one of which may sometimes be acceptable and the other not.

Once it is clear that our goals for him do not coincide with his goals for himself, and once we have used reason and possibly persuasion to convince him (never force), and he still sticks to his own, then as libertarians we must conclude, "It's his life, and I don't own it. I may sometimes use coercion against his will to promote his own ends, but I may never use coercion against his will to promote *my* ends. From my point of view, and perhaps even in some cosmic perspective, my ideals for him are better than his own. But his have the unique distinguishing feature, that they are *his;* and as such, I have no right forcibly to interfere with them." Here, as libertarians, we can stand pat. It is, after all, just another application of Kant's Second Moral Law—that we should always treat others as ends in themselves, never as means toward our own ends.

Notes

1. See, for example, *The Good Samaritan and the Law,* ed. James Ratcliffe (Anchor Doubleday Books, 1966.)

2. See Joel Feinberg, *Social Philosophy,* Chapters 2 and 3 (Prentice-Hall paperback, Foundations of Philosophy series.)

3. Gerald Dworkin, "Paternalism," *The Monist,* Vol. 56 No. 1.

4. See J. Hospers, "Some Problems concerning Punishment and the Use of Force," *Reason,* November 1972 and January 1973 issues.

PART THREE

Liberty and Economics

LUDWIG VON MISES

Market versus Bureaucratic Planning

1. Economic Calculation

The preeminence of the capitalist system consists in the fact that it is the only system of social cooperation and division of labor which makes it possible to apply a method of reckoning and computation in planning new projects and appraising the usefulness of the operation of those plants, farms, and workshops already working. The impracticability of all schemes of socialism and central planning is to be seen in the impossibility of any kind of economic calculation under conditions in which there is no private ownership of the means of production and consequently no market prices for these factors.

The problem to be solved in the conduct of economic affairs is this: There are countless kinds of material factors of production, and within each class they differ from one another both with regard to their physical properties and to the places at which they are available. There are millions and millions of workers and they differ widely with regard to their ability to work. Technology provides us with information about numberless possibilities in regard to what could be achieved by using this supply of natural resources, capital goods, and manpower for the production of consumers' goods. Which of these potential procedures and plans are the most advantageous? Which should be carried out because they are apt to contribute most to the satisfaction of the most urgent needs? Which should be postponed or discarded because their execution would divert factors of production from other projects the execution of which would contribute more to the satisfaction of urgent needs?

It is obvious that these questions cannot be answered by some calculation in kind. One cannot make a variety of things enter into a calculus if there is no common denominator for them.

In the capitalist system all designing and planning is based on the market prices. Without them all the projects and blueprints of the engineers would be a mere academic pastime. They would demonstrate what could be done and how. But they

Reprinted from *Bureaucracy*, Ludwig von Mises (New Haven: Yale University Press, 1957). Used by permission.

would not be in a position to determine whether the realization of a certain project would really increase material well-being or whether it would not, by withdrawing scarce factors of production from other lines, jeopardize the satisfaction of more urgent needs, that is, of needs considered more urgent by the consumers. The guide of economic planning is the market price. The market prices alone can answer the question whether the execution of a project P will yield more than it costs, that is, whether it will be more useful than the execution of other conceivable plans which cannot be realized because the factors of production required are used for the performance of project P.

It has been frequently objected that this orientation of economic activity according to the profit motive, i.e., according to the yardstick of a surplus of yield over costs, leaves out of consideration the interests of the nation as a whole and takes account only of the selfish interests of individuals, different from and often even contrary to the national interests. This idea lies at the bottom of all totalitarian planning. Government control of business, it is claimed by the advocates of authoritarian management, looks after the nation's well-being, while free enterprise, driven by the sole aim of making profits, jeopardizes national interests.

The case is exemplified nowadays by citing the problem of synthetic rubber. Germany, under the rule of Nazi socialism, developed the production of synthetic rubber, while Great Britain and the United States, under the supremacy of profit-seeking free enterprise, did not care about the unprofitable manufacture of such an expensive *Ersatz*. Thus they neglected an important item of war preparedness and exposed their independence to a serious danger.

Nothing can be more spurious than this reasoning. Nobody ever asserted that the conduct of a war and preparing a nation's armed forces for the emergency of a war are a task that could or should be left to the activities of individual citizens. The defense of a nation's security and civilization against aggression on the part both of foreign foes and of domestic gangsters is the first duty of any government. If all men were pleasant and virtuous, if no one coveted what belongs to another, there would be no need for a government, for armies and navies, for policemen, for courts, and prisons. It is the government's business to make the provisions for war. No individual citizen and no group or class of citizens are to blame if the government fails in these endeavors. The guilt rests always with the government and consequently, in a democracy, with the majority of voters.

Germany armed for war. As the German General Staff knew that it would be impossible for warring Germany to import natural rubber, they decided to foster domestic production of synthetic rubber. There is no need to inquire whether or not the British and American military authorities were convinced that their countries, even in case of a new World War, would be in a position to rely upon the rubber plantations of Malaya and the Dutch Indies. At any rate they did not consider it necessary to pile up domestic stocks of natural rubber or to embark upon the production of synthetic rubber. Some American and British businessmen examined the progress of synthetic rubber production in Germany. But as the cost of the synthetic product was considerably higher than that of the natural product, they could not venture to imitate the example set by the Germans. No entrepreneur can invest money in a project which does not offer the prospect of profitability. It is precisely this fact that makes the consumers sovereign and forces the enterpriser to produce what the consumers are most urgently asking for. The consumers, that is, the American and the British public, were not ready to allow for synthetic rubber prices which would have rendered its production profitable. The cheapest way to provide rubber was for the Anglo-Saxon countries to produce other merchandise, for instance, motor cars and various machines, to sell these things abroad, and to import foreign natural rubber.

If it had been possible for the Governments of London and Washington to foresee the events of December, 1941, and January and February, 1942, they would have turned toward measures securing a domestic production of synthetic rubber. It is immaterial with regard to our problem which method they would have chosen for financing this part of defense expenditure. They could subsidize the plants concerned or they could raise, by means of tariffs, the domestic price of rubber to such a level that home production of synthetic rubber would have become profitable. At any rate the people would have been forced to pay for what was done.

If the government does not provide for a defense measure, no capitalist or entrepreneur can fill the gap. To reproach some chemical corporations for not having taken up production of synthetic rubber is no more sensible than to blame the motor industry for not, immediately after Hitler's rise to power, converting its plants into plane factories. Or it would be as justifiable to blame a scholar for having wasted his time writing a book on American history or philosophy instead of devoting all his efforts to training himself for his future functions in the Expeditionary Force. If the government fails in its task of equipping the nation to repel an attack, no individual citizen has any way open to remedy the evil but to criticize the authorities in addressing the sovereign—the voters—in speeches, articles, and books.[1]

Many doctors describe the ways in which their fellow citizens spend their money as utterly foolish and opposed to their real needs. People, they say, should change their diet, restrict their consumption of intoxicating beverages and tobacco, and employ their leisure time in a more reasonable manner. These doctors are probably right. But it is not the task of government to improve the behavior of its "subjects." Neither is it the task of businessmen. They are not the guardians of their customers. If the public prefers hard to soft drinks, the entrepreneurs have to yield to these wishes. He who wants to reform his countrymen must take recourse to persuasion. This alone is the democratic way of bringing about changes. If a man fails in his endeavors to convince other people of the soundness of his ideas, he should blame his own disabilities. He should not ask for a law, that is, for compulsion and coercion by the police.

The ultimate basis of economic calculation is the valuation of all consumers' goods on the part of all the people. It is true that these consumers are fallible and that their judgment is sometimes misguided. We may assume that they would appraise the various commodities differently if they were better instructed. However, as human nature is, we have no means of substituting the wisdom of an infallible authority for people's shallowness.

We do not assert that the market prices are to be considered as expressive of any perennial and absolute value. There are no such things as absolute values, independent of the subjective preferences of erring men. Judgments of value are the outcome of human arbitrariness. They reflect all the shortcomings and weaknesses of their authors. However, the only alternative to the determination of market prices by the choices of all consumers is the determination of values by the judgment of some small groups of men, no less liable to error and frustration than the majority, notwithstanding the fact that they are called "authority." No matter how the values of consumers' goods are determined, whether they are fixed by a dictatorial decision or by the choices of all consumers—the whole people—values are always relative, subjective, and human, never absolute, objective, and divine.

What must be realized is that within a market society organized on the basis of free enterprise and private ownership of the means of production the prices of consumers' goods are faithfully and closely reflected in the prices of the various factors required for their production. Thus it becomes feasible to discover by means of a precise calculation which of the indefinite multitude of thinkable processes of production are more advantageous and which less. "More advantageous" means in this connection: an employment of these factors of production in such a way that the production of the consumers' goods more urgently asked for by the consumers gets a priority over the production of commodities less urgently asked for by the consumers. Economic calculation makes it possible for business to adjust production to the demands of the consumers. On the other hand, under any variety of socialism, the central board of production management would not be in a position to engage in economic calculation. Where there are no markets and consequently no market prices for the factors of production, they cannot become elements of a calculation.

For a full understanding of the problems involved we must try to grasp the nature and the origin of profit.

Within a hypothetical system without any change there would not be any profits and losses at all. In such a stationary world, in which nothing new occurs and all economic conditions remain permanently the same, the total sum that a manufacturer must spend for the factors of production required would be equal to the price he gets for the product. The prices to be paid for the material factors of production, the wages and interest for the capital invested, would absorb the whole price of the product. Nothing would be left for profit. It is obvious that such a system would not have any need for entrepreneurs and no economic function for profits. As only those things are produced today which were produced yesterday, the day before yesterday, last year, and ten years ago, and as the same routine will go on forever, as no changes occur in the supply or demand either of consumers' or of producers' goods or in technical methods, as all prices are stable, there is no room left for any entrepreneurial activity.

But the actual world is a world of permanent change. Population figures, tastes, and wants, the supply of factors of production and technological methods are in a ceaseless flux. In such a state of affairs there is need for a continuous adjustment of production to the change in conditions. This is where the entrepreneur comes in.

Those eager to make profits are always looking for an opportunity. As soon as they discover that the relation of the prices of the factors of production to the anticipated prices of the products seem to offer such an opportunity, they step in. If their appraisal of all the elements involved was correct, they make a profit. But immediately the tendency toward a disappearance of such profits begins to take effect. As an outcome of the new projects inaugurated, the prices of the factors of production in question go up and, on the other hand, those of the products begin to drop. Profits are a permanent phenomenon only because there are always changes in market conditions and in methods of production. He who wants to make profits must be always on the watch for new opportunities. And in searching for profit, he adjusts production to the demands of the consuming public.

We can view the whole market of material factors of production and of labor as a public auction. The bidders are the entrepreneurs. Their highest bids are limited by their expectation of the prices the consumers will be ready to pay for the products. The co-bidders competing with them, whom they must outbid if they are not to go away empty-handed, are in the same situation. All these bidders are, as it were, acting as mandatories of the consumers. But each of them represents a different aspect of the consumers' wants, either another commodity or another way of producing the same commodity. The competition among the various entrepreneurs is essentially a competition among the various possibilities open to individuals to remove as far as possible their state of uneasiness by the acquisition of consumers' goods. The resolution of any man to buy a refrigerator and to postpone the purchase of a new car is a determining factor in the formation of the prices of cars and of refrigerators. The competition between the entrepreneurs reflects these prices of consumers' goods in the formation of the prices of the factors of production. The fact that the various wants of the individual, which conflict because of the inexorable scarcity of the factors of production, are represented on the market by various competing entrepreneurs results in prices for these factors that make economic calculation not only feasible but imperative. An entrepreneur who does not calculate, or disregards the result of the calculation, would very soon go bankrupt and be removed from his managerial function.

But within a socialist community in which there is only one manager there are neither prices of the factors of production nor economic calculation. To the entrepreneur of capitalist society a factor of production through its price sends out a warning: Don't touch me, I am earmarked for the satisfaction of another, more urgent need. But under socialism these factors of production are mute. They give no hint to the planner. Technology offers him a great variety of possible solutions for the same problem. Each of them requires the outlay of other kinds and quantities of various factors of production. But as the socialist manager cannot reduce them to a common denominator, he is not in a position to find out which of them is the most advantageous.

It is true that under socialism there would be neither discernible profits nor discernible losses. Where there is no calculation, there is no means of getting an answer to the question whether the projects planned or carried out were those best fitted to satisfy the most urgent needs; success and failure remain unrecognized in the dark. The advocates of socialism are badly mistaken in considering the absence of discernible profit and loss an excellent point. It is, on the contrary, the essential vice of any socialist management. It is not an advantage to be ignorant of whether or not what one is doing is a suitable means of attaining the ends sought. A socialist management would be like a man forced to spend his life blindfolded.

It has been objected that the market system is at any rate quite inappropriate under the conditions brought about by a great war. If the market mechanism were to be left alone, it would be impossible for the government to get all the equipment needed. The scarce factors of production required for the production of armaments would be wasted for civilian uses which, in a war, are to be considered as less important, even as luxury and waste. Thus it was imperative to resort to the system of government-established priorities and to create the necessary bureaucratic apparatus.

The error of this reasoning is that it does not realize that the necessity for giving the government full power to determine for what kinds of production the various raw materials should be used is not an outcome of the war but of the methods applied in financing the war expenditure.

If the whole amount of money needed for the conduct of the war had been collected by taxes and by borrowing from the public, everybody would have been forced to restrict his consumption drastically. With a money income (after taxes) much lower than before, the consumers would have stopped buying many goods they used to buy before the war. The manufacturers, precisely because they are driven by the profit motive, would have discontinued producing such civilian goods and would have shifted to the production of those goods which the government, now by virtue of the inflow of taxes the biggest buyer on the market, would be ready to buy.

However, a great part of the war expenditure is financed by an increase of currency in circulation and by borrowing from the commercial banks. On the other hand, under price control, it is illegal to raise commodity prices. With higher money incomes and with unchanged commodity prices people would not only not have restricted but have increased their buying of goods for their own consumption. To avoid this, it was necessary to take recourse to rationing and to government-imposed priorites. These measures were needed because previous government interference that paralyzed the operation of the market resulted in paradoxical and highly unsatisfactory conditions. Not the insufficiency of the market mechanism but the inadequacy of previous government meddling with market phenomena made the priority system unavoidable. In this as in many other instances the bureaucrats see in the failure of their preceding measures a proof that further inroads into the market system are necessary.

2. Management under the Profit System

All business transactions are examined by shrewdly calculating profit and loss. New projects are subject to a precise scrutiny of the chances they offer. Every step toward their realization is reflected in entries in the books and accounts. The profit-and-loss account shows whether or not the whole business, or any of its parts, was profitable. The figures of the ledger serve as a guide for the conduct of the whole business and of each of its divisions. Branches which do not pay are discontinued, those yielding profit are expanded. There cannot be any question of clinging to unprofitable lines of business if there is no prospect of rendering them profitable in a not-too-distant future.

The elaborate methods of modern bookkeeping, accountancy, and business statistics provide the enterpriser with a faithful image of all his operations. He is in a position to learn how successful or unsuccessful every one of his transactions was. With the aid of these statements he can check the activities of all departments of his concern no matter how large it may be. There is, to be sure, some amount of discretion in determining the distribution of overhead costs. But apart from this, the figures provide a faithful reflection of all that is going on in every branch or department. The books and the balance sheets are the conscience of business. They are also the businessman's compass.

The devices of bookkeeping and accountancy are so familiar to the businessman that he fails to observe what a marvelous instrument they are. It needed a great poet and writer to appreciate them at their true value. Goethe called bookkeeping by double-entry "one of the finest inventions of the human mind." By means of this, he observed, the businessman can at any time survey the general whole, without needing to perplex himself with the details.[2]

Goethe's characterization hit the core of the matter. The virtue of commercial management lies precisely in the fact that it provides the manager with a method of surveying the whole and all its parts without being enmeshed in details and trifles.

The entrepreneur is in a position to separate the calculation of each part of his business in such a way that he can determine the role that it plays within his whole enterprise. For the public every firm or corporation is an undivided unity. But for the eye of its management it is composed of various sections, each of which is viewed as a separate entity and appreciated according to the share it contributes to the success of the whole enterprise. Within the system of business calculation each section represents an integral being, a hypothetical independent business as it were. It is assumed that this section "owns" a definite part of the whole capital employed in the enterprise, that it buys from other sections and sells to them, that it has its own expenses and its own revenues, that its dealings result either in a profit or a loss which is imputed to its own conduct of affairs as separate from the results achieved by the other sections. Thus the general manager of the whole enterprise can assign to each section's management a great deal of independence. There is no need for the general manager to bother about the minor details of each section's management. The managers of the various sections can have a free hand in the administration of their sections' "internal" affairs. The only directive that the general manager gives to the men whom he entrusts with the management of the various sections, departments, and branches is: Make as much profit as possible. And an examination of the accounts shows him how successful or unsuccessful they were in executing the directive.

In a large-scale enterprise many sections produce only parts or half-finished products which are not directly sold but are used by other sections in manufacturing the final product. This fact does not alter the conditions described. The general manager compares the costs incurred by the production of such parts and half-finished products with the prices he would have to pay for them if he had to buy them from other plants. He is always confronted by the question: Does it pay to produce these things in our own workshops? Would it not be more satisfactory to buy them from other plants specializing in their production?

Thus within the framework of a profit-seeking enterprise responsibility can be divided. Every submanager is responsible for the working of his department. It is to his credit if the accounts show a profit, and it is to his disadvantage if they show a loss. His own selfish interests push him toward the utmost care and exertion in the conduct of his section's affairs. If he incurs losses, he will be their victim. He will be replaced by another man whom the general manager expects to be more successful, or the whole section will be discontinued. At any rate he will be discharged and lose his job. If he succeeds in making profits, he will see his income increased or at least he will not be in danger of losing it. Whether or not a departmental manager is entitled to a share in the profit of his department is not so important with regard to the personal interest he takes in the results of his department's dealings. His fate is at any rate closely connected with that of his department. In working for it, he works not only for his boss but also for himself.

It would be impracticable to restrict the discretion of such a responsible sub-manager by too much interference with detail. If he is efficient, such meddling would at best be superfluous, if not harmful by tying his hands. If he is inefficient, it would not render his activities more successful. It would only provide him with a lame excuse that the failure was caused by his superior's inappropriate instructions. The only instruction required is self-understood and does not need to be especially mentioned: seek profit. Moreover, most of the details can and must be left to the head of every department.

This system was instrumental in the evolution of modern business. Large-scale production in great production aggregates and the establishment of subsidiaries in distant parts of the country and in foreign countries, the department stores, and the chain stores are all built upon the principle of the subordinate managers' responsibility. This does not in any way limit the responsibility of the general manager. The subordinates are responsible only to him. They do not free him from the duty of finding the right man for every job.

If a New York firm establishes branch shops or plants in Los Angeles, in Buenos Aires, in Budapest, and in Calcutta, the chief manager establishes the auxiliary's relation to the head office or parental company only in fairly general terms. All minor questions are to be within the range of the local manager's duties. The auditing department of headquarters carefully inspects the branch's financial transactions and informs the general manager as soon as any irregularities appear. Precautions are taken to prevent irreparable waste of the capital invested in the branch, a squandering of the whole concern's good will and reputation and a collision between the branch's policy and that of headquarters. But a free hand is left to the local management in every other regard. It is practicable to place confidence in the chief of a subsidiary, a department, or a section because his interests and those of the whole concern coincide. If he were to spend too much for current operations or to neglect an opportunity for profitable transactions, he would imperil not only the concern's profits but his own position as well. He is not simply a hired clerk whose only duty is the conscientious accomplishment of an assigned, definite task. He is a businessman himself, a junior partner as it were of the entrepreneur, no matter what the contractual and financial terms of his employment are. He must to the best of his abilities contribute to the success of the firm with which he is connected.

Because this is so, there is no danger in leaving important decisions to his discretion. He will not waste money in the purchase of products and services. He will not hire incompetent assistants and workers; he will not discharge able collaborators in order to replace them by incompetent personal friends or relatives. His conduct is subject to the incorruptible judgment of an unbribable tribunal: the account of profit and loss. In business there is only one thing that matters: success. The unsuccessful department manager is doomed no matter whether the failure was caused by him or not, or whether it would have been possible for him to attain a more satisfactory result. An unprofitable branch of business—sooner or later—must be discontinued, and its manager loses his job.

The sovereignty of the consumers and the democratic operation of the market do not stop at the doors of a big business concern. They permeate all its departments and branches. Responsibility to the consumer is the lifeblood of business and enterprise in an unhampered market society. The profit motive through the instrumentality of which the entrepreneurs are driven to serve the consumers to the best of their ability is at the same time the first principle of any commercial and industrial aggregate's internal organization. It joins together utmost centralization of the whole concern with almost complete autonomy of the parts, it brings into agreement full responsibility of the central management with a high degree of interest and incentive of the subordinate managers of sections, departments, and auxiliaries. It gives to the system of free enterprise that versatility and adaptability which result in an unswerving tendency toward improvement.

3. Personnel Management under an Unhampered Labor Market

The staff of modern large-scale enterprise sometimes includes many hundreds of thousands of clerks and workers. They form a highly differentiated body from the general manager or president down to the scrubwomen, messenger boys, and apprentices. The handling of such a huge body raises many problems. However, they can be solved.

No matter how big a concern may be, the central management deals only with sections, departments, branches, and subsidiaries, the role of which can be precisely determined from the evidence provided by the accounts and statistics. Of course, the accounts do not always demonstrate what may be wrong with a section. They show only that something is wrong, that it does not pay, and must be either reformed or discontinued. The sentences they pass are unappealable. They reveal each department's cash value. And it is cash value alone that matters on the market. The consumers are merciless. They never buy in order to benefit a less efficient producer and to protect him against the consequences of his failure to manage better. They want to be served as well as possible. And the working of the capitalist system forces the entrepreneur to obey the orders issued by the consumers. He does not have the power to distribute bounties at the expense of the consumers. He would waste his funds if he were to use his own money for such a purpose. He simply cannot pay anybody more than he can realize in selling the product.

The same relation that exists between the general manager and his immediate subordinates, the heads of the various sections, pervades the whole business hierarchy. Every section head values his immediate subordinates according to the same principle by which the chief manager values him, and the foreman applies similar methods in appraising his subordinates. The only difference is that under the simpler conditions of the lower units no elaborate accountancy schemes are required for the establishment of each man's cash value. It does not matter whether piece wages or hourly wages are paid. In the long run the worker can never get more than the consumer allows.

No man is infallible. It often happens that a superior errs in judging a subordinate. One of the qualifications required for any higher position is precisely the ability to judge people correctly. He who fails in this regard jeopardizes his chances of success. He hurts his own interests no less than those of the men whose efficiency he has underrated. Things being so, there is no need to look for special protection for the employees against arbitrariness on the part of their employers or their employer's mandatories. Arbitrariness in dealing with personnel is, under the unhampered profit system, an offense that strikes home to its author.

Under an unhampered market economy the appraisal of each individual's effort is detached from any personal considerations and can therefore be free both from bias and dislike. The market passes judgment on the products, not on the producers. The appraisal of the producer results automatically from the appraisal of his product. Each cooperator is valued according to the value of his contribution to the process of production of goods and services. Salaries and wages do not depend on arbitrary decisions. On the labor market every quantity and quality of work is prized to the amount the consumers are ready to pay for the products. It is not a favor on the part of the employer to pay wages and salaries, it is a business transaction, the purchase of a factor of production. The price of labor is a market phenomenon determined by the consumers' demands for goods and services. Virtually every employer is always in search of cheaper labor and every employee in search of a job with higher remuneration.

The very fact that labor is, under capitalism, a commodity and is bought and sold as a commodity makes the wage earner free from any personal dependence. Like the capitalists, the entrepreneurs, and the farmers, the wage earner depends on the arbitrariness of the consumers. But the consumers' choices do not concern the persons engaged in production; they concern things and not men. The employer is not in a position to indulge in favoritism or in prejudice with regard to personnel. As far as he does, the deed itself brings about its own penalty.

It is this fact, and not only constitutions and bills of rights, that makes the receivers of salaries and wages *within an unhampered capitalist system* free men. They are sovereign in their capacity as consumers, and as producers they are, like all other citizens, unconditionally subject to the law of the market. In selling a factor of production, namely, their toil and trouble, on the market at the market price to everybody who is ready to buy it, they do not jeopardize their own standing. They do not owe their employer thanks and subservience, they owe him a definite quantity of labor of a definite quality. The employer, on the other hand, is not in search of sympathetic men whom he likes but efficient workers who are worth the money he pays them.

This cool rationality and objectivity of capitalist relations is, of course, not realized to the same degree in the whole field of business. The nearer a man's function brings him to the consumers, the more personal factors interfere. In the service trades some role is played by sympathies and antipathies; relations are more "human." Stubborn doctrinaires and adamant baiters of capitalism are prepared to call this an advantage. In fact it curtails the businessman's and his employees' personal freedom. A small shopkeeper, a barber, an innkeeper, and an actor are not so free in expressing their political or religious convictions as the owner of a cotton mill or a worker in a steel plant.

But these facts do not invalidate the general characteristics of the market system. It is a system which automatically values every man according to the services he renders to the body of sovereign consumers, i.e., to his fellow men. . . .

4. The Essential Features of Bureaucratic Management

The lawyers, the philosophers, and the politicians look upon the supremacy of the law from another angle than does this book. From their point of view the main function of the law is to limit the power of the authorities and the courts to inflict evils upon the individual citizen and to restrict his freedom. If one assigns to the authorities the power to imprison or even to kill people, one must restrict and clearly circumscribe this power. Otherwise the officeholder or judge would turn into an irresponsible despot. The law determines under what conditions the judge should have the right and the duty to sentence and the policeman to fire his gun. The law protects the people against the arbitrariness of those in office.

The viewpoint of this book is somewhat different. We are dealing here with bureaucracy as a principle of administrative technique and organization. This book looks upon the rules and regulations not merely as measures for the protection of the people and for safeguarding the citizen's rights and freedom but as measures for the execution of the will of the supreme authority. The need to limit the discretion of subordinates is present in every organization. Any organization would disintegrate in the absence of such restrictions. Our task is to investigate the peculiar characteristics of bureaucratic management as distinguished from commercial management.

Bureaucratic management is management bound to comply with detailed rules and regulations fixed by the authority of a superior body. The task of the bureaucrat is to perform what these rules and regulations order him to do. His discretion to act according to his own best conviction is seriously restricted by them.

Business management or profit management is management directed by the profit motive. The objective of business management is to make a profit. As success or failure to attain this end can be ascertained by accounting not only for the whole business concern but also for any of its parts, it is feasible to decentralize both management and accountability without jeopardizing the unity of operations and the attainment of their goal. Responsibility can be divided. There is no need to limit the discretion of subordinates by any rules or regulations other than that underlying all business activities, namely, to render their operations profitable.

The objectives of public administration cannot be measured in money terms and cannot be checked by accountancy methods. Take a nation-wide police system like the F.B.I. There is no yardstick available that could establish whether the expenses incurred by one of its regional or local branches were not excessive. The expenditures of a police station are not reimbursed by its successful management and do not vary in proportion to the success attained. If the head of the whole bureau were to leave his subordinate station chiefs a free hand with regard to money expenditure, the result would be a large increase in costs as every one of them would be zealous to improve the service of his branch as much as possible. It would become impossible for the top executive to keep the expenditures within the appropriations allocated by the representatives of the people or within any limits whatever. It is not because of punctiliousness that the administrative regulations fix how much can be spent by each local office for cleaning the premises, for furniture repairs, and for lighting and heating. Within a business concern such things can be left without hesitation to the discretion of the responsible local manager. He will not spend more than necessary because it is, as it were, his money; if he wastes the concern's money, he jeopardizes the branch's profit and thereby indirectly hurts his own interests. But it is another matter with the local chief of a government agency. In spending more money he can, very often at least, improve the result of his conduct of affairs. Thrift must be imposed on him by regimentation.

In public administration there is no connection between revenue and expenditure. The public services are spending money only; the insignificant income derived from special sources (for example, the sale of printed matter by the Government Printing Office) is more or less accidental. The revenue derived from customs and taxes is not "produced" by the administrative apparatus. Its source is the law, not the activities of customs officers and tax collectors. It is not the merit of a collector of internal revenue that the residents of his district are richer and pay higher taxes than those of another district. The time and effort required for the administrative handling of an income tax return are not in proportion to the amount of the taxable income it concerns.

In public administration there is no market price for achievements. This makes it indispensable to operate public offices according to principles entirely different from those applied under the profit motive.

Now we are in a position to provide a definition of bureaucratic management: Bureaucratic management is the method applied in the conduct of administrative affairs the result of which has no cash value on the market. Remember: we do not say that a successful handling of public affairs has no value, but that it has no price on the market, that its value cannot be realized in a market transaction and consequently cannot be expressed in terms of money.

If we compare the conditions of two countries, say Atlantis and Thule, we can establish many important statistical figures of each of them: the size of the area and of the population, the birth rate and the death rate, the number of illiterates, of crimes committed, and many other demographical data. We can determine the sum of the money income of all its citizens, the money value of the yearly social product, the money value of the goods imported and exported, and many other economic data. But we cannot assign any arithmetical value to the system of government and administration. That does not mean that we deny the importance or the value of good government. It means only that no yardstick can measure these things. They are not liable to an expression in figures.

It may well be that the greatest thing in Atlantis is its good system of government. It may be that Atlantis owes its prosperity to its constitutional and administrative institutions. But we cannot compare them with those of Thule in the same way as we can compare other things, for instance, wage rates or milk prices.

Bureaucratic management is management of affairs which cannot be checked by economic calculation.

5. The Crux of Bureaucratic Management

The plain citizen compares the operation of the bureaus with the working of the profit system, which is more familiar to him. Then he discovers that bureaucratic management is wasteful, inefficient, slow, and rolled up in red tape. He simply cannot understand how reasonable people allow such a mischievous system to endure. Why not adopt the well-tried methods of private business?

However, such criticisms are not sensible. They misconstrue the features peculiar to public administration. They are not aware of the fundamental difference between government and profit-seeking private enterprise. What they call deficiencies and faults of the management of administrative agencies are necessary properties. A bureau is not a profit-seeking enterprise; it cannot make use of any economic calculation; it has to solve problems which are unknown to business management. It is out of the question to improve its management by reshaping it according to the pattern of private business. It is a mistake to judge the efficiency of a government department by comparing it with the working of an enterprise subject to the interplay of market factors.

There are, of course, in every country's public administration manifest shortcomings which strike the eye of every observer. People are sometimes shocked by the degree of maladministration. But if one tries to go to their roots, one often learns that they are not simply the result of culpable negligence or lack of competence. They sometimes turn out to be the result of special political and institutional conditions or of an attempt to come to an arrangement with a problem for which a more satisfactory solution could not be found. A detailed scrutiny of all the difficulties involved may convince an honest investigator that, given the general state of political forces, he himself would not have known how to deal with the matter in a less objectionable way.

It is vain to advocate a bureaucratic reform through the appointment of businessmen as heads of various departments. The quality of being an entrepreneur is not inherent in the personality of the entrepreneur; it is inherent in the position which he occupies in the framework of market society. A former entrepreneur who is given charge of a government bureau is in this capacity no longer a businessman but a bureaucrat. His objective can no longer be profit, but compliance with the rules and regulations. As head of a bureau he may have the power to alter some minor rules and some matters of internal procedure. But the setting of the bureau's activities is determined by rules and regulations which are beyond his reach.

It is a widespread illusion that the efficiency of government bureaus could be improved by management engineers and their methods of scientific management. However, such plans stem from a radical misconstruction of the objectives of civil government.

Like any kind of engineering, management engineering too is conditioned by the availability of a method of calculation. Such a method exists in profit-seeking business. Here the profit-and-loss statement is supreme. The problem of bureaucratic management is precisely the absence of such a method of calculation.

In the field of profit-seeking enterprise the objective of the management engineer's activities is clearly determined by the primacy of the profit motive. His task is to reduce costs without impairing the market value of the result or to reduce costs more than the ensuing reduction of the market value of the result or to raise the market value of the result more than the required rise in costs. But in the field of government the result has no price on a market. It can neither be bought nor sold.

Let us consider three examples.

A police department has the job of protecting a defense plant against sabotage. It assigns thirty patrolmen to this duty. The responsible commissioner does not need the advice of an efficiency expert in order to discover that he could save money by reducing the guard to only twenty men. But the question is: Does this economy outweigh the increase in risk? There are serious things at stake: national defense, the morale of the armed forces and of civilians, repercussions in the field of foreign affairs, the lives of many upright workers. All these valuable things cannot be assessed in terms of money. The responsibility rests entirely with Congress allocating the appropriations required and with the executive branch of the Government. They cannot evade it by leaving the decision to an irresponsible adviser.

One of the tasks of the Bureau of Internal Revenue is the final determination of taxes due. Its duty is the interpretation and application of the law. This is not merely a clerical job; it is a kind of judicial function. Any taxpayer objecting to the Commissioner's interpretation of the law is free to bring suit in a Federal court to recover the amount paid. Of what use can the efficiency engineer with his time and motion studies be for the conduct of these affairs? His stop watch would be in the wrong place in the office rooms of the bureau. It is obvious that—other things being equal—a clerk who works more quickly is a more desirable employee than another who is slower. But the main problem is the quality of the performance. Only the experienced senior clerks are in a position to appreciate duly the achievements of their aides. Intellectual work cannot be measured and valued by mechanical devices.

Let us finally consider an instance in which neither problems of "higher" politics nor those of the correct application of the law are involved. A bureau is in charge of buying all the supplies needed for the technical conduct of office work. This is a comparatively simple job. But it is by no means a mechanical job. The best clerk is not he who fills out the greatest number of orders in an hour. The most satisfactory performance is to buy the most appropriate materials at the cheapest price.

It is therefore, as far as the management of government is concerned, not correct to assert that time study, motion study, and other tools of scientific management "show with reasonable accuracy how much time and effort are required for each of the available methods" and that they therefore "can show which of the possible methods and procedures require the least time and effort."[3] All such things are quite useless because they cannot be coordinated to the quality of the work done. Speed alone is not a measure of intellectual work. You cannot "measure" a doctor according to the time he employs in examining one case. And you cannot "measure" a judge according to the time he needs to adjudicate one case.

If a businessman manufactures some article destined for export into foreign countries, he is eager to reduce the man-hours spent for the production of the various parts of the commodity in question. But the license required for shipping this commodity abroad is not a part of the commodity. The government in issuing a license does not contribute anything to the production, the marketing, and the shipping of this commodity. Its bureau is not a workshop turning out one of the parts needed for the finishing of the product. What the government aims at in making exports depend on the grant of a license is restraint of export trade. It wants to reduce the total volume of exports or the volume exported by undesirable exporters or sold to undesirable buyers. The issuance of licenses is not the objective but a technical device for its attainment. From the point of view of the government the licenses refused or not even applied for are more important than those granted. It would therefore not be to the purpose to take "the total man-hours spent per license" as the standard of the bureau's performance. It would be unsuitable to perform "the operation of processing the licenses . . . on an assembly line basis."[4]

There are other differences. If in the course of a manufacturing process a piece gets spoiled or lost, the result is a precisely limited increase in production costs. But if a license application is lost in the bureau, serious damage may be inflicted upon a citizen. The law may prevent the individual harmed from suing the bureau for indemnification. But the political and moral liability of the government to deal with these applications in a very careful way remains nonetheless.

The conduct of government affairs is as different from the industrial processes as is prosecuting, convicting, and sentencing a murderer from the growing of corn or the manufacturing of shoes. Government efficiency and industrial efficiency are entirely different things. A factory's management cannot be improved by taking a police department for its model, and a tax collector's office cannot become more efficient by adopting the methods of a motor-car plant. Lenin was mistaken in holding up the government's bureaus as a pattern for industry. But those who want to make the management of the bureaus equal to that of the factories are no less mistaken.

There are many things about government administration which need to be reformed. Of course, all human institutions must again and again be adjusted anew to the change of conditions. But no reform could transform a public office into a sort of private enterprise. A government is not a profit-seeking enterprise. The conduct of its affairs cannot be checked by profit-and-loss statements. Its achievement cannot be valued in terms of money. This is fundamental for any treatment of the problems of bureaucracy.

6. Bureaucratic Personnel Management

A bureaucrat differs from a nonbureaucrat precisely because he is working in a field in which it is impossible to appraise the result of a man's effort in terms of money. The nation spends money for the upkeep of the bureaus, for the payment of salaries and wages, and for the purchase of all the equipment and materials needed. But what it gets for the expenditure, the service rendered, cannot be appraised in terms of money, however important and valuable this "output" may be. Its appraisal depends on the discretion of the government.

It is true that the appraisal of the various commodities sold and bought on the market depends no less on discretion, that is, on the discretion of the consumers. But as the consumers are a vast body of different people, an anonymous and amorphous aggregation, the judgments they pass are congealed into an impersonal phenomenon, the market price, and are thus severed from their arbitrary origin. Moreover, they refer to commodities and services as such, not to their performers. The seller-buyer nexus as well as the employer-employee relation, in profit-seeking business are purely matter of fact and impersonal. It is a deal from which both parties derive an advantage. They mutually contribute to each other's living. But it is different with a bureaucratic organization. There the nexus between superior and subordinate is personal. The subordinate depends on the superior's judgment of his personality, not of his work. As long as the office clerk can rely on his chances of getting a job with private business, this dependence cannot become so oppressive as to mark the clerk's whole character. But it is different under the present trend toward general bureaucratization.

The American scene until a few years ago did not know the bureaucrat as a particular type of human being. There were always bureaus and they were, by necessity, operated in a bureaucratic way. But there was no numerous class of men who considered work in the public offices their exclusive calling. There was a continuous change of personnel between government jobs and private jobs. Under civil service provisions public service became a regular career. Appointments were based on examinations and no longer depended on the political affiliation of the applicants. Many remained in public bureaus for life. But they retained their personal independence because they could always consider a return to private jobs.

It was different in continental Europe. There the bureaucrats have long formed an integrated group. Only for a few eminent men was a return to nonofficial life practically open. The majority were tied up with the bureaus for life. They developed a character peculiar to their permanent removal from the world of profit-seeking business. Their intellectual horizon was the hierarchy and its rules and regulations. Their fate was to depend entirely on the favor of their superiors. They were subject to their sway not only when on duty. It was understood that their private activities also—and even those of their wives—had to be appropriate to the dignity of their position and to a special—unwritten—code of conduct becoming to a *Staatsbeamter* or *fonctionnaire*. It was expected that they would endorse the political viewpoint of the cabinet ministers who happened at the time to be in office. At any rate their freedom to support a party of opposition was sensibly curtailed.

The emergence of a large class of such men dependent on the government became a serious menace to the maintenance of constitutional institutions. Attempts were made to protect the individual clerk against arbitrariness on the part of his superiors. But the only result achieved was that discipline was relaxed and that looseness in the performance of the duties spread more and more.

America is a novice in the field of bureaucracy. It has much less experience in this matter than the classical countries of bureaucracy, France, Germany, Austria, and Russia, acquired. In the United States there still prevails a leaning toward an overvaluation of the usefulness of civil-service regulations. Such regulations require that the applicants be a certain age, graduate from certain schools, and pass certain examinations. For promotion to higher ranks and higher salary a certain number of years spent in the lower ranks and the passing of further examinations are required. It is obvious that all such requirements refer to things more or less superficial. There is no need to point out that school attendance, examinations, and years spent in the lower positions do not necessarily qualify a man for a higher job. This machinery for selection sometimes bars the most competent men from a job and does not always prevent the appointment of an utter incompetent. But the worst effect produced is that the main concern of the clerks is to comply with these and other formalities. They forget that their job is to perform an assigned duty as well as possible.

In a properly arranged civil-service system the promotion to higher ranks depends primarily on seniority. The heads of the bureaus are for the most part old men who know that after a few years they will be retired. Having spent the greater part of their lives in subordinate positions, they have lost vigor and initiative. They shun innovations and improvements. They look on every project for reform as a disturbance of their quiet. Their rigid conservatism frustrates all endeavors of a cabinet minister to adjust the service to changed conditions. They look down upon the cabinet minister as an inexperienced layman. In all countries with a settled bureaucracy people used to say: The cabinets come and go, but the bureaus remain.

It would be a mistake to ascribe the frustration of European bureaucratism to intellectual and moral deficiencies of the personnel. In all these countries there were many good families whose scions chose the bureaucratic career because they were honestly intent on serving their nation. The ideal of a bright poor boy who wanted to attain a better station in life was to join the staff of the administration. Many of the most gifted and lofty members of the intelligentsia served in the bureaus. The prestige and the social standing of the government clerks surpassed by far those of any other class of the population with the exception of the army officers and the members of the oldest and wealthiest aristocratic families.

Many civil servants published excellent treatises dealing with the problems of administrative law and statistics. Some of them were in their leisure hours brilliant writers or musicians. Others entered the field of politics and became eminent party leaders. Of course, the bulk of the bureaucrats were rather mediocre men. But it cannot be doubted that a considerable number of able men were to be found in the ranks of the government employees.

The failure of European bureaucracy was certainly not due to incapacities of the personnel. It was an outcome of the unavoidable weakness of any administration of public affairs. The lack of standards which could, in an unquestionable way, ascertain success or nonsuccess in the performance of an official's duties creates insoluble problems. It kills ambition, destroys initiative and the incentive to do more than the minimum required. It makes the bureaucrat look at instructions, not at material and real success.

Notes

1. These observations do not imply any criticism of the prewar policies pursued by the British and American authorities. Only a man who had knowledge of the military events of 1941–43 many years before they occurred would have the right to blame other people for their lack of foresight. Governments are not omniscient, as the planners would have us believe.

2. *Wilhelm Meister's Apprenticeship*, Book I, chap. 10.

3. J. M. Juran, *Bureaucracy, a Challenge to Better Management* (New York, 1944), p. 75.

4. J. M. Juran, *loc. cit.*,pp. 34, 76.

WALTER BLOCK*

A Free Market in Roads

(What would it be like to have a free market in roads?[1]) *All* transport thoroughfares would be privately owned: not only the vehicles, buses, trains, automobiles, trolleys, etc., that travel upon them, but the very roads, highways, byways, streets, sidewalks, bridges, tunnels, crosswalks themselves upon which journeys take place. The transit corridors would be as privately owned as is our fast food industry.

As such, all the usual benefits and responsibilities that are incumbent upon private enterprise would affect roads. The reason a company or individual would want to build or buy an already existing road would be the same as in any other business—to earn a profit. The necessary funds would be raised in a similar manner—by floating an issue of stock, by borrowing, or from past savings of the owner. The risks would be the same—attracting customers and prospering, or failing to do so and going bankrupt. Likewise for the pricing policy; just as private enterprise rarely gives burgers away for free, use of road space would require payment. A road enterprise would face virtually all of the problems shared by other businesses: attracting a labor force, subcontracting, keeping customers satisfied, meeting the price of competitors, innovating, borrowing money, expanding, etc. Thus, a highway or street owner would be a businessman as any other, with much the same problems, opportunities, and risks.

In addition, just as in other business, there would be facets peculiar to this particular industry. The road entrepreneur would have to try to contain congestion, reduce traffic accidents, plan and design new facilities in coordination with already existing highways, as well as with the plans of others for new expansion. He would have to set up the "rules of the road" so as best to accomplish these and other goals. The road industry would be expected to carry on each and every one of the tasks now undertaken by public roads authorities: fill potholes, install road signs, guard rails, maintain lane markings, repair traffic signals, and so on for the myriad of "road furniture" that keeps traffic moving.

Applying the concepts of profit and loss to the road industry, we can see why privatization would almost certainly mean a gain compared to the present nationalized system of road management.

From the *Journal of Libertarian Studies*, Vol. 3 (Summer 1979)
*The Fraser Institute, B. C.

As far as safety is concerned, presently there is no road manager who loses financially if the accident rate on "his" turnpike increases, or is higher than other comparable avenues of transportation. A civil servant draws his annual salary regardless of the accident toll piled up under his domain. But if he were a *private* owner of the road in question, in competition with numerous other highway companies (as well as other modes of transit such as airlines, trains, boats, etc.), completely dependent for financial sustenance on the voluntary payments of satisfied customers, then he would indeed lose out if his road compiled a poor safety record (assuming that customers desire, and are willing to pay for, safety). He would, then, have every incentive to try to reduce accidents, whether by technological innovations, better rules of the road, improved methods of selecting out drunken and other undesirable drivers, etc. If he failed, or did less well than his competition, he eventually would be removed from his position of responsibility. Just as we now expect better mousetraps from a private enterprise system which rewards success and penalizes failure, so could we count on a private ownership setup to improve highway safety. Thus, as a partial answer to the challenge that private ownership would mean the deaths of millions of people in traffic accidents, we reply, "There are, at *present*, millions of people who have been slaughtered on our nation's highways; a changeover to the enterprise system would lead to a precipitous *decline* in the death and injury rate, due to the forces of competition."

Another common objection to private roads is the spectre of having to halt every few feet and toss a coin into a tollbox. This simply would not occur on the market. To see why not, imagine a commercial golf course operating on a similar procedure: forcing the golfers to wait in line at every hole, or demanding payment every time they took a swipe at the ball. It is easy to see what would happen to the cretinous management of such an enterprise: it would very rapidly lose customers and go broke.

If roads were privately owned, the same process would occur. Any road with say, 500 toll booths per mile, would be avoided like the plague by customers, who would happily patronize a road with fewer obstructions, even at a higher money cost per mile. This would be a classical case of economies of scale, where it would pay entrepreneurs to buy the toll collection rights from the millions of holders, in order to rationalize the system into one in which fewer toll gates blocked the roads. Streets that could be so organized would prosper as thoroughfares; others would not. So even if the system somehow *began* in this patchwork manner, market forces would come to bear, mitigating the extreme inefficiency.

There is no reason, however, to begin the market experiment in this way. Instead of arbitrarily assigning each house on the block a share of the road equal to its frontage multiplied by one-half the width of the street in front of it (the way in which the previous example was presumably generated in someone's nightmare vision), there are other methods more in line with historical reality and with the libertarian theory of homesteading property rights.

One scenario would follow the shopping center model: a single owner-builder would buy a section of territory, build roads, and (fronting them) houses. Just as many shopping center builders maintain control over parking lots, malls, and other "in common" areas, the entrepreneur would continue the operation of common areas such as the roads, sidewalks, etc. Primarily residential streets might be built in a meandering, roundabout manner replete with cul-de-sacs, to discourage through travel. Tolls for residents, guests, and deliveries might be pegged at low levels, or be entirely lacking (as in the case of modern shopping centers), while through traffic might be charged at prohibitive rates. Standing in the wings, ensuring that the owner effectively discharges his responsibilities, would be the profit and loss system.

Consider now a road whose main function is to facilitate through traffic. If it is owned by one person or company, who either built it or bought the rights of passage from the previous owners, it would be foolish for him to install dozens of toll gates per mile. In fact, toll gates would probably not be the means of collection employed by a road owner at all. There now exist highly inexpensive electrical devices[2] which can register the passage of an automobile past any fixed point on a road. Were suitable identifying electronic tapes attached to the surface of each road vehicle, there would be no need for a time-wasting, labor costly system of toll collection points. Rather, as the vehicle passes the check point, the electrical impulse set up can be transmitted to a computer which can produce one monthly bill for all roads used, and even mail it out automatically. Road payments could be facilitated in as unobtrusive a manner as utility bills are now.

Then there is the eminent domain challenge: the allegation that roads could not be efficiently constructed without the intermediation of government-imposed eminent domain laws which are not at the disposal of private enterprise. The argument is without merit.

We must first realize that even *with* eminent domain, and under the system of government road construction, there are *still* limits as to where a new road may be placed. Not even a government could last long if it decided to tear down all the skyscrapers in Chicago's Loop in order to make way for yet another highway. The logic of this limitation is obvious: it would cost billions of dollars to replace these magnificent structures; a new highway *near* these buildings, but one which did not necessitate their destruction, might well be equally valuable, but at an infinitesimal fraction of the cost.

With or without eminent domain, then, such a road could not be built. Private enterprise could not afford to do so, because the gains in siting the road over carcasses of valuable buildings would not be worthwhile; nor could the government accomplish this task, while there was still some modicum of common sense prohibiting it from operating completely outside of any economic bounds.

It is true that owners of land generally thought worthless by other people would be able to ask otherwise exorbitant prices from a developer intent upon building a straight road. Some of these landowners would demand high prices because of psychic attachment (e.g., the treasured old homestead); others solely because they knew that building plans called for their particular parcels, and they were determined to obtain the maximum income possible.

But the private road developer is not without defenses, all of which will tend to lower the price he must pay. First, there is no necessity for an absolutely straight road, nor even for one that follows the natural contours of the land. Although one may prefer, on technical grounds, path A, it is usually possible to utilize path B . . . . . Z, all at variously higher costs. If so, then the *cheapest* of these alternatives provides an upper limit to what the owners along path A may charge for their properties. For example, it may be cheaper to blast through an uninhabited mountain rather than pay the exorbitant price of the farmer in the valley; this fact tends to put a limit upon the asking price of the valley farmer.

Secondly, the road developer, knowing that he will be satisfied with any of five trajectories, can purchase *options* to buy the land along each site. If a recalcitrant holdout materializes on any one route, he can shift to his second, third, fourth or fifth choice. The competition between owners along each of these passageways will tend to keep the price down.

Thirdly, in the rare case of a holdout who possesses an absolutely essential plot, it is always possible to build a bridge *over* this land or to tunnel underneath. Ownership of land does not consist of property rights up to the sky or down to the core of the earth; the owner cannot forbid planes from passing overhead, nor can he prohibit a bridge over his land, as long as it does not interfere with the use of his land. Although vastly more expensive than a surface road, these options again put an upper bound on the price the holdout can insist upon.

There is also the fact that land values are usually influenced by their neighborhood. What contributes to the value of residence is the existence of neighboring homes, which supply neighbors, friends, companionship. Similarly, the value of a commercial enterprise is enhanced by the proximity of other businesses, customers, contacts, even competitors. In New York City, the juxtapositon of stock brokerage firms, flower wholesalers, a jewelry exchange, a garment district, etc., all attest to the value of being located near competitors. If a road 150 feet wide sweeps through, completely disrupting this "neighborliness," much of the value of the stubborn landowner's property is dissipated. The risk of being isolated again puts limitations upon the price which may be demanded.

In an out-of-the-way, rural setting, a projected road may not be expected to attract the large number of cash customers necessary to underwrite lavish expenditures on the property of holdouts. However, it will be easier to find alternative routes in a sparsely settled area. Urban locations present the opposite problem: it will be more difficult to find low-cost alternatives, but the expected gains from a road which is expected to carry millions of passengers may justify higher payments for the initial assemblage.

Of course, eminent domain is a great facilitator; it eases the process of land purchase. Seemingly, pieces of land are joined together at an exceedingly low cost. But the *real* costs of assemblage are thereby concealed. Landowners are forced to give up their property at prices determined to be "fair" by the federal bureaucracy, not at prices to which they voluntarily agree. While it appears that private enterprise would have to pay more than the government, this is incorrect. The market will have to pay the full, voluntary price, but this will, paradoxically, be *less* than the government's real payment (its money payments *plus* the values it has forcibly taken from the original owners). This is true because the profit incentive to reduce costs is completely lacking in state "enterprise." Furthermore, the extra costs undergone by the government in the form of bribes, rigged bidding, cost-plus contracts, etc., often would bloat even limited government money outlays past the full costs of private road developers.

Another objection against a system of private roads is the danger of being isolated. The typical nightmare vision runs somewhat as follows: "A man buys a piece of land. He builds a house on it. He stocks it with food, and then brings his family to join him. When they are all happily ensconced, they learn that the road fronting their little cottage has been purchased by an unscrupulous street owning corporation, which will not allow him or his family the use of the road at any but an indefinitely high price. The family may "live happily ever after", but only as long as they keep to their own house. Since the family is too poor to afford a helicopter, the scheming road owner has the family completely in his power. He may starve them into submission, if he so desires."

This does indeed appear frightening, but only because we are not accustomed to dealing with such a problem. It could not exist under the present system, so it is difficult to see how it could be solved by free market institutions. Yet, the answer is simple: no one would buy any plot of land without first insuring that he had the right to enter and leave at will. [3]

Similar contracts are now commonplace on the market, and they give rise to no such blockade problems. Flea markets often rent out tables to separate merchandisers; gold and diamond exchanges usually sublet booths to individual, small merchants; desk space is sometimes available to people who cannot afford an entire office of their own. The suggestion that these contracts are unworkable or unfeasible, on the grounds that the owner of the property might prohibit access to his subtenant, could only be considered ludicrous. Any lawyer who allowed a client to sign a lease which did not specify the rights of access in advance would be summarily fired, if not disbarred. This is true in the present, and would also apply in an era of private roads.

It is virtually impossible to predict the exact future contour of an industry that does not presently exist. The task is roughly comparable to foretelling the makeup of the airline industry immediately after the Wright Brothers' experiments at Kitty Hawk. How many companies would there be? How many aircraft would each one own? Where would they land? Who would train the pilots? Where could tickets be purchased? Would food and movies be provided in flight? What kinds of uniforms would be worn by the stewardesses? Where would the financing come from? These are all questions not only impossible to have answered at that time, but ones that could hardly have arisen. Were an early advocate of a "private airline industry" pressed to point out, in minute detail, all the answers in order to defend the proposition that his idea was sound, he would have had to fail.

In like manner, advocates of free market roads are in no position to set up *the* blueprint for a future private market in transport. They cannot tell how many road owners there will be, what kind of rules of the road they will set up, how much it will cost per mile, how the entrepreneurs will seek to reduce traffic accidents, whether road shoulders will be wider or narrower, or which steps will be taken in order to reduce congestion. Nor can we answer many of the thousands of such questions that are likely to arise.

For one thing, these are not the *kinds* of questions that can be answered in advance with any degree of precision, and not only in transportation. The same limitations would have faced early attempts to specify industrial setups in computers, televisions, or any other industry. It is impossible to foretell the future of industrial events because, given a free market situation, they are the result of the actions of an entire cooperating economy, even though these actions may not be intended by any individual actor. [4] Each person bases his actions on the limited knowledge at his disposal.

Nevertheless, we shall attempt a scenario, though not for the purpose of mapping out, forevermore, the shape of the road market of the future. We realize that such patterns must arise out of the actions of millions of market participants, and will be unknown to any of them in advance. Yet if we are to consider objections to a road market intelligently, we must present a general outline of how such a market *might* function. We will now consider some problems that might arise for a road market, and some possible solutions.

1. Who will decide upon the rules of the road?

This question seems important because we are accustomed to governments determining the rules of the road. Some people even go so far as to *justify* the very existence of government on the ground that *someone* has to fashion highway rules, and that government seems to be the only candidate.

In the free market, each road owner will decide upon the rules his customers are to follow, just as nowadays rules for proper behavior in some locations are, to a great extent, determined by the owner of the property in question. Thus, roller and ice skating emporia decide when and where their patrons may wander, with or without skates. Bowling alleys usually require special bowling shoes, and prohibit going past a certain line in order to knock down the pins. Restaurants demand that diners communicate with their waiter and busboy, and not go marching into the kitchen to consult with the chef.

There are no "God-given" rules of the road. While it might have been convenient had Moses been given a list of the ten best rules for the road, he was not. Nor have legislators been given any special dispensations from on high. It is therefore man's lot to *discover* what rules can best minimize costs and accidents, and maximize speed and comfort. There is no better means of such discovery than the competitive process. Mr. Glumph of the Glumph Highway Company decides upon a set of rules. Each of his competitors decides upon a (slightly) different version. Then the consumer, by his choice to patronize or not, supports one or the other. To the extent that he patronizes Glumph and avoids his competitors, he underwrites and supports Glumph's original decisions. If Glumph loses too many customers, he will be forced to change his rules (or other practices) or face bankruptcy. In this way the forces of the market will be unleashed to do their share in aiding the discovery process. We may never reach the all-perfect set of rules that maximizes the attainment of all conceivable goals, but the *tendency* toward this end will always operate.

2. If a free market in roads is allowed and bankruptcies occur, what will be done about the havoc created for the people dependent upon them?

Bankrupt road companies may well result from the operations of the market. There are insolvencies in every area of the economy, and it would be unlikely for this curse to pass by the road sector. Far from a calamity, however, bankruptcies are paradoxically a sign of a *healthy* economy.

Bankruptcies have a *function*. Stemming from managerial error in the face of changing circumstances, bankruptcies have several beneficial effects. They may be a signal that consumers can no longer achieve maximum benefit from a stretch of land used as a highway; there may be an alternative use that is ranked higher. Although the subject might never arise under public stewardship, surely *sometime* in the past ten centuries there were roads constructed which (from the vantage point of the present) should not have been built; or, even if they were worth building originally, have long since outlasted their usefulness. We *want* a capacity in our system to acknowledge mistakes, *and then act so as to correct them.* The system of public ownership is deficient, in comparison, precisely because bankruptcy and conversion to a more valuable use never exists as a serious alternative. The mistakes are, rather, "frozen in concrete," never to be changed.

Would we really want to apply the present non-bankruptcy system now prevailing in government road management to any other industry? Would it be more efficient to maintain every single grocery store, once built, forevermore? Of course not. It is part of the *health* of the grocery industry that stores no longer needed are allowed to pass on, making room for those in greater demand. No less is true of the roadway industry. Just as it is important for the functioning of the body that dead cells be allowed to disappear, making way for new life, so is it necessary for the proper functioning of our roadway network that some roads be allowed to pass away.

Bankruptcy may serve a second purpose. A business may fail not because there is no longer any need for the road, but because private management is so inept that it cannot attract and hold enough passengers to meet all its costs. In this case, the function served by bankruptcy proceedings would be to relieve the ineffective owners of the road, put it into the hands of the creditors and, subsequently, into the hands of better management.

3. How would traffic snarls be countered in the free market?

If the roads in an entire section of town (e.g., the upper east side of Manhattan), or all of the streets in a small city were completely under the control of one company, traffic congestion would present no new problem. The only difference between this and the present arrangement would be that a private company, not the government road authority, would be in charge. As such, we could only expect the forces of competition to improve matters.

For example, one frequent blocker of traffic, and one which in no way aids the overall movement of motorists, is the automobile caught in an intersection when the light has changed. This situation arises from entering an intersecting cross street, in the hope of making it across so that, when the light changes, one will be ahead of vehicles turning off that street. In the accompanying diagram #1 (see below) a motorist is traveling west along the Side Street. Although the Side Street west of Main Street is chock full of cars, he nevertheless enters the intersection between Main Street and Side Street; he hopes that, by the time Main Street again enjoys the green light, the cars ahead of him will move forward, leaving room for him to leave the intersection.

All too often, however, what happens is that traffic ahead of him on Side Street remains stationary, and the motorist gets caught in the middle of the intersection.

Diagram 1

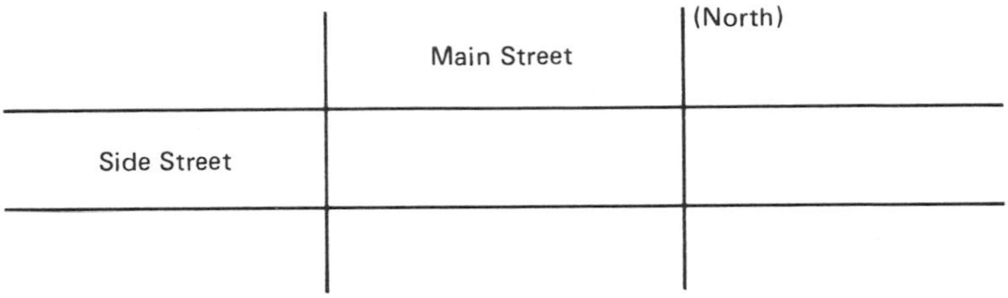

Then, even when the traffic is signaled to move north on Main Street, it cannot; because of the impatience of our motorist, he and his fellows are now stuck in the intersection, blocking northbound traffic. If this process is repeated on the four intersections surrounding one city block (see diagram #2) it can (and does) bring traffic in the entire surrounding area to a virtual standstill.

Diagram 2

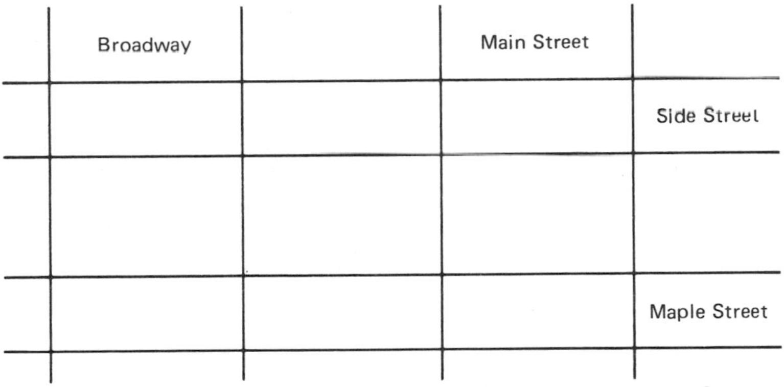

Currently, government regulations prohibit entering an intersection when there is no room on the other side. This rule is beside the point. The question is not whether a traffic system legally *calls for* certain actions, but whether this rule *succeeds* or not. If the mere passage of a law could suffice, all that would be needed to return to the Garden of Eden would be "enabling legislation." What is called for, in addition to the proper rules of the road, is the actual attainment of motorists' conformity with those rules. As far as *this* problem is concerned, private road companies have a comparative advantage over governments. For, as we have seen, if a government fails in this kind of mission, there is no process whereby it is relieved of its duties; whereas, let a private enterprise fail and retribution, in the form of bankruptcy, will be swift and total. Another street company, and still another, if needed, will evolve through the market process, to improve matters.

It is impossible to tell, in advance, what means the private street companies will employ to rid their territories of this threat.

Just as private universities, athletic stadiums, etc., now enforce rules whose purpose is the smooth functioning of the facility, so might road owners levy fines to ensure obedience to rules. For example, automobiles stuck in an intersection could be registered by the road's computer-monitoring system, and charged an extra amount for this driving infraction, on an itemized bill.*

4. What problems would ensue of each street owned by a separate company, or individual?

It might appear that the problems are insoluble. For each owner would seem to have an incentive to *encourage* motorists on his own street to try as hard as they can to get to the next block, to the total disregard of traffic on the cross street. (The more vehicles passing through, the greater the charges that can be levied.) Main Street, in this scenario, would urge its patrons, traveling north, to get into the intersection between it and Side Street, so as to pass on when the next light changed. The Side Street management would do the same: embolden the drivers heading west to try to cross over Main Street, regardless whether there was room on the other side. Each street owner would, in this view, take an extremely narrow stance; he would try to maximize his own profits, and not overly concern himself wtih imposing costs on the others.

The answer to this dilemma is that it could never occur in a free market, based on specified individual private property rights. For in such a system, *all* aspects of the roadway are owned, including the *intersection itself*. In the nature of things, in a full private property system, the intersection must be owned either by the Main Street Company, the Side Street Company, or by some third party. As soon as the property rights to the intersection between the two streets are fully specified (in whichever of these three ways) all such problems and dilemmas cease.

Suppose the Main Street Company had been the first on the scene. It is then the full owner of an unbroken chain of property, known as Main Street. Soon after, the Side Street Company contemplates building. Now the latter company knows full well that *all* of Main Street is private property. Building a cross street to run over the property of Main Street cannot be justified. The Main Street Company, however, has every incentive to welcome a Side Street, if not to build one itself, for the new street will enhance its own property if patrons can use it to arrive at other places. A city street that has no cross street options does not really function as an access route; it would be more like a limited access highway in the middle of a city. The two companies shall have to arrive at a mutually satisfactory arrangement. Presumably, the Side Street Company will have to *pay* for the right to build a cross

---

*I owe this point to David Ramsay Steele, of the Department of Sociology, University of Hull.

street. On the other hand, if the owners of Main Street intend to use it as a limited access highway, then the Side Street Company shall have to build over it, under it, or around it, but not across it. (As part of the contract between the two parties, there would have to be an agreement concerning automobiles getting stuck in the intersection. Presumably this would be prohibited.)

Since original ownership by the Side Street Company would be the same analytically as the case we have just considered, but with the names of the companies reversed, we may pass on to a consideration of ownership by a third party.

If the intersection of the two streets is owned by an outsider, then it is he who decides conflicts between the two road companies. Since his interests would best be served by smoothly flowing traffic, the presumption is that the owner of the intersection would act so as to minimize the chances of motorists from either street being isolated in the intersection as the traffic light changed.

This analysis of the ownership situation concerning cross streets and their intersections will enable us to answer several other possibly perplexing problems.

5. How would green light time be parceled out under free enterprise?

Of course, most street owners, if they had their choice, would prefer the green light for their street 100% of the time. Yet, this would be tantamount to a limited access highway. If it is to be a city street, a road must content itself with less. What proportion of red and green lights shall be allotted to each street?

If all the streets in one neighborhood are owned by one company, then it decides this question, presumably with the intention of maximizing its profits. Again, and for the same reasons, we can expect a more effective job from such a "private" owner, than from a city government apparatus.

In the case of intersection ownership by a third party, the two cross street owners will *bid* for the green light time. *Ceteris paribus,* the presumption is that the owner of the street with the larger volume of street traffic will succeed in bidding for more of the green light time. If the owner of the larger volume street refused to bid for a high proportion of green light time, his customers would tend to patronize competitors—who could offer more green lights, and hence a faster trip.

A similar result would take place with two street owners, no matter what the property dispersal.[5] It is easy to see this if the larger street company owns the intersections. The larger company would simply keep a high proportion (2/3, 3/4, or perhaps even 4/5) of green light time for itself, selling only the remaining small fraction to the intersecting side street. But much the same result would ensue if the smaller road owned the common intersections! Although the relatively lightly traveled road company might like to keep the lion's share of the green lights for itself, it will find that it cannot afford to do so. The more heavily traveled street, representing a clientele willing and able in the aggregate to pay far more for green light privileges, will make it extremely tempting for the small street owner to accept a heavy payment, in order to relinquish most of its green light time. In other words, the customers of the main street, through indirect payments via the main street owner, will bid time away from the smaller number of customers using the minor street. This principle is well established in business, and is illustrated every time a firm sublets space, which it could have used to satisfy its own customers, because it receives more income subletting than retaining the premises for its own use.

The provision of staggered traffic lights (the lights continually turn green, for example, as an auto proceeding at 25 M.P.H. approaches them) may present some conceptual difficulties but, again, they are easily overcome. Of course, there are virtually no problems if either one company owns all the roads, or if the main road (the one to be staggered) is continuously owned. The only question arises when the *side* streets are continuously owned, and it is the main avenues which are to receive the staggered lights. (We are assuming that staggering cannot efficiently be instituted for both north-south *and* intersecting east-west streets, and that staggering is better placed on the main roads than the side ones.)

Under these conditions, there are several possible solutions. For one, the main avenues, being able to make better use of the staggering system, may simply purchase (or rent) the rights to program the lights so that staggering takes place on the main roads. The side roads, even as owners of the intersections, would only be interested in the proportion of each minute that their lights could remain green; they would be indifferent to the necessity of staggering. Since this is precisely what the main roads desire, it seems that some mutually advantageous agreement could feasibly be made.

Another possibility is that the main roads, better able to utilize the staggering capabilities which intersection ownership confers (and perhaps better able to utilize the other advantages bestowed upon their owners) will simply arrange to purchase the intersections outright. If so, the pattern would change from one where the sidestreet corporations owned the intersections to one in which these came under the possession of the main street companies.

Still another alternative would be integration of ownership. We have no idea as to the optimal size of the road firm (single block, single road, continuous road, small city, etc.), so thoughts in this direction can only be considered speculative. With regard to the ease of coordinating staggered light systems, however, it may well be that larger is better. If so, there will be a market tendency for merger, until these economies are exhausted.

Let us recapitulate. We have begun by indicating the present mismanagement of roads by government. We have claimed that improvements, given the status quo of government management, are not likely to suffice. We have briefly explored an alternative—the free market in road ownership and management—and shown how it might deal with a series of problems, and rejected some unsophisticated objections. We are now ready to examine in some detail how private road owners actually might compete in the market place.

How Private Road Owners Might Compete

On the rare occasions when the feasibility of private road ownership has been considered by mainstream economists, it has been summarily rejected, based on the impossibility of competition among private road owners. Seeing this point as almost intuitively obvious, economists have not embarked on lengthy chains of reasoning in refutation. Thus, says Smerk, rather curtly, "Highways could not very well be supplied on a competitive basis, hence they are provided by the various levels of government."[6]

Economists, however, are willing to expound, at great length, upon the need for the conditions of perfect competition, if efficiency is to prevail in the private sector. One of the main reasons the idea of private enterprise for roads has not been accepted is the claim that perfect competition cannot exist in this sphere.

A typical example of this kind of thinking is that of Haveman.[7] Says he:

> A number of conditions must be met if the private sector of the economy—the market system—is to function efficiently. Indeed, these conditions are essential if the private sector is to perform in the public interest. . . . [I]t is the absence of these conditions which often gives rise to demands for public sector [government] action.

These conditions of perfect competition are widely known: numerous buyers and sellers, so that no one of them is big enough to "affect price"; a homogeneous good; and perfect information. One problem with the strict requirement that an industry meet these conditions, or else be consigned to government operation, is that there is virtually *no* industry in a real-life economy that would remain in the private sector! Almost *every* industry would have to be nationalized, were the implicit program of Haveman followed. This is easy to see, once we realize how truly restrictive are these conditions. The homogeneity requirement, by itself, would be enough to bar most goods and services in a modern, complex economy. Except for thumb tacks, rubber bands, paper clips, and several others of this kind, there are hardly any commodities which do not differ, even slightly, in the eyes of most consumers. Perfect information bars even the farm staples from inclusion in the rubric of perfect competition. This can be seen in a healthy, functioning Chicago mercantile exchange. If there were full information available to all and sundry, there could be no such commodities market.

Not "affecting price" also presents difficulties. No matter how small a part of the total market a single individual may be, he can always hold out for a price slightly higher than that commonly prevailing. Given a lack of perfect information, there will usually (but not always) be someone willing to purchase at the higher price.

Therefore, the objection to private roads on the ground that they are inconsistent with perfect competition cannot be sustained. It is true that this industry could not maintain the rigid standards required for perfect competition, but neither can most. In pointing out that *perfect competition* cannot apply to roads, we have by no means conceded that *competition* between the various road owners would not be a vigorous, rivalrous process. On the contrary, were we to allow that perfect competition *could* apply to roads, we would then have to retract our claim that vigorous competition could also ensue. For perfect competition, and competition in the ordinary sense of that word (implying rivalry, attempts to entice customers away from one another) are *opposites*, and inconsistent with each other.[8]

In the perfectly competitive model, each seller can sell all he wants, at the given market price. (This is the assumption that each perfect competitor faces a perfectly elastic demand curve.) A typical rendition of this point of view is furnished by Stonier and Hague:[9]

> The shape of the average revenue curve [demand curve] of the individual firm will depend on conditions in the market in which the firm sells its product. Broadly speaking, the keener the competition of its rivals and the greater the number of fairly close substitutes for its product, the more elastic will a firm's

average revenue curve be. As usual, it is possible to be precise about limiting cases. One limiting case will occur when there are so many competitors producing such close substitutes [the perfectly competitive model] that the demand for the product of each individual firm is infinitely elastic and its average revenue curve is a horizontal straight line. This will mean that the firm can sell as much of its product as it wishes at the ruling market price. If the firm raises its price, then, owing to the ease with which the same, or a very similar, product can be bought from competitors, it will lose all its customers. If the firm were to lower its price, it would be swamped by orders from customers wishing to take advantage of its price reduction. The demand—and the elasticity of demand—for its product would be infinite.

Under these conditions, competition in the usual sense of opposition, contention, rivalry, etc. would be completely lacking. Where is the need to attract the customers of other firms to oneself if each so-called "competitor" can "sell as much of its product as it wishes at the ruling market price?" Why go out and compete if one is guaranteed all the customers one could possibly want? If "competition" is supposed to indicate rivalrous behavior, one would think that "perfect competition" would denote a sort of super-contentiousness. Instead, through dint of misleading definition, it means the very opposite: a highly *passive* existence, where firms do *not* have to go out and actively seek customers.

Again, we can see that rejecting the possibility of perfect competition for a roads industry is by no means equivalent to conceding that there can be no rivalrous competition between the different road owners. Paradoxically, only if perfect competition *were* applicable to roads, might we have to consider the possibility that the process of competition might not be adaptable to highways.

In contrast to the passive notion of perfect competition, which has held center stage in the economics profession for the last few decades, there is a new comprehension of competition, in the *market process* sense, that is now drawing increasing attention.

Instead of concentrating on the maximization of ends, assuming given scarce means, as does the Robbinsian[10] notion of perfect competition, the market process view makes the realistic assumption that the means, although scarce, are in no way *given;* rather, knowledge of them must actively be sought out. The allocation of scarce means among competing ends is a *passive* procedure when the means and the ends are known. All that need be done can be accomplished by a suitably programmed computer. But the active seeking out of the ends and the means in the first place is a task that can be accomplished only by entrepreneurial talent; active, not passive. The entrepreneur, denied his crucial role in the perfectly competitive world view, takes center stage in the market process conception.

Instead of merely economizing, the entrepreneur seeks new and hitherto unknown profit opportunities; not content to allocate given means to already selected ends, the businessman blazes new trails, continually on the lookout for *new* ends, and different means. States Israel Kirzner,[11] one of the pathbreakers in this way of looking at our economy:

> We have seen that the market proceeds through entrepreneurial competition. In this process market participants become aware of opportunities for profit: they perceive price discrepancies (either between the prices offered and asked

by buyers and sellers of the same good or between the price offered by buyers for a product and that asked by sellers for the necessary resources) and move to capture the difference for themselves through their entrepreneurial buying and selling. Competition, in this process, consists of perceiving possibilities of offering opportunities to other market participants which are more attractive than those currently being made available. It is an essentially *rivalrous* process . . . [which] . . . consists not so much in the regards decision-makers have for the likely future reactions of their competitors as in their awareness that in making their present decisions they themselves are in a position to do better for the market than their rivals are prepared to do; it consists not of market participants' reacting passively to given conditions, but of their actively grasping profit opportunities by positively changing the existing conditions.

It is this *competitive market process* that can apply to the road industry. Highway entrepreneurs can continually seek newer and better ways of providing services to their customers. There is no reason why street corporations should not actively compete with other such firms for the continued and increased tolls of their patrons. There may not be millions of buyers and sellers of road transport service at each and every conceivable location (nor is there for *any* industry) but this does not preclude vigorous rivalry among the market participants, however many.

How might this work?

Let us consider, for the sake of simplicity, a town laid out into 64 blocks, as in a checker board (see diagram 3). We can conveniently label the north-south or vertical avenues A through I, and the east-west or horizontal streets 1st through 9th. If a person wants to travel from the junction of First Street and Avenue A to Ninth Street and Avenue I, there are several paths he may take. He might go east along First Street to Avenue I, and then north along Avenue I, to Ninth Street, a horizontal and then a vertical trip. Or he may first go north to Ninth Street, and then east along Ninth Street to Avenue I. Alternatively, he may follow any number of zig-zag paths: east along First Street to Avenue B; north along Avenue B to Second Street; east again, along Second Street to Avenue C; north on C to Third Street . . . etc. Additionally, there are numerous intermediate paths between the pure zig-zag and the one turn.

These possibilities do not open an indefinitely large number of paths, as might be required by the dictates of perfect competition. However, they are sufficiently numerous to serve as the basis for rivalrous competition, where one road entrepreneur, or set of entrepreneurs, seeks to offer better and cheaper channels for transportation than others.

Let us consider the traffic that wishes to go from the junction of First Street and Avenue D to Ninth Street and Avenue D. (Intersections can be seen as whole towns or cities, and streets as actual or potential highways.) If Avenue D is owned by one firm, it might be thought that here, no competition is possible. For the best route is obviously right up Avenue D from First to Ninth Street. Even though this is true, there is still potential competition from Avenues C and E (and even from B and F). If the Avenue D Corporation charges outrageous prices, the customer can use the alternative paths of C or E (or, in a pinch, to B or F, or even A or G, if need be). A second source of potential competition derives, as we have seen, from the

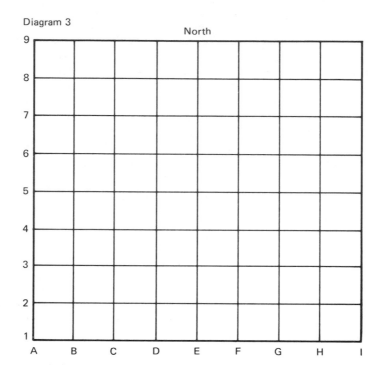

Diagram 3

North

possibility of building another road above the road in question, or tunneling beneath it. Consider again, the management of Avenue D, which is charging an outrageously high price. In addition to the competition provided by nearby roads, competition may also be provided by double, triple, or quadruple decking the road.

The transportation literature is not unaware of the possibility of double decking roads, tunneling, or adding overhead ramps. For example, Wilfred Owen [12] tells us:

> The Port of New York Authority Bus Terminal helps relieve mid-Manhattan traffic congestion. Approximately 90% of intercity bus departures and intercity bus passengers from mid-Manhattan originate at this terminal. The diversion of this traffic on overhead ramps from the terminal to the Lincoln Tunnel has been equivalent to adding three cross-town streets.

John Burchard lauds double decking as follows:

> On one short span of East River Drive [in New York City] there are grassed terraces carried over the traffic lanes right out to the edge of the East River, a special boon for nearby apartment dwellers. The solution was perhaps triggered by the fact that space between the established building lines and the river was so narrow as to force the *superposition of the north and south lanes*. But this did not do more than suggest the opportunity. Applause goes to those who grasped

it, but none to those who with the good example in view so consistently ignored it thereafter. [Emphasis added.][13]

From Burchard's limited perspective, it is indeed a mystery that some should have taken this step and that, once it was taken and proven successful, it should not have been emulated. From the vantage point of a market in roads, the mystery disappears: one bureaucrat stumbled, out of necessity, onto a good plan. Having no financial incentive toward cost minimization, no others saw fit to expand this innovation. *On the market,* given that it is economical to double deck, there will be powerful forces tending toward this result: the profit and loss system.

An authoritative reference to double decking was made by Charles M. Noble, former Director of the Ohio Department of Highways and chief engineer of the New Jersey Turnpike Authority:

> It seems clear that, ultimately, many urban freeways will become double or triple-deck facilities, with upper decks carrying the longer distance volumes, possibly with reversible lanes, and probably operating with new interchanges to avoid flooding of existing interchanges and connecting streets.[14]

It is impossible to foretell exactly how this competition via multiple decking might work out in the real world. Perhaps one company would undertake to build and maintain the roads, as well as the bridgework supporting all the different decks. In this scenario, the road deck owner might sublease each individual deck, much in the same way as the builder of a shopping center does not himself run any of the stores, preferring to sublet them to others. Alternatively, the main owner-builder might decide to keep one road for himself, renting out the other levels to different road companies. This would follow the pattern of the shopping center which builds a large facility for itself, but leases out the remainder of the space.

Whatever the pattern of ownership, there would be several, not just one road company in the same "place"; they could compete with each other. If Avenue D, as in our previous example, becomes multiple decked, then traveling from First Street and Avenue D to Ninth Street and Avenue D need not call for a trip along Avenue C or E, in order to take advantage of competition. One might also have the choice betwen *levels* w,x,y,z, all running over Avenue D!

Let us consider the objections of Z. Haritos:

> There is joint road consumption by consumers with different demand functions. The road is not as good as steel which may be produced to different specifications of quality and dimensions. The economic characteristics necessitate the production of one kind of road for all users at any given place.[15]

This statement is at odds with what we have just been saying. In our view, the double or triple decking of roads *allows* for the production of at least several kinds of road along any given roadway. We would then be forced to reject Haritos's contention. One point of dispute is the equivocation in his use of the word "place."

For in one sense, Haritos is correct. If we *define* "place" as the entity within which two different things cannot possibly exist, then logic forces us to conclude that two different roads cannot exist in the same place. But by the same token, this applies to steel as well. Contrary to Haritos, a road occupies the same logical position as steel. If roads cannot be produced to different specifications of quality and dimensions at any given place, then neither can steel.

But if we reverse matters, and use the word "place" in such a way that two different things (two different pieces of steel, with different specifications) *can* exist in one place (side by side, or close to each other) then steel may indeed be produced to different specifications at any given place, but so may roads! For many different roads, through the technique of multiple decking, can flow along the same pathway, or exist in the same "place."

Another objection charges that competition among roadway entrepreneurs would involve wasteful duplication. Says George M. Smerk: "[C]ompetition between public transport companies, particularly public transit firms with fixed facilities, would require an expensive and undesirable duplication of plant."[16]

This is a popular objection to market competition in many areas; railroad "overbuilding," in particular, has received its share of criticism on this score. However, it is fallacious and misdirected.

We must first of all distinguish between investment *ex ante* and *ex post*. In the *ex ante* sense, *all* investment is undertaken with the purpose of earning a profit. Wasteful overbuilding or needless duplication *cannot* exist in the *ex ante* sense; no one intends, at the outset of his investment, that it should be wasteful or unprofitable.[17] *Ex ante* investment must, of necessity, be nonwasteful.

Ex post perspective is another matter. The plain fact of our existence is that plans are often met by failure; investments often go awry. From the vantage point of history, an investment may very often be judged unwise, wasteful, and needlessly duplicative. But this hardly constitutes a valid argument against private roads! For the point is that *all* investors are liable to error. Unless it is contended that government enterprise is somehow *less* likely to commit error than entrepreneurs who have been continuously tested by the market process of profit and loss, the argument makes little sense. (There are few, indeed, who would be so bold as to make the claim that the government bureaucrat is a better entrepreneur than the private businessman.)

Very often criticisms of the market, such as the charge of wasteful duplication on the part of road owners, stems from a preoccupation with the perfectly competitive model. Looking at the world from this vantage point can be extremely disappointing. The model posits full and perfect information, and in a world of perfect knowledge there of course can be no such thing as wasteful duplication. *Ex post* decisions would be as successful as those *ex ante*. By comparison, in this respect, the real world comes off a distant second best. It is perhaps understandable that a person viewing the real world through perfectly competitive-tinged sunglasses should experience a profound unhappiness with actual investments that turn out to be unwise, or needlessly duplicative.

Such disappointment, however, is not a valid objection to the road market. What must be rejected is not the sometimes mistaken investment of a private road firm, but rather the perfectly competitive model which has no room in it for human error.

An intermediate position on the possibility of road competition is taken by Gabriel Roth. He states:

   . . . while it is possible to envisage competition in the provision of roads connecting points at great distances apart—as occurred on the railways in the early days—it is not possible to envisage competition in the provision of access roads in towns and villages, for most places are served by one road only. A highway authority is in practice in a monopoly position. If any of its roads were to make large profits, we could not expect other road suppliers to rush in to fill the gap. If losses are made on some roads, there are no road suppliers to close them down and transfer their resources to other sectors of the economy.[18]

Here we find several issues of contention. First, it is a rare small town or village that is served by *only one* road, path, or cattle track. Most places have at least several. But even allowing that in many rural communities there is only one serviceable road, let us note the discrepancy in Roth between roads and other services. Most local towns and villages are also served by only one grocer, butcher, baker, etc. Yet Roth would hardly contend that competition cannot thereby exist in these areas. He knows that, even though there is only one grocer in town, there is potential, if not actual competition, from the grocer down the road, or in the next town.

The situation is identical with roads. As we have seen, there is always the likelihood of building another road next to the first, if the established one proves highly popular and profitable. There is also the possibility of building another road above, or tunneling beneath the first road. In addition, competition is also brought in through other transportation *industries*. There may be a trolley line, railroad or subway linking this town with the outside world. If there is not, and the first established road is very profitable, such competition is always open in a free market.

Finally, we come to the statement, "If losses are made on some roads, there are no road suppliers to close them down and transfer their resources to other sectors of the economy." We agree, because a road is generally fixed, geographically. An entrepreneur would no more "move" a no longer profitable road, than he would physically move an equivalently unprofitable farm, or forest. More importantly, even if it were somehow economically feasible to "move" an unprofitable road to a better locale, there *are* no such road suppliers simply because private road ownership is now *prohibited*.

With Roth's statement, we also come to the spectre of monopoly, and to claims that a private road market must function monopolistically. Why are such claims made? There are two reasons usually given. First, indivisibilities—the fact that many factors of production cannot be efficiently utilized at low levels of output. A steel mill or automobile factory cannot be chopped in half and then be asked to produce one-half of the output it had previously been producing.

Says Mohring, "But indivisibilities do exist in the provision of transportation facilities. Each railroad track must have two rails, and each highway or country road must be at least as wide as the vehicles that use it."[19] In similar vein, says Haritos, "To get from A to B, you need a whole lane, not just half, for the full distance, not half of it."[20] And, in the words of Peter Winch, ". . . indivisibility of highways make it impractical to have competing systems of roads, and the responsible authority must therefore be a monopoly."[21]

We do not believe that the existence of indivisibilities is enough to guarantee monopoly, defined by many as a situation in which there is a single seller of a commodity.[22] There are indivisibilities in *every* industry, and in *all* walks of life.

Hammers and nails, bicycles and wheelbarrows, locomotives and elevators, tractors and steel mills, professors and podiatrists, ballet dancers and bricklayers, musicians and motorists, ships and slippers, buckets and broomsticks, none of them can be chopped in half (costlessly) and be expected to produce just half of what they had been producing before. A railroad needs *two* rails (with the exception, of course, of the monorail), not one, or any fraction thereof. Also, in order to connect points A and B, it must stretch completely from one point to the other. It may not end halfway between them, and offer the likelihood of transportation between the two points.

Does this establish the need for government takeover of railroads? Of course not. Yet they exhibit the concept of indivisibilities just as do roads and highways. If indivisibilities justify government involvement in roadways, then they should justify it in *all* other cases wherein indivisibilities can be found. Since the advocates of the indivisibility argument are not willing to extend it to broomsticks, slippers, steel mills, and practically every other good and commodity under the sun, logic compels them to retract it in the case of highways.

Conclusion

So what do we conclude? Having debunked the notion that private ownership of the roads is not "impossible," and that, in fact, it may offer a variety of exciting alternatives to the present system, we return to the question of why should it even be considered. There we come face-to-face again with the problem of safety. A worse job than that which is presently being done by the government road managers is difficult to envision. We need only consider what transpires when safety is questioned in other forms of transportation to see a corollary. When an airline experiences an accident, it often experiences a notable dropping off of passengers. Airlines with excellent safety records, who have conducted surveys, have found that the public *is* aware of safety and will make choices based upon it.

Similarly, private road owners will be in a position to establish regulations and practices to assure safety on their roads. They can impact on the driver, the vehicle, and the road—the key elements of highway safety. They can react more quickly than the government bureaucracy in banning such vehicles as "exploding Pintos." The overriding problem with the National Highway Traffic Safety Administration, and with all similar governmental systems of insuring against vehicle defects, for example, is that there is no competition allowed. Again, in a free market system, opportunities would open up for innovative approaches to safety problems. Should stiffer penalties be shown unsuccessful in reducing unsafe vehicles and practices, an incentive system may be the answer. We cannot paint all the details of the future from our present vantage point. But we do know that "there has to be a better way."

Notes

1. The present author wishes to express a debt of gratitude to the two trailblazers into this subject: Jarret B. Wollstein, *Public Services Under Laissez Faire* (New York: Arno Press, 1974), and Murray N. Rothbard, *For a New Liberty* (New York: Macmillan, 1973), pp. 202-218.

2. William Vickrey, "Pricing and Resource Allocation in Transportation and Public Utilities," *American Economic Review* (May 1963), p. 452; Vickrey, "Breaking the Bottleneck by Sophisticated Pricing of Roadway Use," *General Motors Quarterly* (Spring 1974), p. 24.

3. Says Murray N. Rothbard: "The answer is that everyone, in purchasing homes or street service in a libertarian society, would make sure that the purchase or lease contract provides full access for whatever term of years is specified. With this sort of 'easement' provided in advance by contract, no such sudden blockade would be allowed, since it would be an invasion of the property right of the landowner." *For a New Liberty,* p. 205.

4. F. A. Hayek, *The Constitution of Liberty* (Chicago: University of Chicago Press, 1960), p. 160.

5. We assume away here the presence of psychic income phenomena. See the present author's "Coase and Demsetz on Private Property Rights," *The Journal of Libertarian Studies,* Vol. 1, No. 2 (Spring 1977), p. 111.

6. George M. Smerk, *Urban Transportation: The Federal Role* (Bloomington, Ind.: Indiana University Press, 1965), p. 228.

7. Robert H. Haveman, *The Economics of the Public Sector* (New York: John Wiley and Sons, 1970), p. 23. For a telling criticism of the "control over price" confusion, see Murray N. Rothbard, *Man, Economy and State* (Los Angeles: Nash Pub. Co., 1971), pp. 87-90.

8. Cf. Israel Kirzner, *Competition and Entrepreneurship* (Chicago: University of Chicago Press, 1973).

9. Alfred W. Stonier and Douglas C. Hague, *A Textbook of Economic Theory* (3rd Ed., New York: John Wiley and Sons, 1964), p. 104.

10. See Lionel Robbins, *An Essay on the Nature and Significance of Economic Science* (London: Macmillan, 1932).

11. Kirzner, *Competition and Entrepreneurship,* pp. 122-123.

12. *The Metropolitan Transportation Problem* (Washington, D.C.: The Brookings Institution, 1956), p. 119.

13. John Burchard, "Design and Urban Beauty in the Central City," in J. Q. Wilson, ed., *The Metropolitan Enigma* (Garden City, N.Y.: Doubleday, 1970), p. 245.

14. Charles M. Noble, "Highway Design and Construction Related to Traffic Operation and Safety," *Traffic Quarterly* (November 1971), pp. 546-547.

15. Z. Haritos, "Theory of Road Pricing," 13 *Transportation Journal* (Spring 1974), p. 57.

16. Smerk, *Urban Transportation,* p. 228.

17. Even if someone intends, for some reason, to purposefully invest in a "losing" proposition, we would still deny, *ex ante,* that he intends to worsen his position. That people act in order to benefit themselves is an axiom of economics. If a person intends to lose *money* through his investment, it could only be because, by so doing, he thinks he will increase his *psychic income* by enough to more than compensate himself for his loss of money. In short, he is engaging in charity.

18. Gabriel Roth, *Paying for Roads—The Economics of Traffic Congestion* (Baltimore: Penguin Books, 1967), p. 63.

19. Herbert Mohring, "Urban Highway Investments," in Robert Dorfman, ed., *Measuring Benefits of Government Investments* (Washington, D.C.: The Brookings Institution, 1965), p. 240.

20. Haritos, "Theory of Road Pricing," p. 56.

21. David M. Winch, *Economics of Highway Planning,* (Toronto: University of Toronto Press, 1963), p. 3.

22. For an explanation of "monopoly" as a government grant of exclusive privilege, see Rothbard, *Man, Economy, and State,* pp. 586-619.

ELLEN FRANKEL PAUL

The Just Takings Issue:
Can It Be Resolved by Contemporary
Theories of Justice?

The sanctity of private property as a preserve of individual autonomy free from the overweaning grasp of the state has long been a cherished American myth. In truth, property has never held such an exalted position even in this country, for the government has always intervened in property relationships. In Colonial times real property was held as a grant from the Crown in free and common socage under the provision that the holder pay his rents; while in the immediate post-revolutionary period the new American government engaged in a massive land grant scheme to enrich its meager treasury.[1] However, it is an indubitable fact that in our own day this power of the state over real property has been immeasurably extended. Confronting the individual and his claim of dominion over his own holdings, is the modern Leviathan, whether it be the states or the federal government, with its asserted "police powers."[2] In his defense, the landowner can only furtively cling to the beleaguered and eroded "takings clause" of the Fifth Amendment: "nor shall private property be taken for public use, without just compensation."

The Constitution, obviously, presents no insurmountable barrier to the government's taking of private property, rather, it merely declares that such action must be accompanied by the payment of "just compensation." But this entire "eminent domain" clause has proven notoriously ambiguous and interpretable at the discretion of judges. What qualifies as a "public use" legitimating a taking? What constitutes just compensation? Where ought the line be drawn between uncompensated government regulation under the police power and regulation which becomes so onerous as to amount to a "taking" under eminent domain?[3] This latter query is currently the focus of the takings debate[4] and of this paper.

The practical and juridical issues are undeniably complex, pitting the social needs of an ever more interdependent society against the claims of individuals to

From *Environmental Ethics,* October 1981.
*Bowling Green State University.

their property. Beneath the surface lies a more fundamental issue, that of our basic conceptions of justice as they relate to property acquisition and legitimation. Viewed from this perspective, as essentially a confrontation over theories of justice in property, perhaps it might prove illuminating to examine this "takings" controversy from the vantage point of the two salient and antagonistic theories of justice advanced by philosophers in the 1970's—that of John Rawls' "justice as fairness"[5] and Robert Nozick's "justice as entitlement."[6]

Before embarking upon this analysis of the takings issue as a conflict in basic moral values, let us briefly examine several political developments that have engendered a re-examination of the takings clause. Subsequently, an attempt will be made to isolate a Rawlsian and Nozickian resolution to these troublesome issues.

1) *Zoning*—The development of zoning in the United States is a twentieth century phenomenon having its beginnings in the attempts by cities such as Los Angeles and New York to control the height and spacing of buildings to avoid fire and health hazards. Gradually, the segregation of heavy industrial uses into separate districts became fashionable, largely under the inspiration of Herbert Hoover's advisory committee which drafted a model zoning ordinance now almost universally enacted by the states, the Standard State Zoning Enabling Act. In 1926 the Supreme Court handed down a landmark decision in *Village of Euclid* v. *Ambler Realty Co.*[7] which sanctioned the zoning power as a legitimate exercise of the states' police powers. Barring only regulations of a clearly arbitrary and unreasonable nature, the Court endorsed the doctrine of deference to legislative competence when the legislative intent was considered substantially related to the police powers of protecting public health, safety, morals, or general welfare. This landmark decision has stood the test of time, the Court never, since 1928, having invalidated a zoning regulation for overstepping the police power.[8]

Today, zoning has been employed by localities to further newly recognized social objectives such as limiting urban growth by controlling or prohibiting new development, providing a mix of low and middle income housing in developing communities, and curtailing environmental hazards. The widespread acceptance of zoning as a limitation upon private property is apparent from the fact that Houston, Texas is the only city in the country with a population in excess of a quarter of a million people which has not passed some form of zoning regulation.

The first problematical case posed for the Rawlsian and Nozickian theories of justice concerns a typical kind of zoning dispute:

Hypothetical # 1—In 1972 Alpha purchased land in an undeveloped zone designated residential, intending to build upon it a housing development of single family dwellings. The municipality revised its zoning ordinance in 1973 categorizing Alpha's land as heavy industrial.[9] Consequently, Alpha has been denied the best use of his land and the value of the land has been diminished as a result of the lower market value realizable on industrial sites. No compensation is forthcoming. Assuming that Alpha's procedural due process rights have not been traduced, is this a legitimate exercise of the state's power? If so, does it constitute a compensable taking?

2) *Land Use Restrictions Inspired by Environmentalist Concerns*—While zoning is largely a creature of the 1920s and the challenge posed by it to the takings

clause has been judicially settled in general in favor of the police powers of the states, environmentally inspired land use legislation is a phenomenon of the last decade. This type of legislative initiative cuts at the root of the takings protection, and advocates of broadened powers of the states in the areas of protecting wetlands, natural ecosystems, coastal lands, forests, naturally hazardous lands, and scenic vistas run directly athwart the compensation requirement. Given a broad and traditional interpretation of the takings clause, any state regulation which in essence diminished the use value of land and rendered its market value nugatory would require compensation at the fair market value of the land at its optimum use:

> . . . the takings clause is the major obstacle to effective environmental land use regulation. . . . Since state and local governments cannot afford to acquire by eminent domain all of the land of which harsh land use restrictions are necessary, traditional takings analysis tends to disrupt state land use programs.

Rather than abandoning such legislation, various state courts have attempted to vitiate the compensability requirement of the takings clause. Two cases arising in the Wisconsin and New Hampshire Supreme Courts evince such thinking. In *Just v. Marinette Count,*[10] the Wisconsin Court contended that absent from the bundle of rights possessed by property owners is the right to change the character of a wetland in order to maximize its economic utility. Furthermore, the state's regulation which denied to the plaintiffs the right to use landfill to improve their lakefront property was held to be legitimate because it aimed at prohibiting a harm which, the Court contended, is distinguishable from regulations aimed at the production of public benefits (in which event compensation implicitly would be required). Likewise, in Sibson,[11] the New Hampshire Court declared the protection of wetlands to fall under the legitimate exercise of the police powers, and held, consequently, that no compensation was due no matter how severe the restrictions.[12]

The federal government has entered rather decisively into property regulation with the Federal Water Pollution Control Act, the Clean Air Act, and the National Environmental Policy Act of 1969. The latter mandated the filing of environmental impact statements for all federal or federally subsidized development projects. However, the most comprehensive attempts at land management under the guise of environmental protection have come from the states, with the California Coastal Plan a conspicuous trend setter. Following the passage of Proposition 20 by the voters in 1972, California established a Coastal Commission "to preserve, protect, and where possible, to restore the resources of the coastal zone for the enjoyment of the current and succeeding generations."[13] For three years the Commission was empowered among other things to issue permits for all developments along California's 1,072 mile coast. In 1976 the state legislature enacted the California Coastal Act, the fulfillment of Proposition 20's environmentalist backers' dreams. The Act controls the coastal waters, the scenice beauty of the coast, air quality along the oceanside, regulates power plants, restricts auto access to the beaches, insures public access to beaches, etc. Land uses are particularly affected by the Plan, as all building along the coast must be approved by the Commission (until coastal cities complete their general plans acceptable to the Coastal Commission) to insure "continued development in appropriate areas."[14]

Pursuant to this goal, property owners can be denied building permits because their projects fall afoul of the regional plan. Conspicuously absent from the legislation is any compensatory scheme to mitigate the financial losses of those aggrieved by the Commission and denied their expectations for the enjoyment of their land.

Thus, the following case will be offered for examination by our two theories of justice:

Hypothetical #2—Beta purchased land along the California coast in 1965 hoping to fill in the slightly marshy land and construct the home of his dreams. Financial exigencies forced him to abandon that project until 1977 when, flush from recent business successes, he applied to the California Coastal Commission for a permit to construct his Shangri-La. At the hearings several neighbors appear who have houses on adjoining plots of land filled in the early 1960's. They contend that the new construction would pose hazards to the ecosystem, disturb the scenic beauty of the coastline, and restrict public access to the beaches. [15] Beta is denied his permit to build. He, of course, has the option to sell his land, the value of which has been severely depreciated by the action of the Commissioners.

3) *Urban Renewal and Model Cities Programs*—Urban renewal programs began with the Housing Act of 1949 and gained momentum during the 1960's, culminating in the Demonstration Cities and Metropolitan Development Act of 1966 (42 U.S.C.A. §330). Justified as programs to provide low-income families with decent housing and to redevelop blighted slum areas, the movement fell upon somewhat harder times during the Nixon years with the decentralization of control exemplified in the Housing and Community Development Act of 1974 (42 U.S.C.A. 5305) in which the federal role was limited to funding block grants for locally designed programs.

These programs, in contrast to the environmentalist land use legislation, openly bite the eminent domain bullet by declaring a "taking" and paying compensation to owners for the fair market value of their property. The Fifth Amendment restrictions, then, are not blatantly challenged by such programs, unless one cares to quibble over the legitimacy of the "public use" animating the takings [a quibble seemingly put to rest by the Supreme Court in *Berman v. Parker*, 1348 U.S. 26 (1954)].

Our third hypothetical emerges in the following form: Hypothetical #3— Gamma operates Gamma's Friendly Repair Shop on Vine Street in Cincinnati, a location at which his family has repaired gadgets for three generations, and in a neighborhood inhabited by poor, elderly but loyal customers. The city declares the entire block condemned under its eminent domain powers in order to improve the area by the construction of a high-rise condominium for middle and upper class families. Gamma vigorously protests this plan, but to no avail, Vine Street being in the direct line of the city's redevelopment plans. Despite the offer of fair market value for his building and land, and a relocation allotment, Gamma is still extremely reluctant. He contends that no amount of compensation will repay him for the aggravation of the move, the loss of business resulting from the inability of his elderly clients to travel out of the neighborhood to his new location, and the interruption of the family tradition extending over seventy-five years. Gamma is forced to resettle and is paid the "fair market value"[16] of his property. But what if his property were being taken, not for the construction of private condominiums, but rather for a more explicitly public purpose such as a municipal hospital, highway, or post office; would this make a difference?

The Nozickian Entitlement Theory

Nozick propounds a theory of justice in distribution which is historical; that is, in contrast to what he denominates "current time-slice principles" or "end result principles" of justice which look to a structural principle to determine whether an existent distribution is currently just, the entitlement theory is retrospective. It asks essentially three questions: 1) are the holdings of an individual legitimately acquired under the principle of justice in acquisitions, or 2) are the holdings obtained by transfer from a person entitled to them under (1), or 3) are the holdings acquired under a principle of rectification of injustice.[17]

> In contrast to end-result principles of justice, historical principles of justice hold that past circumstances or actions of people can create differential entitlements of differential deserts to things.[18]

While Nozick avoids an explicit endorsement of Locke's theory of appropriation based upon mixing one's labor with previously unowned things, preferring instead to raise devilish jabs at Locke—e.g., why don't we lose our labor while mixing it with something unowned rather than gaining ownership of the thing—Locke's is apparently the most appealing theory to Nozick. Thus, despite his petulant queries, Locke's theory, we may assume, is the one ultimately (or conditionally?) endorsed, at least by omission of anything better. Along with the Lockean baggage comes the "Lockean proviso," the requirement that for any original act of acquisition to be legitimate "enough and as good" must be "left in common for others." Nozick interprets this to mean that the situation of others must not be worsened beyond a baseline position enjoyed, we may assume, in an unimproved state of nature. Interpreted in the less stringent of two possible ways, Nozick takes this to mean that appropriation is illegitimate if it worsens the condition of other people "by no longer being able to use freely (without appropriation) what he previously could." The more stringent requirement would include this condition plus another: that a person would be made worse off "by losing the opportunity to improve his situation by a particular appropriation or any one."[19]

The weaker proviso does not prohibit acts of acquisition that worsen the position of others due to more limited opportunities to appropriate, or acts which worsen the position of competitors. And even acquisitions which run afoul of the proviso are legitimate if compensation is paid to the affected parties. What this proviso categorically condemns is the appropriation by an individual of the total supply of a good essential for human life. Thus, the principle of transfer is affected, also:

> If my appropriating all of a certain substance violates the Lockean proviso, then so does my appropriating some and purchasing all the rest from others who obtained it without otherwise violating the Lockean proviso. If the proviso excludes someone's appropriating all the drinkable water in the world, it also excludes his purchasing it all.[20]

However, Nozick believes that the "Lockean proviso" will "(almost?) never come into effect," being limited in its application to cases of catastrophe or desert-island situations. Compared to the productiveness of a society based upon appropriation, the base line situation for measuring whether a person is rendered worse off by an act of acquisition is so low that the proviso will not actuate. This is not meant to deny that the proviso casts an "historical shadow" over all property, so that owners may not either independently or in collusion act in such a way as to depress the condition of others below the base line. For example, the individual who owns the only water hole in a desert cannot charge whatever he wills, and likewise the owner of an island cannot cast a shipwrecked seafarer back into the ocean. While the Lockean proviso is a logical possibility, it is little more, for Nozick believes:

> ... that the free operation of a market system will not actually run afoul of the Lockean proviso. ... If this is correct, the proviso will not ... provide a significant opportunity for future state action.[21]

Finally, Nozick's entitlement theory apparently results in the following requirements for a legitimate holding: 1) it must be acquired from previously unowned things by mixing one's labor with it (or by some as yet unspecified Nozickian means), leaving enough and as good in common for others, 2) or it can be acquired by transfer (bequest, purchase, gambling, etc.) from someone who got it by (1) or by previous applications of (2), barring only conglomerations that run afoul of the Lockean proviso, and 3) only acquisitions in accordance with (1) and (2) are justifiable. For society as a whole, then, if each individual's holdings are acquired by entitlement criteria, then the distribution exhibited throughout the society as a whole is just. This, of course leaves us hanging as to the theory of rectification. What ought to be done about acquisitions obtained in violation of the entitlement theory of justice in distribution? Here, Nozick refrains from theorizing. He leaves open the possibility that a society might exhibit such egregious transgressions that transfer payments might be justified: "Although to introduce socialism as the punishment for our sins would be to go too far, past injustices might be so great as to make necessary in the short run a more extensive state in order to rectify them."

Now, where does this leave the entitlement theory in regard to our eminent domain and "takings" issues? Generally, it appears that state action would be necessarily quite circumspect, confined perhaps to instances in which acquisition had been realized by offensive means; i.e., by fraud, theft, threats, or other patently criminal means. This would exemplify the rectification requirement. Other illegitimate means of acquisition would likely include massive government nationalizations or expropriations. Leaving aside these areas of conspicuous injustice, what if any actions of a "takings" type could the government rightfully perform in a society in which property had been acquired according to entitlement principles?

In regard to our Hypothetical #1, in which Alpha has been disadvantaged by a zoning plan alteration removing his land from a residential to an industrial classification without a "takings" compensation, no apparent justification for zoning can be extracted from the entitlement theory. Given the Nozickian market oriented assumptions, individuals who knowingly engage in activities entertain risks, and it would be illegitimate to manipulate the apparatus of the state to attempt to offset them. Thus, a Nozickian would find some aspects of nuisance law also objectionable. For example, in the case of *Spur Industries Inc. v. Del E. Webb Development Co.*,[22] the Arizona Supreme Court enjoined a feedlot from further operation, with compensation to be paid by the plaintiff under the theory that the feedlot constituted a public nuisance even though the developer had consciously continued to build homes in ever nearer proximity to the pre-existing feedlot, presumably relying on some state remedy to enjoin the known risks of his activities. Zoning, which relied on the law of nuisance as its initial justification, would be similarly objectionable. Thus, a Nozickian would eagerly embrace the Houston experience as portrayed by Bernard Siegan in his article, "Non-Zoning in Houston,"[23] as Siegan concludes:

> Economic forces tend to make for a separation of uses even without zoning. . . . When these economic forces do not guarantee that there will be a separation, and separation is vital to maximize profits (or promote one's tastes and desires), property owners will enter into agreements to provide such protection. The restrictive covenants covering home and industrial subdivisions are the most prominent example of this. . . . A non-zoned city is a cosmopolitan collection of property uses. The standard is supply and demand, and if there is economic justification for the use, it is likely to be forthcoming. Zoning restricts the supply of some uses, and thereby prevents some demands from being satisfied. It may likewise impede innovation.[24]

Thus, a Nozickian resolution to the first hypothetical would entail a rejection of the entire zoning framework. The fact that such legislative fiat is usually not considered a compensable taking would only compound the insult.

But what about Beta, whose lifelong dream to construct his personal paradise on the wetlands adjoining the California coast has been forestalled by the California Coastal Commission? Would the Nozickian entitlement theorist confront head-on the Lockean proviso? Are we presented, here, with a genuine desert-island situation? If, in fact, the proviso has been breached, then no legitimate property rights inhere in Beta to this land, and hence no compensation would be required. It would be ironical, indeed, if Nozick's entitlement theory, presumed to represent the archetypal contemporary defense of capitalism, resulted in precisely the kind of erosion of the "takings" clause that proponents of environmentalist land use legislation have been seeking.

The resolution to Beta's hypothetical situation turns upon the meaning of the Lockean "enough and as good" proviso. A case could conceivably be made that the baseline position of Californians and tourists might be impaired by Beta's construction in that their access to beaches or scenic views would be thereby constricted. Furthermore, if the ecosystem of the area would be indeed materially damaged by further construction, and this damage would effect the lifestyles of actual people, this would seemingly place in jeopardy Beta's claim to dominion over the land. If it could be argued that any further construction would so reduce the commons that people would be worse off, this would be sufficient to invalidate Beta's claim to property rights. (This is even a stronger result than the environmentalists have demanded, for presumably Beta's land would return to the commons.) Additionally, if the ecosystem would be so violated by prospective development as to deleteriously affect human life, the property claimant would be akin to the owner of the well in the desert, or the owner of the island, who cannot deny necessities of life to other people; i.e., his property right would be negated. Perhaps, we might also be confronted with Nozick's regress problem under the Lockean proviso; that is, if Y's appropriation falls afoul of the proviso for making Z worse off, then X's appropriation must also be denied, and so on all the way back to A's original acquisition. Under the "strict" interpretation of the proviso, presumably, all of the California coast could fall under a Coastal Plan (and even an outright expropriation) because all acts of acquisition could be considered ultimately suspect once Beta's attempted utilization triggered the Lockean proviso.

Thus, Nozick's conception of the entitlement theory, which includes a Lockean theory of acquisition qualified by the proviso, places all property ownership under a "shadow," a shadow which intrudes immediately under the "strict" interpretation and eventually even under the "weak" version. Nozick, in recent years, has contemplated abandoning the Lockean proviso. Clearly, an entitlement theory without any "enough and as good" baggage would find entirely inhospitable such uncompensated takings of property as manifested by the California Coastal Plan. If Beta's ownership was legitimately acquired by admixture of his labor with virgin land or by transfer from a legitimate owner, no claims of social utility could ever suffice to negate his privilege to use and dispose of his property as he willed. The only apparent restriction would arise under elements of nuisance law prohibiting the infliction upon others of actual harms—so he could not belch noxious pollutants onto his neighbors' property, or take actions which would cause flooding or fires upon adjoining land.

Gamma's predicament—of compensation being coercively proffered by the state for the condemnation of his business to make way for a condominium (or hospital, or highway)—may similarly run afoul of the Lockean proviso, but the state's case would have to be in extremis. If a nuclear power plant could only be constructed on your land, and such power were absolutely required for the very survival of some elements or all of the population (say, your land was the only plot not subject to earthquake faults in the area), then a legitimate takings under the proviso would be conceivable. Compensation? Probably not for the land itself, which you would, under the proviso, not rightfully own, but certainly for the additional value produced by your labor on the land. Perhaps the proviso could be breached in the less extreme case of the construction of a hospital, although Nozick himself would undoubtedly demur. He would, presumably, rely upon his dubious distinction between 1) denying somebody a life-saving medicine derived from readily available chemical elements, which would not, he claims, make anyone worse off, and 2) depriving someone of water when you are the owner of a solitary oasis in the desert. The hospital construction allegedly would fall under the first case, and hence, not abridge the proviso, Gamma not being in the position of harming others by depriving them of their common entitlement, but simply of denying them a benefit.[25]

Bereft of the Lockean proviso, entitlement theory leads to the conclusion that no governmental eminent domain taking, even a compensable one, will (ever?) be justified. It is conceivable that if a private business were operated in such reckless disregard for human life and it persisted in these excesses despite warnings—e.g., as with the Arizona factory leaking radioactive titium—a taking would be justifiable. But barring such extreme cases, takings for condominiums, highways, or hospitals against the will of property owners would be proscribed. This leaves open the question of whether governments should legitimately engage in eminent domain activities even with the willing acquiescence of compensated property owners.

The entitlement theory expounded in *Anarchy, State, and Utopia* which embraces the Lockean proviso can be utilized to validate environmentalist land use legislation given the proper fact situations, and it does so without such regulations constituting a compensable taking.[26] Model cities or urban renewal type takings with compensation for the increased value of labor might also be justifiable under certain extreme circumstances. Curiously enough, the much less severe kind of regulation entailed by zoning seems to be unjustified unless some direct worsening of the baseline position of individuals can be demonstrated. Once the Lockean proviso is renounced, however, the picture changes rather drastically. Then, forced eminent domain proceedings and all lesser uncompensated takings including land use legislation and zoning must be condemned.

Rawlsian Justice as Fairness

"Justice as fairness" emerges from Rawls' reasoning about a hypothetical "original position," an imagined state of nature. If one envisions persons placed behind a veil of ignorance, which deprives them of knowledge of their natural assets, position in society, psychological propensities, and conception of the good, what basic principles of justice will they choose to regulate their society? The fundamentals of the Rawlsian argument have been well rehearsed in the literature[27] and there is no need to belabor them here. What evolves from this hypothetical contract are two principles of justice, with the first being lexically superior to the second. The full statement of the two principles of justice for institutions is as follows:

First Principle
Each person is to have an equal right to the most extensive total system of equal basic liberties compatible with a similar system of liberty for all.
Second Principle
Social and economic inequalities are to be arranged so that they are both:
a) to the greatest benefit of the least advantaged, consistent with the just savings principle (this is the difference principle), and
b) attached to offices and positions open to all under conditions of fair equality of opportunity.
First Priority Rule (The Priority of Liberty)
The principles of justice are to be ranked in lexical order and therefore liberty can be restricted only for the sake of liberty. There are two cases:
a) a less extensive liberty must strengthen the total system of liberty shared by all;
b) a less than equal liberty must be acceptable to those with the lesser liberty.
Second Priority Rule (The Priority of Justice over Efficiency and Welfare)
The second principle of justice is lexically prior to the principle of efficiency and to that of maximizing the sum of advantages; and fair opportunity is prior to the difference principle. There are two cases:
a) an inequality of opportunity must enhance the opportunities of those with the lesser opportunity;
b) an excessive rate of savings must on balance mitigate the burden of those bearing this hardship.

General Conception

> All social primary goods—liberty and opportunity, income and wealth, and
> the bases of self-respect—are to be distributed equally unless an unequal
> distribution of any or all of these goods is to the advantage of the least
> favored. [28]

The major difficulty in applying the two principles to actual societies arises from
the fact that all such societies have evolved in ways which depart rather markedly
from the Rawlsian scenario. Rawls, however, does not wish to curtail the applicability of his theory of justice to "ideal" situations solely, rather he argues that the
two principles with their priority rules can be profitably utilized to adjudicate
questions of justice in "nonideal" systems.

> In practice we must usually choose between several unjust, or second best,
> arrangements; and then we look to nonideal theory to find the least unjust
> scheme. Sometimes this scheme will include measures and policies that a
> perfectly just system would reject. Two wrongs can make a right in the sense
> that the best available arrangement may contain a balance of imperfections, an
> adjustment of compensating justices. [29]

Let us begin with an analysis of the second hypothetical; i.e., the case of Beta
and the California Coastal Commission. Public goods are, Rawls argues, characterized by indivisibility and publicness, with the result that if anyone is to enjoy
their benefits they must be supplied through the political process and not the
market. [30] Even in the most favorable circumstances where it could be assumed
that everyone shares the same sense of justice and that the public good is to
everyone's advantage, coercive action by the state would be necessary to avoid the
problem of free-riders. Thus, the government could legitimately concern itself
with such economic functions as: 1) the rate of savings and the direction of
investment, 2) the fraction of national wealth devoted to conservation and to
elimination of irremediable injuries to future generations, and 3) the husbanding
of natural resources and the preservation of the environment. [31] Thus, government
can rearrange market relationships to rectify the problem of externalities in order
that public and environmental harms shall be ameliorated. A Rawlsian analysis
ostensibly would look rather favorably upon the mission of the Coastal Commission. But a closer examination is in order.

Taken first from the perspective of ideal theory, how would Beta's dispute be
resolved? While Rawls contends that both a private property system and market
socialism would be compatible with justice as fairness, [32] the ideal scheme he
adumbrates takes as its basis market arrangements; what Rawls terms a property-
owning democracy. In order to secure the requirements of justice—the liberties of
equal citizenship, fair equality of opportunity, and a government guaranteed social
minimum—four basic institutional branches are required:

1. *An allocation branch* which keeps the price system workably competitive and
prevents unreasonable market power. Its tools for accomplishing this objective
include taxes, subsidies, and revisions in the scope and definition of property
rights. If prices fail to measure accurately social costs and benefits, property rights
can be redefined. [33]

2. *A stabilization branch* to bring about reasonably full employment and maintain the efficiency of the market economy.

3. *A transfer branch* which would take needs into account and provide for the social minimum to the least advantaged through transfer payments in such a way as to maximize their long-run expectations.

4. *A distributive branch* to preserve justice in distributive shares by means of inheritance and gift taxes and readjustments in rights of property in order to prevent concentrations of power detrimental to the fair value of political liberty and fair equality of opportunity.

These four branches would satisfy the requirements of justice, but if subsequently the citizens decide that they desire further public expenditures a fifth branch, *the exchange branch,* could be added but it would have to operate as a representative institution taking all interests into account and requiring virtual unanimity to make further changes.[34] This branch would only operate where the justice of the existing distribution of income, wealth, and property rights had been previously guaranteed.

It would appear, then, that Beta's predicament would fall under this exchange branch if we assume an ideal system. The California Coastal Plan, having been approved by a referendum initially, subsequently passed by the legislature, and operated by Commissioners presumably representative of divergent interests, would fall short of the virtual unanimity requirement unless we further assume for the sake of argument resounding majorities at each stage. If we make that assumption, would compensation be due to Beta if a virtually unanimous citizenry felt that to benefit the interests of future generations and to maximize the advantage of the least well-off beyond what mere justice would dictate, his construction privileges must be denied? But what criteria should be employed by the citizenry in making such decisions? Does the "theory of benefits" employ justice criteria? Two possible interpretations of Rawls present themselves. On the first, assuming that Beta is not among the least advantaged in society, his assertion of a putative right to build his dream house would seemingly have to meet the criteria specified in the difference principle. Unless his exercise of construction rights would benefit the least advantaged over the long run, it could be argued that he would not, in fact, have had such a right, and consequently, no compensation was due upon a denial of a building permit. Given the preponderant sentiment among the citizenry and the Commissioners that the least advantaged and future generations would be better served by the preservation of beach access and environmental purity, Beta's claim of a property privilege (not a right) would dissolve and there would be no grounds for compensation.

The foregoing analysis seems rather unsatisfying. Since this excess saving demanded of Beta goes beyond the dictates required by the theory of justice and is discretionary, should Beta be held to the standards of the difference principle? Should he not be assuaged by compensation from those who desire to go beyond mere justice? Perhaps not. If all citizens were aware that property was held as a public trust under the principles of justice as fairness, it would be difficult to argue that anyone's legitimate expectations, a concern for Rawls, or his due process rights under the rule of law principle of legality, another Rawlsian concern, had been violated. However, even then, if one individual were being treated differently and forced to sacrifice disproportionately for the benefit of others, some compensation ought to be forthcoming.

To complicate the Rawlsian analysis even further, couldn't it be argued that Beta's predicament falls not under the exchange branch, but rather under the purview of the allocation branch? If Beta's situation can be subsumed under the latter category, property could simply be redefined to take into account social costs, and then on a police power argument no unanimity would be required, no property right would be breached, and hence no compensation would be necessary.

The more interesting and perplexing problems arise in our actual, non-ideal system. How ought Beta's affairs be resolved here, where he has not been forewarned of the possible curtailment of his property rights conceived as a public trust? Here, I believe Rawlsianism breaks down into what I would call Left-wing Rawlsianism and Right-wing Rawlsianism. How do we balance the "two wrongs can make a right," and resolve an "adjustment of compensating injustices?" Given that we have a system that bears some relationship to the Rawlsian ideal (at least the first principle of justice has been largely realized), the Left Rawlsian might focus upon the second principle of justice and the second priority rule. Since the second principle (i.e., the difference principle and fair equality of opportunity) is lexically prior to efficiency, one might argue that although efficiency might be hampered by disruptions in the expectations of property owners when their exercise of heretofore sacrosanct property rights could be curtailed in the future, this is of less concern than the preservation of future possibilities for the least advantaged and future generations. Thus, if the least advantaged will benefit from the Coastal Plan's preservation and planned growth strategy, Beta as a member of the more advantaged group would have no legitimate right to hinder their improvement. The Left Rawlsian would be adverse to compensation, citing the lack of a physical taking, and the possibility that Beta could use his land for other socially beneficial purposes such as a public park, or beach. The case might be strengthened further by citing the lexical priority of fair equality of opportunity to the difference principle and, hence, to efficiency. Then, the argument could be made that allowing property owners total discretion over their coastal lands would deny to others their fair equality of opportunity rights by curtailing future positions of economic advantage on the coastline to those already in a privileged position. Part of the Coastal Commission's mission is to insure that housing and apartments for those in lower economic groups will be available along the coastline, and this would be enthusiastically endorsed by the Left Rawlsian.

A Right Rawlsian might assess the situation quite differently. An explicit component of the first principle of justice, that which decrees equal compatible liberties for all, is the traditional notion of the rule of law which dictates in part: 1) that laws be enacted in good faith and that this good faith be recognized by those subject to the enactments; 2) that similar cases be treated similarly, and 3) that laws ought not be retroactive. Rawls terms this "justice as regularity,"[35] and he concludes that the rules of a legal system ought to serve to organize social behavior by providing a basis of legitimate expectations. Given that Beta bought the land before anyone conceived the Coastal Plan, the retroactivity prohibition has been violated. Likewise, Beta would hardly acknowledge the good faith of those denying him his previously legitimate expectations, nor would similar cases be treated similarly if the homes of his neighbors were allowed to stand in the abutting terrain, while his permit to build anything on his land was gainsaid. The Right Rawlsian, however, is still not a Nozickian champion of the sanctity of property, and the first principle is designed to protect almost exclusively the civil and political liberties, not the right to property. Therefore, he would not wish to prohibit the activities of the Coastal Commission; rather, he would argue for some principle of compensation.[36] Such compensation would be due only to individuals in Beta's predicament, those who owned property before the Coastal Plan was even a prospect. Clearly, for those who acquire land after the Plan has come into force, the Rawlsian would not see any need for compensation at all unless unforeseeable changes in the plan were enacted. Such future alterations even if unforeseeable might not require compensation if they were promulgated in furtherance of the second principle by a majority of the legislature. Unanimity would not be required because of the non-ideal nature of the system. The reason why aggrieved acquisiters after the Plan's inception would not deserve compensation is that the market price of land would already be discounted for the uncertainty element of the Plan.

The only unresolved issue is the extent of compensation due prior owners. This would only present a short-term problem, as previously indicated, and perhaps the Commission could give less compensation to even prior owners as time went on, under the theory that their legitimate expectations could be readjusted over time. This, however, might present insurmountable problems with property owners proffering ersatz proposals in the near-term to gain the higher compensation for the Commission's refusal. Leaving this problem aside, it seems that a Right Rawlsian would contend for something less than full market value or best use value as the standard of compensation. He might, as some have argued,[37] endorse the concept of transferable development rights (TDR's). Under a TDR system an owner denied a building permit on his land could sell his unused construction rights to other owners who would then apply it to their property enabling them to exceed such zoning restrictions' height limitations on their property. Another alternative would be to compensate Beta only for the price originally paid for the land. Again, this might be so trivial an amount as to vitiate Beta's rule of law expectation, or else it might be so large as to render the entire Coastal Plan prohibitively expensive. The Rawlsian theory of justice would provide little assistance in prescribing the actual amount of fair compensation; however, it does set the boundaries of a just resolution.

Hypothetical #1, the zoning ordinance case, presents no fundamentally new issues for Rawlsian non-ideal theory. Because it represents less of a taking than the Coastal Plan hypothetical, Alpha would have less of a claim to redress, even from the Right Rawlsian. Given that zoning pertained at the time of purchase, and that alterations of some kind in the zoning plan are not unforeseeable, and that the injury is only of a slight monetary nature, social concerns implicit in the second principle would handily override Alpha's protestations even without compensation. Just as no one is guaranteed the profitability of his product in the market, a Rawlsian might argue that no one ought to be viewed as having a compensable property right in the perpetuation of existing zoning practices.

Hypothetical #3, the sad tale of Gamma forced by a Model Cities block renewal program to relocate his business against his will but with full compensation, does raise new issues. The resolution to this case turns upon the second principle of justice. Does this exercise of eminent domain further the long-run advantage of those least well-off? But who are the relevant least advantaged? Are they the old folks who live in the neighborhood of the small shops who will be disadvantaged by having lost access to convenient shopping facilities? Are they all the poor people in the county, state, or country who might, arguably, benefit from the increased jobs, general prosperity, and aesthetic improvement engendered by projects such as this one? And what about the claims of future generations of disadvantaged? Rawls contends that saving and replenishment of the capital stock are obligations each generation owes the next. Will this sacred trust be met by allowing decaying neighborhoods to degenerate further simply to serve the convenience of the presently disadvantaged? What renders Rawlsianism so difficult to operationalize is precisely these kinds of dilemmas—of how to identify the relevant "least advantaged," and of how to resolve questions of intergenerational equity.

Again, putting these reservations aside, evidently for a Rawlsian, if Gamma and his neighbors were being inconvenienced for the construction of a public hospital that would serve the health needs of the poor the taking with compensation could be felicitously resolved. Such a taking would clearly serve the interests of the least well-off. But the proposed example of the luxury condominiums, a dubious exercise of the takings privilege for "public use" at best, would in all likelihood fall thunderously athwart the difference principle.

Conclusion

Can either of these contemporary theories of justice resolve the takings issue? Nozickian entitlement theory bereft of the Lockean proviso does offer a clear resolution to takings problems, but it is a resolution the implications of which most legal theorists, legislators, judges, and environmentalists would find extremely unpalatable. Such a truncated and radicalized entitlement theory would deny to government any power of eminent domain under practically all conceivable circumstances, and consequently proscribe all lesser takings, whether compensable or not.

Nozickian theory as it presently stands atop the Lockean proviso does, curiously enough, offer land use proponents a fairly clear standard to determine whether a taking is legitimate and, furthermore, whether it requires compensation. Under the proviso, restrictions of construction along the California Coast that did not compensate owners for their loss of expectations could be justified by invalidating the claims of the owners as violations of the "enough and as good" left for others stipulation. Thus, contrary to some of Nozick's critics who view him as an antediluvian throwback to nineteenth century *laissez faire*, Nozickian entitlement theory can serve to justify the most radical forms of land use legislation.

Rawlsian theory suffers from problems of indeterminacy and interpretability when applied to ideal systems, and the difficulties only proliferate when the fairness criteria are applied to non-ideal situations. At least when interpreted in the Right Rawlsian manner, justice as fairness offers a greater barrier to plans like that in California than does Nozickian entitlement theory, because it demands compensation, partial perhaps, in all cases of the taking of land acquired prior to the instigation of a land use plan. What makes Rawlsian principles so elusive despite the addition of priority rules is that disputes can be seen as either falling under the purview of the first or second principle of justice with equal cogency, depending upon the extent of one's disposition to view property rights as intrinsically related to the principle of liberty.

Notes

1. See: Jonathan Hughes, *The Governmental Habit* (New York: Basic Books, 1977), Ch. 1.

2. The claim by the state to intervene in private relationships in order to protect the health, safety, morals, or general welfare of the community; a doctrine which developed in the courts after the Civil War.

3. Supreme Court decisions on this issue have followed a decidedly *ad hoc,* case by case deliberative process eschewing the adoption of general principles. The result has been confusion. See: "Developments in the Law: Zoning," *Harvard Law Review,* 91(1978):1464, in which recent case law from the lower courts was examined. The results of this survey are a mixed bag of incompatible rulings founded upon disparate tests, eg. (1) "the degree of economic loss imposed by the challenged measure," (2) "a balancing of the measure's public benefits against its private harms," (3) "the diameter of the conduct prohibited by the regulation and its impact on society," (4) "various formulations of fairness concerns," (5) "the expectations of the aggrieved property holder," and (6) "whether a physical intrusion has occurred." In fact, these first two tests can be traced to Justice Holmes' decision in *Pennsylvania Coal Co. v. Mahon,* 260 U.S. 393 (1922). Here, a law prohibiting coal companies from mining in order to protect surface properties from subsidence was declared unconstitutional as a taking of property without just compensation. The tests Holmes invoked have been recited in countless subsequent cases on the state and federal levels. Both a "diminution in value" test and a "balancing" test were invoked by Holmes and not carefully distinguished. Property values can be diminished by police power measures (i.e., measures to protect the health, safety, morals, and general welfare) to a certain degree, but if that loss becomes too severe a "takings" results and compensation must be forthcoming or else the measure becomes invalid. This encouraged a case by case scrutiny of the facts in each litigation, and, naturally, a crazy quilt of decisional law in which cases seemingly analogous are distinguished on arbitrary grounds (see the decisions dealing with the federal navigational servitude), and other cases in which slight damages are compensated (eg., if a strip of land is taken for a sidewalk) while catastrophic losses are left completely uncompensated (eg., if a sand and gravel pit is declared a public nuisance and prohibited (*Goldblatt v. Town of Hempstead,* 369 U.S. 590 (1962)).

4. For discussions of the takings issue in the recent literature, see: Sax, "Takings and the Police Power," *Yale Law Journal* 74 (1964); 36, Michelmaw, "Property, Utility, and Fairness: Comments on the Ethical Foundation of 'Just Compensation' Law," *Harvard Law Review* 80 (1967): 1156; Coase, "The Problem of Social Cost," *Journal of Law and Economics,* 3 (1960); Hoskins, "Police Power and Compensable Takings—A Landmark Decision Clarifies the Rule," *Connecticut Law Review,* 11 (1979); 279; "Developments in the Law: Zoning," *Harvard Law Review* (which offers extensive references); Costonis, " 'Fair' Compensation and the Accomodation Power: Antidotes for the Takings Impasse in Land Use Controversies," *Columbia Law Review* 75 (1975): 1021.

5. John Rawls, *A Theory of Justice* (Cambridge: Harvard University Press, 1971).

6. Robert Nozick, *Anarchy, State, and Utopia* (New York: Basic Books, 1974).

7. *Village of Euclid* v. *Ambler Realty Co.* 279 U.S. 365 (1926).

8. In *Nectow* v. *City of Cambridge,* 277 U.S. 183 (1928), the court did invalidate a zoning regulation because, under investigation by a master, it was found to deprive the affected land of any possible use compatible with its designation as zoned (i.e., residential); and no necessity was found to justify the restriction as a police power measure (i.e., in furtherance of the health, safety, or general welfare). But this finding certainly did not undercut the Court's *Euclid* endorsement of the legitimacy of zoning under the police power, but rather reemphasized the limits to that power adumbrated in *Euclid.* In *Nectow,* Justice Sutherland wrote for the Court: "The governmental power to interfere by zoning regulation with the general rights of the landowner by restricting the character of its use, is not unlimited, and other questions aside, such restrictions cannot be imposed if it does not bear a substantial relation to the public health, safety, morals, or general welfare." 277 U.S. 183, 188.

9. Let us assume that this reorganization has not been accomplished in a manner that would violate procedural due process. That is, it was not done by administrative fiat, but rather by the legislature, in accordance with a comprehensive plan, and not retroactively.

10. *Just* v. *Marinette County*, 56 Wis. 2d 7, 201 N.W. 2d 761 (1972).

11. *Sibson* v. *State of New Hampshire*, 115 N.H. 124, 336 A. 2d 239 (1975). For a discussion of this case see: Ackerman, *Private Property and the Constitution* (New Haven: Yale, 1977).

12. In reaching this conclusion the New Hampshire court invoked several currently fashionable theories which have the effect of expanding the scope of permissible police power regulation: 1) The Sax test (Sax, "Takings, Private Property and Public Rights," 81 Yale L.J. 149 (1971)—that if the state action proscribes activities that could harm the public it is a valid exercise of the police power and, hence, noncompensable, but if it appropriates property for the public use, the property owner must be indemnified, and 2) a balancing test—in which the importance of the public benefit sought to be promoted is weighed against the seriousness of the restriction of a private right, and the legislation is sustained unless the benefit is of such a minor nature as to render the restriction on the landowner unreasonable. For a recent discussion of the wetlands issue, see: Donald W. Steever, Jr., "Trends in Wetland Litigation," *Environmental Comment*, (August, 1977): 9-12.

13. From Proposition 20, as quoted in Tom Hazlett, "A Case of Coastal Piracy," *Inquiry*, (March 1979): 17.

14. For a detailed discussion of the California Coastal Plan, see: David B. Zulob, "The California Coastal Plan," *Environmental Policy and Law* 2 (April 1976).

15. Not a preposterous hypothetical situation at all. See: Hazlett "A Case of Coastal Piracy." Standing to bring an objection before the Commission is broadly extended to all interested parties under the Coastal Act.

16. This hypothetical is, in substance, based upon an actual incident. See: *Cincinnati Enquirer*, May 4, 1979, "Shop Keepers Find Some Happiness in Dislocation."

17. Nozick, *Anarchy, State, and Utopia*, pp. 151, 153.

18. *Ibid.*, p. 155.

19. *Ibid.*, p. 176.

20. *Ibid.*, p. 179.

21. *Ibid.*, p. 182.

22. *Spur Industries, Inc.* v. *Del E. Webb Development Co.*, 494 P. 2d 700, 4 ERC 1052 (1972).

23. Bernard H. Siegan, "Non-zoning in Houston," *The Journal of Law and Economics*, 13 (April 1970): 71-147. See also: Ellickson, "Alternatives to Zoning: Covenants, Nuisance Rules, and Fines as Land Use Controls," *University of Chicago Law Review*, 40 (1973): 681; and Ross, "Land Use Control in Metropolitan Areas: The Future of Zoning and a Proposed Alternative," *Southern California Law Review*, 45 (1972): 335.

24. *Ibid.*, Siegan, p. 142.

25. However, this distinction appears of rather dubious merit. The doctor who is the only person who can perform a lifesaving operation on you and refuses, seems to fall into the identical category with the oasis owner who refuses you water from his well. Both are denying you benefits to which they claim sole property rights to be utilized at their discretion. Hence, if the inaction of one is legitimate, so is the other, or else they are both illegitimate.

26. One ought to note that Nozick allows for compensation on the part of would-be property owners who fall afoul of the Lockean proviso in order to buy the acquiesence of disadvantaged parties. For our purposes, this seems to be irrelevant since the state has interposed itself between all other offended parties and the property acquirer. In the case of the California Coastal Plan, one could argue that the California voters by implication denied to property pursuers this option.

27. R. Fullinwider, "A Chronological Bibliography of Works on John Rawls' *Theory of Justice*," *Political Theory*, 5 (November 1977): 561-570.

28. Rawls, *A Theory of Justice*, pp. 302-303.

29. *Ibid.*, p. 279; also, pp. 264, 303.

30. *Ibid.*, see the discussion of public goods, pp. 266-274.

31. *Ibid.*, p. 271.

32. *Ibid.*, pp. 271-274.

33. *Ibid.*, p. 276.

34. *Ibid.*, pp. 282-4.

35. *Ibid.*, pp. 235-238.

36. Michelman, "Property, Utility, and Fairness: Comments on the Ethical Foundations of 'Just Compensation' Law". According to one model Michelman offers, his Rawlsian basic fairness model, an uncompensated taking is not unfair so long as the disappointed claimant ought to see how such decisions will, in the long-run, pose less risk to people like him than would any alternative program. If the offended party can reasonably be viewed as having his category of individuals placed in a worse situation than under alternative land use proposals, compensation would be due (pp. 1221-23).

37. See: J. Costonis, "Development Rights Transfer: An Explanatory Essay," *Yale Law Journal* 83 (1973): 75; Note, "The Unconstitutionality of Transferable Development Rights," *Yale Law Journal* 85 (1975): 1101.

TIBOR R. MACHAN*

Dissolving the Problem of
Public Goods:
Financing Government without
Coercive Measures

Among those who regard liberty as the highest, or primary public value, there are some who believe that government is, by its very nature, a morally unacceptable institution.[1] Others hold, as I do, that government is precisely that institution that should be established so as to protect and preserve the liberty at issue in this context, namely, the liberty accorded to human beings when their fellows refrain from initiating force in human encounters.[2] The first group, "anarcho-libertarians," share something with statists: the belief that government *requires* the initiation of physical force (and its threat). The anarchists conclude from this that no government is justifiable, whereas statists conclude that the allegedly required coercion is justifiable. There are some libertarians, however, who reject the premise that government entails the initiation of coercion. To make out their case, they face some unique problems. Of these I wish to take just one, namely, whether it is possible to provide government with financial support adequate for its task without relying on any institutional coercive measures such as taxation, which is the expropriation of wealth from citizens by force for purposes of funding the work of governments.

The services provided by governments are commonly regarded as public goods, since, if provided, such services can be enjoyed even by those who would not

*SUNY, Fredonia and UCSB

choose to pay for them. The most frequently cited example of such a public good is national defense. Once it is secured, everyone can easily benefit without having to contribute to the cost of production. As John Rawls notes, "A citizen receives the same protection from foreign invasion regardless of whether he has paid his taxes."[3] Such public goods, then, might never be produced if we relied on voluntary support, since too many members of the community might count on a free ride, believing that *their* support of national defense isn't required in order for it to be produced and thus available to them. As Rolf Sartorius observes, if

> each agree[s] to cooperate contingently upon others doing likewise [then] . . .
> each reasons that either enough others so agree and the public good thus
> becomes available to him free of charge, or enough others do not and thus there
> would have been no point to agreeing in the first place.
> Individuals would not voluntarily cooperate toward [the support of govern-
> ment], and observing the principle that no one may be deprived of his property
> without his consent would prevent the state from compelling him to do so,
> either by way of compulsory taxation or conscription.[4]

The conclusion facing the nonanarchist (or archist) libertarian is that either we have such public goods as national defense—and governmental compulsion of payment for them—or we must do without such goods. Both of these are unacceptable for those libertarians who regard government, in its proper form, an essential and valuable institution of a human community.

The problem of public goods—i.e., that there can be so many who plan on free riding that the goods may not be produced at all—is easily dismissed when we are not speaking of political matters. Some public goods, so called, have nothing to do with politics, citizenship, or government. People walking in "public" places, namely where many who live nearby or far gather or commute, are free riders in their enjoyment of the way others dress or look, yet no one worries about this because there is no assumption here about such benefit being essential. If others find it too costly to make themselves good-looking at their own expense, so be it. Similarly, if it costs too much to produce television signals capable of being received by those not paying for them, they might not get produced; but again, television signals are by no means essential public goods. National defense and other political values, however, are demonstrably essential for the very survival and functioning of a free society, at least in terms the nonanarchist libertarian conceives of human community life. This is why the public goods problem must be solved before the libertarian who considers government vital can rest assured that his conception of political life is possible, let alone preferable, to all others.

To a large extent the public goods/free rider problem grows out of the familiar assumption of contemporary economic theory, namely, that everyone is a utility maximizing individual, motivated solely by the desire to pursue private gains. Assuming that a public good is one that an individual would desire, but only at the minimal expense (of his wealth or time) necessary for its attainment, then any opportunity to become a free rider would be seized. This may not require, according to Mancur Olson, "the selfish, profit maximizing behavior that economists usually find in the market place . . . [since] even if the number of a large group were to neglect his own interests entirely, he still would not rationally contribute towards the provision of any collective or public good, since his own contribution would not be perceptible."[5] It seems, however, that this result still requires something akin to the economists' assumption, since without it we can easily imagine some citizens contributing to the provision of the public good as a matter of principle. Moreover, we can imagine that recognition and discussion of the public goods problem would spur the members of the group in question, if all were not solely eager to secure for themselves what they value at the lowest cost, to make arrangements to overcome the problem. This is what frequently happens when a group of people engage in the selection of a restaurant for dinner—some of them, realizing that not everyone's preference can be satisfied, simply withdraw from the discussion about what restaurant to choose. When a check is brought for the entire group, those who had lower priced meals will often agree to an even divying up of the bill. The value of keeping things going, of fraternity, and of related matters that correspond in some measure to public goods is great enough to forgo the chance of getting the best possible deal on the meal.

As Richard Tuck has noted, "the free-rider problem is not in fact a problem of *political* theory alone—it is merely a particular application of a general logical problem," that of the paradox of the Sorites: "One stone does not make a heap; but the addition of one stone to something that is not a heap can never transform it into a heap." Tuck argues that "we have to treat minute increments as non-negligible, even though the Sorites argument seems to establish that they ought to be treated as [negligible]." With respect to public goods, Tuck observes that "universal confidence in (say) stable property ownership or continued personal freedom is desirable; . . . a particular defection from such a universal practice in the interest of local utility would not sap that confidence, though iterated defection would."[6] And except on the assumption of narrow selfishness, whereby everyone is obsessed with getting away with a free ride, such iterated defection need not be counted upon.

The solution that I am proposing, however, does not depend on how many members of society would defect just in case they could get away with it. Rather, I want to suggest an approach to understanding the nature of government as a public good that would undercut the problem associated with the provision of such public goods as national defense by the recognition that the provision of other, nonpublic (government provided) goods depends on providing the former, as well. Let me first sketch how this suggestion solves the problem of government financing.

The key to this idea is that a libertarian government would provide crucial yet unique private goods as well as public goods, and this would make it possible to secure the financing of government voluntarily. The provision of the private goods can be linked directly to the consumer, who would need to pay for it. Yet, given that the private good is a uniquely political good, providable only by or within the framework of a political/legal institution such as government, it would afford the opportunity to collect support for the public good that is also required. For example, the protection of contracts is a private good that government provides at some level of the adjudicatory process in contractual disputes. (Even if a dispute is handled by a private arbitration board, the government/legal framework must be there "in the wings" to assure due process in such matters as arrest, trial, imprisonment, and seizure of property, should the decision of the arbitrators be rejected by one of the parties.) The national defense that government would provide is, of course, the classic public good. But government provides both goods, and payment for the former would also serve to fund the latter. In an imperfect analogy, this is similar to the way in which Coca Cola buyers pay for the overhead and security provisions at the bottling plants even though, if asked to contribute money for these purposes, they might well refuse—on standard public goods grounds!

In spelling this proposal out a bit, let us first recall that the justification and need of government arises from the objective value to all members of society of living with others without personal militarization, ad hoc adjudication of disputes, and the general insecurity that goes with lawlessness. Individuals who recognize the value of social life readily acknowledge the value of establishing an agency to provide them with the protection and preservation of their rights in the context of a system of objective law.[7]

Take contracts, for example. One of the benefits of social life is the possibility of extensive promise making for a variety of purposes—artistic, commercial, romantic, scientific, educational, recreational, athletic, and so forth. Sometimes relations among human beings are such that trust, danger of bad reputation, loss of friendship, etc., do not adequately assure against loss of value, against inadequate return on considerable investment, or against the performance of outright victimization and injury. Some of these concerns can be handled by turning to insurance agencies. But sometimes, when matters are important and complex—and they very frequently are—satisfaction is obtainable only through legal protection, e.g., against the violation of rights. Here, it is not simply some service, but some service *aiming at justice*, that is sought. Contracts are one way of insuring against serious loss and supporting efforts toward recovery, but by means that remain attentive to human dignity, that is, to the fact that no one is officially permitted to abridge the natural human rights of individuals in the community. Justly upholding the terms of contract is one government service. Government is the institution of a community specifically responsible for maintaining justice among members as members. This task is frequently accomplished only by the use of physical force, which government, by virtue of its unique adherence to the principle of due process— e.g., stringent rules of evidence, clear and present danger, probable cause, speedy and fair trial provisions, etc.—is established to carry out.

Promise breakers could have good reason for breaking their promises, but they would have even better reason to reassure their trading partners about the recovery of investment or avoidance of serious losses. Thus, even in usual utility-maximizing terms, members of society would ordinarily find it beneficial to secure the private good of government protection and enforcement of contracts (even if government is involved only as the ultimate protector—see the above discussion of arbitration). Especially in a human community in which traders do not know each other personally, then, the prospect of entering into enforceable contractual relationships is of considerable objective value to practically everyone.

For these and related reasons, it is plausible that the private good of having one's own liberty protected and preserved in the context of contractual relationships would be one of the most widely sought services of government in a free society. Every valid contract imposes a burden on the legal system and its administrators, for the "machinery" for interpreting and enforcing contracts, should disputes arise, must be in place. So providing this protection requires expenditures on the part of government. A system of contract fees, collected at the time of the signing or registering of contracts—from the most simple trades to elaborate corporate arrangements—with provisions for further payment in case of special services generated throughout the period of the contractual relationship, would provide funding for this government activity. Even the faintest appreciation for the staggering number of contracts drawn in contemporary societies within the span of just one day will suggest the revenue-obtaining potential of government work.

Like contract protection, other governmental services are deliverable to individuals, so fees for the services rendered could be established. Among such potentially individualized services are securing criminal justice and defending private homes and businesses or supervising such defense by private security agents so that due process of law is preserved.[8] Not only would it be possible to require payment for particular services rendered, but, if criminal actions are involved, burdens could be distributed in line with the determination of legal responsibility. For example, court costs could be imposed on guilty parties, and criminals could be required to cover other costs, such as police services.

For government to be able to carry out these functions, however—to stand ready for purposes of adjudicating disputes, defending persons and property, issuing warrants for arrest, seeking reparations, imposing penalties or imprisonment—it must be stable and secure. Government, in other words, has overhead costs, including those associated with providing for the defense of *the system of laws* itself. Foreign aggression, usually aimed at the country as a whole, is obviously a threat to this system. Once a country has been conquered, the foreigners take over the administration of justice and, with appropriate alterations (though by no means with even very dramatic ones), continue the business of state, good or ill. Against this eventuality a government should protect the community, including itself—or, the institution of government must be so constituted that its protection of its own functions is provided for as a necessary means towards its provision of the protection and preservation of the rights of its citizens. Accordingly, its charges for the provision of its various services would reasonably include some amount to cover the cost of defense against foreign aggression. In this respect, the situation would be much like Coca Cola paying for security guards and other overhead costs from earnings from the sale of such clearly individually consumed goods as bottles of Coke.

It might be thought that in this way the principles of a free society, as conceived along libertarian lines, would be breached. First, would not everyone be required to pay for services? Second, would not those who might wish to compete in the provision of government's private services be forcibly excluded?

Regarding the fear of reintroducing coercive financing, it must be observed that entering into contractual agreements, for example, is an entirely voluntary matter. Anyone can, literally, simply accept a handshake or friendly wink and not bother with contracts, just as one can avoid marriage vows and simply leave it at being lovers. Yet the existence of a legal system makes possible the legal protection of relations beyond the state of promises, should one desire this firmer protection. And such private goods, obtainable from government, would reasonably carry the burden of supporting the public good of national defense.

But what about the objection that in a free society government could not legitimately bar others from providing, say, contract protection. And then those others could offer it at a lower price, not having the national-defense overhead costs to worry about. So government would lose its private-goods customers, and this would still leave us with the public goods problem.[9]

This objection, usually advanced by economists with an anarchist libertarian viewpoint, can be met by noting that government is the political institution which is established and authorized to pursue justice in the social realm, making it a monopoly both in the sense of classic natural monopolies and in the sense of the requirement for internal integrity in the administration of justice. That is, on the one hand, the same services provided outside the legal framework would not be as valuable without provisions of due process of law. On the other hand, the ethical justification of establishing government implies that in human relations, where disputes often arise and sometimes culminate in conflict, an institution be invoked which is capable of providing for the most peaceful, least rights-violating procedures required for problem solving. In short, there will very likely be greater demand for government-backed arbitration proceedings, and the very logic of establishing government (from the ethical point of view of why they *should* be established) would generate this demand.[10]

Outside the context of a libertarian conception of government, this solution might be challenged on grounds, among others, that governmental costs are enormous and the very existence of deficit spending in most modern societies indicates that not even taxation can secure enough funding for government. In libertarian theory, however, the scope of government is severely confined to securing the protection and preservation of Lockean natural (individual human) rights. That is, only protecting and preserving everyone's Lockean rights are legitimate governmental concerns.[11] Although such a service is a public good that can be made private in its particular delivery (as detailed earlier), it is still a public good in the sense of its provision being good for members of the community as such, for citizens as citizens. But because there is a definite constraint on what constitutes such a public good, it should be plausible, at least, that its provision will not involve so much cost as is now commonly associated with governmental operations that range from some bona fide public goods—e.g., criminal law and national defense—to such nonpublic goods as national public radio, mail service, and the printing of money.[12]

In short, then, competition in providing *legal* protection and adjudication of contracts would be impossible because this good is not solely an economic but also a political good, the provision of which requires the existence and maintenance of an integrated legal system, including national defense.[13] To prohibit the provision of this good apart from the legal system is tantamount to prohibiting vigilante groups, lynching, and similar paralegal processes which always involve third parties whose rights are seriously endangered without the full protection of due process of law.

The fee-for-services-plus-overhead solution is not the only one that could be invoked to finance the administration of governments in a free society. As Ayn Rand has suggested,[14] emergency funds could be raised through lotteries or by appealing for contributions, e.g., in time of war. The integrity of the system would be evident all along, so a genuine threat to the system requiring military action could be demonstrated readily in public debate conducted by a free press, the educational and scientific communities, and so forth. When it is recalled that liberal democratic regimes are closest to the polity envisioned by libertarians (and they have all along received relatively solid popular support) the probability of support for the libertarian system—including extraordinary support in times of trouble—may also be assumed. But what is crucial is something else, namely, that it is not inherently impossible to secure the public good of the maintenance of justice, including the protection and preservation of the rights of citizens from domestic and foreign aggression, without disregarding those very values.

There is, of course, no guarantee that a government of a libertarian society *would be* voluntarily financed. Spells of neglect could settle in, or there could be periods during which government is not needed, when the world of the anarchist libertarian might be realized, at least for a brief period.[15] Yet, whenever the challenge is posed to provide such a guarantee, it must be noted that coercive funding of government is anything but a guarantee against governments' going bankrupt, waging unsuccessful and unwarranted wars, neglecting various related obligations, etc. Richard Tuck observes:

> It has been customary for political theorists to accept that [the free rider-public goods] argument is a good one, and to direct their energies toward devising strategies to cope with it. The most popular has undoubtedly been some mechanism of social coercion, despite the fact that such mechanisms characteristically depend on cooperative action by the people concerned, and that the argument is therefore likely to turn into a *regressusu ad infinitum.*[16]

If the false and impossible ideal of guaranteed provision of public goods is rejected, as it should be, then the solution offered along lines sketched above will have to be assessed comparatively[17] It will have to be judged in accordance with how well it would secure for members of human communities the values they should seek from a legal system, granting that all such proposals carry risks of abuse and neglect, risks the elimination of which from human affairs is not only impossible but dangerous to pursue.

Notes:

*Discussions with Rolf Sartorius, David Friedman, and Lester H. Hunt have helped me in formulating my case, which isn't to say that they would be satisfied with the result. I wish to thank Marty Zupan for her advice, support, and editorial assistance in my completion of this essay.

1. See, e.g., Murray N. Rothbard, *Power and Market* (Menlo Park, Calif.: Institute for Humane Studies, 1970). See also his essay in this volume, "Society without a State."

2. I provide a moral case for such a libertarian government, as well as a case against the anarchist libertarian position, in *Human Rights and Human Liberties* (Chicago: Nelson-Hall, 1975)

3. John Rawls, *A Theory of Justice* (Cambridge, Mass.: Harvard University Press, 1971), p. 267.

4. Rolf Sartorius, "Limits of Libertarianism," in R. L. Cunningham, ed., *Liberty and the Rule of Law* (College Station, Texas: Texas A & M University Press, 1979), pp. 92, 122.

5. Mancur Olson, *The Logic of Collective Action* (Cambridge, Mass.: Harvard University Press, 1965), p. 64.

6. Richard Tuck, "Is there a free-rider problem, and if so, what is it?" in R. Harrison, ed., *Rational Action* (Cambridge, Eng.: Cambridge University Press, 1977), pp. 152-56.

7. Perhaps I should say that they *should* and probably will acknowledge the value of such an agency. This brings up the issue of how a government is properly established, something

that comprises a crucial feature of the libertarian framework but is beyond the scope of the present essay. But see my "Human Rights, Feudalism, and Political Change," in A. Rosebaum, ed., *The Philosophy of Human Rights* (Westport, Conn.: Greenwood Press, 1980), pp. 207-51.

8. In some cases, the possibility of differentiating in service delivery may depend on technological developments, although it is more likely that it would simply require people's willingness to modify standard commercial practices to the services in question. Skeptics may wish to check out the method of customer differentiation devised by a private provider of fire protection. See Robert W. Poole, Jr., "Fighting Fires for Profit," *Reason*, May 1976, pp. 6-11.

9. See, e.g., David Friedman, *The Machinery of Freedom* (New York: Harper & Row, 1973), chapter 34 .

10. Machan, op. cit., *Human Rights and Human Liberties*.

11. For the view that libertarian natural rights are not the familiar Lockean rights which impose only negative duties on others—e.g., the obligation to refrain from initiating physical force against others—but that they instead "involve providing people with positive benefit," see James W. Nickel, "Is There a Human Right to Employment?" *Philosophical Forum* 10 (Winter-Summer 1978-79): 164. But this view is mistaken, and the mistake stems from the belief that human rights are rights against government as distinct from rights that should be respected by all and for the protection and preservation of which governments should be established. See my "Wronging Rights," *Policy Review* 17 (Summer 1981): pp. 37-58.

12. I develop the argument for this in "Rational Choice and Public Affairs," *Theory and Decision* 12 (September 1980): 229-58.

13. For more on this see, David Kelley, "The Necessity of Government," *The Freeman* 24 (April 1974): None of this precludes the free operations of security services, arbitration groups, etc., which are ultimately accountable to government and do not undertake the enforcement of decisions independently of government.

14. Ayn Rand, "Government Financing in a Free Society," in E. S. Phelps, ed., *Economic Justice* (Baltimore: Penguine Books, 1973), pp. 363-67.

15. Certain periods of individualist anarchism have occurred throughout human history. See, for an example, Joseph R. Peden, "Property Rights in Celtic Irish Law," *Journal of Libertarian Studies* 1 (Spring 1977): 81-95

16. Tuck, *op. cit.*, "Free-rider Problem," pp. 147-48.

17. Further details and refinements of this and related tasks of a libertarian political system are, of course, required but it is usual for those to emerge only after the basic framework proposed is deemed workable. The political science and legal elaboration of libertarianism presuppose the basic plausibility of the general system.

PART FOUR

Liberty and Morality

DOUGLAS DEN UYL*

Freedom and Virtue

Modern political thinkers have consistently agreed that the goal of social action is freedom. Spinoza, for example, states that "the purpose (*finis*) of the state is really freedom."[1] Rousseau's opening comments of the *Social Contract* indicate that he is concerned with the liberation of mankind. J. S. Mill, in the introductory chapter of *On Liberty,* argues that the conflict between liberty and authority is the central political issue. Ancient political philosophy, on the other hand, is characterized by a rather different attitude toward the purpose of the state. Aristotle, in fact, criticizes the democrat who places liberty and equality above all social values.[2] For the ancients, virtue constituted the end to be sought. It is "for the sake of good actions . . . that political associations must be considered to exist."[3] The fundamental political choice, therefore, seems to be between a regime that promotes freedom and one that promotes virtue. Are these mutually exclusive alternatives?

I

If a free society is defined as one in which each person may live his life as he chooses so long as he does not infringe on the rights of others by the initiation of physical force, then the classical attitude on what a political regime should seek to secure would seem to be the most defensible in all cases. Given a society whose institutions conformed to the above principle, there would be no question of the promotion of freedom. A free society could not promote freedom, because that society would already *be* free. That is to say, that freedom would not be something a society or its members could aspire to. Freedom would instead characterize their condition or state of existence. The promotion of freedom only makes sense in societies that are unfree. Virtue, on the other hand, is something that can always serve as an object of one's aspirations. A man may be born free, but he is never born virtuous. For this reason, all societies are in a position to consider the promotion of virtue. Free societies can seek to maintain their freedom, but freedom will not

This is a significantly revised version of the paper "Freedom and Virtue," *Reason Papers,* No. 5 (Winter 1979).
*Bellarmine College.

serve as a further goal for the members of that society. The answer given by the ancients to the question of what constitutes the central social goal is, therefore, a most profound one; for, unlike the goal of freedom, virtue is an ever-present concern even in an ideally free society.

It might be objected that people always desire to purge themselves of such social burdens as poverty, disease, and ignorance. We desire to be free of these burdens; and since actions must be taken to achieve this type of freedom, freedom can be promoted in a free society. This objection, however, is not without difficulties. In the first place, it is true that the relief of poverty, disease, and ignorance can serve as goals in any society. Yet freedom conceived in terms of the relief of burdens cannot be a primary sense of freedom. The mere aspiration to relieve certain burdens implies nothing about the context in which those burdens are to be relieved. That is to say, such aspirations would be present in any social context whether the society was rich, poor, politically repressive, politically liberal, etc. And since the aspiration to relieve certain burdens is present in any (actual) society, the criterion of relieving burdens cannot serve as the most essential standard for distinguishing a free from an unfree society. Thus one is compelled to search for a more fundamental conception of freedom that will set the context for legitimizing any secondary senses of freedom. One must be able to claim, in other words, that the institutional arrangements of a society (in which particular goals are sought) are themselves free. The definition of freedom given above qualifies as a candidate for a first-order, or primary, conception of freedom (there may be other candidates). That definition does not suffer from a need for a setting in which the conditions demanded by the definition can be met. The definition itself determines such a setting. In short, the relief-of-burdens view of freedom must be derivative from or dependent upon a more fundamental conception of freedom, since the aspiration to relieve burdens begs one to search for the proper context for that relief.

But suppose we grant that the relief of burdens cannot serve as a fundamental standard for determining which societies are free. Nevertheless, the objection could be re-phrased to read: given a primary conception of freedom, is it not still possible to pursue freedom in a free society by relieving burdens which are admittedly secondary freedoms? This reformulated objection brings us to the second major defect of the relief-of-burdens view of freedom. To relieve burdens requires action, and the mere desire to obtain such relief does not specify the nature of the actions to be taken. We could, for example, solve the problems of poverty, disease, and ignorance simply by doing away with whoever is poor, sick, or stupid. Some knowledge is, therefore, required in order to distinguish between right and wrong actions. Yet once we become concerned with the distinction between right and wrong, we are no longer considering freedom but rather virtue. Right action or virtue can be promoted, but the *actual* relief of burdens cannot. To be without burdens is, once again, to be in a certain existential condition. Actions conducive to securing that condition can be promoted in order to obtain the desired result, but the result itself cannot properly be considered without giving attention to the means necessary for the achievement of that result. Thus, a society cannot literally promote freedom from any burden and cannot properly promote a certain set of means for the relief of burdens without first having a clearly defined set of ethical principles that justify the means under consideration. In some sense, therefore, the relief of burdens presupposes the promotion of virtue—that is, right action.

A second objection to the conclusion that freedom cannot be the central social goal might be that a society could promote freedom by insuring the freedom to *do* certain things, such as obtaining a better job, receiving an education, or having the leisure to travel. The freedom to engage in certain activities, however, is also a second-order view of freedom and suffers the same defects as noted above. The freedom to do X(s) calls for a determination of the context in which X will be done. Moreover, the freedom to an X raises the question of whether X is good for human beings and the question of the appropriate means for pursuing X. Once these questions are raised, one is compelled to search for both a more fundamental conception of freedom and some standards for determining which things are worthy of our aspirations. The latter concern again raises the issue of virtue; for the virtuous person is able to distinguish the good things from the bad. [4]

The foregoing arguments indicate that reflection moves us to transcend the concern with secondary senses of freedom. We must justify that primary context in which our actions will take place and determine those moral principles that establish the permissible within that context. Concern for the relief of certain burdens and the attainment of certain goods must give way to a concern for gaining the wisdom necessary to understand what must be secured to relieve *any* burden or gain *any* good. Wisdom, in this sense, means not only practical knowledge of the means to certain ends but, most importantly, knowledge of those principles that should guide and set the context for all of our actions. Right action is itself dependent upon wisdom; for it would make no sense to claim that one ought to do A and, at the same time, have no conception of why alternatives to A are either wrong or less than satisfactory. Knowledge of moral principles is thus more fundamental than concrete moral acts. In the end, one comes to recognize the myopic nature of doctrines formulated exclusively in terms of secondary freedoms.

The promotion of virtue is of fundamental importance because persons stand in need of standards to guide their actions. A society without a sense of its own fundamental moral principles is one in which the members of that society are not able to perceive clearly the worthiness of their actions. Moreover, as indicated above, a society whose sole focus is upon the secondary freedoms is one out of touch (or soon to lose touch) with more fundamental concerns. The United States is today a country that has lost sight of its earlier concern with a primary conception of freedom. [5] Instead, the secondary freedoms now dominate the public consciousness. Since the "pursuit" of secondary freedom is argued for on moral grounds, the interesting question is whether a primary sense of freedom is compatible with the demands of moral virtue. The foregoing discussion has argued for the importance of moral virtue and has also shown the deficiencies inherent in an exclusive concern with secondary freedom. Thus, can a primary conception of freedom (such as mutual non-interference) also set the context for the advancement of virtue in society? In the next section I argue that moral virtue cannot be achieved by the coercive measures so common in contemporary social life. I conclude that freedom in the primary sense not only depicts the proper setting for social interaction, but also specifies the conditions for a meaningful sense of moral virtue.

II

"Virtue" is a moral term—that is, a term understood within an ethical or moral context. The nature of the ethical theory one adopts is therefore likely to determine one's view of virtue. Without developing a full ethical theory here or even outlining one, I can look into a specific moral question that is relevant to our present theme. The conclusions drawn below should be sufficient to indicate the necessary connection between freedom and virtue.

Given the assumption that freedom ought to be maintained and virtue promoted (i.e., given the argument of the first section), the question whether there might be some conflict between freedom and virtue still remains. This question arises because freedom, as earlier defined (mutual non-interference), seems too weak a condition for securing virtue. The apparent weakness of mutual non-interference has led many to call upon certain coercive agencies to act in behalf of virtue or moral goodness. We shall, therefore, examine the moral significance of the methods used by that agency which puts checks on our freedom for the sake of the "morally proper"—namely, we shall examine the methods employed by government. Government is an institution often utilized by those who seek to undertake moral actions. Certain individuals claim moral worth or credit for actions that employ the coercive power of government. The question under consideration is whether, in fact, one does deserve moral worth or credit when utilizing the coercive power of government to perform certain alleged "good deeds."

If it can be shown that the employment of coercive methods can never be morally worthy (and is indeed morally unworthy), then freedom and virtue will not be in conflict *politically,* since it will be for ethical reasons that this traditional role of government will be criticized. Our primary definition of freedom, in other words, will not only serve to define the context in which other secondary senses of freedom might obtain, but that definition will also serve to define the ethical context in which virtuous actions must derive their meaning. Thus, mutual non-interference will be primary with respect to both freedom and virtue and will serve as the condition that must be presupposed before any meaningful sense can be given to freedom and virtue. Freedom and virtue, therefore, will be seen as inextricably linked.[6]

Coercion can be defined as the use (or threat) of physical force. There are two types of coercion. The first is initiatory—the initiation of (or threat of) the use of physical force. Most present-day governments are greatly expanding their use of initiatory coercion. Initiatory coercion can be distinguished from the second type—retaliatory coercion, or the retaliatory use of physical force (e.g., self-defense). I cannot undertake here a discussion of retaliatory coercion, except to note that retaliatory coercion may not be inconsistent with the definition of freedom given above. The rights people possess would have little practical significance if it were not possible to ensure the protection of those rights. Retaliatory coercion may therefore be necessary to counter the destructive effects of initiatory coercion. Moreover, retaliatory coercion may be the morally proper response to initiatory coercion.

The argument below will concern only initiatory coercion, which has traditionally been considered consistent with a virtuous and moral society. We shall first examine whether those who initiate coercion (or advocate that initiation) for the sake of some "good" thereby gain or deserve moral worth. We shall then examine whether coercion ought ever to be employed.

The notion of responsibility can be considered the central concept for a proper understanding of morality and human rights. Moral consideration cannot be given to a person's deeds unless that person was responsible for doing those deeds—that is, was the moral agent of the deed. There can be no good or bad deeds without actual doers of the deeds; and in order to qualify as a doer (i.e., moral agent) of a deed, one must be responsible for the deed done. Yet this seemingly obvious point has been almost completely ignored in contemporary society.

A word needs to be said here about the relation of moral agency, or responsibility, to moral predicates (terms such as "good," "bad," "noble," "just," etc. applied to persons and their acts). We have already assumed that if a person is not responsible for taking an action, that person cannot be held morally responsible for the act. "Moral agency" is thus a notion whose full intelligibility necessarily depends upon the notion of responsibility. To be responsible or to act responsibly means to be an adult human being who undertakes an action by his own choice.[7] A person is not held responsible for an act if he was forced to do that act or if he is mentally defective or incompetent. By the same token, if a person does not do an act he is not responsible for the act (e.g., when we find out someone else did the act). On the basis of these conceptual relationships it thus seems reasonable to conclude that if a person did not do an act or was forced to do it, moral worthiness or unworthiness cannot be attributed to that person.

Now just as a man cannot be held responsible for an act he did not do or was forced to do, the act itself cannot be of any moral significance if there are no responsible agents performing the act. In a community of sleepwalkers or zombies, there would be no morally good or bad acts. The reason for this is connected to the slogan "ought implies can." In order for an act to be called good or bad, that act must be of the sort that would allow one to say, "one ought to do this" or "one ought not do that." It would make no sense to tell sleepwalkers or zombies that they ought or ought not do X, because they are not responsible agents—that is, they have no choice in what they do.

To apply the point further: if all the agents involved in an action (call them group A) were performing the action under coercion, "ought" and "ought not" would not be applicable to them *or to anyone else not in group A*. It makes no sense to say of those being coerced (group A) that they ought or ought not do X, since they have no real choice in the matter.[8] Moreover, one cannot propose to anyone outside of group A that he ought to take action X in the same way and under the same conditions that the members of group A are taking the action. The reason for this last statement is that one cannot recommend, "you ought to do X" *and also* (in the "same breath") recommend, "the way you ought to do X is by being coerced to do X." The second recommendation negates the first. When one is coerced to do X, one does not have any choice in doing X; but when one asserts that "one ought to do X" one necessarily implies that the proposed action is open to choice. One *can* choose to be coerced into getting X done; but one cannot be considered to be *doing* X in the sense of being responsible for X.[9] This last line of reasoning points to the following: there is something strange (to say the least) about the proposition, "one ought to be coerced into doing good deed X." The strangeness, I believe, stems from the separation of choice from the applicability of an ought statement. Since moral recommendations presuppose choice, the actions of a coerced party lack moral significance.

It is necessary to point out that actions with no responsible agents may have beneficial or deleterious consequences; thus the actions that produce those consequences might in everyday speech be called good or bad. For example, a sleepwalker might aid someone in his walking, and we might therefore conclude that a "good" action was done. The sleepwalker's "good" action is without any real moral force, however, since it is not possible to say of that action that one ought to perform it. [11]

One may wonder why we should ever be concerned with the moral issue. Why not simply seek to produce benefits and avoid harm? The justification for the necessity of a serious consideration of moral issues is a complicated one and beyond the scope of what can be accomplished here. Nevertheless, I did indicate in section one that to focus only upon secondary freedoms (benefits) ignores certain substantive questions that demand attention. Moreover, unless one is willing to claim that moral virtue is the same as the reception of a benefit, a concern for the advancement of virtue in society will necessarily be a concern for more than the mere production of benefits. And finally, if choice and morality are inextricably linked, it does not seem possible to escape the moral issue. For even if only a few are producing benefits by coercing the majority of people in society, those few are still acting by choice and thus subject to moral appraisal. [12]

Let us now take the case of a prejudiced white homeowner who refuses to sell his house to a black man. [13] The selling of the house would seem to be good, for if the man could be convinced to sell, he should be praised for overcoming his prejudice. The selling of the house might, furthermore, lead to racial harmony, since those who live in the neighborhood could come to recognize that there is nothing inherently wrong with blacks. Let us also suppose, however, that there is a law that prohibits such refusal of sale. In this case there would be four principal actors: the homeowner (H), the black man (B), the police who enforce the law (P), and the legislators who made the law (L). Let us suppose further that because of L, P forced H to sell to B. Now if we ask who is the moral agent (or responsible agent) in the actual selling of the house, we find that our answer to this question must be, nobody. H is not responsible for "selling" the house, because he was coerced into the "sale." L and P are not responsible agents for the "sale," because they did not sell the house, since it was not theirs to sell. B, of course, does not figure into the selling act. We have, therefore, the peculiar picture of the performance of a supposedly good act without any morally responsible agents of the act.

It is true that L and P (and also H and B) are responsible in one sense, namely, *that* the house was "sold." The fact that L and P were responsible that the house was "sold," however, in no way entitles them to any moral credit. In order to discover the reason for this last assertion let us draw a distinction between "responsibility-that" and "responsibility-for." Responsibility-that an action occurs refers to the causal mode which brought about the action. Responsibility-for an action will include certain features of responsibility-that but adds the moral element of whether and in what sense the agents of the action acted by choice. There can be responsibility-that without responsibility-for. The case of the prejudiced homeowner is one example, and so is the case of the sleepwalker who is responsible-that the lamp fell on the floor, but not responsible for the lamp ending up there.

Yet it was noted earlier that there can be good or bad acts only when there is (to use our new term) responsibility-for. It is possible to be confused about whether someone is responsible-that an action occurred or responsible-for that action, but these practical difficulties do not affect the fact that we attach moral significance only to the latter form of responsibility.

To deserve moral credit, an action taken by an agent must be a good action. The only way any of the actions in the home-seller example could qualify as good actions would be if one were prepared to accept the notion that there can be morally good or bad actions apart from there being any agent responsible-for those actions. I have previously indicated some problems with this position. Since no one is responsible-for the "selling" of the house, the act of "selling" the house no longer qualifies as a good act (though it may well have conferred a benefit). One cannot say, in other words, that the "selling" of the house is a morally good act and one that others ought to perform. "Ought" has no meaning when applied to H or anyone else in H's position. Even *if* it were possible to say that the fact that the house was "sold" was morally good (which it is not), the fact that no one was responsible-for the "sale" of the house means that no one can claim moral credit for that "sale."[14]

The implications of the above argument are sweeping. If someone claims that he or she is about to do or advocate on moral grounds some action for the "public good," and that coercive methods will be employed to secure the desired end, then the action that results from the coercion and for which the advocate of coercion attempts to claim some moral worth is not a morally worthy action.[15] Thus, a very large percentage of current political events do not deserve to be viewed as enhancing the moral status of those who proposed those events.[16] Having offered some rationale for the impermissibility of ever linking coercion to the morally good, let us now see if coercion must be considered morally bad.[17]

From the homeowner example at least two additional arguments can be advanced on why a society seeking virtue would not want to employ coercion. In the first place, to coerce people is to remove the possibility of moral praise from those being coerced. Thus in a society of complete coercion no one (except perhaps the coercers) could be praised for his actions. By contrast, a completely voluntary society would leave open the possibility that everyone could be praised. Now surely a society in which all have the possibility for praise is preferable to one where none or only some do.

But the response might be that if all have the possibility for praise, all have the possibility for blame as well; and surely it is better to have a social order where some "good" acts are enforced, rather than leave open the possibility that all acts might be evil. The cost of not being able to praise all is worth paying to keep us from lapsing into total depravity. While there is plausibility to this response, the response nevertheless fails on two counts. First, a free society (as defined above) will not lapse into *total* depravity, since no act of initiatory coercion will be allowed (e.g., murder, theft, rape, etc.). On the other hand, once coercion is taken to be appropriate in some circumstances it becomes difficult to see why coercion may not be appropriate in any and all circumstances—thus raising the spectre of totalitarianism.[18] This is especially true if those in positions of authority are convinced that the ends justify the means (i.e., that voluntary participation is not a necessary consideration when formulating social policy), for then it does not matter whether the result is coercively achieved or not. It is true that the fear of totalitarianism may prevent a society from explicitly endorsing a totalitarian end; but fear of totalitarianism is not an argument directed specifically against any new act of coercion that might be proposed. Thus each additional coercive measure may chip away at freedom until the feared end arrives anyway. Therefore, the real possibility of one form of complete moral depravity (totalitarianism) is present in the mixed regime (coercive and free). On that basis it is no longer obvious that the attempt to avoid depravity by allowing some coercion is less costly than not allowing any.

It is only apparent, secondly, that we have a middle ground between freedom and totalitarianism in moral matters. It is true that if left free people may not voluntarily do what is best. But when they are coerced that possibility is removed entirely. And since rewards are proportionate to risk, the mixed social order removes the possibility of a robustly virtuous society in favor of, at best, a social order of thin virtue. Coercion cuts off the possibility of moral peaks for those forced into the "actions" they take. Their "actions" are less laudatory than they could otherwise have been, if they had chosen those "actions" voluntarily.[19] Thus *only* a free society holds out the possibility of full virtue, and again it is no longer obvious that the chance for complete excellence is not worth the risks of complete freedom.

The second major argument I wish to make takes a somewhat different tack. In order to assert that coercion is good, one must be able to argue that, at least in some circumstances, coercive acts ought to be undertaken. When one recommends the moral propriety of coercive acts, one implies the following proposition. "One ought to act such that the situation created by the coercive action renders the term 'ought' (or 'ought not') inapplicable to the action to be done by the coerced, no matter what the nature of the action may be."[20] The foregoing proposition is a necessary implication of the recommendation to coerce, because of the argument given in the first part of this second section. To give an example, if a gunman sticks you up, it makes no moral sense to tell you (the coerced) that you "ought" to give the gunman your money; for one of our previous conclusions was that moral oughts are inapplicable to persons who are being coerced. Let us carry our analysis a bit further.

It is possible (a) to translate the word "ought" by substituting the word "good" (any other positive moral value term would work as well for our purposes). For example, when one asserts, "You ought to do X," one normally means that it is good that you do X. Let us (b) also translate "the coerced" in the proposition of the preceding paragraph to "the other party to the relation." If we first apply translation (b), and then (a) with (b), to the proposition under consideration we would move from, "One ought to act such that the situation created by the coercive action renders the term 'ought' inapplicable to the action to be done by the other party to the relation, no matter what the nature of the action may be," to, "It is good to act such that the situation created by the coerced action renders the term 'good' inapplicable to the action to be done by the other party to the relation, no matter what the nature of that action may be." The problem with this translation is that the power of the first "good" of the translation loses its force or meaning by the time we reach a consideration of the results of the action. It seems meaningless, in other words, to say that the first action of a relationship between two people is good (namely, A's coercion of B) if the second act (e.g., B's giving A the money) cannot bear any relationship to the moral quality of the first act. What could the first "good" possibly mean here? Does it make sense to assert that one ought to engage in a relationship with another person, who is necessary to achieve some end, when no matter what that other person does, his actions cannot be called good?

In the example under consideration it is impossible for the actions of A and B to have the same moral status. And if it is impossible for the actions of A and B to have the same moral status, then no positive moral quality can be attached to the relationship between A and B. Since there is a *relationship* between A and B, the only way that relationship could be deemed a good one is if it were *possible* (at least) that the actions of both parties to the relationship could be good—otherwise (if it were not possible) there could be no morally good *relationship* between A and B. In short, coercive acts make it impossible for the term "good" to be applied to all parties to the relationship; and if a positive moral term, such as "good," cannot be applied to *all* aspects of a relationship, then the relationship itself is suspect.

The kind of problem we ran into above does not arise if one begins with the supposition that coercion is bad or that one ought not to coerce. It is, indeed, meaningful to say that "One ought not to act such that the situation created by the coercive action renders the term 'ought' (or 'ought not') inapplicable to the action to be done by the coerced, no matter what the nature of the action may be." (We can, of course, substitute "it is bad that" for "ought not" in the above.) In this last case, the entire force of the "ought not" is maintained. One can use "ought not" either to indicate that something is bad or to indicate that a relevant feature of an action may not be good. We usually use this second sense of "ought not" when we lack knowledge. For example, one might say that one ought not to do X because it is not known whether a relevant feature of that act is bad or good. But in situations in which coercion is used, we do know that a relevant feature of an action *cannot* be called good (by the argument above). Thus, whether "ought not" is applicable to coercive acts because those acts are positively bad or because it is not meaningful to say one ought to coerce, the result is the same—coercive acts ought not to be undertaken. The initial force of the "ought not" generates no paradox. We must conclude, therefore, that the only way to characterize coercion is an action that ought not to be undertaken.

So far we have shown the following: those coerced into an action cannot be said to deserve praise (or blame), only a free society offers the possibility of a completely virtuous society, and a coercive relationship between two parties does not allow both parties to equally achieve the same moral status. With respect to the last point a utilitarian (for example) might say, "So be it. The fact that both parties to the relationship cannot achieve the same moral status does not show that the act of coercion was itself wrong." Yet I believe that the preceding argument does in fact give us a good reason for condemning the coercive act. Coercion is a relative concept, a concept that refers to a *relationship* between two (or more) individuals. Since our argument has shown that the parties to the relationship cannot (no matter what) achieve equal moral status, the only remaining alternative is that those advocating a coercive relationship are advancing a type or moral elitism. I say elitism because, if the coercive act is considered good, the coercer has established a situation in which only the coercer has the opportunity of moral excellence to the exclusion of any others in the relationship. Therefore, the necessary inequity of a coercive relationship is a good reason for abandoning that type of relationship altogether.[2]

But perhaps the objection to my argument cuts somewhat deeper. Have I not assumed all along too close a connection between an evaluation of the act and an evaluation of the person? We often say, for example, that an act was wrong, but the person doing it is excused for such and such a reason. Thus it would seem that we have a case where the act was wrong but there was no responsible agent of the act. Moreover, a utilitarian might say that since all that matters in evaluating acts are the consequences, the coercive or non-coercive character of the act is irrelevant. If an act is good, the act *must* be performed even if coercive measures are needed to secure it.

Before responding to these criticisms I should like to emphasize again that my arguments are meant to apply to initiatory coercion. Incarcerating individuals for violent crimes or enforcing contractual obligations are acts of retaliatory coercion and would have to be dealt with separately. By the same token, my arguments are not necessarily applicable to the relationship between children and adults. They may be, but since it is not clear that children deserve the same moral responsibilities as adults, we shall ignore the question here.

Two meta-ethical assumptions stand behind the arguments advanced so far. I shall not argue for these assumptions, since they are not without their own inherent plausibility; and to argue for more would take us too far afield. Nevertheless, I shall try to outline below some implications of these assumptions as they bear directly on the recent criticisms of my argument. The two assumptions are, 1) actions do not exist apart from actors, and 2) the moral order is instantiated by an act of choice.[22]

It is common in textbooks on moral philosophy to distinguish action morality from agent morality. But if the first meta-ethical assumption is correct, this common distinction is essentially an artificial one. Actions are not "writ large" in some Platonic heaven or Kantian noumenal order. Actions only exist when taken by concrete individual human beings. To assume otherwise is to create a dualism in the moral order comparable to that found in some theories of the mind/body relation. In both cases the human person is divested of unity, since an evaluation of his behavior is subject to two different modes of analysis. Thus is it misleading, at best, to speak of the rightness (or wrongness) of an act apart from any reference to the actor—that is, if the first assumption is correct.

I do not want to be understood as claiming that the distinction between agent and action morality is useless. Just as Aristotle claimed that the distinction between soul and body was useful for analytic purposes, so also analysis may justify the distinction between agent and action morality. It is, for example, often helpful in teaching moral philosophy to ignore motives and intentional choices in order to help clarify and categorize actions. Yet when we engage in such abstractions we are ignoring part of the reality rather than grasping a different one. That is to say, if we focus on the action to the exclusion of the agent, we are saying, in effect, that "given a normal set of motivations, intentions, and choices, action X is right (or wrong)," or "*ceterus paribus,* action X is right (or wrong)," or "*if* we ignore the agent himself, then action X is right (or wrong)." All these statements indicate that the full reality is not described by focusing on the action alone. Indeed, in the strictest sense the term "action" would include *both* the individual's behavior and his psychological disposition.[23]

As to the second meta-ethical assumption, the moral good is distinguished from the non-moral good by the fact that the moral good is chosen. An animal may achieve the good by catching its prey, but this good is not a moral one because the animal (presumably) did not act from an intentional choice. Rather, the animal was directed by instinct. In contrast, what makes any good achieved by a human being a moral good is the fact that it was chosen. Thus, if we take the agent's motivations on one side and the act itself on the other, it is choice which links the two sides together and instantiates an event capable of moral evaluation. The importance of choice to human morality cannot be overemphasized. Even if we infallibly knew, for example, that God dictates X as good and Y as evil, such knowledge would not become part of the moral enterprise until someone chose to follow or not follow God's dictates.[24]

In applying these meta-ethical principles to the criticisms mentioned earlier, let us begin with excuses. The ordinary analysis of excusing someone runs as follows:[25] the act was wrong, but you are free of blame because of N facts or circumstances. On this analysis the act remains wrong, but the agent is free of blame. Thus cases of excusing seem to cast doubt on my first meta-ethical assumption. But I wish to propose another analysis of excusing—one that accords more readily with that assumption. Under the new proposal, a person is excused when, a) there is some basis for questioning the propriety of an action(s) and b) the person's action(s) is found to be (upon further inquiry) morally right or morally acceptable.

Consider two examples. Jones sees smoke pouring out of a window at the rear of some building. He is unable to take a closer look, so he pulls the fire alarm on the box next to him and calls the fire department. It turns out that the fire department was called needlessly, since the smoke came only from an overheated frying pan. In the second case, Smith is walking through the woods near Brown's property. Brown will not tolerate trespassing, and Smith respects that right. He notices an old stump that marks the edge of Brown's property and steers clear of it. Smith was not aware that that morning Brown bought the property that extended beyond the stump and included the area where Smith was walking. In both cases, Smith and Jones would be excused.

With the Jones example we have a case where Jones did in fact undertake the morally correct action. Jones acted with the fullest use of his rational faculties and on the basis of the most complete information. Had another person been present at the time Jones saw the smoke, it would have been appropriate to say, "you ought to pull the fire alarm" and "you did the right thing by calling the fire department." The truth of these propositions is not changed with hindsight. The reason we may now feel inclined to say that the false alarm was wrong (though excusable) is because we compare our judgment of the act in question to propositions about normal actions (e.g., "calling in false alarms is wrong"). We forget these "normal" assessments are contingent—that is, *given* normal circumstances the act is wrong. But under the circumstances discussed, Jones did the right thing. The Smith example can be analysed similarly, though we are less inclined to say Smith acted rightly. We might say instead that Smith's action was morally acceptable. On this theory, then, excusable actions are those actions called into question by their apparent conflict with paradigm cases of moral propriety, but where the action is nevertheless found to be at least morally acceptable. All that has been abandoned in this theory versus the traditional analysis is the unreasonable demand that we ape the stance of God when making moral evaluations.

Notice that both Smith and Jones were responsible-for the actions they took.

And given the preceding argument, moral evaluations can be given to their acts. This is quite different from the case of "selling" the house discussed above. There no one was responsible-for the act of "selling" the house, though someone was responsible-for the act of coercion that caused the house to change hands. Thus, unlike Jones who could be praised for taking decisive action under limited conditions, we still cannot praise L for "selling" the house.

The utilitarian might still insist that what is relevant to morality is only that the act be done by whatever mode is necessary to accomplish that end. In this case our second assumption is applicable and cannot be ignored by the utilitarian. If consequences alone were sufficient to establish the moral propriety of an action, then presumably moral evaluations ought to be extended to animals and machines. They too do things which have consequences. The utilitarian however, apparently wants to restrict the realm of moral responsibility (and thus evaluation) to human beings.[26] It seems that the most plausible way to accomplish this is to accept the truth of our second assumption. We would therefore extend our moral evaluations only to human beings, because only they choose to act according to the standards demanded by utilitarian theory (whether act or rule). We expect, in other words, a person to understand what it means to maximize overall social utility and to make the conscious choice to be guided by such considerations. Utilitarianism qualifies as a moral doctrine precisely because it attempts to guide and evaluate actions that human beings can *choose* to make. If the fundamentality of choice is ignored, there would be little basis for morally blaming criminals but not tornados for evil consequences. Thus the utilitarian must also recognize that the ascription of virtue presupposes choice.

While the utilitarian must admit the importance of choice to morality and virtue in some general sense, it still remains true that *this* act of coercion by *this* agent was chosen, and the foregoing arguments have not shown directly that coercion itself is wrong. This last point is accurate. Only a theory of rights could show that coercion itself is unjustified, and no theory of rights has been advanced here. But one must recall what we set out to prove and what has been done toward that end. We have shown that virtue cannot be ascribed to those who act under coercion. Thus the more coercion there is, the less virtuous a society becomes. We have also shown that those who coerce cannot lay claim to the "virtuous" consequences of the coercion, since they were not responsible-for those consequences. They may be praised (or blamed) for the value of the coercive act itself, but not the goodness that allegedly results therefrom. Moreover, coercive relationships are inherently unequal with respect to the moral status of all parties involved. And finally morality cannot concentrate exclusively on the act to the exclusion of considering the choices of the agent of the act.

Now since the overall goal of this essay was to show that freedom and virtue are inexorably linked together, the argument that I have not shown that a particular action of coercion by a particular coercer to be wrong carries little power. In the first place, if the act of coercion is itself good such that we can attribute virtue to the coercer, it must be because the coercer freely chose to coerce. The fact that the action was freely chosen only supports my general theme rather than refutes it. And secondly, we have so limited what a coercer can morally lay claim to that the only possibility left open to those who coerce is that coercion can somehow be *inherently* good. I am willing to rest my case on the evident absurdity of attributing any inherent goodness to any act of coercion.

The foregoing arguments imply that the kinds of governmental initiatives that are justified on moral grounds are not in the best interests of promoting virtue in society. Many contemporary political thinkers conceive of their task as one of balancing the requirements of freedom with those of morality and virtue. This balancing procedure presupposes a fundamental conflict between these two values. Yet if the above analysis is correct, then—fundamentally at least—there is no conflict. Mutual non-interference serves as a necessary condition for both a free and a moral or virtuous, society. If this is so, our task becomes one of seeking voluntary means to secure those secondary freedoms spoken of earlier. This is a demanding task, but one whose undertaking thereby enters the realm of the noble.

Notes

1. *Tractatus-Theologico Politicus*, A. G. Wernham (ed.), (Oxford, 1958), Chap. 20, p. 231.

2. *Politics* 5, 9. 1310a25-38

3. *Ibid.*, 3, 9. 1281a3-4.

4. See Aristotle's *Nicomachean Ethics* 6, 5. 1140a24-1140b30.

5. See my article, "Government and the Governed," *Reason Papers*, No. 2 (Fall 1975, pp. 41-64.

6. It must be noted, of course, that mutual non-interference does not guarantee a virtuous society, but serves only as necessary condition for a truly virtuous society. Once this primary condition is secured, more would have to be done to secure a fully virtuous society. Though I also believe that a society based upon mutual non-interference is more likely to secure virtue, I shall not argue for that here.

7. The fundamental significance of choice in morality goes back at least as far as Aristotle. See the *Nicomachean Ethics* 3, 1. 1109b30-33: "Since virtue is concerned with passions and actions, and on voluntary passions and actions praise and blame are bestowed, on those that are involuntary pardon, and sometimes also pity, to distinguish the voluntary and the involuntary is presumably necessary."

8. I recognize the possibility of certain emergency cases (e.g., war) where the context is so radically altered that our above analysis may not fully apply. For the proper attitude toward such cases, see Ayn Rand, "The Ethics of Emergencies," in *The Virtue of Selfishness* (New York, 1964), pp. 43-49.

9. It would seen that the foregoing could lead to the following problem: given the general drift of our argument, it appears that one could absolve oneself of moral responsibility by asking to be coerced into an immoral action (e.g., "coerce me into stealing from X"); for if one was coerced, one would not be responsible for the act. This case is only apparently a problem. Basically, there are two ways to consider this case: either one is free to back out of the deal to be coerced (in which case one is not coerced), or one is at core actually being coerced—that is, one is not free to back out or change one's mind. In the latter case one *would not* be fully responsible for what one did (though one may be responsible for initiating the situation). The point is that one's being coerced and one's not being coerced are mutually exclusive states of affairs. One cannot have the characteristics of both states at the same time. If one uncoercedly asks at time t_1 to be coerced at t_2, one is either uncoercedly following the conditions established at t_1 or one is actually being coerced at t_2. One cannot at the same time ask to be coerced and actually be coerced, because whether one is or is not coerced is a decision or action one cannot make oneself. One is coerced only and exclusively as a result of the decisions and actions of others.

10. I emphasize the qualificaitons made in note 8 above.

11. It should be apparent from what has been said that the view offered here is not a utilitarian one. I cannot undertake a critique of utilitarianism here, though something is said later in the essay. It should be clear that the production of benefits does not function as the basis of my moral theory. For more on my own view see, "Ethical Egoism and Gewirth's PCC," *The Personalist* 56 (1975), sec. 1.

12. Some thinkers, such as B. F. Skinner, have supposed that the leaders themselves could be subject to their own legislation and thus escape being considered any more of a coercer

than any other citizen. But this conception is simply a fantasy, since if a society has any authority at all (and it is naive to suppose otherwise, except perhaps in the case of anarcho-capitalism), there will be those in a position to either change (or not apply) the rules or at least keep them in force by choice.

13. I am not arguing in favor of racial prejudice, which I consider to be wholly immoral. I chose this particular case only so that I would not be open to the charge of selecting examples that gloss over hard cases.

14. At this point the following question may arise: if L is not morally praiseworthy for the good act he produced, then would he be morally blameworthy if he coerced another to perform a *bad* act? It could appear by the above argument that he would not be morally blameworthy for the resultant bad act. If this is the implication of my argument, then that argument must be mistaken. This is not an implication of my argument, however. In our above case with L, H, P, and B, the mode of action taken by L (ignoring P for the sake of simplicity) ends with H. In other words, the following sort of relation obtains: L (coerces) H (non-coerces) B. This schema helps indicate that L is not the responsible moral agent in "selling" the house and that the mode of activity which L utilizes (coercion) ends with H and not B. Insofar as L is morally responsible, it is with respect to H and not to B. While H must "sell" the house to B, B thus has the option of refusing to take the house. Yet now consider the schema for P coercing R to steal from Q: P (coerces) R (coerces) Q. Because the mode of activity is the same between (P and R) and (R and Q), and because P initiated the sequence, the moral agency of P now extends through R to Q. P is thus responsible for what happens to Q.

15. The advocacy of coerced actions on moral grounds is quite common among philosophers. For example, the following give but a minute sample of the articles available: Lord Patrick Devlin, "Morals and the Criminal Law," in *Ethics and Public Policy,* ed. Tom L. Beauchamp (Englewood Cliffs, N. J., 1975), pp. 246-48; Burton M. Leiser, *Liberty, Justice, and Morals* (New York, 1973), Ch. 12; Peter Singer, "Famine, Affluence, and Morality," in *World Hunger and Moral Obligation,* ed. William Aiken and Hugh La Follette (Englewood Cliffs, N. J., 1977) pp. 22ff; Jan Narveson, "Aesthetics, Charity, Utility and Distributive Justice," *Monist* 56 (1972): 527-551; J. Brenton Stearns, "Ecology and the Indefinite Unborn," *ibid,* pp. 612-625; and B. J. Diggs, "The Common Good as Reason for Political Action," *Ethics* 83 (1973): 283-293. Most of the arguments put forth by these authors are stated in impersonal terms—that is, they recommend that certain actions be taken by the state or the government. But since the state is run by individuals, the implications of their arguments are clear: those who contribute to the coercively enforced actions advocated by these authors should consider their acts to be of positive moral worth.

16. Needless to say, the argument above does not apply to retaliatory coercion, but rather to the initiatory use. I shall ignore those cases where the two sorts of coercion are mixed (e.g., when people are conscripted to defend themselves).

17. Many references to such arguments could be given, but the positions closest to my own is given in Tibor R. Machan, *Human Rights and Human Liberties* (Chicago, 1973).

18. The slippery slope argument about the gradual erosion of freedom can be made on legal and economic grounds as well. In the legal area, the role played by precedent is bound to grease the slope. Each case decided in favor of coercive intervention by the state serves as a precedent for many other future cases. And since these other cases will contain features at least slightly different from the original, further intervention (and thus new precedents) will be required to draw these cases in line with the original decision. This is one reason why F. A. Hayek is so concerned to stress the importance of integrity in the legal system (cf. *Law, Legislation and Liberty* [Chicago, 1973] Vol. 1, Ch. 3). On the economic side, intervention in the market causes distortions in the market. These distortions must be corrected either by removing the original cause or with another act of intervention. Since the latter course of action is the overwhelming choice of governments, new distortions are created which must in turn be corrected by more intervention. (cf. Ludwig von Mises, *Planning for Freedom,* Libertarian Press, 1962).

19. The scare quotes around "action" are designed to indicate my reluctance to call coerced behavior an action. Coercion involves the substitution of one person's will or intention by another's such that the coerced loses his autonomy and becomes, in effect, a tool of the coercer. This is easy enough to appreciate in cases where one is literally physically

bound and forcibly placed in circumstances that are not a part of his own choice. But in cases of threatened violence the coercive factors may appear more ambiguous. It does seem that some element of choice or voluntariness is present when one is given the alternative of "your money or your life." Nevertheless, the appearance of choice is largely an illusion. When violence is threatened, one must assume that the threat is serious. Indeed, all too often the threat is carried out no matter what the coerced does. Thus the choices being made are on the part of the coercer who has chosen to threaten rather than initiate violence. He may do so because of a fear of more severe penalties or because of some perverse desire to watch another human being beg for mercy and look frightened. Whatever the motives, taking a coercer's threats seriously implies considering the actions of the coerced *as if* they were being executed under violent compulsion. No other consideration is possible, unless we have grounds for supposing the threats to be made with less than full sincerity. One of the reasons we allow for difference in penalties between threatened and actual violence is that the latter allows for no contingencies. But this difference does not imply that we should lessen our judgment that threatened and actual violence are both equally coercive.

Coercion has sometimes been defined in terms of restricting alternatives or being faced with undesirable alternatives. But surely these criteria are too broad, since natural events and everyday social circumstances can restrict our alternatives or present us with undesirable choices. But even if we were to accept some broader definition of coercion than one constructed in terms of the initiatory use of physical force, there is a hierarchical principle to consider. Physical violence must be considered as the most fundamental form of coercion, because such violence threatens to obliterate the very possibility of any form of moral behavior. Thus to initiate an act of physical violence (e.g., a law) to correct another form of "coercion" (e.g., an employer paying below market wage rates) is to correct a lesser evil with a greater one.

20. I refer the reader again to note 9 above.

21. If the coercive act is bad, there is still the inequity. But that is just a further reason for abandoning coercion.

22. Although I believe in the fundamentality of choice for morality, I am not trying to imply any particular solution to the free will/determinism debate.

23. Eric Mack has made a similar point (albeit more formally) in "Campbell's Refutation of Egoism," *Canadian Journal of Philosophy,* Vol. III, No. 4, June 1974. These kinds of abstractions I am mentioning here are common in other areas beside morality. We can, for example, speak of the color of an object apart from the object itself (or any other such quality or quantity). But here again the separation is merely conceptual and not actual.

24. More detail on these points can be found in my "Nozick on the Randian Argument," *The Personalist,* April 1978, Sections I and II.

25. To be excused is not the same thing as being pardoned or forgiven. The latter acts presuppose authority, whereas being excused does not.

26. My point remains valid, I believe, even in those cases where some utilitarians (e.g., Peter Singer) wish to include animals in the set of those who may be affected by the consequences of one's actions. But there is a difference between widening the scope of consequential affectations and making a determination of who is subject to moral evaluation. It is one thing, in other words, to consider the consequences of one's actions upon animals and quite another to hold animals morally responsible for the consequences of *their* actions upon us. Presumably we do not demand the latter, since there is no reason to believe that animals understand the happiness principle (and the norms that follow from it) in such a way that they choose to direct their behavior according to those norms.

This is a revised version of a paper first published in *Reason Papers* No. 5 (Winter 1979). The paper was later read at a conference on "Freedom and Virtue" in Santa Barbara (Spring 1980). The revisions owe much to that conference, and I wish to thank all the participants, especially Eugene Miller, Tibor Machan, Lansing Pollock, Michael Gorr, Danny Shapiro, and Gilbert Harman.

GILBERT HARMAN*

Libertarianism and Morality

Libertarianism is in part a thesis about the limits of governmental action. In its strictest form, it holds that governments may legitimately protect people from each other but may not legitimately impose taxes and other restrictions merely for the sake of projects aimed at advancing general welfare. Governments may prevent people from injuring each other, they may protect property rights, they may enforce contracts. But they may not prevent people from injuring themselves, they may not interfere with immoral acts that do not affect others, and they may not require those who are better off to help those who are worse off.

Governmments may, in other words, enforce only certain aspects of morality. Morally, one should not only keep one's contracts and avoid injury to others and their property but also develop one's own talents, refrain from injuring oneself, and help others who need help. Libertarianism allows governments to enforce some of those duties but not others.

Now, consider the following justification that might be offered for this strict libertarian thesis about the limits of government:

Ideally, there would be no need for government. We would be able to rely entirely on morality. People would be motivated by morality to avoid harm to others, to help those who need help, and so on. If everyone acted morally, things would work out as well as could be expected without the enormous costs of government. The trouble is that the ideal situation in which everyone acts morally is too unstable. Situations will arise in which someone is tempted by considerations of personal gain to fail to help someone who needs help or is tempted to steal from someone else or tempted to fail to keep a contract or tempted to use physical force against someone else. It is only to be expected that people will occasionally give in to such temptations. Now, the existence of scattered occasions on which one person fails to help another may not be too serious, since others will be able to provide the needed help. But a few acts of stealing, of broken contracts, or of injury will have serious consequences, since they can lead to a breakdown in trust and to a need for

This paper grew out of a conference on Virtue and Liberty sponsored by Liberty Fund, Inc., held at the Reason Foundation, Santa Barbara, California.
*Princeton University.

elaborate precautions and protections. These breakdowns are likely to lead to acts of retaliation and then to feuding, which will only make things worse. Therefore some enforcement of morality is needed in order to preserve stability and this is where government comes in. But there is no argument here for government enforcement of other aspects of morality, such as the duty to help others who need help.

This line of thought presupposes that in a libertarian society there would be a shared morality which, among other things, would motivate people to help those who need help. It collapses if (as I suspect) the establishment of a strictly libertarian society would lead members of the society to attach less importance to those aspects of morality not enforced by government so that, in particular, they would cease to care very much about those less fortunate than themselves and would come to attach little importance to the duty to help those who need help. This would undermine the suggested justification of the strict libertarian thesis since it would mean that those aspects of morality the libertarian does not wish to enforce are as unstable as those aspects of morality the libertarian does wish to enforce.

Whether the establishment of strict libertarianism would have such a result needs to be discussed. But first I want to mention a different argument for libertarianism, one which appeals more directly to morality, that is, to ordinary moral views. This argument rests on the fact that we ordinarily attach much greater importance to the negative aspects of morality than to its positive aspects. We normally take it to be much worse to injure someone than to fail to save someone from injury. We take it to be much worse to steal something from another than to fail to give someone something. We normally suppose one cannot violate a negative duty in order to perform a positive duty even where more is gained than lost. For example, we think it would be wrong for a doctor to try to save five patients by seizing and cutting up a healthy person and distributing his or her organs to the others, since that would be to violate a negative duty not to harm the healthy patient in order to fulfill a mere positive duty to save the others. [1] On the other hand, we do not ordinarily think it wrong for people to sacrifice themselves for others. The duty not to harm oneself has the strength of a positive duty rather than that of a negative duty.

The point is sometimes made in terms of rights. One has a right to one's property, one has a right to what another has agreed to supply, one has a right not to be injured by others. But a person in need does not have a right to another person's help. Perhaps the other person ought to help, but he or she does not absolutely have to help. The first person does not have a right to the second person's aid unless for example they had earlier agreed they would help each other in times of need. Similarly, even though we normally suppose one ought not to harm oneself, one does not have a right not to be harmed by oneself. People may sacrifice themselves in order to save others. That violates no one's rights. But the doctor may not seize and cut up a healthy visitor to the hospital in order to save five patients. The patients have no rights to another person's organs and the healthy visitor's rights would be certainly violated by such an action.

Now, these aspects of ordinary moral views seem to support strict libertarianism:

One person can be forcibly prevented from violating someone else's rights but not forcibly required to pay taxes to benefit others, since these others have no right to the first person's money. Only the first person has a right to that money. To force that person to pay taxes to benefit others is to violate that person's right to the money. There is a negative duty of the strong sort not to violate that right. The duty to help others is the weaker sort of positive duty. The imposition of forced taxation for this purpose is as wrong as the doctor's sacrificing the healthy visitor for the sake of the five patients. Similarly, a person cannot be forcibly prevented from harming him or herself. If a person harms him or herself, no one's rights are violated, but a person has a right not to be forcibly deprived of liberty. It is wrong to violate a strong negative duty, by using force against someone, merely to prevent that person from violating a weak positive duty by harming him or herself. Although a government may forcibly prevent people from injuring others, it may not forcibly prevent them from injuring themselves. A government may perhaps require taxes from its citizens in order to support a police force that protects people's rights, it may not require payment of taxes in order to support a system of welfare.

Commonsense morality may therefore appear to imply strict libertarianism.

The issue is complicated, however, and commonsense morality is not consistently libertarian. Most people in the United States seem to think that some governmental welfare programs are justified and that the government is justified in taxing its citizens in order to support these programs. Many would even say that people have a right to adequate medical care, a decent education, at least a minimal income, and so forth. Ordinary moral views therefore do not yield a clear-cut verdict in favor of libertarianism. The best that can be said is that some aspects of commonsense morality seem to imply libertarianism and other aspects do not. There appears to be a conflict between these aspects of commonsense morality. If one recognizes this conflict in one's own moral view and tries to resolve it by modifying one's moral views in the way that seems most appropriate, one may be led to adopt the strict libertarian thesis. But that is not the only possibility. One might instead be led to modify or attach less importance to those aspects of morality that speak in favor of libertarianism. One might come to reject the distinction between positive and negative duties in favor of a general utilitarianism. Or one might allow some force to that distinction but observe that it is not an absolute distinction. The doctor is not justified in cutting up the healthy visitor to save five patients, but that is not to say a person's rights may never be violated in order to save someone else. One might be justified in forcibly taking the only life preserver around in order to throw it to a drowning swimmer, even over the objections of the life preserver's owner. Similarly, the government might be justified in forcibly taking income and wealth from its citizens in order to save people from disease or poverty or ignorance.

It can also be objected that, even if reflection on commonsense morality leads one to adopt a position that approximates strict libertarianism, this shows only that libertarianism is built into this morality and does not show that libertarianism is right. This merely pushes the problem of justification back one step: We must now ask what justifies those aspects of commonsense morality that support strict libertarianism. It is true that justification must always come to an end somewhere.

And it may be that there is no deeper justification than seeing whether a view is sustained by one's considered reflection on common sense. Still we would like to know *why* we distinguish positive and negative duties as we do. What is our reason for this? Is there a rational basis for this distinction? Or is it, as some would argue, merely part of bourgeois ideology imposed by the ruling class as a way of sustaining its power. Here again is an issue to which we will have to return.

A third argument for strict libertarianism cites the unhappy consequences of allowing government more power than it should have according to strict libertarian principles.

(1) Government welfare programs will appreciably lower overall production and (2) the administration of these programs will inevitably be bungled. Total production will be lowered for two reasons. First, the extra taxation needed to support government welfare programs reduces the after-tax money someone gets for a unit of work. Anyone who is just willing to do an extra unit of work to receive the pretax amount of money will not be willing to do that extra unit for the lesser after tax amount. Since less productive work will be done given the tax than would be done without the tax, less will be produced.

Furthermore, the benefits of the government program will, for a similar reason, reduce the incentives to work of those who receive the benefits. Any such person who was before just willing to do a unit of work for a given amount of money will no longer be willing to do so, because that extra money is not worth as much to the person in question, given the unearned benefit received from the government. And this loss of production will be magnified by any tax on earnings or by any loss of welfare benefits that results from increased earnings.

The administration of the new government programs will inevitably be bungled because of the lack of economic incentives. This will lead to more inefficiency and even corruption that would occur in a business that must compete with other businesses.

As for government restrictions on people harming themselves, the argument from decreased production does not seem to apply directly. Indeed it could be argued that an effective prohibition on gambling or the use of alcohol might increase total production in society. But enforcement of such restrictions is extremely difficult when compared with enforcement of laws against stealing, violence, and fraud. There are not in the same way victims who will complain if they are vicitimized. People will be willing to cooperate with each other to violate the law. There is a much greater risk of payoffs to the police to allow illegal gambling or drinking to continue. This will tend to corrupt the police and therefore to weaken their effectiveness even in enforcing the laws against fraud, stealing, and violence.

This sort of argument from consequences is powerful but inconclusive. Consider the last point. Antilibertarians will be quick to point out that the *cost* of enforcement of paternalistic laws must be weighed against their *benefits*. It may be that increases in production more than make up for the costs of enforcement—and in addition people may be generally better off not intoxicated, not gambling.

As for government welfare programs a number of things must be said. First, the benefits of these programs must not be ignored but must be weighed against any costs. Second, the effects of taxation on productive work are not so easy to determine. An income tax will reduce one's whole after-tax income, so the value of extra money will be greater; this may or may not counteract the effect of the tax on the money one would get for an extra unit of work. Economists disagree about this.[2]

Third, long term and short term effects must be distinguished. In the long term one adapts to a system of taxation and government benefits. That changes what one values. One will take for granted a certain level of income, one will be very unwilling to settle for less, one will think of more than that as an extra delight. After-tax behavior therefore cannot be predicted on the basis of pretax values. For example, the receipt of welfare benefits establishes a floor which represents what the recipient now expects, a higher floor than previously existed. As a result it is quite unclear whether we should predict that after receiving government benefits, the recipient will be more or less willing to do an extra unit of work for a given amount of money.

Fourth, although government welfare programs can be inefficient and biased, the same is true of private charities. It may well be that the public accountability of governmental programs can keep them more efficient and fairer than private charities that are not accountable to anyone but their rich contributors.

Here libertarians often invoke history and note the many disasters that have resulted when governments have gone beyond what libertarianism permits. The trouble is that defenders of the welfare state appeal to history too by noting disasters that have resulted when governments have not gone beyond what libertarianism permits. There are horrors on both sides. Furthermore, the same horrors are sometimes cited as evidence by both sides! History tells us that horrors have occurred. Only theory can say why they have occurred—whether too much or too little governmental intervention or some other factor. But, as I have indicated, theory fails to give a clear answer.

I have now mentioned what I think are the three most promising sorts of justifications that can be offered for strict libertarianism—(1) the argument that we can make do with morality alone without government except where government enforcement of morality is needed for the sake of stability, to protect people against violence, fraud, and theft; (2) the argument that ordinary commonsense morality supports strict libertarianism; (3) the argument that the consequences of adhering to strict libertarian principles are much better than the consequences of not doing so.

Some libertarians take the basic libertarian principles to be self-evident, but that is best thought of as a version of the appeal to commonsense morality. (The principles are not literally self-evident since many thoughtful people explicitly reject them.) Many libertarians prefer not to discuss the problem of justification at all, saying merely that libertarianism depends on certain basic assumptions which one can either accept or not. That too is probably best considered a version of strategy (2), appealing to ordinary commonsense morality.

The distinction between (1), (2), and (3) is somewhat arbitrary. (1), which argues that we can rely on morality for the most part, needing government enforcement only of certain aspects of morality that are otherwise unstable, might be offered as an argument for (or as a special case of) (3), which says strict libertarianism has better consequences than alternatives. (1) and/or (3) might be said to be what explains the moral intuitions appealed to in (2)—and these moral intuitions might therefore be said to provide evidence for (1) or (3). I suspect that the three arguments stand or fall together, although I also believe it is useful to separate issues in the way I have suggested.

I now want to look more closely at questions left over from our discussion of the first and second strategies. In particular, I want to consider the following two issues: First, how stable are those aspects of morality that strict libertarianism would not enforce? In a libertarian society, would people help those who need help, for example, or would this aspect of moral behavior tend to diminish? Second, what accounts for the libertarian aspects of ordinary commonsense morality? Is there a good reason for them or are they rather imposed somehow by the "ruling class"?

To answer this second group of questions first, I want to suggest both that, in a way, the libertarian aspects of morality are imposed by the "ruling class" and also that there are good reasons for these aspects of morality. In suggesting this I assume there is no a priori source of morality, nor any source in God or human nature. I have argued elsewhere that morality arises from something like convention. People accept moral principles and values because it is in their interest to do so given that others do so. It is useful that there be widely accepted moral conventions. The content of these conventions cannot be settled ahead of time but depends on continuing implicit negotiation, bargaining, and compromise. The relevant conventions change over time because of new knowledge, changing interests, and shifting coalitions. Morality is in certain ways like politics. [3]

In our ordinary commonsense morality, negative duties are stronger than positive duties. We consider it much worse to harm someone else than to fail to help someone, worse to steal than to fail to give, worse to lie than to fail to reveal information. The reason for this, I suggest, is that our ordinary commonsense morality is the result of an implicit continuing compromise between people of different powers and resources. Prohibitions against harm, theft, and fraud are in everyone's interest equally, but a positive duty to help those who need help benefits mainly the poorer and weaker members of society, who will be needing most of the help, rather than the relatively richer and stronger members who have more resources for providing help. The stronger and richer members would prefer strong prohibitions against harm, theft, and fraud and no duty to help those who need help. The poorer and weaker members would prefer a strong duty to help as well as a strong prohibition against harm, theft, and fraud. One would expect the continual implicit bargaining between these groups to yield as a compromise the strong prohibition against harm, which everyone wants, plus a somewhat weaker duty to help, since not everyone favors such a duty. This, of course, is just what we have in our society.

So, I suggest, to some extent it is true that libertarian aspects of ordinary commonsense morality are there because they have been imposed (or at least influenced) by the "ruling class", that is by those with relatively more power and resources. I would not expect to find such libertarian aspects in the morality of a completely egalitarian society. In such a society, the duty to help others should be as strong as the duty not to harm them. But that is not to say there is no justification for the libertarian aspects of *our* morality. For I see no other source of justification than current convention, no *a priori* morality. If that is right, then the fact that different principles from ours would be accepted under different conditions does not undermine our principles. Those other principles are not our principles and cannot be relevant to what we ought morally to do. What a person has moral reasons to do depends on the principles and values that person actually accepts, not on the principles and values that person or someone else would accept under different conditions.

This is, however, not a complete vindication of strict libertarianism. I have aleady mentioned that ordinary commonsense morality has nonlibertarian aspects. In particular, it allows the government to tax its citizens in order to support various welfare programs—and this may be crucial to the current moral compromise. This may be part of the price required for important groups to accept current morality. But then it cannot be said that taxation for this purpose is morally wrong. In order to argue against taxation for those programs one could not appeal directly to morality but would for instance have to point out unintended bad consequences of the system of taxation and welfare.

I claim that morality must be conventional in this way if morality is to give people reasons to do things. These reasons cannot come from reason alone or from human nature since there are clearly people—such as certain successful criminals—who have no reason to follow ordinary commonsense morality. The moral reasons a person has must derive from that person's acceptance of certain principles and values. People who for one reason or another do not accept the relevant principles and values have no reasons of that sort to act in that way, although they may have other reasons to do so. People accept certain values and principles, when they do, mainly because it is in their interests to do so, given that others also do. It is in their interest because it makes possible certain benefits of social cooperation available only to those accepting the relevant values and principles, where merely pretending to accept the values and principles is too much trouble and too risky.

This is not to say that the resulting moral motivation is self-interested motivation. It is not. For self-interested reasons people can acquire non-self-interested concerns. It is in their interest to acquire these concerns. Once they acquire such concerns they are no longer motivated entirely by self-interest.

Since these non-self-interested moral concerns can help motivate continued adherence to moral conventions and can even lead one to support certain changes in current conventions, it is oversimple to say (as I just did) that self-interest is what gives people reasons to accept moral conventions. But self-interest remains a powerful motivation and it is unlikely many people will long accept moral conventions if it is not in their interests to do so.

(Here it is appropriate to note an ambivalence or tension in some libertarian thinking, where on the one hand, it is insisted that people are basically motivated by self-interest and, on the other hand, it is said that in the absence of governmental regulations people who are better off will offer help to those who need help!)

I have suggested that the libertarian aspects of ordinary commonsense morality are there because this morality represents a current compromise among people of different powers and resources. I have noted this implies that such a distinction would not arise in a completely egalitarian society. In such a society the duty of helping those who need help ought to be just as strong as the duty of not harming others.

Now recall the first justification I considered for strict libertarianism, which argues that government must enforce laws against violence, fraud, and theft, because morality is unstable in this area. Without some government enforcement, people cannot rely on moral conventions alone. But, it is argued, other aspects of morality are not unstable in this way. Private immoral acts between consenting adults do not threaten others. If one person refuses a request for aid, someone else can help.

This, I suggest, is implausible. Consider a completely egalitarian society in which the duty to help others is as strong as the duty not to harm them. If the government in such a society is limited as strict libertarianism recommends, then we can expect that the society will not remain an egalitarian society for very long. Some people will use their liberty to provide things and services that others want in a way that will yield a good profit. Others will not do as well. The society will very quickly become a society of people of different powers and resources. As Robert Nozick remarks, it would seem that this can be prevented only by outlawing "capitalistic acts between consenting adults,"[4] and libertarian principles rule out such government restriction. But then, if I am right, when the society has become less egalitarian, moral concerns will change. Those better off will successfully bargain for a weaker duty to help others. So if I am right, there is after all an instability in this aspect of morality too. This seems clearly true for the morality of an egalitarian society: if there is no regulation of capitalistic acts so as to guarantee that the society will remain egalitarian, then morality will change as society becomes less egalitarian.

Similarly, consider a society where there are some differences in powers and resources in which there are also government welfare programs financed by progressive taxation. Here too, if the government is then limited in the way libertarianism requires, we should expect greater inequalities to occur, which will make it even more in the interest of the rich and powerful to minimize the positive duty of charity, which should result in a weakening of the force of that duty in the morality of that society.

This, by the way, is not to say that there will be less private charity in a libertarian society than in a society with government welfare programs. There might well be more private charity in the more libertarian society. The point is that there will be less overall charity in the libertarian society. In the society with government welfare programs, people are taxed to support those programs of government charity. This means not only that there will be less need for private charity, but also that people will have fewer resources for private charity. It is therefore to be expected then that there will be more private charity in the more libertarian society even though the total amount of charity—public and private—is much less. In the nonlibertarian society, the duty to help others is stronger but is mainly discharged in paying one's taxes so that little if any private charity is required. In the libertarian society, the duty to help others is weaker but it is not discharged in paying one's taxes, so a certain amount of private charity is required.

None of this means strict libertarianism must be rejected as unjustified. A libertarian may reject those aspects of ordinary commonsense morality that conflict with strict libertarianism and have excellent reasons for doing so. But that does rule out one sort of moral argument for libertarianism. To say that people ought morally to refrain from interfering in the lives of others except to prevent fraud, violence, or theft and to say that it is morally wrong of people to interfere with others for other reasons is to say that the people in question have moral reasons not to interfere in this way—and that is to presuppose shared moral principles or values that provide such reasons. It is no good simply to abandon ordinary principles and then judge people morally on the basis of libertarian principles they do not accept, for the speaker's acceptance of certain principles does not by itself give the other people any reason to observe those principles if they do not accept them.

A libertarian who does not wish to abandon the moral case for libertarianism cannot simply reject the current moral consensus but must instead accept it for what it is while advocating a change in the consensus in the direction of strict libertarianism. Libertarians have self-interested reasons to try to bring about such a change, because libertarians tend to be relatively well off in a given society, or at least believe they have good prospects of becoming relatively well off, and, as I have argued, strict libertarian principles are in the interests of those who are relatively well off. (Of course those who are well off may also feel a concern for others which may give them a strong reason not to advocate libertarianism.)

What is the best strategy for advocates of a more libertarian morality? An appeal to allegedly self-evident or *a priori* moral principles or natural rights is I think shortsighted. Belief in an *a priori* morality can lead one as easily (perhaps more easily) to utilitarianism or egalitarianism as to libertarianism. In any event, there is no point to trying to hide the libertarian's self-interested reasons for urging adoption of that morality, since everyone is aware of these reasons and to refuse to speak of them is to encourage the false view that such self-interested reasons are disreputable. Libertarians ought rather to *insist* on this point about self-interest and to insist on its legitimacy as a reason for them to favor libertarianism. They can also point this consideration out to others who are relatively well off who may be confused about it or unsure whether it is a legitimate thing to appeal to. They can also play up the unseen costs of governmental regulation and taxation. Finally, libertarians can try to create as large a coalition as possible of those who would support modifying the overall moral (and political) consensus in that direction and then can bargain hard with those that are left so as to accept the minimum compromise away from libertarianism that is at this time relatively stable.

Such tactics are openly used, without apology, on the other side on behalf of the poor and weak: "consciousness raising," in other words appeals to self-interest, in order to promote coalitions in favor of changing the moral consensus towards egalitarianism. Libertarians should follow suit. This would end a certain hypocrisy and would help to bring the real sources of morality—of moral consensus—out into the open.

Notes

1. I am oversimplifying here. See Judith Jarvis Thomson, "Killing, Letting Die, and the Trolley Problem," *Monist* 59 (1976) pp. 204-217.

2. Edward Cowen, "Economic Model Due on Tax-Cut 'Incentives'," *New York Times,* February 18, 1980, pp. D1, D3.

3. Gilbert Harman, "Moral Relativism Defended," *Philosophical Review* 84 (1975) pp. 3-22; "Relativistic Ethics," *Midwest Studies in Philosophy* 3 (1978) pp. 109-121; and "What Is Moral Relativism?" in *Values and Morals,* eds. Goldman and Kim (Dordrecht, Holland; D. Reidel: 1978) pp. 143-161.

4. Robert Nozick, *Anarchy, State, and Utopia* (New York, Basic Books: 1974) p. 163.

H. B. ACTON

The Ethics of Competition

Competition, strife and rivalry

Critics of competitive markets often contrast the competition that is essential to such markets with non-competitive cooperation. They believe that competition goes along with such characteristics as aggression, emulation, rivalry, conflict and strife, and that cooperation belongs with mutual aid, benevolence, modesty and harmony. In their view it follows, therefore, that economic competition is morally inferior to cooperative, non-competitive modes of commercial and industrial organisation. Right-minded people, it is assumed, are against strife and in favour of harmony and mutual aid. Modestly conducted cooperation, therefore, is superior to aggressive competition, and hence collectivist organisation is to be preferred to what these critics call 'the law of the jungle'. Collectivists are on the side of the angels while supporters of competitive markets are the Devil's disciples, helping him to bring misfortunes on the hindmost. Some, even, of those who support capitalism do so in a shamefaced way,[1] as they are convinced that in itself collectivism, being a form of cooperation and harmony, is morally superior to capitalism, even though, alas, human egoism makes capitalism inevitable.

We must now ask whether competition in free markets does have the morally obnoxious features we have just mentioned. Is it a species of strife, rivalry, emulation? Is it opposed to altruism, cooperation, and harmony? Is the only moral justification for competitive markets and capitalism that socialism is an ideal beyond human capacity to realise?

According to Dr. Samuel Johnson, competition is 'the action of endeavouring to gain what another endeavours to gain at the same time.' Johnson expresses this definition in morally neutral terms and brings out the central idea that in competition two or more people want and try to get what only one can have. He does not say anything about *how* they try to get it, since this depends upon what it is that they

Reprinted from *The Morals of Markets* (Atlantic Highlands, N.J.: Humanites Press, 1971). Used by permission.

want and how it *can* be got. There certainly are what we might call competitive jungle situations in which animals seize food and run away with it or fight among themselves for it. Human beings sometimes do similar things, as when the members of a Bingo Club jostled each other as they pillaged presents intended for children at a Christmas party. Those who gain them do so as a result of strength or agility, but although some animals fight to the death, human beings generally confine their scramble within rules. With animals there may be no rules at all, and no conception of what is fair or unfair.[2] When 'all's fair in love or war' human beings approach the jungle situation.

But let us now consider the sort of situation in which human beings compete for a prize or a job. In such situations the competitors may not meet one another and may not even know one another. When a prize is offered, say, for the best essay on Balzac or for the first correct solution of a mathematical problem, the winner of the competition is the competitor who does the required thing best or first. There has to be an awarding authority which makes the award according to certain rules. The essay has to be of such and such a length and has to be sent in by such and such a date. Applicants for a job have to submit accounts of their qualifications, specimens of their work, and so on. If there is only one prize or only one job, then at least one competitor has to be unsuccessful.

We may now compare prize competition situations with competitive jungle situations. In the latter, let us suppose, there are no rules and no awarding authorities. In the absence of rules, jungle competition may take place when there is enough for all even though it is intensified when there is a scarcity. In prize competition situations, there is never enough for all, and there must be losers. Jungle competition often takes place by means of fighting, but this is not necessary to it, since by eating its food or occupying its space, a group of animals may destroy another group it does not come into contact with. For competition of either sort to involve rivalry, the competitors have to know one another, for when 'rivalry' does not mean the same thing as 'competition', it means the attempt of individuals or groups to outdo other individuals or groups, and this requires the rivals to have some knowledge of one another. It is possible to compete without knowing that one is competing, for someone might endeavour to obtain a prize or job without knowing that others are after it too. The essence of competition is that each competitor strives after what he wants. The essence of rivalry is that each competitor strives to outdo the others. In competition, the failure of the losers is a consequence of the success of the winners not something that the winners aim to secure. Rivals, on the other hand, set out to *defeat each other* as well as to win the prize. To aim at defeating someone else comes somewhat closer to malevolence than mere competition does. Someone who endeavours to write the best essay in order to win the prize, may have no desire to defeat anyone else, but rivals do endeavour to defeat one another. Friendly rivalry is possible, as in games, but even this can easily spill over into hostility.

In jungle competition, then, the competing parties may fight, and may act as rivals to one another. But even in this primitive kind of competition, fighting *need* not occur, and does not when a species of animal unwittingly destroys the food of another species. In prize or job competition, there is an awarding authority proceeding according to rules, as there is not in jungle competition. As in some sorts of jungle competition, the competitors for prizes or jobs may not know one another or have any personal contact with one another. If they know one another they can behave as rivals. Rivals can be friends, as in games, but rivalry has kinship with hostility and malevolence, because rivals endeavour to outdo one another as well as to do what will win them the prize. The existence of rules for competitions for prizes and jobs limits the things that can be done to win. Competitors at local flower shows have been known to destroy their rivals' blooms. But this sort of behaviour is against the rules.

How, then, is economic competition related to the forms of competition we have now considered? It shares one important presupposition with them, that there is not an abundance of everything for everybody. If everyone could always get everything that he wanted, there would be no economic activity and no competition. Competition of all sorts presupposes scarcity, or at any rate a *belief* that what is wanted is scarce. (There might be enough food for all the animals who fight for it, but they fight because they do not know this.) Now competitive markets are not places where people fight, nor places where they pursue their rivalries. We have already seen that the attempts to outwit one another in what is called 'oriental' bargaining are not features of developed markets, but can only make sense for parties who are ignorant of conditions of supply and demand. Rivalry comes in when political considerations are important, as with pre-emptive purchases in time of war. But in general, economic behaviour in competitive markets is a peaceful sort of thing. Piracy and confiscation are uncommercial activities and trade flourishes when goods can be inspected and moved about without danger from marauding bands. Exchange, as we have seen, is morally preferable to spoliation or entreaty.

These, however, are very general considerations, and we must now consider some forms of economic activity in more detail, in order to see what morally relevant forms of economic competition may take. Let us consider, then, competition between firms for a contract, competition in the labour market, and competition to sell to ultimate consumers.

(a) Competition for Contracts

When firms compete for a contract they are in a situation analogous to that between competitors for a prize or a job. Each firm tries to get the order for itself by considering its own technical resources and probable costs in relation to what it considers the ordering firm is willing to pay. Its knowledge that other firms are tendering discourages it from asking too much, and its desire to make as good a profit as possible makes it unwilling to ask too little. Knowledge, intelligence and luck all affect the success of the enterprise. Rivalry need not enter into the situation at all, although, of course, it often does. A spirit of rivalry could cloud the judgment of a firm or individual and lead to unprofitable courses. In trying to obtain an order, of course, the tendering firm does more than quote its price, it will laud its product. Its representative may entertain the potential buyer and flatter him. But a buyer who signs a contract because of the charm of the salesman rather than because of the economic merits of the deal may come to regret it and certainly will do so if he makes a practice of acting in that way. Both parties will judge the success of the contract in terms of eventual profit or loss and, in a competitive situation, are led by the hope of profit to cut their costs as much as they can.

It should be noted that there is impersonal competition between firms, just as there is impersonal competition between animals in the jungle. We have said a group or species of animal, even without fighting, may deprive another group or species of its food or space, and in so doing may lead to its extinction. In the process of natural selection those animals which do not succeed in adapting themselves to their circumstances eventually die out. They may be devoured by others, or they may just be deprived of what they need by others which do not ever meet or recognise them. Something analogous happens between firms. A firm which makes and uses a new invention may cause other firms to go out of business or even bring about the extinction of a whole industry. The defeated firms or industries are not assaulted or threatened; they just cease to get orders. But the extinction of a firm or an industry is not the same sort of thing as the extinction of an animal or a species. When the last are rendered extinct, particular animal organisms die and have no descendents. Physical death occurs. But the extinction of firms and industries does not necessarily involve the physical death of human organisms, even though a stockbroker may jump from the roof or handloom weavers die of hunger.[3] Bankruptcy may be described as economic death, but it is quite different from physical death. Firms themselves, indeed, may survive by changing the scope of their activities, and even if they are extinguished, the men who direct the work for them go elsewhere and work for other firms. Herbert Spencer's phrase 'the survival of the fittest' applies, therefore, to firms as well as to animals and animal species, but in its economic application it does not imply the physical death of those that fail to survive, but only the cessation of some groupings and activities and the assumption and organisation of new ones.

(b) Competition between suppliers of labour

We may now consider some moral implications of competition in the market for labour. When workmen compete with one another for jobs and firms compete with one another for workmen, wages vary in terms of its supply and of the demand for labour. It is well known that for several generations from the end of the eighteenth century employers in industrial countries had the upper hand over those who worked for them. The population was increasing, new industrial methods were making traditional skills useless to those who had them, and combinations among workmen were legally regarded as criminal conspiracies. Furthermore, the society within which the industrial revolution was taking place was already divided into classes and accustomed to the exercise of authority from above. In these circumstances workmen tended to be the losers in wage bargaining, and their situation was improved when legal obstacles to the formation of trade unions were removed, and improved still more when trade unions were given legal immunity from claims for damages.

Nowadays groups of employers negotiate with trade unions and in many industries no workman can get a job if he does not belong to a union, and may lose it if he does not strike when his union gives the order. Furthermore, it is a function of unions to prohibit unusually productive or efficient workmanship on the part of its members, and in this way competition between more efficient and less efficient workmen is prevented. Because of their need for votes, democratic political parties dare not seem to falter in advocating full employment. When there are more jobs than there are workmen to fill them, employers bid among one another for skilled men and in this way the total wages paid are often much higher than those negotiated between unions and employers' associations. At the same time there has been a growth of egalitarian sentiment, so that workmen are less inclined to fall in with their employers' wishes than they were in the nineteenth-century aftermath of aristocratic society.

(c) *Competition between employers of labour*

When there is full employment and unions bargain on behalf of men who have little fear of losing their jobs, there is competition between firms for the skilled labour they find it difficult to obtain, but little competition between workmen applying for jobs. If competition promotes efficiency, then the absence of competition among workers is likely to lessen their working efficiency. Trade unions, furthermore, tend to discourage speed and efficiency of work, and in so doing they tend to diminish pride in achievement and workmanship. In such conditions unions are not the protectors of the workers against grasping employers—the employers may *want* to grasp, but they just cannot do so—but aggressive foment-ers of increased claims. If they did not act in this way they would not retain their members, since the terms of trade favour the workers in any case. The trade unions are thus tempted to require all workers to become union men and to regard themselves as united claimants from what the employers wilfully withhold from them. It is no longer a question of individuals competing for jobs as if they were prizes, but of the whole group extorting a collective prize for everyone. Bargaining comes into its own again, and the employers do well if they manage to settle for something less than the original demand. Instead of individuals competing with one another for scarce jobs, there are large organisations, manoeuvring, compromising, bluffing and striking to secure collective transfers of wealth. Instead of competing with one another, the workers support organisations which threaten and fight for them.

Under conditions of full employment, then, employers compete for labour, even when they do not compete with one another in other ways. Employees, however, do not compete among themselves, but pay spokesmen to bargain for collective benefits on their behalf. It is not a situation of emulation and rivalry between individuals, but one of conflicting collectivities. But even in these conditions the *impersonal* competition I mentioned above still continues. As invention proceeds, for example, some industries decline by comparison with others. Thus oil and gas gain by comparison with coal and road transport by comparison with the railways. Declining private industries may get state subsidies, declining nationalised industries may get both subsidies and other privileges. But unless they can be kept in being as museum pieces, like the Swiss Guards at the Vatican, they are reduced or eliminated just like the unsuccessful firms in competitive market conditions. This competition is inseparable from the attempt to improve. Whenever someone tries to do something in a better way than it has been done before, others are faced with the choice of doing likewise or of being squeezed out. There may be no rivalry, no emulation, no struggle, no fighting, but just an exercise of originality or ingenuity by someone who has no intention of competing with or outdoing anyone.

(d) Competition to sell to consumers

We now come to competition to sell to ultimate consumers and the ethics of the relationships involved. There is a sense in which the ultimate consumers compete among themselves, in that a buyer who is unwilling to buy at the price that is asked may realise that there are others who will pay that price. The sellers, of course, compete with one another in providing what the consumers want at prices they will pay. The sellers also compete with one another in offering the consumers commodities they had not thought of before.

Competition between sellers is not unlike competition between firms for contracts and raises no new issues except those connected with advertising. Competition between buyers is hardly felt as such in competitive markets. This is because most consumers arrange their purchases according to their means, and go to those shops where the things they can afford are on sale. In societies divided into classes, few individuals think much about expenditures outside or beyond their ability to pay. But the situation is rather different when everyone thinks it possible or thinks it right that he should buy everything that is on offer. Then he may come to regard the rich man who pays high prices as competing against him, with superior buying power, for goods that he would like to have but is prevented from affording. When there is a single,classless market, the feeling of being, so to say, 'out-bought' by others is engendered. This encourages both demands for higher pay and demands for reductions in the spending-power of the richer consumers. I suggest that competition between consumers is not emulative when they think of their budgets in terms of their resources. It tends to become emulative when they take seriously the idea of expenditure beyond the limits of their present income. In the nineteenth century and earlier twentieth, those who had such ambitions aimed first to acquire the money necessary to satisfy them. They tried to get better paid jobs and they saved. Buy many consumers now hope for these results by collective measures exerted through trade unions and political parties. This is the reason why hopes and demands outrun resources and intensify the struggle for them. Whereas in the earlier forms of free competition individuals were encouraged to rely on their own efforts and abilities, in the system of cooperative conflict that has now emerged individuals hope to satisfy their desires by collective protection and pressure groups. The activities of individuals are merged into those of groups and masses.

Opponents of competitive markets often criticise the part played by advertisements in stimulating desire and demand. They assert that when competing firms advertise in order to encourage expenditure on their goods they stimulate a materialistic outlook and mould men's lives in doing so. It is true that advertisement can lead to increased sales,[4] but commercial advertisement is only part of the apparatus of persuasion that operates so massively in contemporary society. Ever since the eighteenth century political leaders have been saying that each individual has the right to pursue his happiness, and the results of this belief are being experienced in our day. The 'scramble' for consumption goods is due to the misleading belief that there is increased wealth to be had effortlessly for all rather than to economic competition. Individuals would be less willing to buy what advertisers tell them if they were more inclined to accept limitations on their desires. When, furthermore, governments encourage inflation, thrift becomes pointless except for those with very large incomes or very small outgoings or both. The inflation characteristic of our day results from the happiness-seeking moral outlook of our time as well as from clumsy attempts to apply Keynesian economic theories in democratic societies. Indeed, Keynes's economic theory was in part an expression of his opposition to the strenuous moralism of the Victorian era when it was generally considered right first to save and then to spend. This comes out in a passage of *The General Theory of Employment, Interest and Money* (Macmillan, 1936) where he writes, with reference to Mandeville's criticisms of the evils of saving:

> No wonder that such wicked sentiments called down the opprobrium of two centuries of moralists and economists who felt much more virtuous in possession of their austere doctrine that no sound remedy was discoverable except in the utmost of thrift and economy both by the individual and the state. Petty's 'entertainments, magnificent shows, triumphal arches, etc.' gave place to the penny-wisdom of Gladstonian finance, and to a state system which 'could not afford' hospitals, open spaces, noble buildings, even the preservation of its ancient monuments, far less the splendours of music and the drama, all of which were consigned to the private charity or magnanimity of improvident individuals.[5]

In *The Fable of the Bees*, Mandeville called prodigality 'that noble sin', and elaborated this by saying: 'I mean the unmixed prodigality of heedless and voluptuous men, that being educated in plenty, abhor the vile thoughts of lucre.' Keynes, like his friend (and rival) Lytton Strachey, disliked the puritanism inculcated in Victorian times, and Mandeville's easygoing hedonism was congenial to him. It has now become congenial to large sections of the population and in doing so has served to increase both the effective demand for consumer goods and the belief that they ought to be available for the asking. It is in this moral climate that advertisers of consumer goods operate, and there will be a 'scramble' for them as long as this fundamental weather does not change. There is no consistency, and little honesty, in criticising competitive advertising and at the same time proclaiming the right of everyone to as much as they can enjoy.

Market commodities and non-market goods

It can be argued that casualties of the competitive market system, those who are unable to maintain themselves by their own exertions, may need to be supported by non-market means. Children as such are hardly casualties, but, apart from family allowances and school tuition and meals, and medical care, they are supported by their parents, and, to a decreasing extent, incapacitated parents are supported by their children. Insurance is a means of dealing with casualties within the market mechanism itself, and in this way both firms and individuals may guard themselves against the effects of death, accident, illness and other human risks. If there are people who cannot afford to pay the premiums, and if there are misfortunes that the market cannot insure against, then casualties may have to be helped by other than market means to enter the market, except that the incapacitated may need personal care in kind.

It was because the market was thought incapable of helping people in need of help that poor relief, unemployment benefit and medical care was provided, by private charity, voluntary insurance or publicly financed agencies. Thus people get incomes they do not work for, to pay for food and clothing they could not otherwise buy. They also get subsidised lodging and 'free' medical treatment, although they might have money (or vouchers) to pay for them.[6] Sometimes, but rarely, the gratuitous benefits are forced from private individuals in what amounts to confiscation, as happens when the rents of private houses are controlled at uneconomic rates and the landlords in consequence have to house their tenants at their own expense. But for the most part, the casualties of the system receive help paid for by money collected in rates and taxes. As incomes rise the casualties become fewer because they can insure against sickness, accident, death and other uncertainties. When we say that the market cannot deal with the casualties of the system we are faced with the possibilities of voluntary private provision (charity), involuntary private provision (enforced gifts, as with some controlled rents), voluntary public provision (as with public appeals for victims of natural disasters), and involuntary public provision (as with taxation). It is the last that people generally have in mind when they speak of providing for needs outside the market.

We need not spend time considering the ethics of involuntary private provision. There is no morally defensible reason at all for forcing some individuals, irrespective of their incomes or circumstances, to give pecuniary help to beneficiaries whose incomes and circumstances have not been inquired into. In this way benefits are provided for people who may not need them by people who may not be in a position to afford them. The public at large say that certain classes of people should be helped, and then take no steps to see that the help goes to those who need it or that it is provided by those who, in equity, should provide it. The existence of this system is a sign of moral abdication, and those who oppose its abolition can have no concern for justice.

For the charitable methods of helping the casualties of the market to be feasible there must be wealthy people and wealthy organisations, or there must be a widespread ability and willingness on the part of friends and neighbours to help their unfortunate fellows. In contemporary society families are so scattered and friendships are so dispersed, that less help comes from personal and family loyalties. Fewer people think they ought to help one another in these ways, although they are increasingly able to do so, and people in distress no longer expect to obtain much help this way. No doubt this unconcern has been encouraged by the establishment of public relief organisations, but whatever the reasons for it, the fact remains. When help is dispensed by charities and other organised bodies, enquiries may have to be made into the extent and nature of the need. But these bodies may not have the power to obtain the necessary information, and in any case their representatives may think that too close enquiry will destroy the charitable atmosphere. They may prefer to be deceived by some artful dodger rather than to probe too far into his affairs, and as a result honest need may pass unnoticed and unhelped. Furthermore, when the subservience of immediately post-aristocratic society diminishes, many of those in need have an aversion to receiving gifts of this sort. They know they have no *right* to gifts, and they think they do have a right to some other sort of assistance. Givers, even those giving to relieve distress, can give to whom they please. People in distress who are *not* relieved naturally come to think they are unjustly overlooked. Thus there arises the belief that those in distress have a right to receive assistance.

It is at this stage that it comes to be accepted that such assistance should be provided by monies raised through taxation. For if the indigent have a right to assistance, and if there is no one in particular against whom this right can be claimed, then it is the public at large who have to fulfill it. Agencies of the government can demand the information necessary to distribute assistance to those who need it in proportion to their need. In this way, the help is less subject to private whim and accident than private charity would be. Indeed, in large populations it might not be possible for charity to provide the necessary help on the requisite scale. In a democratic community the citizens are presumed to approve of the expenditure they pay their taxes to meet, and in general the presumption is well-founded.[7] The plight of the needy is brought to their attention and they do not wish to see them starved or rendered desperate.

But in housing, medicine, and education the matter has been taken further than this. Let us take first the example of housing. At one time private bodies such as the Peabody Trust built blocks of flats to be let at cheap rents to those who could not afford unsubsidised accommodation. Local authorities then joined in and financed such accommodation by sudsidies from the rates. Then the central government added to these subsidies and a position was reached in which a considerable proportion of the population live in publicly subsidised dwellings. In some areas, indeed, a majority of the population are so provided for. It then comes to be said that housing is and ought to be a 'social service' and should not be left to be bought and sold in markets. This might be put forward as part of an argument for a socialist system of society, but we are not now discussing it in that light. The arguments we are concerned with are (1) that when housing is scarce it should be distributed in accordance with need, just as food should be rationed in times of famine, and (2), that housing is something very special, in that without places to live in people cannot go about their other affairs. The assumption here is that some things are too fundamental and important for individual survival for them to be left to be settled by market decisions.

On the first of these two arguments, we need to know about the nature and causes of the scarcity before we decide that rationing of subsidised housing by officials is the only way out. Scarcity is a function of effective demand, and if large numbers of people who cannot afford them nevertheless demand *new* houses, there are likely to be difficulties in supplying them. In general, the idea that everyone has a right to accommodation of the sort that he considers desirable is bound to lead to the idea and even to the creation of a shortage. Again, the legislation controlling rents has made it very unlikely that private companies will build houses to rent. Thus the legislation controlling rents has forced the provision of such houses on to the public sector. Once the local governments and central government agencies are organised for this purpose, interests are built up in our society which regard it as natural that they should expand and extend. These do not consist only of the officials and administrators, but also of the 'experts', that is to say, specialists who know about the organisation and statistics of the matter. Once local authorities have large housing departments, they regard extension of them as the most natural and effective way of dealing with housing shortages, and do not ask whether other measures could be taken which would lessen or remove the responsibilities of their departments. The combination of large organisations, interested 'experts' and lazy-minded good nature forms a public opinion that is unlikely to be critical.

It is the second argument, however, that takes us to the heart of the problem. If the most fundamental and important things must not be left to be supplied and bought in markets, then it is not housing alone that will be claimed as essentially a social service. Similar, indeed, more extensive claims, are made in respect of medical care and of education. There are at present no influential voices calling for the abolition of private house ownership, but there are many who say that no one should be allowed to buy or sell medical attention or education. Medical attention is a matter of life or death and education or the lack of it can make or mar a whole career. (Food or the lack of it is also a matter of life or death, but the nationalisation of food provision is not advocated on that ground.) Such important matters, it is said, should not be left to be settled by the purse, for if they are, the better-off will live longer, healthier lives and have better careers than the poorer members of the community.

Before we consider the moral issues involved in this attitude, it will be as well to notice a similarity between housing, medical care and education. In all three cases a large organisation has been first set up, 'experts' have collected around it, and what was first regarded as a rescue operation for some is now regarded as a right or perhaps even a necessity for all. Now that the National Health Service has been working for twenty years it is suggested that it is *morally wrong* for individuals to pay for medical care. The main argument used is that in so doing they divert to their own use medical skill which, if used in the National Health Service, would be used for people most in need rather than for those who can pay for it. What began as an organisation for ensuring that no one would go without medical care for lack of means may possibly turn into the only permitted source of such care. People would then be prevented from paying for better medical care. When, several years ago, doctors withdrew from the National Health Service in order to provide medical care for a group of paying patients, they were criticised on the ground that they were diminishing the amount of care available in the National Health Service and providing their paying patients with more than their due.

Similarly, the organised network of local authority schools is gradually ousting fee-paying schools, even though public education was first provided in order to ensure that parents should not escape their obligation to see that their children are educated. It is now being claimed that it is wrong for people to pay for education outside the public system. For in doing so, it is argued, they are unfairly buying advantages and privileges for their children at the expense of those whose parents are less well-off. It appears that when the public bodies concerned with education and health grow very large, arguments are produced for swallowing up the remaining private concerns. Perhaps it is only because millions of people now own their houses and many children still hope to inherit from them that it is not likewise being argued that in buying a house for himself a man is 'jumping the queue' and obtaining unfair advantages for himself and his family.

An interesting example of the way in which this institutional imperialism works may be seen from the arguments devised in order to equate the relief of taxation allowed for interest payments on house mortgages with subsidies for council houses. The tax reliefs were granted at a time when house-ownership was being encouraged and when well-off people tended to buy houses for cash. Owing to inflation and high taxation it pays many more people than it used to to buy their houses by means of mortgages, and a good sum of money would be saved by the Treasury if this concession were withdrawn. Because of this, it is said that the wealthy are being subsidised in buying their houses just as the poor are subsidised by having houses at less than their economic rents. But the wealthy came to use this system of finance because inflation and high taxation made it financially advantageous for them to do so. Furthermore, if house-ownership were still regarded as a worthy object of public policy then it could be encouraged among the less well-off. As it is, the major effort is put into subsidised rented housing, and critics of this policy are then told that well-to-do house-buyers are also being subsidised. Yet it is public policy by way of inflation, high taxation and publicly provided housing that has made it appear that tax relief on house mortgages is a form of subsidy.

We must now consider the argument that some needs are so fundamental that their satisfaction should not be left to the market, but should be provided publicly. This amounts to saying that in what concerns their basic needs people should not be left to fend for themselves. Social reformers in the past have said that no one should be allowed to go without shelter, medical care and education of some kind. But now the view is that no one should be allowed to *buy* these things for himself, but should be allotted his fair share of them under a publicly organised scheme. Taxes would be paid in accordance with ability, and benefits allotted in accordance with need. In this way the communist rule 'from each according to his ability, to each according to his need', would be applied, not to economic activity, but to the sphere of welfare. Not to organise things this way would be to support injustice, privilege, discrimination.

My first comment is that this dual system of economic inequality and welfare contains within itself, to use Saint-Simon's expression, 'the seeds of its own destruction'. For few people, in the long run, are likely to work and contrive their utmost if they are to be in no better position, as regards the fundamentals of living, than the helpless, the lazy or the unlucky. The more egalitarian the welfare distribution, the less enthusiasm there is likely to be for the competitive economic activities that produce the wealth. Within the system of competitive capitalism the individual is supposed to do the best he can 'for himself', which generally means also for his family and any causes he has set his heart on. But if he is prevented from using his income or his profits for things that *he* wants, if he is forced to send his children to schools he does not like and to go to a doctor he does not trust, then he may well wonder whether his business activities are worth while. He would be discouraged still further if housing became entirely a matter of welfare, to be allocated only in accordance with need. Thus, the extension of welfare and so-called 'fair shares' from one field to another is not compatible with the system of competitive capitalism. Believers in capitalism who set no limits to the extension of the 'fair shares' principle are helping to stake out the ground in which their graves will be dug.

It will be said, however, that it is wrong to wish to buy privileges with superior wealth. We may now see the issue in this way: it is said by some that education and medical care are so important and fundamental that they ought not to be bought and sold, and by others that, just because they are so important and fundamental, they should be the responsibility of each individual. The conflict would appear to be between these two policies: (a) providing basic welfare at public expense and in accordance with need, and (b) each individual regarding himself as responsible for providing his own and his family's basic welfare according to his resources and his wishes.

Now it should be remarked in the first place that (a) is a much more cumbrous way of proceeding than (b). For under (a), the money has to be collected in taxes and used to pay for the doctors and hospitals to which the individual taxpayers then present themselves, whereas under (b) they pay the doctors and the hospitals direct. What reasons are put forward for preferring the roundabout way?

One reason is that it is a means of making the well-off pay towards the welfare of the poor. But this would only justify taxation to cover the welfare expenses of those who could not afford to pay for themselves. Yet what is being advocated is taxation to provide a service which is to be the *sole* service for everyone. Why, then, should those who can afford to, not pay for the welfare services they require for themselves and their families? Having contributed towards others, shouldn't they be free to look after themselves with what remains to them? Two reasons are given for answering these questions in the negative. The first is that if the better-off members of the community paid for private welfare services for themselves and their families, they would be enticing skill and other resources away from the state system and in this way lowering the level of the services it can provide. The second reason is that it is unjust that some people should have different and better welfare services than others, since welfare should be in accordance with need, not in accordance with ability to pay.

The first of these reasons is the less radical. It depends on the fact that a state system already exists, and is then put forward as the claim that nothing should be available outside it. It can be answered in the following way. Either only a few want services outside the state system, or many do. If only a few, then the effect on the whole system is small and there is no need to trouble about it. If many want services outside the system, this shows that many people can and do wish to be responsible for their own arrangements, even after they have been taxed to provide for others. Furthermore, the more people there are who wish for private provision, the fewer there are who need public provision. Again because they are paying for it themselves, those who opt out of the system are likely to employ existing resources more economically than do those who remain in the system.

Of course, it is the second, more radical reason that moves most of those who object to the buying and selling of medical care and education. They think it is unjust for people to spend money on schooling or medical care for themselves or their children, for in doing so they are buying privileges, and privileges should not be bought. If a privilege is merely an advantage, then the more intelligent and shrewder people are constantly buying privileges, since they constantly buy to better advantage than other people. If, however, a privilege is an *unjust* advantage, then to talk of buying privileges in these connections, is merely to assert that it is wrong to buy medical care or education.

Which things, then, is it right to buy and sell, and which things should be excluded from markets altogether? Professor R. M. Titmuss[8] thinks that human blood should not be bought and sold, but rather given and taken, and then only within the British National Health Service. Not many people object to the selling of human hair, although Kant thought the practice 'not entirely free from blame'.[9] All civilised peoples think it wrong to buy and sell human beings, yet these same societies regard the selling of one's labour, which is an activity of one's self even if not a part or organ, as morally acceptable. One can list some objects and activities which are universally regarded as morally unsuitable for purposes of buying and selling, e.g. votes, knowledge that would be useful to a foreign power, knowledge about a friend which would be of interest to a newspaper and its readers, sexual complaisance or sexual activity, a man's services as thief or killer. There are some things and activities which by their very nature *could* not be bought or sold. Love and tenderness, for example, presuppose a spontaneous concern on the part of the person who, as we say, *gives* them, and just could not be made available in return for a payment offered. On the other hand, care and attention can be bought, even though they can only be sold by someone who is conscientious and skilful.

However, we are not here concerned with any argument to the effect that medical care and education *cannot* be bought or sold, but with the argument that, like votes, knowledge acquired in friendship, and one's country's military secrets, they *should not* be. The last two are forms of betrayal and the first is bribery, and the relevant actions are wrong because betrayal and bribery are. Selling one's services as a thief or murderer are wrong because theft and murder are wrong, and prostitution is wrong because it denies human dignity on the part of both supplier and customer. Betrayal of a friend in the way mentioned above is not a *criminal* offence, but fidelity is not regarded as open to financial offers.

On the face of it, education and medical care are not, like treachery, bribery or theft, morally wrong or criminal and hence not rightly bought or sold for that reason. For many generations private doctoring and private schooling were not only tolerated, but were highly respected activities. Has anything happened, then, to change their moral quality? I suggest that it is the growth of the large state organisations connected with them that has led many people to change their moral attitudes towards them. When in the past a doctor set up in practice or a scholar opened a school, all he had to consider were his patients, pupils or colleagues. But nowadays the state educational and medical systems, and the 'experts' associated with them, join to accuse him of antisocial behaviour. It is not enough for him to help a number of particular individuals who pay him to do so, for it is said, there are other individuals who need the help more, and in any case the people's representatives and the state apparatus they control know better than he does where doctoring and schooling can best be deployed. It is not the business of the law to interfere with a man's choice of a car, a diet,[10] or a form of sexual behaviour, but education and medical care are held to be quite different; inequality is permissible in the former, but not in the latter, because in the latter they are too important to be left to individual choice. Buying education is, indirectly, buying chances in life, and buying medical care is, in effect, buying life itself. The implication is that life chances ought to all be equal, that health and life should be equally considered through public authority, and that these equalities can in practice be achieved in these ways.

Now the critic of this outlook may deny that equality can be achieved in these ways. He may suggest that powerful people, politicians and their hangers-on prominent among them, would get advantages for themselves and their families which in the free system had been obtained by rich people. He may also suggest that sometimes those who pay for what they consider better things may be very much mistaken. But the main line of criticism, I suggest, ought to go to the implications of imposing an equality as regards education and health and of leaving individuals to pursue freely chosen lives in other ways. I have already suggested that equalised welfare and a competitive economy are not likely to be able to exist together for very long. I now suggest that when they do live together their union is morally questionable. Broadly speaking, what is advocated is forcible communal and equalised provision of what is considered most fundamental to the individual, and freedom as regards the less fundamental, particularly the inessentials and luxuries. The government consider this to be 'getting our priorities right,' since they see themselves organising the people so that they *receive* the fundamentals before they can concern themselves with anything else. The priorities are those of the government and presuppose that the government controls what people can do. But from the point of view of the individual the moral situation looks very different. Under the compulsory welfare system we are considering, schooling and medical care are organised in ways over which the individual has little control. They are not among the things that *he* has to work and save for—or so it seems to him, for the money for them is taken from him before he receives his pay. In the very process, therefore, of being made *social* or *governmental* priorities, education and medical care cease to be *individual* priorities in the economy of the individual. As he is not allowed as an individual to spend money on these things, whatever sense of priorities he may have must be expressed in other directions. His responsibility in the spending of his money starts only after these fundamental services have been provided for him.

The consequences of publicity providing people gratis with services which would be of fundamental personal and moral importance if they had to provide them for themselves, are likely to be very far-reaching indeed. When the government imposes *its* priorities it alters the balance of the choices which the individual can make for himself. In the past it has been regarded as an individual's responsibility to direct his expenditure in the best possible way. This involved him in ensuring that he had dealt with essentials before he embarked on inessentials and luxuries. Some people made a better job of this than others, and there were, as we have emphasised, some whose mistakes or misfortunes made them casualties. But under the system we are now considering, no one is to be allowed to have personal control of his expenditure on some of the basic matters. But the more his needs are satisfied in this way, the more important will his expenditures on other things seem to him. Some of these other expenditures, such as those on food[11] and clothing, will be important enough, but luxuries and superfluities will play a large part among them. His sense of responsibility for what he is not allowed to decide for himself is likely to diminish, and it is possible that he will be less concerned for his health and his children's education than for his amusements. The very quality of his amusements, it may be suggested, varies in accordance with whether they are engaged in after he has himself provided for the fundamentals of his life, or whether they are the major part of the mere residue of personal choice allowed to him by a paternalistic society.

Let us consider the situation of a man who is not allowed to spend from his own income on his health or his children's education. Let us suppose, too, that his housing is subsidised and is of the standardised type usual for such accommodation. His control over the medical attention he and his family get, and over his children's schooling and his house is small. He can vote at national and local elections, and he can sometimes change his doctor or make protests about how the schools are organised. A man in this situation would give expression to his personal aims in spending the income he takes home from work after taxes have been deducted. Because his taxes are paid on his behalf by his employer, and because they finance what is publicly provided for him, his take-home pay appears to him to be his total pay. From this he has to buy food, clothing and furniture, but apart from such items it is amusements and luxuries that his 'wages' appear to buy for him. A likely consequence of this would be that the connection between work and the provision of the state-provided fundamentals is obscured. The individual would be encouraged to believe that provision for such fundamentals as health and education is not his concern. When he presses for increased wages what he is likely to have in mind is the income he can spend as an individual, and he will probably think that the pre-empted taxation gets in the way of this. Unless he has strong religious convictions, or a concern for public work or for the exercise of some skill or artistic ability, he is likely to think that work is for food and amusement. Adam Smith said that 'it is perfectly self-evident' that 'consumption is the sole end and purpose of all production',[12] but to the inhabitant of a secularised Welfare State, it is amusement and luxury that are likely to appear as the main ends of production. For in such a society the system of taxation and of welfare expenditure conceals the connection between work and production on the one hand, and the consumption of welfare services on the other. We may call this the mystification of the Welfare State. If, on the other hand, people pay directly for their doctor and for their children's education, they are likely to approach the rest of their expenditure in a different and perhaps a more responsible manner.

Monopoly and cooperation

We have already discussed the idea that economic competition is a form of strife or rivalry and should therefore be morally condemned. We may now briefly consider the idea that competition is bad because it is opposed to cooperation which, as a form of harmony in human affairs, ought to be promoted as much as possible.

Deliberately organised cooperation is not, in itself, necessarily good. A cabal or gang may cooperate most amicably in carrying out an evil design, and hence the purpose for which the cooperators deliberately harmonise their actions and policies is relevant to the goodness or badness of what they are doing. Furthermore, people may cooperate without deliberately setting out to do so. This indeed is what generally happens when commodities are produced under competitive market conditions. In his *Harmonies Economiques,* Bastiat wrote of the mining, smelting, manufacturing, transporting, financing and storing involved in producing a cheap lamp for sale to a French workman. Firms and individuals all over the world had worked together in producing it, but no one man or body of men had organised all these processes so as to fit them together into a whole. There was detailed cooperation in hiring men, miners or metal-workers or dockers, buying materials, moving finished or semifinished products, and so on. But there was no single plan for lamp-manufacturing, organised from a single centre and requiring the acquiescence, obedience or enthusiasm of all the participants. The mineowner, the miner, the metalworker, the carrier, each pursued his own ends, and, without even considering the lamps that resulted, cooperated in producing them and getting them to the shops and to the purchasers. Competitive cooperation, therefore, is not a contradiction in terms, if we mean by it the working together that takes place without conscious participation in some comprehensive plan. There must, of course, be deliberate cooperation within firms, and between firms that contract with one another, but in a competitive economy the firms are not cooperating to execute a plan agreed between them all or imposed upon them.

Competition, then, is not opposed to cooperation, but rather to deliberate and comprehensively organised forms of it, as described, for example, by Engels in his *Fundamental Principles of Communism* (1847) in the words: 'When industry is conducted in common and in accordance with plans determined by the whole of society . . .'[13] Competition then, is not opposed to cooperation but is opposed to monopoly. There may be occasions when a monopoly is justified, as, for example, when the cost of producing a commodity is very much less when the total output is produced by one firm and there are substitutes to which consumers may turn if the price goes too high. But competition is not compatible with agreements between firms for limiting or eliminating it. On the practical effects of legislation to prevent monopoly, I am not competent to judge. But it should be emphasised that when there are substitutes for the monopolised commodity, and when it is open to new firms to come into the market, undesirable monopolies are not likely to persist. A competitive economy can put up with some monopolies and even publicly organise some to its own advantage. It is when competition has already been seriously undermined that calls for anti-monopoly legislation are heard, and then it may be too late for them to be of much effect. Such may be the situation in Great Britain today.

Notes

1. See again Catherwood, *Britain with the Brakes Off*. In *The Christian in Industrial Society* (London, Tyndale, 1964) Mr. Catherwood had proposed the setting up of what were later called 'Little Neddies' (p. 37).

2. Animals do generally confine their fights within rules, and so may be said to have some conception of what is permissible.

3. The bankrupt stockbroker is generally 'hammered' and the employees of dying industries are nowadays retrained, redeployed or pensioned.

4. Ralph Harris and Arthur Seldon, *Advertising in Action,* Hutchinson for the Institute of Economic Affairs, London, 1962.

5. P. 362. Cf. the passage from the *Treatise on Money* (1930) quoted in Sir Roy Harrod's *The Life of John Maynard Keynes* (Macmillan, 1951), pp. 406-7, where the relation of thrift to enterprise and profit is most carefully stated. The anti-Victorian ambit of Keynes's outlook is made clear by Harrod in chapter 5 and elsewhere.

6. Ralph Harris and Arthur Seldon, *Choice in Welfare* (IEA, 1963 and 1965); A. T. Peacock and J. Wiseman, *Education for Democrats* (IEA, 1964); E. G. West, *Education and the State* (IEA, 1963).

7. Recent research suggests, however, that the public does not generally approve of indiscriminate 'universal' social benefits, Arthur Seldon, *Welfare and Taxation,* (IEA, 1968).

8. In *Choice and 'The Welfare State',* Fabian Tract No. 370, Feb. 1967, pp. 13-16. According to Professor Titmuss *sellers* of blood try to sell too much and so weaken themselves.

Furthermore they tend to be 'Skid Row' characters and their blood is not always up to standard.

9. *The Metaphysics of Morals* (1796) in *Werke* (Prussian Academy Edition) Vol. 6, p. 423. Kant thought that to 'give away or sell a tooth' or 'to submit oneself to castration in order to gain an easier livelihood as a singer' were somewhat akin to self-murder. Hair, as a *part* but not an *organ* of the body, was rather different, but even so, in selling it, an individual was treating a part of himself (and hence himself?) as a means rather than as an end in itself. Blood seems to be neither an organ nor a part of the body. In *The Price of Blood* (IEA, 1968), Michael H. Cooper and Anthony J. Culyer argue that 'payment, provided that it is separated from donation, would induce further supplies', and that 'payment for blood can be both sensible and humane' (p. 45).

10. Of course the state has a duty to require standards of food production and manufacture, since buyers are frequently unable to ascertain whether the food is poisonous, adulterated, etc. Similarly, the state justifiably requires school teachers, doctors, etc., to have certain qualifications.

11. Diet is of great importance for individual health ('man ist was er isst', said Feuerbach), but no one proposes that diets should be publicly devised and imposed, even though bad diet must increase the calls upon the National Health Service. Subsidised school meals, however, have been defended on the ground that parents may fail to provide nourishing meals for their children.

12. *The Wealth of Nations*, Book 4, ch. 8.

13. *Marx-Engels: Werke* (Dietz Verlag, Berlin, 1964), Vol. 4, p. 376.

ANTONY FLEW*

Libertarians versus Egalitarians

Let me begin by distinguishing some different interpretations of equality. For not every ideal of equality constitutes a threat to liberty. On the contrary: the most fundamental of these ideals is itself essentially connected with respecting every individual's right *to choose*, in as many respects as is practically consistent with the corresponding equal rights of everyone else.

The first basic distinction is between, on the one hand, ideals or norms and, on the other hand, facts or putative facts. The second paragraph of the American Declaration of Independence begins: *"We hold these truths to be self-evident, that all Men are created equal. . . ."* But it would be quite wrong on this account to discredit the Signers with some foolish belief that babies come identical, that there are no genetically determined differences of physique, of temperament, and of ability. For those wise men at once glossed the phrase "all Men are created equal" with an explanation showing that this was for them a matter, not of what allegedly *is* the case, but of what ideally *ought* to be. The complete sentence thus reads:

> We hold those truths to be self-evident, that all men are created equal, that they are endowed by their Creator with certain unalienable Rights, that among these are Life, Liberty, and the Pursuit of Happiness.[1]

No statement of the first *(is)* kind by itself either logically presupposes or entails any proclamation of the second *(ought)* sort. As an illustration of the nature and an indication of the significance of this first basic distinction, it is perhaps worth repeating yet once more that this necessary truth provides one of two independently decisive reasons why immoral conclusions about the propriety of discriminating either for, or against, individuals upon grounds of racial group membership cannot be validly deduced from premises stating only that certain racial groups are, on average, either superior or inferior to others in their natural endowments.

This essay was first published in September 1978 in *Encounter* under the title "The Procrustean Ideal."
*University of Reading.

(The second of these often neglected yet both independently quite decisive reasons is that nothing about the particular characteristics of a particular member of a group follows from any general statement about the average of that group: you may be a dwarf or a giant or neither, and yet still happen to belong to a group which is on average either very tall or very short or neither.)[2]

When J. V. Stalin said to a visiting American Senator, "You believe that men are equal, I know that they are not," Stalin had missed the point. What he knew, his visitor knew too. People are in fact born with very unequal potentialities. What, apparently, Stalin did not know was that the Signers were neither asserting nor presupposing a false proposition in biology or psychology. They were instead demanding that certain very general basic rights ought to be guaranteed.

The second basic distinction is between three different ideals of equality. The first and hardest to define seems to have no accepted distinguishing label—perhaps partly for those reasons. Until and unless something better is suggested, let us call this, baldly, *personal equality.* The second is usually called *equality of opportunity,* although it might be better described as fair and open competition for scarce opportunities. Ths is what the great French Revolution of 1789 meant by "the career open to the talents." The third is, by contrast with the second, *equality of outcome* or *equality of result.*

The first of these three ideals can best be introduced as a secularised version of the traditional Judaeo-Christian insistence that every soul is of equal value in the eyes of God. However much we actually do differ and perhaps should differ in other ways, we all have our lives to live and our decisions to make; and in this most fundamental respect we ought all to recognise one another as equals. As a less poetic, sexually more scrupulous poet might have written: "A person is a person for a' that. . . ." It was this ideal, in a fully secularised form, which Immanuel Kant was expressing when he laid down "The Formula of the End in Itself." After taking "rational nature" or—as we would be more likely to say—personality as "something *whose existence* has *in itself* an absolute value," Kant's Categorical Imperative becomes:

> Act in such a way that you always treat humanity, whether in your own person or in the person of any other, never simply as a means, but always at the same time as an end.[3]

Once the next two ideals have been picked out and docketed, they may seem to be unconfusably different both from the first and from each other. They are, nevertheless, quite commonly assumed to be compatible companions, even where they are not actually mistaken to be the same. Thus the Editors of a recent sourcebook on *The "Inequality" Controversy* write, without a qualm of historical conscience, of America's traditional "commitment to equality of opportunity *and to equality of results*." They really ought to know better. But they even go on to say of one of their contributors that he examines this "concept of equality of opportunity" and "traces the development of the concept to its logically inevitable definition as equality of results."[4]

Yet for most people, though not for all, a large part, though not the whole of the point of equality of opportunity lies in its being opportunity to better the condition of themselves and their families; whether this is for them a matter of being better off than they are now or would otherwise be, or whether it is for them also or alternatively a matter of relativities and hence essentially of being better off in the future than (certain) others then are. For this perhaps deplorable majority the intrinsic rewards to be found in developing and using talents are as nothing compared with the further and extrinsic rewards which they hope by these means to win. Suppose that you first offer equality of opportunity; and then explain that, as a devout egalitarian of the third sort, you also propose to ensure that, whatever opportunities are or are not taken, everyone is going to be ground down and kept down to your ideal of equality of results. You will not be very warmly or widely thanked for your first offer, I think, once your second intention is fully understood. For, as Confucius really did say, without cynical exaggeration and with traditional Chinese realism: "It is not easy to find a man who has studied for three years without aiming at pay."[5]

It is, I suspect, mainly because they are themselves perhaps rather guiltily aware of the wide unpopularity of some of the implications of their Procrustean ideal that our contemporary egalitarians of outcome so often confound it with equality of opportunity.

One instructive method is by tripping over that favourite cliché *"life chances."* Jean Floud, for instance, who is much respected as a social engineer, does this in a recent article under the characteristic and revealing title "Making Adults More Equal: The Scope and Limitations of Public Educational Policy." She defines the key expression *"life-chances"* in a perfectly straightforward way, "in terms of people's economic and social opportunities." But then, like so many others, she forthwith proceeds to identify differences in educational opportunity with differences in achieved education, life-chances with actual lives. What she is talking about is correlations (reported by Christopher Jencks) between achieved education and achieved income. Yet she insists on calling differences in the former, differences in educational opportunity, while differences in the latter are correspondingly equated with differences in life-chances:

> . . . differences of educational opportunity do not explain much of the variation in individual incomes. Measures of the independent influence of educational opportunity on people's life-chance give different results.[6]

Connoisseurs of doctrinaire high-handedness will now appreciate an example of an even shorter way of collapsing this fundamental distinction; and consequently identifying the third with the second ideal of equality—equal life-chances with equal lives. "Surely," one Swedish philosopher suggests, "we could always define 'real chance' in such a way that it becomes analytically true that if two members of a society have the same real chance to achieve equality of economic welfare, then their actual economic welfare level will be the same."[7] Yes indeed, nothing easier. Nor more wanton and more wrong.

Personal Equality

After this briefly illustrated account of the differences between three current ideals of equality, we are now in a position to consider whether and, if so, how and how far any of these various ideals are enemies to liberty. Of the first it is obvious that the contrary is the truth. The same ideal also demands a measure of democracy, which itself in turn necessitates respect for at least the most fundamental individual liberties.

I suggest that democrats are in any case best advised to ground their—and my—convictions upon the splendid Kantian ideal to which I have just attached the colourless label "personal equality." To do this is to appeal—not to the false and silly doctrine that the majority is always, or even most often, right—but to the true and crucial fact that it is everyone's lives which government is governing. It is the appeal which was superbly put in the 1640s by the russet-coated Captain Rainborough in the Putney Debates of the New Model Army:

> Really I think that the poorest he that is in England hath a life to live as the greatest he; and therefore truly, Sir, I think it is clear, that every man that is to live under a government ought first by his own consent to put himself under that government; and I do believe that the poorest man in England is not at all bound to that government that he hath not had a voice to put himself under.[8]

He here, as so often, should embrace she!

The connection between democracy and certain minimum individual liberties is logically necessary. For these are those which are the preconditions of its being truly said that citizens made and implemented their decisions on how to cast their votes freely. These preconditions include, for instance, effective guarantees against intimidation. Again, it must be possible to get and to spread relevant information, to discuss issues with other people, and to organise opposition. Besides the minimal civil liberties which are in this way logically necessary to democracy it may be that other and especially economic liberties are also contingently required. For, though it is obviously possible to have a pluralist economy without democracy, there are very strong reasons for believing that a fully socialist (Clause IV) setup is in practice incompatible with authentic (*i.e.* Western: "vote-the-scoundrels out") democratic institutions.

Certainly this contention about the economic preconditions of political pluralism is not peculiar to Milton Friedman, F. A. Hayek, and Sir Keith Joseph.[9] It has also been accepted, albeit with a somewhat sullen inertia, by such right-wing social democrats as Anthony Crosland and Roy Jenkins. And it is seen as a manifest and agreeable lesson of experience by the most powerful and persistent contemporary enemies of democracy—thus the Institute of Marxism-Leninism in Moscow sketches a programme for achieving total and irremovable Communist domination by following "United Front" or "Broad Left" tactics:

> Having once acquired political power, the working class implements the liquidation of the private ownership of the means of production. . . . As a result, under socialism, there remains no ground for the existence of any opposition parties counterbalancing the Communist Party.[10]

We, however, must put this question aside in order to notice that very illiberal decisions may be reached by impeccably democratic procedures. At some times and in some countries—but not, it seems, in Britain today[11]—a referendum held after a great national debate might well reaffirm legislation refusing the "right to die" to the degradingly senile and the unrelievably ill. Similar referenda might impose and extend various choice-denying monopolies, and all manner of other legal restrictions not needed to safeguard the maximum equal freedoms of every citizen. In the words of John Stuart Mill's classic essay *On Liberty:*

> The "people" who exercise the power are not always the same people with those over whom it is exercised; and the self-government spoken of is not the government of each by himself, but of each by all the rest. [12]

All this is as true as it is important. But what is relevant here is that no such illiberal policies are dictated by the first sort of ideal of equality. If anything it forbids them. For what is the categorical imperative never to treat anyone *"simply as a means, but always at the same time as an end"* if it is not an insistence upon everyone's equal right to make their own decisions in the light of their own chosen ends? (Kant's own attempt to derive therefrom an absolute embargo upon suicide is manifestly factitious and unsound, an unhappy product of his own too conservative first-order ethical preconceptions.)

Choice and Inequality

Unavoidable conflicts with the claims of liberty begin with the second ideal of equality: equality of opportunity. There are two complications which we need to disentangle at once. First, we need to make up our minds whether it really is equality which we are talking about, or only a minimum without a maximum. The idea of a "welfare floor," a state-provided safety-net, is most familiar from other areas of social policy. It was indeed a main theme of Sir Winston Churchill's domestic speeches during his years as Leader of the Conservative Party.

As an ideal this is essentially different from that of a compulsory ceiling, or of anything else requiring measures to pull excellers back (notwithstanding that in practice such safety-nets are usually financed in part from progressive direct taxation). Nor is this safety-net ideal at all the same as the egalitarian ideal of state monopoly provision, provision which shall be at the same time both the minimum and the maximum, equal for all. [13] Applying these distinctions to our present area of interest it is easy to see that safety-net measures to spread and increase educational opportunity are measures to extend and to raise the floor rather than to enforce a uniform equal provision. Guided by this different ideal, and by a commitment to liberty, libertarian democrats want to defend, while their egalitarian opponents long to destroy, alternatives to and within the state system.

We also have to ask at what stage in the human life-cycle it is proposed that the desired "equality of opportunity" should begin. There is a world of difference between, at one extreme, applying this notion to adult job applicants or to candidates for tertiary education, and, at the other extreme, applying it to newborn babies or even the freshly fertilised egg. The clashes here are with actual or possible parental liberties and they are the more serious and the more general the nearer the point of application of the idea is put to the moment of the child's conception. The trouble is that to have been, and to be, raised in a good home is in so many ways so much an advantage. Indeed the criteria of goodness here are, for the most part, at the same time criteria of such advantage.

So, if you want to achieve ideal equality of opportunity from the very beginning, then you have to abolish the home and the family in favour of the universal compulsory comprehensive *crèche*. Failing that, your next best bet is to find ways of minimising home influences, and/or of intruding compensatory measures to offset the advantages of above-average and the disadvantages of below-average homes. Any of this must involve substantially circumscribing, if not outright abolishing, the freedom of parents to make homes, and to bring up their children as they see fit; and/or most if not all of the point of their labouring so to do.

The most extreme proposals of this kind are not at present, I believe, on any British agenda. For most of those for whom true equality of opportunity from the earliest stage is a value, it remains one value which can and has to be traded off against others. Yet the intractable inevitability of clashes between this ideal and that of the family with substantial parental rights, and duties, can be illustrated with an example which belongs to the stuff of present-day British educational politics.

Until a few years ago the stock objection to any defence of parental choice in education was to say that in this country real choice is confined to a privileged few able to afford the fat fees of private schools. Although it perhaps did too little justice to the differences between the denominational and the more secular schools within the state system—and although by overlooking the number of those who could afford such fees but preferred to spend their money in other ways it certainly underestimated the size of this minority—this objection was still substantially correct in what it said. What were wholly wrong, and to any lover of liberty utterly obnoxious, were the supplementary suggestions: that liberties can be of value only to those who are themselves able and willing to make direct use of them; and that no one ought to be allowed to do anything which not everyone can do, or wants to do.

But now market-minded radicals associated with the Institute of Economic Affairs are plugging at the idea of educational vouchers.[14] This promises a vast extension of genuine family choice either within the state sector only, or both within and outside it. To this lively liberalising idea the standard response of the wooden authoritarian Left, and of their allies entrenched in the educational bureaucracies, is to protest. First, that, since a lot of parents—and particularly working class parents—are ignorant and indifferent, such a system, even if it were—like its American anticipators—confined to the public sector, would be bound to produce inequalities as between sump and quality comprehensives. And, second, that (since we know the previous proposition to be true) it must on no account be subjected to the experimental test which might show that a voucher system both tended to raise educational standards and pleased the public. So, when a *Daily Telegraph* editorial advocated just such an experiment, the Secretary of the Working Constituency Labour Party wrote:

> We should worry less about "parental choice." . . . The voucher system, which you claim offers freedom of choice to parents, can only operate at the expense of denying children the equality of opportunity they ought to enjoy in a civilised society. Under this system we would very soon have good schools packed with the fortunate children of competent, caring parents with deprived children from disadvantaged homes languishing in sink schools.[15]

To that I want to reply that this is not, it seems, what actually is happening in those US school areas which are operating a voucher system: that in Britain we already have all too many sink schools; that under a voucher system, outstanding examples, such as William Tyndale School, would be identified, and could be reformed, more quickly; and, finally, that the supercilious, and—in the usual purely abusive sense—elitist suggestions of working-class indifference are grossly unfair to all those obviously working-class parents who during that Tyndale affair protested publicly and appeared before the television cameras. Yet my main reason for giving that quotation is to bring out that the two ideals I have described must indeed be ultimately incompatible. For people in fact are, from the beginning, incorrigibly different. So, where they are permitted to make choices, their choices will not always be in the same sense; and such differences cannot but produce, in some dimensions, inequalities.

Absolute Equality?

The third kind of equality is that of outcome or results. This ideal needs to be considered in the light of a further distinction, developed by Rousseau in the second paragraph of his Dissertation *On the Origin and Foundation of the Inequality of Mankind* (1755). On the one hand, Rousseau says, there is the inequality "which I call natural or physical, because it is established by nature, and consists in a difference of age, health, bodily strength, and the qualities of mind or of the soul." On the other there is what nowadays would be called social inequality, which "depends on a kind of convention, and is established, or at least authorised, by the consent of men." Most contemporary engineers of equality concentrate upon the social, while giving occasional and peripheral attention to schemes for compensating socially by starts and handicaps for whatever natural inequalities they can bring themselves to admit. But Christopher Jencks is clearly right in his protest:

> For a thoroughgoing egalitarian . . . inequality that derives from biology ought to be as repulsive as inequality that derives from early socialisation. [16]

Although this third idea of equality is today widely cherished, and cherished perhaps especially among political intellectuals, [17] it is hard to find any principled statement of which possible human differences are and are not to be condemned as inequalities—or even of why inequalities are supposed to be, as such, evil. It is also true that those who upon this ground urge in particular the reduction of (certain) differences in wealth and income rarely want to advocate an absolute equality in these respects. Bernard Shaw was very much the exception among socialists in advocating a strict equality of incomes. He remained, however, altogether typical in his inflexible refusal to set a costly personal example by surrendering his own very substantial, and therefore on his own account very unjust, surplus above average. But we must not by either of these two observations be misled to conclude that equality of outcome is not being held as a value; that it is not, that is to say, being accepted as a good in itself, good not just as a means but as an end.

Certainly there are those for whom particular egalitarian measures are solely means to other ends. In his robust exposition of *Utilitarian Ethics* Anthony Quinton, for instance, points out that:

> In most imaginable circumstances the distribution of a hundred oranges among a hundred people that will bring about the greatest total utility is that in which each person gets only one. . . . [For] like most objects of desire oranges are subject to the law of diminishing marginal utility. [18]

Those for whom equality is thus a means to the utilitarian end will have no inhibitions on accepting incentive inequalities which tend to maximise not just the minimum but the general welfare. But equally certainly there are now many other people for whom equality is a good in itself, perhaps even the preeminent or sole good. Thus on 30 December 1974 the editorialist of *The Guardian,* who presumably knows his readers, laid it on the line:

> Nearly all of us want to get through 1975 with the least damage to social equality.

Again, writing as a supporter of the Liberal Party, A. T. Peacock makes a point of first dismissing the consideration just now seen in Quinton, before proceeding to insist that Liberal support for progressive taxation is based upon "a positive dislike of gross inequality."[19]

Nor are the facts that people want to abolish *some* differences and not others and that even in those *some* they repudiate absolute equality sufficient to show that they are not committed to equality as a value. The first shows that for them it is a value only in certain contexts. But this limitation leaves it none the less a value. The second indicates no more than that its claims are not for them indefeasible, that trade-offs against other values may be tolerated.

"Can urban, industrial, bureaucratic societies like ours realise the promise of equality and social justice . . . without sacrificing the liberties which they have so far attained?" That was the apt question put about "Equality" in a series of articles in *New Society* on the values proclaimed in the famous motto of successive French republics. Although the author, David Donnison, seems to have been too embarrassed to offer so much as a single illustration of the possible conflict, his conclusion was bold and correct: "That is the central question."[20]

Donnison is an outstandingly suitable spokesman for the socialist establishment brand of British egalitarianism. Right-hand man and later successor to Richard Titmuss at the London School of Economics, eponymous chairman of the Donnison Committee and formerly member of other bodies working towards a uniform and universal system of compulsory comprehensive education, appointed to his present top Whitehall job by a Labour Minister of Health and Social Security, he has been honoured (along with Paul Streeten, Michael Young and Alex Ramsay) as one of the four great equalisers.

> Apart from any influence their writings may have had, those four must by now have planned, directed or managed several billion dollars' worth of three or four countries' capital resources, mostly to the purpose . . . of reducing inequalities. They are ambitious men at the top of severely competitive professions. . . . As far as I know each pays his taxes, takes home two or three times the average family income . . . and would work as well for a great deal less if more equal societies required that.[21]

Even the unhallowed ranks of Tuscany can scarce forbear to cheer "how splendid!" before proceeding, after taking careful aim, to launch an explosive missile question. Upon what grounds of principle are those four just men proposing *not* to yield up their own remaining unequal (and, we must presume, from their own account, socially unjust) excess—until and unless they shall be so compelled by law?

At the end of his original article Donnison asserts that the possible conflict between Freedom and Equality is "the central question." Yet it was an article remarkable for not finding need or space to make the distinctions which I have presented as being fundamental. Donnison did, however, have the grace to begin by conceding that the egalitarianism for which he was speaking is "muddled"; and suggesting, in a usefully provocative way, that it is "muddled because its academic spokesmen were never challenged by sufficiently tough opposition to compel them to clarify their views. . . ." Having thus originally concluded that the possible incompatibility between Freedom and Equality is "the central question," Donnison went on two weeks later in the Correspondence columns—having perhaps been, in the meantime, shaken by the unfamiliar experience of meeting tough academic opposition—to dismiss all libertarian objectors with contempt:

> It is nonsense to tell us that nations which have more of one necessarily have less of the other.

Suppose that we are talking about Freedom and Equality in some purely voluntary organisation such as an Israeli kibbutz. Or suppose that we are being presented with a private moral ideal, which adherents will strive first to reach themselves, and afterwards recommend to others by example and by argument. Then there might indeed be no necessary conflict. But that is not how it is. This ideal of "equality and social justice" is in fact one which has been approached, and which it is proposed to continue to approach, primarily, if not quite exclusively, by legal and administrative measures rather than by individual conversion and self-sacrificing self-discipline. It is also in one of its aspects, as I and others have recently been arguing, the Ideology of a New Class of social administrators—people professionally involved in (and personally advanced by) the business of enforcing it.

All this being so, the true nonsense is to pretend that there is no inverse necessary connection between imposed equality of outcome and liberties for the citizen. Of course there has to be compulsion if everyone is to be got and kept either up or down, as individually appropriate, to the officially approved average level of whatever it may be which is being equalised. No one is suggesting, surely, that those "several billion dollars' worth of . . . resources" were the freewill offerings voluntarily made available by people who share the ideals and ambitions of the four just men?

It is equally obvious that the public provision of a welfare floor or safety net must involve some restriction of some possible liberties. For there will have to be taxes, that is to say, compulsory exactions, to pay for this too. But these exactions, these restrictions on liberty, will be modest compared with those needed to finance non-selective services available to all without any test of means. Still greater exactions must be required to finance monopoly services; in which the maintenance of the monopoly also itself inevitably involves further and different restrictions on liberty. The uniform monopoly service—admitting no element of consumer choice and hence no possibility of diversity—is at the same time and necessarily both the most constrictive of individual liberties and the most congenial to the ideal of equality of outcome.

It is, therefore, no accident that those who harbour ideals of this sort are forever pressing for always more (and never less) state monopoly in health, education, and welfare services: as well as, for that matter, over "the means of production, distribution, and exchange." Ralph Harris and Arthur Seldon, reviewing the first twenty years of the Institute of Economic Affairs,[22] understood well why every suggestion made by their writers for more *selectivity* and more *choice* in welfare services has run into unrelenting opposition from the Titmuss camp. For, for them, equality and not freedom or even welfare is the name of the game.

Two further observations ought to be made, especially in view of the fact that one party in these disputes is so often supposed both to have all the compassion and to be wholly disinterested. First, a selective welfare system will almost always be cheaper than a non-selective, and a state-floor system cheaper than a state monopoly. So if we admit selectivity and permit choice, we can the more easily afford to provide a higher and more extensive floor. A steady opposition to such selectivity, and still more the opposition to choice, is therefore likely to be motivated by something other than a simple compassionate concern to relieve the most urgent human needs. Secondly, the expansion of non-selective and perhaps ultimately monopoly services provides more scope and more promotion for more social administrators—who then, in turn, strengthen the powerful and effective lobby pressing for still further expansion.

"Who Will Equalise the Equalisers?"

Apart from whatever particular limitations of liberty must be essentially involved in any particular programme for compulsory equalisation—or, for that matter, in any programme for compulsory *anything*—there are good general reasons to believe that a strenuous, sustained, and extensive policy for imposing this ideal, especially in those areas which happen to be of most concern to the subjects, will as a matter of fact call for a highly authoritarian and widely repressive form of government.

I have already referred to the case for holding that a fully socialist economy must be, in practice, incompatible with a "Western" democratic political regime, and with those minimum liberties required to make effective elections possible. Now it is precisely such a centralised, socialist, command economy which is necessary in order to make possible—though it alone will certainly not be sufficient to guarantee—the imposition and maintenance of any approved pattern of distribution. This socialist presupposition of the enforcement of "equality and social justice" comes out very clearly in some revealing words of the Chairman of a recent BBC series on *Whatever Happened to Equality?* (words uttered some time before his elevation to a Labour life peerage). He was confronted with:

> the idea that the state should determine everyone's rewards according to some system of fairness, and should determine prices accordingly . . . this is the acceptance of the view that there is a rational system of social justice which it is the business of the state to enforce.

John Vaizey agreed wholeheartedly:

> That's a view I should embrace very strongly. I believe that this is the way one ought to think about society.[23]

This confession may be compared with one of the findings of a much recommended sociological study of *Class Inequality and Political Order* (1972). The author, Frank Parkin, seems to be one of those clear-headed and honest socialists who make little or no pretence of being concerned about freedom as well as equality. Parkin concludes:

> Egalitarianism seems to require a political system in which the state is able to hold in check those social and occupational groups which, by virtue of their skills or education or personal attributes, might otherwise attempt to stake claims to a disproportionate share of society's rewards. The most effective way of holding such groups in check is by denying them the right to organise politically, or in other ways, to undermine social equality. This presumably is the reasoning underlying the Marxist-Leninist case for a political order based upon the "dictatorship of the proletariat."

Yet there is a most remarkable, and at the same time most commonplace, deficiency in this conclusion. Nowhere in his whole book does it ever seem to cross Parkin's mind that, even in the somewhat unlikely event that such an uncriticisable and irremovable Power Elite were to subdue all temptations to appropriate massive prerequisites and privileges for its own members, still its absolute power over, and its total control of, the rest of the society must in itself constitute the greatest possible offence to any genuine ideal of personal equality or even of equality of outcome.

So there is one key question which needs to be pressed and pressed and pressed again, not only against the Leninists but also against all the other, if milder, "engineers of the soul," the whips of compulsory equality. (Leninists are, after all, openly committed to absolute rule by the elite vanguard; and, privately at least, never forget to ask with Lenin "Who/whom?")

That one key question is: "And who will equalise the equalisers? . . ."

Notes

1. For a study of the background beliefs of the Founding Fathers on these issues, see: Wilhelm Sjöstrand, *Freedom and Equality as Fundamental Educational Principles in Western Democracy from John Locke to Edmund Burke* (1973), Ch. 2.

2. Both these two fallacies (and "racism" in the sense implicitly defined above) are in fact totally repudiated by Arthur Jensen and H. J. Eysenck, two psychologists who have in recent years been ferociously abused for daring to question the assumption that there are no such average differences. Compare "The Jensen Uproar" in my *Sociology, Equality, and Education* (1976).

3. *Groundwork of the Metaphysic of Morals*, in *The Moral Law*, translated by H. J. Paton (1948), pp. 90-91.

4. D. M. Levine and M. J. Bane, *The "Inequality" Controversy* (1975), pp. 5, 198; but compare and contrast p. 11. Italics added.

5. *The Analects of Confucius,* edited and with a translation by W. E. Soothill (1910), p. 399 (VIII §2).

6. In P. R. Cox, H. B. Miles, and J. Peel (eds.), *Equalities and Inequalities in Education* (1975), pp. 37, 41.

7. Lars Ericsson, *Justice in the Distribution of Economic Resources* (1976), p. 130: inverted commas added.

8. *The Clarke Papers,* edited by C. H. Firth (1891), vol. 1, p. 301.

9. Milton Friedman, *Capitalism and Freedom* (1962). F. A. Hayek, *The Road to Serfdom* (1944) and *The Constitution of Liberty* (1960). Keith Joseph, *Stranded on the Middle Ground* (1976).

10. Quoted in *The Economist* (London), June 17, 1972, p. 23. I possess a photo copy of the complete Russian text.

11. A recent National Opinion Poll revealed a four-to-one majority in favour of the legalisation of voluntary euthanasia.

12. J. S. Mill, *On Liberty,* Everyman edition (1910), p. 67.

13. These two quite different ideals are clearly confounded in the publisher's puff for Mr. Frank Field's *Unequal Britain* (1977): "As Director of the Child Poverty Action Group, he draws together evidence from all the major social reports to ask if there is a cycle of inequality in which a large number of people are trapped." Seeing not scarcity but inequality as the evil, Field is, like most of the ideologues of social justice, understandably unconcerned about wealth creation. But it should be remarked that both unconcern and any commitment to impose and lower a ceiling are, in different ways, incongruous with the stated aims of the organisation which he heads. For it claims, surely, to be concerned with a floor not a ceiling, and with absolutes more than relativities.

14. The original suggestion, which would surely have won the instant support of J. S. Mill, came from Milton Friedman. But it seems to have been developed for a British context first in A. T. Peacock and J. Wiseman, *Education for Democrats* (1964). Compare: E. G. West, *Economics, Education and the Politician* (1968), *Choice in Welfare* (1970), and A. Maynard, *Experiment with Choice in Education* (1975).

15. November 25, 1975: sneer quotes original.

16. Christopher Jencks, *Inequality* (1972), p. 73.

17. On "equality and social justice" as the ideology of this New Class, see Robert Nisbet, "The Fatal Ambivalence," in *Encounter,* December 1976; compare my "Equality *or* Justice," in P. A. French (ed.), *Studies in Ethical Theory.*

18. *Utilitarian Ethics* (1973), pp. 75-76.

19. The last two quotations are borrowed: the first from Terry Arthur, *Ninety-Five Percent Is Crap* (1975), p. 183; and the second from F. A. Hayek, *The Constitution of Liberty* (1960), p. 518.

20. *New Society,* November 20, 1975, p. 424.

21. H. Stretton, *Capitalism, Socialism and the Environment* (1976), p. vi.

22. *Not from Benevolence. . . : 20 Years of Economic Dissent* (1977), Ch. 4.

23. Printed in *The Listener* (London), May 5, 1974, p. 566.

ROBERT NOZICK*

Entitlements and Patterns

The Entitlement Theory

The subject of justice in holdings consists of three major topics. The first is the *original acquisition of holdings,* the appropriation of unheld things. This includes the issues of how unheld things may come to be held, the process, or processes, by which unheld things may come to be held, the things that may come to be held by these processes, the extent of what comes to be held by a particular process, and so on. We shall refer to the complicated truth about this topic, which we shall not formulate here, as the principle of justice in acquisition. The second topic concerns the *transfer of holdings* from one person to another. By what processes may a person transfer holdings to another? How may a person acquire a holding from another who holds it? Under this topic come general descriptions of voluntary exchange, and gift and (on the other hand) fraud, as well as reference to particular conventional details fixed upon in a given society. The complicated truth about this subject (with placeholders for conventional details) we shall call the principle of justice in transfer. (And we shall suppose it also includes principles governing how a person may divest himself of a holding, passing it into an unheld state.)

If the world were wholly just, the following inductive definition would exhaustively cover the subject of justice in holdings.

1. A person who acquires a holding in accordance with the principle of justice in acquisition is entitled to that holding.
2. A person who acquires a holding in accordance with the principle of justice in transfer, from someone else entitled to the holding, is entitled to the holding.
3. No one is entitled to a holding except by (repeated) applications of 1 and 2.

The complete principle of distributive justice would say simply that a distribution is just if everyone is entitled to the holdings they possess under the distribution.

A distribution is just if it arises from another just distribution by legitimate

From *Anarchy, State and Utopia* (New York: Basic Books, 1974)
*Harvard University.

means. The legitimate means of moving from one distribution to another are specified by the principle of justice in acquisition.* Whatever arises from a just situation by just steps is itself just. The means of change specified by the principle of justice in transfer preserve justice. As correct rules of inference are truth-preserving, and any conclusion deduced via repeated application of such rules from only true premises is itself true, so the means of transition from one situation to another specified by the principle of justice in transfer are justice-preserving, and any situation actually arising from repeated transitions in accordance with the principle from a just situation is itself just. The parallel between justice-preserving transformations and truth-preserving transformations illuminates where it fails as well as where it holds. That a conclusion could have been deduced by truth-preserving means from premises that are true suffices to show its truth. That from a just situation a situation *could* have arisen via justice-preserving means does *not* suffice to show its justice. The fact that a thief's victims voluntarily *could* have presented him with gifts does not entitle the thief to his ill-gotten gains. Justice in holdings is historical; it depends upon what actually has happened. We shall return to this point later.

Not all actual situations are generated in accordance with the two principles of justice in holdings: the principle of justice in acquisition and the principle of justice in transfer. Some people steal from others, or defraud them, or enslave them, seizing their product and preventing them from living as they choose, or forcibly exclude others from competing in exchanges. None of these are permissible modes of transition from one situation to another. And some persons acquire holdings by means not sanctioned by the principle of justice in acquisition. The existence of past injustice (previous violations of the first two principles of justice in holdings) raises the third major topic under justice in holdings: the rectification of injustice in holdings. If past injustice has shaped present holdings in various ways, some identifiable and some not, what now, if anything, ought to be done to rectify these injustices? What obligations do the performers of injustice have toward those whose position is worse than it would have been had compensation been paid promptly? How, if at all, do things change if the beneficiaries and those made worse off are not the direct parties in the act of injustice, but, for example, their descendants? Is an injustice done to someone whose holding was itself based upon an unrectified injustice? How far back must one go in wiping clean the historical slate of injustices? What may victims of injustice permissibly do in order to rectify the injustices being done to them, including the many injustices done by persons acting through their government? I do not know of a thorough or theoretically sophisticated treatment of such issues.[1] Idealizing greatly, let us suppose theoretical investigation will produce a principle of rectification. This principle uses historical information about previous situations and injustices done in them (as defined by the first two principles of justice and rights against interference), and information about the actual course of events that flowed from these injustices, until the present, and it yields a description (or descriptions) of holdings in

---

*Applications of the principle of justice in acquisition may also occur as part of the move from one distribution to another. You may find an unheld thing now and appropriate it. Acquisitions also are to be understood as included when, to simplify, I speak only of transitions by transfers.

the society. The principle of rectification presumably will make use of its best estimate of subjunctive information about what would have occurred (or a probability distribution over what might have occurred, using the expected value) if the injustice had not taken place. If the actual description of holdings turns out not to be one of the descriptions yielded by the principle, then one of the descriptions yielded must be realized.*

The general outlines of the theory of justice in holdings are that the holdings of a person are just if he is entitled to them by the principles of justice in acquisition and transfer, or by the principles of rectification of injustices (as specified by the first two principles). If each person's holdings are just, then the total set (distribution) of holdings is just. To turn these general outlines into a specific theory we would have to specify the details of each of the three principles of justice in holdings: the principle of acquisition of holdings, the principle of transfer of holdings, and the principle of rectification of violations of the first two principles. I shall not attempt that task here. (Locke's principle of justice in acquisition is discussed below.)

Historical Principles and End-Result Principles

The general outlines of the entitlement theory illuminate the nature and defects of other conceptions of distributive justice. The entitlement theory of justice in distribution is *historical;* whether a distribution is just depends upon how it came about. In contrast, *current time-slice principles* of justice hold that the justice of a distribution is determined by how things are distributed (who has what) as judged by some *structural* principle(s) of just distribution. A utilitarian who judges between any two distributions by seeing which has the greater sum of utility and, if the sums tie, applies some fixed equality criterion to choose the more equal distribution, would hold a current time-slice principle of justice. As would someone who had a fixed schedule of trade-offs between the sum of happiness and equality. According to a current time-slice principle, all that needs to be looked at, in judging the justice of a distribution, is who ends up with what; in comparing any two distributions one need look only at the matrix presenting the distributions. No further information need be fed into a principle of justice. It is a consequence of such principles of justice that any two structurally identical distributions are equally just. (Two distributions are structurally identical if they present the same profile, but perhaps have different persons occupying the particular slots. My having ten and your having five, and my having five and your having ten are structurally identical distributions.) Welfare economics is the theory of current time-slice principles of justice. The subject is conceived as operating on matrices representing only current information about distribution. This, as well as some of the usual conditions (for example, the choice of distribution is invariant under

---

*If the principle of rectification of violations of the first two principles yields more than one description of holdings, then some choice must be made as to which of these is to be realized. Perhaps the sort of considerations about distributive justice and equality that I argue against play a legitimate role in *this* subsidiary choice. Similarly, there may be room for such considerations in deciding which otherwise arbitrary features a statute will embody, when such features are unavoidable because other considerations do not specify a precise line; yet a line must be drawn.

relabeling of columns), guarantees that welfare economics will be a current time-slice theory, with all of its inadequacies.

Most persons do not accept current time-slice principles as constituting the whole story about distributive shares. They think it relevant in assessing the justice of a situation to consider not only the distribution it embodies, but also how that distribution came about. If some persons are in prison for murder or war crimes, we do not say that to assess the justice of the distribution in the society we must look only at what this person has, and that person has, and that person has, . . . at the current time. We think it relevant to ask whether someone did something so that he *deserved* to be punished, deserved to have a lower share. Most will agree to the relevance of further information with regard to punishments and penalties. Consider also desired things. One traditional socialist view is that workers are entitled to the product and full fruits of their labor; they have earned it; a distribution is unjust if it does not give the workers what they are entitled to. Such entitlements are based upon some past history. No socialist holding this view would find it comforting to be told that because the actual distribution A happens to coincide structurally with the one he desires D, A therefore is no less just than D; it differs only in that the "parasitic" owners of capital receive under A what the workers are entitled to under D, and the workers receive under A what the owners are entitled to under D, namely very little. This socialist rightly, in my view, holds onto the notions of earning, producing, entitlement, desert, and so forth, and he rejects current time-slice principles that look only to the structure of the resulting set of holdings. (The set of holdings resulting from what? Isn't it implausible that how holdings are produced and come to exist has no effect at all on who should hold what?) His mistake lies in his view of what entitlements arise out of what sorts of productive processes.

We construe the position we discuss too narrowly by speaking of *current* time-slice principles. Nothing is changed if structural principles operate upon a time sequence of current time-slice profiles and, for example, give someone more now to counterbalance the less he has had earlier. A utilitarian or an egalitarian or any mixture of the two over time will inherit the difficulties of his more myopic comrades. He is not helped by the fact that *some* of the information others considered relevant in assessing a distribution is reflected, unrecoverably, in past matrices. Henceforth, we shall refer to such unhistorical principles of distributive justice, including the current time-slice principles, as *end-result principles* or *end-state principles*.

In contrast to end-result principles of justice, *historical principles* of justice hold that past circumstances or actions of people can create differential entitlements or differential deserts to things. An injustice can be worked by moving from one distribution to another structurally identical one, for the second, in profile the same, may violate people's entitlements or deserts; it may not fit the actual history.

Patterning

The entitlement principles of justice in holdings that we have sketched are historical principles of justice. To better understand their precise character, we shall distinguish them from another subclass of the historical principles. Consider, as an example, the principle of distribution according to moral merit. This principle requires that total distributive shares vary directly with moral merit; no person should have a greater share than anyone whose moral merit is greater. (If moral merit could be not merely ordered but measured on an interval or ratio scale, stronger principles could be formulated.) Or consider the principle that results by substituting "usefulness to society" for "moral merit" in the previous principle. Or instead of "distribute according to moral merit," or "distribute according to useful-ness to society," we might consider "distribute according to the weighted sum of moral merit, usefulness to society, and need," with the weights of the different dimensions equal. Let us call a principle of distribution *patterned* if it specifies that a distribution is to vary along with some natural dimension, weighted sum of natural dimensions, or lexicographic ordering of natural dimensions. And let us say a distribution is patterned if it accords with some patterned principle. (I speak of natural dimensions, admittedly without a general criterion for them, because for any set of holdings some artificial dimensions can be gimmicked up to vary along with the distribution of the set.) The principle of distribution in accordance with moral merit is a patterned historical principle, which specifies a patterned distribu-tion. "Distribute according to I.Q." is a patterned principle that looks to information not contained in distributional matrices. It is not historical, however, in that it does not look to any past actions creating differential entitlements to evaluate a distribu-tion; it requires only distributional matrices whose columns are labeled by I.Q. scores. The distribution in a society, however, may be composed of such simple patterned distributions, without itself being simply patterned. Different sectors may operate different patterns, or some combination of patterns may operate in different proportions across a society. A distribution composed in this manner, from a small number of patterned distributions, we also shall term "patterned." And we extend the use of "pattern" to include the overall designs put forth by combinations of end-state principles.

Almost every suggested principle of distributive justice is patterned: to each according to his moral merit, or needs, or marginal product, or how hard he tries, or the weighted sum of the foregoing, and so on. The principle of entitlement we have sketched is *not* patterned.* There is no one natural dimension or weighted sum or combination of a small number of natural dimensions that yields the distributions generated in accordance with the principle of entitlement. The set of holdings that results when some persons receive their marginal products, others win at gam-bling, others receive a share of their mate's income, others receive gifts from foundations, others receive interest on loans, others receive gifts from admirers,

---

*One might try to squeeze a patterned conception of distributive justice into the framework of the entitlement conception, by formulating a gimmicky obligatory "principle of transfer" that would lead to the pattern. For example, the principle that if one has more than the mean income one must transfer everything one holds above the mean to persons below the mean so as to bring them up to (but not over) the mean. We can formulate a criterion for a "principle of transfer" to rule out such obligatory transfers, or we can say that no correct principle of transfer, no principle of transfer in a free society will be like this. The former is probably the better course, though the latter also is true.

Alternatively, one might think to make the entitlement conception instantiate a pattern, by using matrix entries that express the relative strength of a person's entitlements as measured by some real-valued function. But even if the limitation to natural dimensions failed to exclude this function, the resulting edifice would *not* capture our system of entitlements to *particular* things.

others receive returns on investment, others make for themselves much of what they have, others find things, and so on, will not be patterned. Heavy strands of patterns will run through it; significant portions of the variance in holdings will be accounted for by pattern-variables. If most people most of the time choose to transfer some of their entitlements to others only in exchange for something from them, then a large part of what many people hold will vary with what they held that others wanted. More details are provided by the theory of marginal productivity. But gifts to relatives, charitable donations, bequests to children, and the like, are not best conceived, in the first instance, in this manner. Ignoring the strands of pattern, let us suppose for the moment that a distribution actually arrived at by the operation of the principle of entitlement is random with respect to any pattern. Though the resulting set of holdings will be unpatterned, it will not be incomprehensible, for it can be seen as arising from the operation of a small number of principles. These principles specify how an initial distribution may arise (the principle of acquisition of holdings) and how distributions may be transformed into others (the principle of transfer of holdings). The process whereby the set of holdings is generated will be intelligible, though the set of holdings itself that results from this process will be unpatterned.

The writings of F. A. Hayek focus less than is usually done upon what patterning distributive justice requires. Hayek argues that we cannot know enough about each person's situation to distribute to each according to his moral merit (but would justice demand we do so if we did have this knowledge?); and he goes on to say, "our objection is against all attempts to impress upon society a deliberately chosen pattern of distribution, whether it be an order of equality or of inequality."[2] However, Hayek concludes that in a free society there will be distribution in accordance with value rather than moral merit; that is, in accordance with the perceived value of a person's actions and services to others. Despite his rejection of a patterned conception of distributive justice, Hayek himself suggests a pattern he thinks justifiable: distribution in accordance with the perceived benefits given to others, leaving room for the complaint that a free society does not realize exactly this pattern. Stating this patterned strand of a free capitalist society more precisely, we get "To each according to how much he benefits others who have the resources for benefiting those who benefit them." This will seem arbitrary unless some acceptable initial set of holdings is specified, or unless it is held that the operation of the system over time washes out any significant effects from the initial set of holdings. As an example of the latter, if almost anyone would have bought a car from Henry Ford, the supposition that it was an arbitrary matter who held the money then (and so bought) would not place Henry Ford's earnings under a cloud. In any event, *his* coming to hold it is not arbitrary. Distribution according to benefits to others *is* a major patterned strand in a free capitalist society, as Hayek correctly points out, but it is only a strand and does not constitute the whole pattern of a system of entitlements (namely, inheritance, gifts for arbitrary reasons, charity, and so on) or a standard that one should insist a society fit. Will people tolerate for long a system yielding distributions that they believe are unpatterned?[3] No doubt people will not long accept a distribution they believe is *unjust*. People want their society to be and to look just. But must the look of justice reside in a resulting pattern rather than in the underlying generating principles? We are in no position to conclude that the inhabitants of a society embodying an entitlement conception of justice in holdings will find it unacceptable. Still, it must be granted that were people's reasons for transferring some of their holdings to others always irrational or arbitrary, we would find this disturbing. (Suppose people always determined what holdings they would transfer, and to whom, by using a random device.) We feel more comfortable upholding the justice of an entitlement system if most of the transfers under it are done for reasons. This does not mean necessarily that all deserve what holdings they receive. It means only that there is a purpose or point to someone's transferring a holding to one person rather than to another; that usually we can see what the transferrer thinks he's gaining, what cause he thinks he's serving, what goals he thinks he's helping to achieve, and so forth. Since in a capitalist society people often transfer holdings to others in accordance with how much they perceive these others benefiting them, the fabric constituted by the individual transactions and transfers is largely reasonable and intelligible.* (Gifts to loved ones, bequests to children, charity to the needy also are nonarbitrary components of the fabric.) In stressing the large strand of distribution in accordance with benefit to others, Hayek shows the point of many transfers, and so shows that the system of transfer of entitlements is not just spinning its gears aimlessly. The system of entitlements is defensible when constituted by the individual aims of individual transactions. No overarching aim is needed, no distributional pattern is required.

To think that the task of a theory of distributive justice is to fill in the blank in "to each according to his ———" is to be predisposed to search for a pattern; and the separate treatment of "from each according to his _____" treats production and distribution as two separate and independent issues. On an entitlement view these are *not* two separate questions. Whoever makes something, having bought or contracted for all other held resources used in the process (transferring some of his holdings for these cooperating factors), is entitled to it. The situation is *not* one of something's getting made, and there being an open question of who is to get it. Things come into the world already attached to people having entitlements over them. From the point of view of the historical entitlement conception of justice in holdings, those who start afresh to complete "to each according to his ———" treat objects as if they appeared from nowhere, out of nothing. A complete theory of justice might cover this limit case as well; perhaps here is a use for the usual conceptions of distributive justice.[4]

So entrenched are maxims of the usual form that perhaps we should present the entitlement conception as a competitor. Ignoring acquisition and rectification, we might say:

> From each according to what he chooses to do, to each according to what he makes for himself (perhaps with the contracted aid of others) and what others

---

*We certainly benefit because great economic incentives operate to get others to spend much time and energy to figure out how to serve us by providing things we will want to pay for. It is not mere paradox mongering to wonder whether capitalism should be criticized for most rewarding and hence encouraging, not individualists like Thoreau who go about their own lives, but people who are occupied with serving others and winning them as customers. But to defend capitalism one need not think businessmen are the finest human types. (I do not mean to join here the general maligning of businessmen, either.) Those who think the finest should acquire the most can try to convince their fellows to transfer resources in accordance with *that* principle.

choose to do for him and choose to give him of what they've been given previously (under this maxim) and haven't yet expended or transferred.

This, the discerning reader will have noticed, has its defects as a slogan. So as a summary and great simplification (and not as a maxim with any independent meaning) we have:

From each as they choose, to each as they are chosen.

How Liberty Upsets Patterns

It is not clear how those holding alternative conceptions of distributive justice can reject the entitlement conception of justice in holdings. For suppose a distribution favored by one of these non-entitlement conceptions is realized. Let us suppose it is your favorite one and let us call this distribution D_1; perhaps everyone has an equal share, perhaps shares vary in accordance with some dimension you treasure. Now suppose that Wilt Chamberlain is greatly in demand by basketball teams, being a great gate attraction. (Also suppose contracts run only for a year, with players being free agents.) He signs the following sort of contract with a team: In each home game, twenty-five cents from the price of each ticket of admission goes to him. (We ignore the question of whether he is "gouging" the owners, letting them look out for themselves.) The season starts, and people cheerfully attend his team's games; they buy their tickets, each time dropping a separate twenty-five cents of their admission price into a special box with Chamberlain's name on it. They are excited about seeing him play; it is worth the total admission price to them. Let us suppose that in one season one million persons attend his home games, and Wilt Chamberlain winds up with $250,000, a much larger sum than the average income and larger even than anyone else has. Is he entitled to this income? Is this new distribution D_2, unjust? If so, why? There is *no* question about whether each of the people was entitled to the control over the resources they held in D_1; because that was the distribution (your favorite) that (for the purposes of argument) we assumed was acceptable. Each of these persons *chose* to give twenty-five cents of their money to Chamberlain. They could have spent it on going to the movies, or on candy bars, or on copies of *Dissent* magazine, or of *Monthly Review*. But they all, at least one million of them, converged on giving it to Wilt Chamberlain in exchange for watching him play basketball. If D_1 was a just distribution, and people voluntarily moved from it to D_2, transferring parts of their shares they were given under D_1 (what was it for if not to do something with?), isn't D_2 also just? If the people were entitled to dispose of the resources to which they were entitled (under D_1), didn't this include their being entitled to give it to, or exchange it with, Wilt Chamberlain? Can anyone else complain on grounds of justice? Each other person already has his legitimate share under D_1. Under D_1, there is nothing that anyone has that anyone else has a claim of justice against. After someone transfers something to Wilt Chamberlain, third parties *still* have their legitimate shares; *their* shares are not changed. By what process could such a transfer among two persons give rise to a legitimate claim of distributive justice on a portion of what was transferred, by a third party who had no claim of justice on any holding of the others *before* the transfer?* To cut off objections irrelevant here, we might imagine the exchanges occurring in a socialist society, after hours. After playing whatever basketball he does in his daily work, or doing whatever other daily work he does, Wilt Chamberlain decides to put in *overtime* to earn additional money. (First his work quota is set; he works time over that.) Or imagine it is a skilled juggler people like to see, who puts on shows after hours.

Why might someone work overtime in a society in which it is assumed their needs are satisfied? Perhaps because they care about things other than needs. I like to write in books that I read, and to have easy access to books for browsing at odd hours. It would be very pleasant and convenient to have the resources of Widener Library in my back yard. No society, I assume, will provide such resources close to each person who would like them as part of his regular allotment (under D_1). Thus, persons either must do without some extra things that they want, or be allowed to do something extra to get some of these things. On what basis could the inequalities that would eventuate be forbidden? Notice also that small factories would spring up in a socialist society, unless forbidden. I melt down some of my personal possessions (under D_1) and build a machine out of the material. I offer you, and others, a philosophy lecture once a week in exchange for your cranking the handle on my machine, whose products I exchange for yet other things, and so on. (The raw materials used by the machine are given to me by others who possess them under D_1, in exchange for hearing lectures.) Each person might participate to gain things over and above their allotment under D_1. Some persons even might want to leave their job in socialist industry and work full time in this private sector. Here I wish merely to note how private property even in means of production would occur in a socialist society that did not forbid people to use as they wished some of the resources they are given under the socialist distribution D_1.[5] The socialist society would have to forbid capitalist acts between consenting adults.

The general point illustrated by the Wilt Chamberlain example and the example of the entrepreneur in a socialist society is that no end-state principle or distributional patterned principle of justice can be continuously realized without continuous interference with people's lives. Any favored pattern would be transformed into one unfavored by the principle, by people choosing to act in various ways; for

---

* Might not a transfer have instrumental effects on a third party, changing his feasible options? (But what if the two parties to the transfer independently had used their holdings in this fashion?) I discuss this question below, but note here that this question concedes the point for distributions of ultimate intrinsic noninstrumental goods (pure utility experiences, so to speak) that are transferrable. It also might be objected that the transfer might make a third party more envious because it worsens his position relative to someone else. I find it incomprehensible how this can be thought to involve a claim of justice. On envy, see Chapter 8, *Anarchy, State, and Utopia* (New York: Basic Books, 1974).

Here and elsewhere in this chapter, a theory which incorporates elements of pure procedural justice might find what I say acceptable, *if* kept in its proper place; that is, if background institutions exist to ensure the satisfaction of certain conditions on distributive shares. But if these institutions are not themselves the sum or invisible-hand result of people's voluntary (nonaggressive) actions, the constraints they impose require justification. At no point does *our* argument assume any background institutions more extensive than those of the minimal night-watchman state, a state limited to protecting persons against murder, assault, theft, fraud, and so forth.

example, by people exchanging goods and services with other people, or giving things to other people, things the transferrers are entitled to under the favored distributional pattern. To maintain a pattern one must either continually interfere to stop people from transferring resources as they wish to, or continually (or periodically) interfere to take from some persons resources that others for some reason chose to transfer to them. (But if some time limit is to be set on how long people may keep resources others voluntarily transfer to them, why let them keep these resources for *any* period of time? Why not have immediate confiscation?) It might be objected that all persons voluntarily will choose to refrain from actions which would upset the pattern. This presupposes unrealistically (1) that all will most want to maintain the pattern (are those who don't, to be "reeducated" or forced to undergo "self-criticism"?), (2) that each can gather enough information about his own actions and the ongoing activities of others to discover which of his actions will upset the pattern, and (3) that diverse and far-flung persons can coordinate their actions to dovetail into the pattern. Compare the manner in which the market is neutral among persons' desires, as it reflects and transmits widely scattered information via prices, and coordinates persons' activities.

It puts things perhaps a bit too strongly to say that every patterned (or end-state) principle is liable to be thwarted by the voluntary actions of the individual parties transferring some of their shares they receive under the principle. For perhaps some *very* weak patterns are not so thwarted. Any distributional pattern with any egalitarian component is overturnable by the voluntary actions of individual persons over time; as is every patterned condition with sufficient content so as actually to have been proposed as presenting the central core of distributive justice. Still, given the possibility that some weak conditions or patterns may not be unstable in this way, it would be better to formulate an explicit description of the kind of interesting and contentful patterns under discussion, and to prove a theorem about their instability. Since the weaker the patterning, the more likely it is that the entitlement system itself satisfies it, a plausible conjecture is that any patterning either is unstable or is satisfied by the entitlement system.

Notes

1. See, however, the useful book by Boris Bittker, *The Case for Black Reparations* (New York: Random House, 1973)

2. F. A. Hayek, *The Constitution of Liberty* (Chicago: University of Chicago Press, 1960), p. 87.

3. This question does not imply that they will tolerate any and every patterned distribution. In discussing Hayek's views, Irving Kristol has recently speculated that people will not long tolerate a system that yields distributions patterned in accordance with value rather than merit. (" 'When Virtue Loses All Her Loveliness'—Some Reflections on Capitalism and 'The Free Society,' " *The Public Interest*, Fall 1970, pp. 3-15.) Kristol, following some remarks of Hayek's, equates the merit system with justice. Since some case can be made for the external standard of distribution in accordance with benefit to others, we ask about a weaker (and therefore more plausible) hypothesis.

4. Varying situations continuously from that limit situation to our own would force us to make explicit the underlying rationale of entitlements and to consider whether entitlement considerations lexicographically precede the considerations of the usual theories of distributive justice, so that the *slightest* strand of entitlement outweighs the considerations of the usual theories of distributive justice.

5. See the selection from John Henry MacKay's novel, *The Anarchists,* reprinted in

Leonard Krimmerman and Lewis Perry, eds., *Patterns of Anarchy* (New York: Doubleday Anrchor Books, 1966), in which an individualist anarchist presses upon a communist anarchist the following question: "Would you, in the system of society which you call 'free Communism' prevent individuals from exchanging their labor among themselves by means of their own medium of exchange? And further, Would you prevent them from occupying land for the purpose of personal use?" The novel continues: "[the] question was not to be escaped. If he answered 'Yes!' he admitted that society had the right of control over the individual and threw overboard the autonomy of the individual which he had always zealously defended; if on the other hand, he answered 'No!' he admitted the right of private property which he had just denied so emphatically. . . . Then he answered 'In Anarchy any number of men must have the right of forming a voluntary association, and so realizing their ideas in practice. Nor can I understand how any one could justly be driven from the land and house which he uses and occupies . . . every serious man must declare himself: for Socialism, and thereby for force and against liberty, or for Anarchism, and thereby for liberty and against force.' " In contrast, we find Noam Chomsky writing: "Any consistent anarchist must oppose private ownership of the means of production," "the consistent anarchist then . . . will be a socialist . . . of a particular sort." Introduction to Daniel Guerin, *Anarchism: From Theory to Practice* (New York: Monthly Review Press, 1970), pages xiii, xv.

FRED D. MILLER, JR.*

The Natural Right to
Private Property

All serious issues of public policy eventually turn on questions of property rights. For example, in order to provide a sound theoretical foundation for public policies dealing with the "energy crisis," we must find, and justify on ethical grounds, answers to the following sorts of questions: "Who properly holds title to reserves of such natural resources as petroleum, natural gas, and coal? Who is entitled to the capital and technology which have been developed in the energy industries? Who is entitled to the profits ('windfall' or ordinary) earned by business people and corporations?" And sound answers to these questions presuppose a justification of the libertarian principle that individuals have a natural right to private property.

Ethical issues concerning property rights are a part—an *inseparable* part, I shall argue—of a broader set of issues concerning the moral status of assets of any sort. The moral status of assets is *the* fundamental issue in ethics and social philosophy. Competing theories of value prescribe the ends to which assets are to be employed: for example, the ends of "the greatest happiness for the greatest number" or of individual enlightened self-interest. Theories of virtue prescribe the manner in which they are to be employed: for example, productiveness and rationality. "Morals," in the popular sense, are largely concerned with self-regarding or private uses of assets: for example, sexual practices, abortion, and the use of drugs. Theories of justice define rules for establishing entitlement to assets and for transferring and enforcing titles to them. It is not surprising, then, that the disagreements between the two theories of justice which are currently most influential in Anglo-American philosophy, those of John Rawls and Robert Nozick, converge on the issue of the moral status of assets. And this controversy over the nature of justice has important policy implications. For Rawls's treatment provides a rationale for a continuation and expansion of the liberal welfare state, whereas

This paper grew out of a conference sponsored by the American Association for the Philosophic Study of Society held in Ann Arbor, Michigan.

*Department of Philosophy, Bowling Green State University.

Nozick's libertarian account purportedly entails a radical reorientation toward free-market "capitalism between consenting adults."

Assets are assumed to fall into two distinct categories: *Natural assets* include the intelligence, talent, and physical advantages of human beings resulting from their individual genetic endowments; and *nonhuman resources* include geographical regions, transportable physical objects, and tangible and intangible products of human labor. (*The right to private property* is hereafter understood as *the entitlement to nonhuman resources.*) These two categories of assets are treated quite differently in many ethical theories. Thus Locke states, "Though the earth and all inferior creatures be common to all men, yet every man has a property in his own person; this nobody has any right to but himself." On such a view, nonhuman assets might be distributed or redistributed so as to maximize utility, but it would not be permissible to enslave individuals, i.e., to coerce them to use their natural assets to maximize utility. Rawls has argued, however, that these two sorts of assets really cannot be distinguished in this way. Just as the fact that a person possesses certain private property is a contingent historical fact, the fact that a person possesses certain mental or physical advantages is a contingent natural fact. Such a person has been "favored by nature" or has won in the "natural lottery," so that differences involving natural abilities and talents are just as much the result of "chance contingencies" as differences in wealth and income are the result of "historical and social fortune." Rawls concludes, ". . . once we are troubled by the influence of either social contingencies or natural chance on the determination of distributive shares [in the benefits and burdens of social cooperation], we are bound, on reflection, to be bothered by the influence of the other. From a moral standpoint the two seem equally arbitrary."[1] Robert Nozick has, quite justifiably, objected against Rawls' ambiguous uses of the expression, "arbitrary from a moral point of view." Just because a fact is morally arbitrary in the sense that "there is no moral reason why the fact ought to be that way," it does not *obviously* follow that "the fact's being that way is of no moral significance and has no moral consequences."[2] Nevertheless, Rawls's reasoning seems to contain a grain of truth. There is no significant, morally relevant difference between facts involving an individual's natural assets and facts involving that individual's nonhuman possessions. This suggests the following principle of parity:

> (I) Entitlements to natural assets and entitlements to nonhuman resources should be determined by the same sorts of normative principles.

Rawls argues that the benefits of the distribution of natural assets and nonhuman assets among individuals in society are subject to a conception of justice which is, essentially, egalitarian. This conception is expressed in two principles of justice: "the first requires equality in the assignment of basic rights and duties, while the second holds that social and economic equalities, for example inequalities of wealth and authority, are just only if they result in compensating benefits for everyone, and in particular for the least advantaged members of society."[3] Rawls defends this conception of justice as more reasonable than any other on the grounds that "rational persons in the initial situation would choose its principles over those of the other for the role of justice."[4] This defense relies upon crucial presumptions about how the original position should be characterized and about the theory of rational choice bearing on contractual arrangements. These presumptions have, of course, undergone the most intense critical examination. But Rawls also maintains that the conception of justice which is supported by such a contractarian defense should also square with the moral judgments "which we now make intuitively and in which we have the greatest confidence."[5] The premiss of the contractarian defense and our "considered moral judgments" should, ultimately, be in a state of "reflective equilibrium" or form, together, "one coherent view."[6] Rawls is, therefore, committed to arguing that his egalitarian conception of justice involves "principles which match our considered judgments duly pruned and adjusted."[7] Rawls tries to meet this commitment in a section entitled, "The Tendency to Equality." He claims that his second principle, the difference principle, is acceptable to all, "from the standpoint of common sense." He emphasizes that he is not trying in this section to present an "argument" for his principle, "since in a contract theory arguments are made from the point of view of the original position. But these intuitive considerations help to clarify the nature of the principle and the sense in which it is egalitarian."[8] This is rather misleading. For while it is true that these "intuitive considerations" are, for Rawls, no substitute for a *contractarian* argument, nevertheless, they cannot, by his own lights, be merely elucidative. For Rawls is committed to providing an argument to show that the conclusions of his contractarian argument are in substantial agreement with "intuitive" or "common sense" moral judgments.

Rawls takes his difference principle to represent, "in effect, an agreement to regard the distribution of natural talents as a common asset and to share in the benefits of this distribution whatever it turns out to be."[9] On this account the aptitude and potentialities which individuals possess as part of their genetic endowment are regarded as a common or "collective asset."[10] Rawls seems to suppose that human beings can be treated as clusters of capacities and potentialities. It is a contingent matter, depending upon facts of heredity, natural environment, and social circumstance, whether an individual cluster contains any specific capacity or potentiality. Even a person's "character depends in large part upon fortunate family and social circumstances for which he can claim no credit."[11] It is difficult to avoid the implication, which Rawls does not explicitly draw, that human beings themselves are simply collections of natural resources. Presumably, in *normal* circumstances[12], this would not justify treating people as collections of spare parts such as corneas and kidneys who could be "cannibalized" against their wills for the benefit of the less advantaged, namely, of people who are blind or without kidneys and cannot find voluntary donors. But, on Rawls' account, it clearly *does* justify pooling *all* benefits, including material goods and social advantages, resulting from the employment of these natural assets, together and allocating these benefits according to principles of distributive justice. "Those who have been favored by nature, whoever they are, may gain from their good fortune only on terms that improve the situation of those who have lost out."[13]

Rawls argues that the agreement to regard the distribution of natural abilities as a common asset is coherent with "intuitive considerations." He considers the objection that individuals are entitled to their advantages, because they deserve them as the fruits of their natural assets and superior character. Against this, Rawls appeals to the "considered judgment" that "no one deserves his place in the distribution of natural endowments, any more than one deserves one's initial starting place in society." Considerations of character receive similar, if somewhat cavalier, treatment. Rawls's reply proceeds:

> The notion of desert seems not to apply to these cases. Thus the more advantaged representative man cannot say that he deserves and therefore has a right to a scheme of cooperation in which he is permitted to acquire benefits in ways that do not contribute to the welfare of others. There is no basis for his making this claim. From the standpoint of common sense, then, the difference principle appears to be acceptable both to the more advantaged and to the less advantaged individual.[14]

This reasoning is expressed in such a loose and informal manner that it is difficult to determine its intended force. But it seems possible to distinguish three main stages of argument:

(1) An individual does not deserve his or her natural assets.
(2) There is no reason to assign an individual exclusive title to his or her natural assets.
(3) Everyone has title to the individuals' natural assets.

The implication is that (2) follows from (1) and that (3) follows from (2).

This reasoning involves serious difficulties. There is, in the first place, the difficulty, pointed out by Nozick, that the inference from (1) to (2) relies upon the very dubious unstated assumption that people are entitled only to what they deserve.[15] Nozick objects that the notion of entitlement is deeper than the notion of desert, for people deserve what they have produced insofar as they have employed assets to which they are entitled. The fact that Rawls is making this assumption is not obvious, because his argument is couched within a response to an objection. The *objector* is made to presume desert as the basis for entitlement to natural assets. But to refute this one objector is not to establish that "there is *no* basis" for claiming entitlement. There is an important consideration here regarding the burden of proof. Rawls, not Nozick, assumed the burden of proving that his contractarian principles had implications coinciding with "considered moral judgments." And the claim that people are entitled only to what they deserve is strikingly counter-intuitive. It is not at all necessary, "from the standpoint of common sense," to prove that I deserve my left kidney, in order to have a basis for claiming that it shouldn't be reallocated to contribute to the welfare of others. From this standpoint, the fact that it is part of my body and is therefore *mine* provides a sufficient basis for a title to its continued possession.

However, the attempt to derive (3) from (2) is also problematic. Even if there were no moral reason to assign me exclusive title to my left kidney, would it *follow* that it is a common asset, i.e. that "everyone" had a collective title to it? The latter would imply that it would be morally wrong for me to resist attempts to allocate my left kidney so as to contribute to the welfare of others, such as those unfortunate with malfunctioning kidneys. This pattern of argument—*Not I, so Everyone*—occurs in other contexts. For example, Alan Goldman has argued that "our moral intuitions rebel" at the "unhindered operation of a free market economy as sole distributor of advantages," because ". . . we cannot see why children should be *held responsible* for the sins or omissions of their ancestors . . ."[15] He goes on to argue that voluntary exchanges of assets may have the result that children are "deprived" to such an extent that they cannot satisfy their basic needs." In such a case their needs give rise to the right to interfere in the free, noncoercive economic activities of others. In response to the Nozickian objection that this would entail the violation of libertarian side constraints, Goldman argues:

> To refuse to violate the absolute freedom of those who fail to recognize the rights of others arising from basic needs, is to press the distinction between positive and negative duties to an irrational point. It amounts here to *a refusal to accept responsibility* for an unjust state of affairs when the means to alter it are known.[17]

Goldman seems to be using the following implicit sort of reasoning: Children who have unequal holdings as a result of facts of history over which they have no control are *not responsible* for lacking them and do not *deserve* to suffer.[18] Therefore, *everyone is responsible* for the fact that the children have unequal holdings. If others have a responsibility toward those who are worse off, it is, of course, permissible to coerce them into meeting that responsibility. The claims of collective responsibility permit Goldman to describe the children as "deprived"—they have been deprived of their basic needs by others. And he can claim that "the ability and freedom to frame a meaningful life plan for oneself . . . [are] *denied* to those who lack conditions that render such plans predictable."[19] They have obviously been denied these things by the insensitive and irresponsible free marketeers who should have been looking out for them.[20] The crux of his argument is the move, "I'm not responsible, so everyone is."

How persuasive is this pattern of argument. *Not I, so Everyone?* The two ways in which the pattern of argument can most naturally be understood are both quite implausible. (A) One might argue that since there is no reason to assign an individual exclusive title to his or her natural assets and resulting benefits, this is, in itself, a reason for assigning to everyone a *collective* title to the individual's natural assets. This interpretation is suggested by Rawls's language of "sharing" in the benefits of "collective assets." Unfortunately, the argument, so construed, is totally unconvincing. For from the fact that individuals do not stand in some relation R to themselves it certainly does not, as a general rule, follow that all individuals stand in relation R to each individual. For example, from the fact that an individual is not the cause of his or her natural assets, it scarcely follows that *everyone* is the collective cause of that particular individual's natural assets. Hence, even if Rawls were right that "there is no basis" for the entitlement claims of individuals, this would not provide any basis for *collective* entitlement claims. No "intuitive considerations" provide a basis for such an inference. (B) Another interpretation involves *the presumption of egalitarianism*. According to Goldman, "That this presumption operates on the level of moral intuition is clear from the fact that, although we feel uncomfortable if persons are treated differently or gain different benefits when no relevant difference between them has been found, we do not feel uncomfortable about treating people the same or giving them equal shares without finding a relevant sameness (other than a common humanity)."[21] The reasoning will evidently proceed: Since there is no reason to assign an individual exclusive title to his or her natural assets, this is, in itself, reason for assigning to each person *equal* title to the total supply of natural resources. Many ethical writers take this reasoning to be as self-evident as anything in ethics can be. Nevertheless, it is of very suspect parentage. For it is the normative offspring of a notorious metaphysical dictum: *the principle of sufficient reason.* For example, Parmenides used the principle to demonstrate that the universe could not have had an origin in time. For if the universe came into existence at t_o, there should be a reason why it existed at t_o and any instant thereafter rather than at any instant before t_o. But there *is* no such good reason, if it is the first event. Hence, every instant has an equal claim to be an instant when the universe existed, exists, or will exist. It follows from this temporal egalitarianism that the universe could not have come into existence and cannot cease to exist. This may seem an easy way to refute the big-bang theory without benefit of telescope, but it raises obvious questions. If, as quantum physics suggests, there is no sufficient reason why the nucleus of a tritium atom decays at one instant rather than another, should it not follow from the principle that it either never decays or that it always decays? These examples suggest a need for caution. Even if we have no reason for assigning a fact to one time rather than another, it may be a basic truth, for which we have no deeper explanation, that this fact *does* belong to one time rather than another. The absence of a sufficient reason is no argument for egalitarianism. An analogous point can be made in ethics. The absence of a sufficient reason for assigning an individual exclusive title to his or her natural assets is, in itself, no argument for egalitarianism.

In view of the preceding objections, there is no reason to accept the arguments of Rawls, Goldman, and other egalitarian theorists that each individual's natural asset should be regarded as collectively owned property. Are there, on the other hand, any arguments for the view that each individual properly is entitled to his or her own natural assets? The most important source of such arguments has been the *natural rights* tradition which reaches back to the ancient Greek philosophers, especially Aristotle, and which in modern times has formed the ethical foundation for the political philosophy of libertarianism.[22] A persuasive argument for individual natural rights is made by the philosopher Ayn Rand.[23] The following formulation represents a highly simplified restatement of her complex argument.

The first stage of the argument is a biocentric theory of value: ". . . the fact that living entities exist and function necessitates the existence of values and of an ultimate value which for any given living entity is its own life." Here "life" should be understood not in the sense of "brute survival" but as referring to a higher order good which *includes* the various first order goods of human life, such as intellectual fulfillment, productive work, friendship, etc. In this sense it is comparable to Aristotle's notion of happiness or ενδαιμονια. Life is *continuous purposive activity including all specific goods.* It thus is comparable to Aristotle's notions of ενεργεια (activity) and εντελεχεια (complete reality). Rand's argument is not the crude *non sequitur* that life is the ultimate value because values can be attained only if the agent survives till attainment. Rather, the key premiss is that values can exist only if it is true that one ought to promote life (in the sense of engaging in continuous purposive activity). How does one establish such a premiss? Rand's theory is explicitly naturalist: "the validation of value judgments is to be achieved by reference to the facts of reality." The theory does not, however, attempt to deduce an "ought" naively from an "is." Rather, it seeks to establish an ultimate value by uncovering a principle which is *presupposed* in all valuing; so that anyone who makes value judgments without accepting the principle is committing "the fallacy of the stolen concept."

Reasoning of this sort is *dialectical* or "negative demonstration" in the same sense as Aristotle's defense of the law of noncontradiction against his sophistic opponents. There is a close, instructive parallel between the Aristotelian and Randian arguments.[24] Aristotle's argument proceeds "You cannot think or speak unless the law of noncontradiction is true. So, in speaking or thinking you are committed to the law of noncontradiction." Aristotle recognizes the futility of trying to prove every principle *in vacuo* or to convince a totally unreasoning being or "vegetable," but he contends that a plausible negative argument can be mounted from a starting-point: the interlocutor says something which is significant for himself and another. The word "man" is significant only if it can be provided one meaning and *not* another, but without the law of noncontradiction this is not assured. (We would not be able to rule out the following: The word means *man* but not *cabbage;* and the word means *cabbage!*) So in speaking one is committed to the law of noncontradiction. The argument for life as an ultimate value has a similar structure: "You cannot value unless it is true that one ought to promote life." Again, one cannot prove the principle *in vacuo* or persuade a vegetable or an entity devoid of values of the principle. But the argument can be directed to an interlocutor who holds any value (in Rand's sense of value: that which one acts to gain or keep). What makes this a valuation rather than random behavior? "Because this promotes *my* life, i.e. serves *my* purposes, and one ought to promote one's life." So in the act of valuing one is committed to the principle that one ought to promote one's life.

Nothing in this argument of course is meant to show that anyone must value something or that in valuing one always acknowledges principles to which one is committed. Human beings differ from other organisms in that, even though only one ultimate value is possible, it must be chosen, and this makes it possible for humans to be *moral* beings: "A code of values accepted by choice is a code of morality."

From the thesis that life is an ultimate value presupposed by all other values, Rand derives a theory of natural rights. "Life is a process of self-sustaining and self-generated action: the right to life means the right to engage in self-sustaining and self-generated action—which means: the freedom to take all the actions required by the nature of a rational being for the support, the furtherance, the fulfillment and the enjoyment of his own life." The connection is defended between the value of life and rights in general. The rights of one individual are moral constraints upon *others* not to aggress against this individual. These constraints can be derived from the principle that life is an ultimate value for each organism or that each person ought to act to pursue his or her own purposes. In an ingenious article, "Egoism and Rights," Eric Mack has argued that this principle places a moral constraint on one's actions. For if an agent aggresses against other persons and thereby impedes them from acting in their own interest, that agent acts as if the universal principle, "Each person ought to act to pursue his or her own purposes," were untrue, because one is forcibly *preventing* the principle from being implemented. But one is not acting in a justified manner if one is acting on a principle *and* acting as if the principle were false. Other persons can appeal to this principle as a constraint on the aggressor's behavior, i.e., claim *rights* which the agent ought to respect. The principle, thus construed, implies that one has the negative right not to be aggressed against but not that one has positive "welfare rights."[25]

These arguments provide a plausible basis for the claim that individuals have a right to their natural assets. They provide, in the first place, a basis for

(II) Every person is an end in himself or herself.

This principle entails, as has been shown, that persons ought not to have their purposes forcibly subordinated to the purposes of others, so long as the others have not themselves attempted to subordinate the purposes of other persons. The *natural* rights approach, which treats a person as a flesh and blood organism rather than as a disembodied transcendental ego, also requires:

(III) A person is a living human being with essential mental and physical characteristics.

To deny a given individual's exclusive title to his or her natural assets is to make it possible for others to establish morally justified property rights in that individual person given principle (III). In such a case it would be morally justified to use force to uphold such rights and thus subordinate the will of persons in a manner which, according to (II), cannot be morally justified. From these two principles it follows, therefore, that:

(IV) Each individual has an unconditional title to a particular set of natural assets.

But some philosophers, following John Locke, accept such a conclusion that individuals have exclusive title to their own natural assets, and nevertheless, reject the corresponding thesis about private property, that:

(V) Each individual has an unconditional title to a particular set of nonhuman resources.

Even some present day libertarian defenders of capitalism seem to distinguish between property rights and personal rights. Nozick, for example, goes much further than most twentieth century theorists in defending the rights of individuals to acquire titles to holdings, to transfer titles in the form of gratitudes or free market exchanges, and to recover holdings which are subject to one's entitlement but not one's possession; but even Nozick qualifies his theory of entitlement to nonhuman holdings with what he calls "the Lockean proviso." "A process normally giving rise to a permanent bequeathable property right in a previously unowned thing will not do so if the position of others no longer at liberty to use the thing is thereby worsened." Nozick interprets this proviso as the requirement that no person can appropriate part of a natural (nonhuman) resource if others would thereby lose opportunity to improve their situation by using without appropriation what they otherwise could—unless something else counterbalances the diminution in opportunity. In order to explain this "unless" clause, Nozick introduces the notion of a "base line" for comparison, which is, evidently, the highest level a given person would be at if property were not privately appropriated. Critics of Nozick have correctly identified this Lockean proviso as the Achilles' heel of his theory of entitlement. Some of them have challenged his suggestion that the base line approximates the subsistence level and have, instead, pegged it so high as to justify a drastic redistribution of property holdings. Moreover, in contrast to Locke, Nozick takes the proviso to constrain subsequent actions, even if the initial acquisition is in accordance with Locke's proviso. For example, even if a person justly acquires title to a water hole, if all the other water holes in the desert but his dry up, this "brings into operation the Lockean proviso and limits his property rights." Thus, anyone's claim to *any* natural resources can be challenged at any given time by the argument that the private possession of this resource places others below their base line. Thus, the proviso leaves the door open for a vast welfare state, supervising perpetual, extensive transfers of income and property, on the basis of Nozick's theory. Another criticism concerns the internal coherence of Nozick's theory. Nozick maintains that his "historical entitlement" conception of justice involving the distribution of natural resources in society excludes patterned or end state rules of justice.[26] Yet, as Hillel Steiner has persuasively argued, Nozick's proviso introduces a principle of compensation from welfare economics. For a property holder must compensate others for any diminution of opportunity which places them below their base line. This principle, specifying a *welfare* baseline for everyone, is a *patterned* principle of justice, imposing *structural* considerations on the size of permissible holdings.[27]

Significantly, Nozick takes the Lockean proviso as intuitive and does not discuss *Locke's* reasons for stating it. Locke includes the proviso in his theory of property acquisition, so that there is "left no room for controversy about the title, nor for encroachment on the right of others."[28] Locke's solution is that the acquisition of property must satisfy three necessary conditions which are jointly sufficient: (1) "Whatsoever . . . the appropriator removes out of the state that nature hath provided and left it in, he hath mixed his labor with, and joined to it something that is his own, and thereby makes it his property"[29]; (2) ". . . there is enough, and as good left in common for others"[20]; and (3) "as much as anyone can make use of to any advantage of life before it spoils, so much he may by his labor fix a property in."[31] The second of these conditions amounts to the Lockean proviso, to which Nozick is deeply committed. Now, Locke makes it very clear why he is deeply committed to the proviso. He sees the problem of the acquisition of property as the problem of "how men might come to have a property in several parts of that which *God gave to mankind in common,* and that without any express compact of all the commoners."[32] Locke infers that "the earth and all that is therein" originally "belong to mankind in common."[33] He reasons that his conditions on acquisition provide a solution to the problem: "God gave the world to men in common; but since He gave it to them for their benefit, and the greatest conveniences of life they were capable to draw from it, it cannot be supposed He meant it should always remain common and uncultivated."[34] Thus Locke *assumes,* on religious grounds, that natural resources were originally *common assets,* and that normative principles directed that these resources be used to advance the common benefit of humankind. Locke believes that the private appropriation of property, subject to his conditions, is justified under these principles. Thus, it is clear why Locke is deeply committed to the Lockean proviso. It is less clear why *Nozick* is deeply committed to the Lockean proviso. Nozick, like Locke, is concerned about whether the private holding of property will violate the rights of others[35], but for Locke this question arises because the property being appropriated belongs to a *collective asset* to which "everyone" has a claim. It is doubtful whether Nozick would want to accept Locke's assumption that the earth belongs to all humankind or whether, without Locke's special religious dogmas, he could make such a claim plausible.

Hillel Steiner has defended an egalitarian interpretation of the Lockean proviso, according to which "it imposes an egalitarian structure on individuals' appropriative entitlements, prescribing to each a quantitatively and qualitatively similar bundle of natural objects."[36] He contends that the spirit of this proviso "is captured in the requirement that *each individual has a right to an equal share of the basic non-human means of production.*"[37] He defends this egalitarian proviso against Nozick's general objection to patterned principles of justice by distinguishing between manmade and natural resources. He accepts Nozick's argument that "our commonsense view of what is just—of what is owed to individuals by right—is inextricably bound up with what they *have done*,"[38] so that it is wrong to treat *manmade* objects "as if they appeared from nowhere, out of nothing."[39] But, he argues, in contrast to manmade objects, "the objects of appropriative rights *do* appear from nowhere and out of nothing and are *not* the results of individuals' past actions."[40] Nozick can appeal to the notion of desert in connection with manmade objects, but nobody can be said to deserve a parcel of natural resources which he or she has not personally produced. Thus, everyone has an *equal* claim to the available stock of natural resources, which should be parcelled out, so far as possible, in equal, homogeneous lots. (This principle obviously poses intractable practical difficulties, in terms of identifying equal exchange values for different grades and kinds of resources, or of providing for claims of future generations.) But this argument leads to a serious inconsistency in Steiner's theory of natural rights: "Natural or human rights are . . . rights to human bodies and natural objects. The kind of rule required to prescribe the first of these in a universal and inalienable form is, uncontroversially, one prohibiting slavery. What we have now to consider is what kind of right to natural objects can be enjoyed universally and inalienably."[41] Steiner agrees with Nozick that people have an unconditional claim to their natural assets, but he contends that the title to nonhuman resources is subject to egalitarian constraints. But the argument which he uses to establish his claim for nonhuman resources could be used to establish the same claim for human assets. I certainly cannot say I *deserve* my left kidney; from the point of view of *my* actions it did "appear from nowhere and out of nothing." Should we infer, then, that each individual has a right to an equal share of the available stock of kidneys, and that I am obliged to give up my left kidney if someone else needs one?

According to principle (I) above there is a basic moral parity between natural assets and nonhuman resources. Hence, if some version of the Lockean proviso places constraints upon the possession and use of nonhuman resources, it will place similar constraints upon the possession and use of our natural assets. For any argument that the distribution of nonhuman resources is a "common asset," there will be a similar argument for our natural *human* assets. It has already been shown that the arguments which Goldman and others have offered for "collective entitlement" to the natural assets of individuals and for a presumption of equal entitlement to the natural assets of all individuals are fallacious. These arguments do not improve when they are applied to nonhuman resources. I can see no good reason for supposing that all persons have a collective title to all available natural resources or that all persons have an equal claim to the stock of available natural

resources. The parity principle implies, rather, that the right to nonhuman resources is on the same footing as the right to human assets (see principles (IV) and (V) above). Both are imbedded equally deeply in the fundamental right to life (see principles (II) and (III) above).

These are, of course, important differences between holdings of natural assets and holdings of nonhuman resources. But these seem to be due to contingent facts about us as human beings and about most resources. The fact that all of us, except for Siamese twins, are unambiguously sealed within a single stretch of epidermis prevents territorial disputes from arising. Nozick has pointed out the difficulties that arise in appropriating property, in connection with defining precise boundaries.

> What are the boundaries of what labor is mixed with? If a private astronaut clears a place on Mars, has he mixed his labor with (so that he comes to own) the whole planet, the whole uninhabited universe, or just a particular plot? Which plot does an act bring under ownership?[42]

Problems about vague boundaries are obviously important but similar problems could arise for persons whose physiology happened to differ from that of human beings, such as gaseous entities which were capable of spatial overlap. And problems of vague boundaries arise in connection with our natural assets as well. Where does one draw the line between the oxygen which is circulating through one's body and, therefore, part of one's "person" and the fresh oxygen flowing into one's mouth and trachea? (It is hard to see what is established by such arguments from vagueness. The fact that one has no answer to the question, "How few hairs must a man have before he is bald?" does not prove that there are no bald men.) It is also becoming increasingly difficult to draw the line in the case of bodily parts. Is a surgically implanted pacemaker a part of one's natural assets? Certainly, in the case of an organ which was organically grown and then "accepted" by the recipient's body after transplantation, it would be hard not to accept it as part of the person's own body. But why should the question of whether it is made of "organic tissue" be the deciding factor? Is that not arbitrary? But if it is not the deciding factor, on what grounds do we rule out prosthetic limbs, or walking sticks, or spectacles, or hearing aids, or even clothing? The reason we cannot draw a sharp line between property rights and more "basic" human rights is that human beings are organisms occupying a place in the natural world and existing by interacting with their environment. No moral philosopher concerned with human rights should overlook that fact. There is, in the theory of rights, a continuum from basic rights of free thought and expression, to the property rights of shareholders of petroleum corporations to petroleum reserves discovered, and capital and technology developed, by their agents. No framer of public policy concerned with issues such as "the energy crisis" should overlook *that* fact.[43]

Notes

1. John Rawls, *A Theory of Justice* (Cambridge, Mass.: Harvard University Press, 1971), p. 75.

2. Robert Nozick, *Anarchy, State and Utopia* (Oxford: Basil Blackwell, 1974), p. 227.

3. Rawls, pp. 14-15.

4. *Ibid.*, p. 17

5. *Ibid.*, p. 19.

6. *Ibid.*, p. 21.

7. *Ibid.*, p. 20. Rawls' use of the words "match" and "coincide," to describe the relationship involved in reflective equilibrium, makes it clear that, by "coherence," Rawls does not *simply* mean logical compatibility. There should be a substantial equivalence between judgments about entitlement to assets which are justified on the contractarian approach and "intuitive" judgments about entitlement.

8. *Ibid.*, p. 104.

9. *Ibid.*, p. 101.

10. *Ibid.*, p. 179.

11. *Ibid.*, p. 104.

12. Rawls insists on the priority of the equal liberty principle (which assigns to citizens "freedom of the person along with the right to hold (personal property)" as well as other civil liberties) over the difference principle (pp. 61, 244). There can be no trade-off between liberty and economic well-being so long as conditions of at least moderate scarcity prevail. But Rawls does allow that equal liberty can be denied, but "only if it is necessary to enhance the quality of civilization so that in due course the equal freedoms can be enjoyed by all" (p. 542). If "social conditions do not allow the effective establishment of these rights," then they may be limited (p. 152).

13. *Ibid.*, p. 101.

14. *Ibid.*, p. 104.

15. Nozick, p. 225.

16. Alan Goldman, "The Entitlement Theory of Distributive Justice," *The Journal of Philosophy* 73 (1976), p. 824; my emphasis.

17. *Ibid.*, pp. 833-834; my emphasis.

18. Cf. *ibid.*, p. 835.

19. *Ibid.*, pp. 827, 829.

20. At one point Goldman suggests that "the system is responsible" and should not "allow" such things to happen (pp. 832, 825)—but, unfortunately, *persons*, not systems, are coerced to fulfill moral obligations.

21. *Ibid.*, p. 832. It is hard to know what to make of this "we." Is it the editorial "we"? The imperial "we"? This "we" does not include libertarians and other nonegalitarians. (See Nozick's remarks on the egalitarian presumption, pp. 223, 233 ff.) Is it necessary to point out how problematic the technique is of basing ethical theories on ungrounded challengeable "intuitions"?

22. See Tibor R. Machan, "Some Recent Work in Human Rights Theory," *American Philosophical Quarterly* 17 (1980), pp. 103-116 and David Gordon, "Contemporary Currents in Libertarian Political Philosophy," *Literature of Liberty* 4 (1981), pp. 7-35 for very useful bibliographies and critical discussions of natural rights arguments. The exegesis provided here of Ayn Rand's theory has affinities with the reconstructions of Tibor Machan, Eric Mack, Douglas Rasmussen and Douglas Den Uyl.

23. Ayn Rand, "The Objectivist Ethics" and "Man's Rights," in *The Virtue of Selfishness* (New York: New American Library, 1964), pp. 16-17, 24, 23, 93-94.

24. See Aristotle *Metaphysics* IV, c. 4-8. For a full appreciation of this parallel I am especially indebted to Douglas B. Rasmussen, "A Groundwork for Rights: Man's Natural End," *Journal of Libertarian Studies* 4 (1980), pp. 65-76.

25. Eric Mack, "Egoism and Rights," *The Personalist* 54 (1973), pp. 5-33.

26. Nozick, pp. 178, 177, 181-182, 180, 153-155.

27. Hillel Steiner, "The Natural Right to the Means of Production," *The Philosophical Quarterly* 27 (1977), pp. 45-46. The baseline also poses intractable difficulties of implementation, which will not be pursued here.

28. John Locke, *Second Treatise of Government*, Ch. 5, sec. 51.

29. *Ibid.*, sec. 27; cf. sec. 31.

30. *Ibid.*, sec. 27.

31. *Ibid.*, sec. 26; cf. sec. 31.

32. *Ibid.*, sec. 25.

33. *Ibid.*, sec. 26.

34. *Ibid.*, sec. 27.

35. Nozick, p. 179 *n* (cf. Locke, *op. cit.*, sec. 51) where Nozick invokes the proviso in order to criticize the theory of property rights in Ayn Rand "Man's Rights." My own approach is closer to Rand's, if I have understood her correctly.

36. Steiner, p. 45.

37. *Ibid.*, p. 49; Steiner's emphasis.

38. *Ibid.*, p. 49.

39. Nozick, p. 160.

40. Steiner, p. 49.

41. *Ibid.*, p. 44.

42. Nozick, p. 174.

43. This paper was inspired by a course on Rawls and Nozick which I team taught with Louis I. Katzner at Bowling Green State University. I wrote the first draft while I was a visiting assistant professor at the Johns Hopkins University. I read it, under the title, "Natural Assets in Rawls and Nozick," to the American Association for the Philosophic Study of Society in Milwaukee in 1977, where Jeffrey Paul offered helpful comments, and to the philosophy club at MIT in 1978. I have also received helpful criticisms from John O. Nelson.